# THE ESSENTIAL BIBLE DICTIONARY

**Essential Bible Companion Series**

*Essential Bible Atlas*

*Essential Bible Companion*

*Essential Bible Companion to the Psalms*

*Essential Bible Dictionary*

*Essential Companion to Life in Bible Times*

# THE ESSENTIAL BIBLE DICTIONARY

MOISÉS SILVA

ZONDERVAN®

ZONDERVAN.com/
AUTHORTRACKER
*follow your favorite authors*

ZONDERVAN

*Essential Bible Dictionary*

Requests for information should be addressed to:

Zondervan, Grand Rapids, Michigan 49530

---

Library of Congress Cataloging-in-Publication Data

Essential Bible dictionary / Moisés Silva, general editor.
p. cm.—(Essential Bible companion series)
ISBN 978-0-310-27821-4 (softcover)
1. Bible—Dictionaries. I. Silva, Moisés.
BS440.E75 2011
220.3—dc22 2010034653

---

*Cover design: Kirk Douponce, DogEaredDesign.com*
*Art Direction: Tammy Johnson*
*Cover photography: Istockphoto*
*Interior design: Matthew VanZomeren*

*Printed in China*

---

11 12 13 14 15 16 17 18 /CTC/ 23 22 21 20 19 18 17 16 15 14 13 12 11 10 9 8 7 6 5 4 3 2 1

# Contents

# Preface

The *Essential Bible Dictionary* is designed to provide quick but reliable information on the most important names and concepts found in the Bible, as well as explanations for selected terms that modern readers find difficult to understand.

Unlike comparable works in the market, the *EBD* does not include words that are readily found in English dictionaries (e.g., *adhere, foul, lad, prey, thither*) unless a special biblical usage requires comment. On the other hand, it includes a larger number of proper names than one usually finds in Bible dictionaries for students. Moreover, many of the entries provide a fuller description, based on the forthcoming *Zondervan Illustrated Bible Dictionary.*

The New International Version (NIV, 1984 ed.) serves as the primary basis of this work, although alternate renderings and spellings of proper names are often given, especially from Today's New International Version (TNIV) and the King James Version (KJV).

Cross-references are set in SMALL CAPS, indicating that the term in question has a separate entry in the dictionary. Thus when the reader comes across an unfamiliar name or concept, he or she can tell immediately whether the term is described elsewhere.

The pronunciation of biblical names is based on W. O. Walker Jr., *The Harper Collins Bible Pronunciation Guide* (1989), which uses a simple system for indicating English sounds, as shown here.

## Pronunciation Key

| | | | |
|---|---|---|---|
| a | **c**a**t** | n | **n**ot |
| ah | f**a**ther | ng | si**ng** |
| ahr | l**ar**d | o | h**o**t |
| air | c**ar**e | oh | g**o** |
| aw | j**aw** | oi | b**oy** |
| ay | p**ay** | oo | f**oo**t |
| b | **b**ug | *oo* | b**oo**t |
| ch | **ch**ew | oor | p**oor** |
| d | **d**o | or | f**or** |
| e, eh | p**e**t | ou | h**ow** |
| ee | s**ee**m | p | **p**at |
| er | **er**ror | r | **r**un |
| f | **f**un | s | **s**o |
| g | **g**ood | sh | **s**ure |
| h | **h**ot | t | **t**oe |
| hw | **wh**ether | th | **th**in |
| i | **i**t | *th* | **th**en |
| *i* | sk**y** | ts | **ts**etse |
| ihr | **ear** | tw | **tw**in |
| j | **j**oke | uh | **a**go |
| k | **k**ing | uhr | h**er** |
| kh | **ch** as in German *Buch* | v | **v**ow |
| ks | ve**x** | w | **w**eather |
| kw | **qu**ill | y | **y**oung |
| l | **l**ove | z | **z**one |
| m | **m**at | zh | vi**s**ion |

*Stress accents are printed after stressed syllables:*

ʹ primary stress

ʹ secondary stress

# Abbreviations

## General Abbreviations

| | | | |
|---|---|---|---|
| AD | Year of our Lord | KJV | King James Version |
| BC | Before Christ | Mt. | Mount |
| c. | about, approximately | NIV | New International Version |
| cent. | century | NRSV | New Revised Standard Version |
| cf. | compare | NT | New Testament |
| e.g. | for example | OT | Old Testament |
| Gk. | Greek | RSV | Revised Standard Version |
| Heb. | Hebrew | TNIV | Today's New International Version |

## Abbreviations of Biblical Books

| | | | | | |
|---|---|---|---|---|---|
| Gen. | Genesis | Isa. | Isaiah | Rom. | Romans |
| Exod. | Exodus | Jer. | Jeremiah | 1 Cor. | 1 Corinthians |
| Lev. | Leviticus | Lam. | Lamentations | 2 Cor. | 2 Corinthians |
| Num. | Numbers | Ezek. | Ezekiel | Gal. | Galatians |
| Deut. | Deuteronomy | Dan. | Daniel | Eph. | Ephesians |
| Josh. | Joshua | Hos. | Hosea | Phil. | Philippians |
| Jdg. | Judges | Joel | Joel | Col. | Colossians |
| Ruth | Ruth | Amos | Amos | 1 Thess | 1 Thessalonians |
| 1 Sam. | 1 Samuel | Obad. | Obadiah | 2 Thess. | 2 Thessalonians |
| 2 Sam. | 2 Samuel | Jon. | Jonah | 1 Tim. | 1 Timothy |
| 1 Ki. | 1 Kings | Mic. | Micah | 2 Tim. | 2 Timothy |
| 2 Ki. | 2 Kings | Nah. | Nahum | Tit. | Titus |
| 1 Chr. | 1 Chronicles | Hab. | Habakkuk | Phlm. | Philemon |
| 2 Chr. | 2 Chronicles | Zeph. | Zephaniah | Heb. | Hebrews |
| Ezra | Ezra | Hag. | Haggai | Jas. | James |
| Neh. | Nehemiah | Zech. | Zechariah | 1 Pet. | 1 Peter |
| Esth. | Esther | Mal. | Malachi | 2 Pet. | 2 Peter |
| Job | Job | Matt. | Matthew | 1 Jn. | 1 John |
| Ps. | Psalm(s) | Mk. | Mark | 2 Jn. | 2 John |
| Prov. | Proverbs | Lk. | Luke | 3 Jn. | 3 John |
| Eccl. | Ecclesiastes | Jn. | John | Jude | Jude |
| Cant. | Canticles (Song of Songs) | Acts | Acts | Rev. | Revelation |

# A

**Aaron** (air′uhn). Brother of MOSES and MIRIAM (Num. 26:59). Aaron and his wife Elisheba had four sons (26:60; see NADAB). God appointed him to be Moses' spokesman (Exod. 4:14–16), and he later became the first HIGH PRIEST in Israel (ch. 28). Although highly regarded, Aaron is also faulted for his part in the incident of the golden calf (32:1–25) and for his criticism of Moses (Num. 12:1–9). He died without being allowed to enter the Promised Land (20:12, 22–29). In the NT, the author of Hebrews regards Aaron as a foreshadowing of Christ (Heb. 5:1–5), but explains that the Aaronic priesthood was only temporary, whereas Christ's ministry is eternal (7:11–28).

**Aaron's staff (rod).** When KORAH and his confederates challenged the leadership of MOSES and AARON (Num. 16–17), Moses placed the staffs of the tribal leaders, including Aaron's, inside the TABERNACLE. The next day Aaron's staff was found to have budded, vindicating his divine authority as high priest; it was then placed before the ARK in the HOLY OF HOLIES "as a sign to the rebellious" (17:6–10). The staff referred to is very likely the same shepherd's staff Moses was carrying at the time of his call (Exod. 4:2–4; called "the staff of God" in v. 20).

**Abaddon** (uh-bad′uhn). This Hebrew name means "[place of] destruction, ruin." With its Greek equivalent Apollyon, it is used once in the NT with reference to the evil angel who reigns over the infernal regions of the ABYSS (Rev. 9:11).

Mt. Hor. The structure on top of the mountain is known as Aaron's Tomb.



**Abana** (ab′uh-nuh). The name of a river (today called Barada) that flows through DAMASCUS and makes the area lovely and fertile. It was mentioned by NAAMAN when he objected to bathing in the JORDAN (2 Ki. 5:12).

**Abarim** (ab′uh-rim). The region E of the JORDAN, and specifically a mountain range in NW MOAB that includes Mount NEBO. The Israelites encamped here just before crossing the Jordan, and from one of its peaks MOSES saw the Promised Land (Num. 33:47–48; Deut. 32:49).

A

**Abba** (ah'buh, ab'uh). An ARAMAIC term meaning "father," used with the corresponding Greek term three times in the NT as a way of addressing God (Mk. 14:36; Rom. 8:15; Gal. 4:6). It is probable that Jesus used this word also in many of the instances where the Gospels record that he referred to God as FATHER.

**Abdon** (ab'duhn). The eleventh mentioned JUDGE of Israel; he ruled eight years (Jdg. 12:13–15).

**Abednego** (uh-bed'ni-goh). The Babylonian name given to AZARIAH, one of the three Israelite youths who were companions of DANIEL (Dan. 1:7). The other two were SHADRACH and MESHACH. Daniel and his three friends belonged to the Hebrew royal family and determined not to defile themselves with the pagan diet (vv. 8–15). Later, the three youths were appointed provincial administrators (2:49). Because they refused to worship the pagan image set up by King NEBUCHADNEZZAR, they were cast into a fiery furnace, but they were miraculously delivered (3:1–30). The NT alludes to them when it mentions the heroes of faith who "quenched the fury of the flames" (Heb. 11:34).

**Abel** (ay'buhl). **(1)** ADAM and EVE's second son, who was murdered by his brother CAIN because God looked with favor on Abel's offering (Gen. 4:1–12; see Heb. 11:4; 12:24). **(2)** Shortened form of Abel Beth Maacah, a town in the extreme N of Palestine (2 Sam. 20:18; see vv. 14–15).

**Abel Meholah** (ay'buhl-mi-hoh'luh). The hometown of ELISHA the prophet (1 Ki. 19:16; also mentioned in Jdg. 7:22, etc.).

**Abiathar** (uh-bi'uh-thahr). Son of the high priest AHIMELECH. After his father's death, Abiathar joined DAVID (1 Sam. 22:20–23), and later he served as high priest along with ZADOK (2 Sam. 15:24–29). When David was near death, Abiathar supported ADONIJAH rather than SOLOMON (1 Ki. 1:7), so when the latter ascended the throne, Abiathar was banished (2:22–27).

**Abib** (ay'bib, ah-veev'). TNIV Aviv. The first month in the Jewish religious CALENDAR (corresponding to March–April), during which the Passover took place (Exod. 13:4; 23:15; 34:18; Deut. 16:1). Abib is the older name for the month of Nisan (Neh. 2:1; Esth. 3:7).

**Abigail, Abigal** (ab'uh-gayl, ab'uh-gal). **(1)** The wise and beautiful wife of NABAL, a rich man who refused to give provisions to DAVID. After Nabal died, Abigal married David and bore his second son, KILEAB (1 Sam. 25:2–42; 2 Sam. 3:3). **(2)** A sister of King David and the mother of AMASA (2 Sam. 17:25; 1 Chr. 2:16–17).

**Abihu** (uh-bi'hyoo). Second son of AARON; he and his older brother NADAB, who were priests, presented a type of offering that God had forbidden, and for that reason God took their lives (Exod. 6:23; Lev. 10:1–2).

**Abijah, Abijam** (uh-bi'juh, uh-bi'juhm). The name of several persons, especially a son of REHOBOAM who became the second king of Judah after the division of the kingdom (1 Ki. 14:31–15:8 [where the Heb. text calls him "Abijam"]; 2 Chr. 12:16–14:1). Abijah followed the evil ways of his father and reigned only three years.

**Abilene** (ab'uh-lee'nee). A region in SYRIA near the Antilebanon mountains (see LEBANON); it was ruled by Lysanias when JOHN the Baptist began his ministry (Lk. 3:1).

**Abimelech** (uh-bim'uh-lek). TNIV Abimelek. **(1)** A PHILISTINE king of GERAR who took SARAH to marry her; after being warned by God in a dream, he immediately returned her to ABRAHAM (Gen. 20:1–18). The name Abimelech may be a title. **(2)** A second king of Gerar, probably the son of the previous Abimelech; he rebuked ISAAC for trying to pass off REBEKAH as his sister (Gen. 26:1–11). **(3)** The son of GIDEON by a concubine; after murdering all but one of his half brothers, he became king of SHECHEM (Jdg. 8:31; 9:1–57). **(4)** A Philistine king mentioned in the title of Ps. 34; he is very likely the same as ACHISH king of GATH (1 Sam. 21:10–22:1).

**Abinadab** (uh-bin'uh-dab). **(1)** A brother of DAVID (1 Sam. 16:8; 17:13). **(2)** A son of SAUL who died with his father in battle with the PHILISTINES (1 Sam. 31:2). **(3)** A man of KIRIATH JEARIM at whose place the ARK of the covenant remained; three of his sons, including UZZAH, had responsibilities guarding the ark (1 Sam. 7:1; 2 Sam. 6:3–4).

**Abishag** (ab'uh-shag). A woman who nursed DAVID in his old age (1 Ki. 1:3). After David died, ADONIJAH sought to marry her (2:13–25).

**Abishai** (uh-bi'shi). A brother of JOAB and loyal warrior under DAVID (1 Sam. 26:6–9; 2 Sam. 3:30; 16:9–11; 23:18–19).

**Abishalom.** See ABSALOM.

**Abner** (ab'nuhr). Cousin (or uncle) of King SAUL and commander in chief of the Israelite army (1 Sam. 14:50). At Saul's death, Abner had ISH-BOSHETH made king over Israel (2 Sam. 2:8), but he later went over to DAVID's side (3:8–13). When JOAB found out, he accused Abner of being a spy and murdered him (3:23–27).

**abomination.** This English term, applied to that which causes disgust or hatred, occurs frequently in the OT in the KJV, but modern versions prefer other renderings, such as the adjective *detestable.* Two main Hebrew words are involved. One of them is used of idols (e.g., 2 Ki. 23:24; Jer. 7:30), of forbidden practices (e.g., 2 Ki. 23:24), and generally of anything contrary to the worship and religion of the Lord (e.g., 2 Chr. 15:8; Isa. 66:3; Jer. 4:1). A second and more common term is applied to wider areas of life: things related to idols (Deut. 7:25; 27:15), forbidden sexual practices (e.g., Lev. 18:22, 26–27), offering blemished animals in sacrifice (17:1), and heathen divination (18:9, 12).

**abomination of desolation.** Also "abomination that causes desolation." This expression, which can be rendered "appalling sacrilege" or the like, occurs several times in Daniel (Dan. 9:27; 11:31; 12:11) and is usually understood as a reference to the profanation of the Jerusalem TEMPLE by Antiochus IV in 165 BC. Jesus used the phrase when speaking of the future (Matt. 24:15; Mk. 13:4); it is debated whether he was referring to the destruction of Jerusalem in AD 70 or to the end times (cf. 2 Thess. 2:3–4, 8–10).

**Abraham** (ay'bruh-ham). The father of the Hebrew nation. The name is interpreted as "father of a multitude" (cf. Gen. 17:5, perhaps a play on words); his original name

This monument in Golan (NE of the Sea of Galilee) is known as a dolmen, a unique form of burial that Abraham may have encountered when he reached Palestine.

A

(used from Gen. 11:26 to 17:5) was Abram, possibly meaning "my father is exalted." He and his family, living in UR OF THE CHALDEANS, had an idolatrous background (Gen. 11:31; Josh. 24:2). At age seventy-five he was commanded by God to leave all and go out into the unknown, sustained only by the divine promise that his descendants would become a great nation and that he would be a blessing to all the peoples of the earth (12:1–4). God reaffirmed his COVENANT with Abraham on several occasions (esp. chs. 15 and 17). After many years of waiting for a child, Abraham and SARAH became impatient and he fathered ISHMAEL through the servant HAGAR (ch. 16). Finally, when Abraham was a hundred years old, Sarah gave birth to ISAAC (21:1–7). Years later, God tested Abraham's FAITH by instructing him to sacrifice his beloved son, though an angel prevented him from doing so (22:1–18). The NT focuses on Abraham as the father of Christian believers (Rom. 4; Heb. 11:8–16; Jas. 2:21–23).

**Abraham's bosom (side).** A figure of speech used by Jesus in the parable of Lazarus and the rich man to designate blessedness in the afterlife (Lk. 16:22–23). Reclining on a person's side indicates close fellowship (cf. Jn. 1:18; 13:23).

**Abram.** See ABRAHAM.

**Absalom** (ab'suh-luhm). Third son of DAVID (2 Sam. 3:3; called Abishalom in 1 Ki. 15:2, 10). His sister TAMAR was raped by their half brother AMNON, David's eldest son (2 Sam. 13:1–20). Absalom treacherously plotted Amnon's assassination (13:21–29), and some years later he used his good looks to incite a revolt against his own father (14:25–26; 15:1–13). In battle, Absalom's long hair got tangled in a tree and JOAB used the opportunity to kill him, an act that caused David deep grief (ch. 18).

**abstain, abstinence.** These terms refer to the avoidance of a particular action or practice, usually as an expression of self-denial. The decree of the COUNCIL of Jerusalem commanded abstinence from certain practices that offended Jewish Christians (Acts 15:20, 29). The Bible urges believers to abstain from sinful behavior and desires (1 Thess. 4:3; 5:22; 1 Pet. 2:11). However, it condemns those who teach abstinence from foods that "God created to be received with thanksgiving" (1 Tim. 4:3). The modern expression "total abstinence" refers to the practice of avoiding alcoholic beverages completely.

**abyss.** A great gulf or pit that is (or appears to be) bottomless. The NIV uses the term as a name for the place where the demons and other evil forces are held (Lk. 8:31 [KJV "the deep"]; Rev. 9:1–2, etc. [KJV "the bottomless pit"]). The corresponding Greek term, *abyssos*, is also used once by PAUL (Rom. 10:7 [KJV and NIV "the deep"]).

**acacia.** A term applied to various trees and shrubs native to warmer climates. The acacia (or *shittim*) wood is durable and close-grained, and it was used for the construction of the TABERNACLE and the ARK of the covenant (Exod. 25–27, 35–38; Deut. 10:3).

**acceptance.** The act of receiving something or someone with approval. In the Bible the most vital need of the person is to be acceptable to God. SIN separates; acceptance is a condition of restoration to God. The OT sacrifices were not sufficient for this task, but God provided full access to himself through Jesus Christ by his cross (Eph. 2:18; 3:12). See JUSTIFICATION. Believers can offer themselves acceptably to God (Rom. 12:1); and their spiritual sacrifices, such as acts of praise and well-doing, are acceptable through Christ (Phil 4:18; Heb. 13:15–16; 1 Pet. 2:5). Because God has received believers, moreover, they are to forgive and accept each other in the fellowship of LOVE (Eph. 4:32; 5:2).

**Acco** (ak′oh). Also Accho, Akko. A Canaanite-Phoenician coastal city, known as Ptolemais in NT times, and today as Acre, some 8 mi. (13 km.) N of Mount CARMEL (Jdg. 1:31; Acts 21:7).

**accord.** See UNITY.

**accursed.** See ANATHEMA.

**Aceldama.** See AKELDAMA.

**Achaia** (uh-kay′uh). The name of a region, later a Roman PROVINCE, in S GREECE (Acts 18:27, etc.); CORINTH was its capital. The areas N of Achaia were districts of MACEDONIA, and the phrase "Macedonia and Achaia" generally means all Greece (Acts 19:21; Rom. 15:26; 1 Thess. 1:7–8).

**Achan** (ay′kan). Also called Achar (1 Chr. 2:7). An Israelite who was stoned to death for violating the ban (see ANATHEMA) during the conquest of JERICHO (Josh. 7:1–26). Achan had stolen silver, gold, and an expensive garment, even though JOSHUA had devoted the metals to God and made clear that everything else must be destroyed (6:17–19).

**Achaz.** See AHAZ.

**Achish** (ay′kish). A PHILISTINE king of GATH to whom DAVID fled for protection (1 Sam. 21:10–15; 27:1–12; 29:1–11). In the title to Ps. 34 Achish is called ABIMELECH, which may have been a dynastic name of Philistine kings.

**Achor** (ay′kohr). The valley in which ACHAN was stoned to death because he had taken forbidden booty (Josh. 7:24–26). God's promise of future blessing is expressed by saying that he will turn the Valley of Achor

Aerial view of the city of Acco. 

Remains of Herod's palace in Caesarea, a city that figures prominently in the book of Acts. © Baker Publishing Group

(which means "trouble") into "a door of hope" (Hos. 2:15).

**acrostic.** A composition in which the first letters of consecutive lines follow the alphabet or form words. The OT contains fourteen acrostic poems, with the twenty-two letters of the Hebrew alphabet appearing in order at the beginning of each line or stanza (Ps. 9; 10; 25; 34; 37; 111; 112; 119; 145; Prov. 31:10–31, Nah. 1:2–10; and each chapter of Lamentations).

**Acsah** (ak′suh). Also Achsah, Aksah. A daughter of CALEB who was given in marriage to OTHNIEL (Josh. 15:16–19; Jdg. 1:12–15; 1 Chr. 2:49).

**Acts of the Apostles.** A NT book that gives the history of early Christianity from the ASCENSION OF CHRIST to PAUL's imprisonment in ROME. It is the second of a two-volume work (the first volume being the Gospel of LUKE) addressed to a man named THEOPHILUS. It aims to present what Jesus Christ, after ascending to heaven, continued to do through the APOSTLES by the power of the HOLY SPIRIT (Acts 1:1–8). Approximately the first half of the book, which focuses on the ministry of PETER, deals mainly with the growth of the CHURCH in JERUSALEM and surrounding areas. The rest of the book focuses on PAUL's missionary work outside of PALESTINE.

**Adah** (ay′duh). **(1)** Wife of LAMECH and mother of Jabal and Jubal (Gen. 4:19–21). **(2)** Wife of ESAU and daughter of Elon the HITTITE (Gen. 36:2). This marriage introduced Canaanite blood and influence into ISAAC's family.

**Adam** (ad′uhm). In Hebrew this term can function as a generic noun meaning "man, humanity" (cf. Gen. 1:26–27), but it is also the name given to the first man (5:3), whom God created from the dust of the ground

## OVERVIEW OF ACTS

**AUTHOR:** Anonymous, but traditionally attributed to LUKE the physician.

**HISTORICAL SETTING:** Covers the period from the ASCENSION OF CHRIST (AD 30 or 33) to PAUL's imprisonment in ROME (c. 61–63). The book was probably written in Rome soon after the last events narrated, but some date it to the 70s or even later.

**PURPOSE:** To provide a historical-theological account of the early CHURCH, focusing on the rapid expansion of Christianity as a result of the powerful outpouring of the HOLY SPIRIT.

**CONTENTS:** Promise and fulfillment of the Spirit's power (Acts 1–2). Spread of the GOSPEL in JERUSALEM, JUDEA, SAMARIA, and ANTIOCH, with emphasis on the ministry of PETER (chs. 3–12). Spread of the gospel in Asia Minor and Europe as far as Rome, with emphasis on the ministry of Paul (chs. 13–28).

(2:7). Adam was made in the image of God, provided with a garden and a wife, and given work to do (2:15, 22). His rejection of God's authority led to the breaking of communion with God, expulsion from the garden, and a life of toil (ch. 3; see FALL, THE). From the physical descendants of Adam and EVE the human race emerged. In the NT, Adam is presented as the representative of humanity and contrasted with Jesus as the representative of the new humanity (Rom. 5:12–19; 1 Cor. 15:20–22, 45–49).

**adamant.** This English noun, referring to an extremely hard stone (such as diamond), is used twice in the KJV (Ezek. 3:9; Zech. 7:12); the Hebrew word possibly refers to flint.

**Adar** (ay'dahr). The twelfth month (late February to early March) in the Babylonian CALENDAR used by Israel after the EXILE (Ezra 6:15; Esth. 3:7, 13; 8:12; 9:1, 15–21).

**Admah** (ad'muh). One of the cities of the plain near the DEAD SEA, marking CANAAN's southern border (Gen. 10:19; 14:2); it was destroyed by God (Deut. 29:23; Hos. 11:8). See SODOM.

**Adonai** (ad'oh-n*i*'). A divine name usually translated "the Lord." See JEHOVAH.

**Adonijah** (ad'uh-n*i*'juh). The name of several men in the OT, but especially the fourth son of DAVID (2 Sam. 3:4). When David was near death, Adonijah attempted but failed to seize the throne. SOLOMON pardoned him, but later Adonijah sought to marry ABISHAG, David's nurse in his last illness. Solomon became suspicious and had Adonijah killed (1 Ki. 1:5–2:25).

Reconstruction of the tabernacle with the altar out front. Upon hearing of Solomon's rise to the throne, Adonijah went to the tabernacle, which had been set up in Jerusalem, and held on to the horns of the altar until the king made an oath not to put him to death (1 Ki. 1:51).

Todd Bolen/www.BiblePlaces.com

A

**Adoniram** (ad'uh-n*i*'ruhm). Also known as Adoram and Hadoram. An official in charge of forced labor under DAVID (2 Sam. 20:24), SOLOMON (1 Ki. 4:6; 5:14), and REHOBOAM (1 Ki. 12:18; 2 Chr. 10:18). Rehoboam sent him on a mission of some kind to the rebel tribes of Israel, who stoned him to death.

**Adoni-Zedek** (uh-doh'n*i*-zee'dek). AMORITE king of JERUSALEM when the Israelites invaded Canaan; he invited four other kings to join him in attacking GIBEON, but JOSHUA defeated and killed them on the day when the sun and moon stood still (Josh. 10).

**adoption.** The act of taking a child of other parents as one's own child (e.g., MOSES, Exod. 2:10). In the NT, PAUL uses the Greek term meaning "adoption" to describe the relationship that believers enjoy with God (Rom. 8:15; Gal. 4:5; Eph. 1:5). See also REGENERATION.

**Adoram.** See ADONIRAM.

**Adramyttium** (ad'ruh-mit'ee-uhm). Ancient port city of MYSIA in Asia Minor (modern Turkey). PAUL began his voyage to ROME in a ship of Adramyttium (Acts 27:2).

**Adria, Adriatic Sea** (ay'dree-uh, ay'dree-a'tik). The entire body of water lying between ITALY on the W and GREECE on the E; it extends into the central MEDITERRANEAN SEA to include the waters where PAUL's ship encountered the storm on the voyage to ROME (Acts 27:27).

**Adullam** (uh-duhl'uhm). A very ancient city in the lowland of PALESTINE, between the hill country of JUDAH and the sea, 13 mi. (21 km.) SW of BETHLEHEM (Gen. 38:1, 12, 20; Josh. 15:35). DAVID hid with his family and about four hundred men in one of the many limestone caves near this town at a time when SAUL sought his life (1 Sam. 22:1–2).

**adultery.** Voluntary sexual intercourse between a married person and someone other than his or her spouse. One of the Ten COMMANDMENTS forbids it (Exod. 20:14; Deut. 5:18). From the earliest times, even outside the people of God, adultery was regarded as a serious sin (Gen. 26:10; 39:9). Jesus said it was possible to commit adultery in the heart (Matt. 5:27–28). MARRIAGE is a COVENANT relationship (e.g., Mal. 2:14) that imposes obligations on the partners; thus the Bible draws a comparison between adultery and religious APOSTASY (e.g., Isa. 57:3; Jer. 3:8–9; Matt. 12:39; Mk. 8:38).

**advent.** This English term, which refers to the arrival of someone or something important, is used especially of the coming of CHRIST at the INCARNATION. In the church calendar it refers to the period that begins the fourth Sunday before Christmas. The term is also used with reference to Jesus' second coming.

**adversary.** An opponent or enemy. See SATAN.

**adversity.** See TRIBULATION.

**advocate.** One who pleads the cause of another. See HOLY SPIRIT.

**Aeneas** (i-nee'uhs). A man who had been bedridden with paralysis for eight years and who was miraculously healed by PETER (Acts 9:33–35).

**Aenon** (ee'nuhn). A place near SALIM where JOHN the Baptist was baptizing during the time Jesus ministered in Judea (Jn. 3:22–23). Its location is uncertain.

**affliction.** See TRIBULATION.

**Agabus** (ag'uh-buhs). One of the prophets from JERUSALEM who went to ANTIOCH of Syria and predicted a severe famine (Acts 11:27–30). He is probably the same man who years later warned PAUL that he would be imprisoned if he persisted in going to JERUSALEM (21:10–11).

**Agag** (ay'gag). An important king of AMALEK mentioned in BALAAM's prophecy (Num.

24:7). Some believe this prediction was fulfilled when SAUL defeated a king by that name (1 Sam. 15:1–33), but it is possible that Agag was a dynastic title.

**agape.** A Greek word for LOVE used frequently in the NT. It is also used in Jude 12 of common meals that cultivated brotherly love among Christians.

**Agar.** See HAGAR.

**Agrippa** (uh-grip′uh). **(1)** King Herod Agrippa I, referred to simply as Herod in Acts 12, was the grandson of HEROD the Great. He killed JAMES (brother of JOHN the apostle) and also tried to execute PETER. **(2)** His son, King Herod Agrippa II, is referred to simply as Agrippa in Acts 25–26. He found no fault in PAUL when the apostle appeared before him.

**Agur** (ay′guhr). Son of Jakeh; an otherwise unknown writer of maxims who may have been from a place named MASSA (Prov. 30:1; the meaning of this verse is debated).

**Ahab** (ay′hab). **(1)** Son of OMRI and seventh king of the northern kingdom of ISRAEL; he reigned twenty-two years, 874–853 BC (1 Ki. 16:28–22:40). Politically, Ahab was one of the strongest kings of Israel, but he owes his prominence in the OT to the religious APOSTASY that occurred in Israel during his reign. His marriage to JEZEBEL, daughter of the king of SIDON, was politically advantageous but religiously disastrous. At this critical period in the history of Israel, God raised up ELIJAH, whose faithful ministry culminated in the conflict with the prophets of BAAL on Mount CARMEL (ch. 18). **(2)** Son of Kolaiah; a false prophet guilty of immorality (Jer. 29:21–23).

**Ahasuerus** (uh-hash′yoo-er′uhs). See XERXES.

**Ahava** (uh-hay′vuh). The name of a canal and its surrounding area in BABYLON; it served as a gathering place for the Israelites returning to Jerusalem with EZRA (Ezra 8:15, 21, 31).

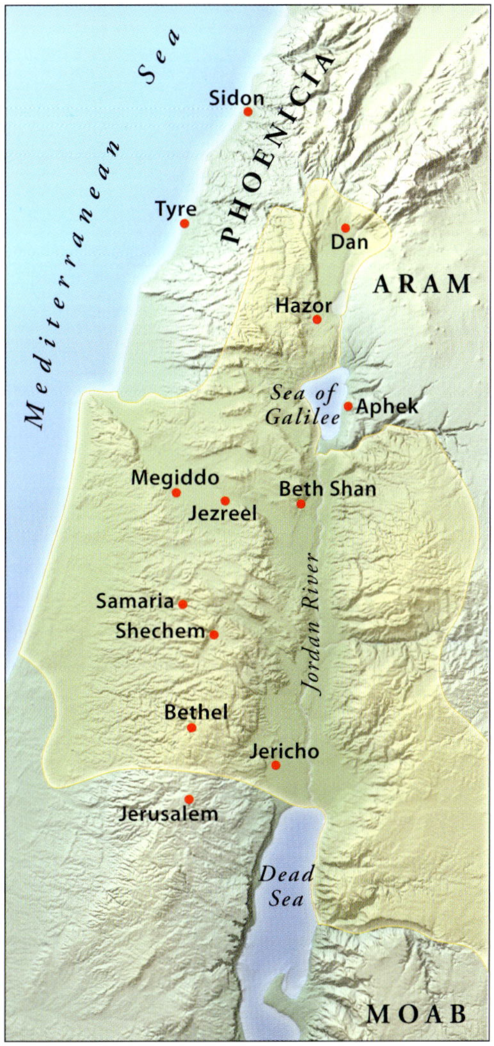


The Northern Kingdom of Israel.

**Ahaz** (ay′haz). KJV NT Achaz. **(1)** Reigning over the southern kingdom of JUDAH c. 735–715 BC, Ahaz son of Jotham was a king of great significance both historically and theologically (2 Ki. 16; 2 Chr. 28; Isa. 7). As a result of his policies and unbelief, the people of God became vassals of ASSYRIA, and never again did the throne of DAVID exist in its fully sovereign right. **(2)** Son of Micah and great-grandson of King SAUL (1 Chr. 8:35–36; 9:41–42).

**Ahaziah** (ay′huh-*zi*′uh). **(1)** Son of AHAB and JEZEBEL; he was the eighth king of ISRAEL, reigning only two years c. 853–852 BC (1 Ki. 22:49–53; 2 Ki. 1:1). Ahaziah was a worshiper of JEROBOAM's calves and of his mother's idols. He died as a result of injuries sustained when he fell from his upper room. **(2)** Son of JEHORAM and ATHALIAH; he was the sixth king of JUDAH, reigning only one year c. 842 BC (2 Ki. 8:25–29; 9:21–27; called Jehoahaz in 2 Chr. 21:17 and 25:23). He followed the idolatrous practices of his grandfather Ahab. Judgment came on him through the hand of JEHU.

**Ahijah** (uh-*hi*′juh). **(1)** A priest who consulted the oracles of God for SAUL (1 Sam. 14:3, 18–19); the same as AHIMELECH. **(2)** A prophet from SHILOH who predicted to JEROBOAM that he would reign over ten of the twelve tribes (1 Ki. 11:29–39; 12:15); later he foretold Jeroboam's death. (14:1–18). He was also the author of a historical document (2 Chr. 9:29).

**Ahikam** (uh-*hi*′kuhm). A royal secretary during the reign of King JOSIAH and a prominent man in the following decades (2 Ki. 22:12, 14; 25:22; 2 Chr. 34:20; Jer. 26:24; 39:14; 40:5–41:18; 43:6).

The Greek Monastery of St. Onuphrius lies on the southern edge of Jerusalem's Hinnom Valley and marks the traditional site of Akeldama.



**Ahimaaz** (uh-him′ay-az). Son of ZADOK the high priest (1 Chr. 6:8). During ABSALOM's rebellion he served as messenger between DAVID and HUSHAI (2 Sam. 15:24–27; 17:15–22) and later brought news of victory (18:19–28).

**Ahimelech** (uh-him′uh-lek) TNIV Ahimelek. A priest in NOB who gave assistance to DAVID by offering him the SHOWBREAD (1 Sam. 21:1–9); when SAUL learned of this aid, it cost Ahimelech his life (22:9–19). Also known as AHIJAH (14:3, 18).

**Ahinoam** (uh-hin′oh-uhm). **(1)** Wife of SAUL (1 Sam. 14:50), thus the first queen of Israel. **(2)** A different Ahinoam became the wife of DAVID and bore him his first son, AMNON (1 Sam. 25:43; 27:3; 30:5; 2 Sam. 2:2; 3:2; 1 Chr. 3:1).

**Ahithophel** (uh-hith′uh-fel). DAVID's counselor who joined the conspiracy of ABSALOM (2 Sam. 15:12, 31; 16:15, 20–21). The wisdom of his advice was proverbial (16:23), but David's prayer turned his counsel into foolishness (15:31). When his counsel was rejected, he went to his home and hanged himself (17:1–23).

**Ai** (*i*, ay′*i*). A city of central PALESTINE, E of BETHEL, near which ABRAHAM pitched his tent when he arrived in CANAAN (Gen. 12:8). Ai was the second Canaanite city taken by the forces under JOSHUA (Josh. 7–8). There was also an Ammonite city by the same name (Jer. 49:3).

**Aijalon** (ay′juh-lon). KJV also Ajalon. A city about 13 mi. (21 km.) NW of JERUSALEM mentioned by JOSHUA when he prayed for the sun and moon to stand still (Josh. 10:12). SAUL and JONATHAN won a great victory against the PHILISTINES in the vicinity of Aijalon (1 Sam. 14:31). (There was also a town by the same name in ZEBULUN, Jdg. 12:12.)

**Akeldama** (uh-kel′duh-muh). Also Aceldama and Hakeldama. An ARAMAIC name meaning "Field of Blood," referring to the field purchased with the money JUDAS Iscariot received for betraying Christ (Acts 1:18–19). Matthew, with a fuller account of the purchase, says the priests bought it, apparently in Judas's name, the money having been his (Matt. 27:3–10).

**Akkad** (ak′ad). Also Accad. One of the cities or districts of NIMROD's kingdom in SHINAR (Gen. 10:10). Akkad perhaps should be identified with ancient Agade, a major city in northern BABYLONIA.

**Akko.** See ACCO.

**alabaster.** A white or light-colored mineral used to make vases for holding perfumed ointments (Matt. 26:7; Mk. 14:3; Lk. 7:37).

**alamoth** (al′uh-moth). Probably the name of a musical tune (1 Chr. 15:20; Ps. 46, title); the term may indicate a women's choir or musical instruments set in a high pitch.

**alcoholism.** See DRUNKENNESS.

**aleph** (ah′lef). The first letter of the Hebrew alphabet (א, transliterated as '), used to begin each verse in Ps. 119:1–8.

**Alexander** (al′ig-zan′duhr). **(1)** Alexander the Great (356–323 BC) was a Macedonian king who conquered much of the ancient world, making possible the spread of Greek culture. Many believe he is mentioned in Dan. 8:5–8, 21. **(2)** Son of Simon of CYRENE (Mk. 15:21). **(3)** A member of the high-priestly family (Acts 4:6). **(4)** The Jewish spokesman at the time of the riot in EPHESUS (Acts 19:33). **(5)** A man who denied the Christian faith (1 Tim. 1:20). **(6)** A coppersmith who did PAUL great harm and opposed his message (2 Tim. 4:14).

**Alexandria** (al′ig-zan′dree-uh). A city founded by Alexander the Great in 332 BC; it became the capital of EGYPT and a great educational center (several other cities elsewhere were also named Alexandria by him). It included a large Jewish population. The city and its inhabitants are mentioned in the NT (Acts 6:9; 18:24; a ship in 27:6; 28:11).

This statue of Alexander the Great is dated to the 3rd cent. BC.
Todd Bolen/www.BiblePlaces.com

**algum.** See ALMUG.

**allegory.** An extended metaphor or a narrative that makes use of symbols. In this sense, allegory is a literary device used extensively in Scripture, for example in Isa. 5:1–7 (but it should be distinguished from PARABLE). The term often refers, however, to the expression of hidden, mysterious truths by the use of words that also have a literal meaning.

**alleluia.** See HALLELUJAH.

**alliance.** See COVENANT.

**allotment.** Distribution, assignment. This term is used in reference to the allocation of the land of PALESTINE to the tribes of Israel (Josh. 15–17). See LOTS.

**Almighty.** A divine title referring to God's absolute power.

**alms.** A gift (such as money, food, clothing) intended to relieve the needs of the poor.

**almug.** A type of wood (perhaps the red sandalwood or a species of juniper) mentioned in 1 Ki. 10:11–12 as an import from OPHIR. In 2 Chr. 2:8 and 9:10–11 the word appears as "algum," probably a spelling variant.

**aloe.** A shrubby plant containing juices that were used by the ancients for embalming (John 19:39) and other purposes. The OT references to aloes (Num. 24:6; Ps. 45:8; Prov. 7:17; Cant. 4:14) may indicate a large tree known as the eaglewood, whose resin was used in making perfumes.

Canaanite round altar in Megiddo (c. 2500 BC). © Willam D. Mounce

**alpha and omega** (al′fuh, oh-mayg′uh). The first and last letters of the Greek alphabet (roughly equivalent to English *a* and *o*). The phrase "I am the Alpha and the Omega" occurs only in the book of Revelation (Rev. 1:8; 21:6; 22:13), indicating divine and eternal greatness.

**Alphaeus** (al-fee′uhs). **(1)** The father of MATTHEW (Levi, Mk. 2:14). **(2)** Father of JAMES, one of the twelve disciples (Matt. 10:3; Mk. 3:18; Lk. 6:15; Acts 1:13); Alphaeus's name is included to distinguish this James from the son of ZEBEDEE.

**altar.** A platform or similar structure used for WORSHIP, especially for offering SACRIFICES. The first altar we read about was erected by NOAH after leaving the ark (Gen. 8:20); ABRAHAM and the other patriarchs also built simple altars (12:7–8; 13:4, 18; 22:9; 26:25; 35:1–7). Later, with the erection of the TABERNACLE, elaborate altars were constructed by the Hebrews for sacrifices (Exod. 27:1–8) and also for the burning of INCENSE (30:1–10).

**Al-taschith** (al-tas′kith). A term found in the KJV in the titles of Ps. 57–59 and 75; it is a Hebrew phrase meaning "Do not destroy," and it may be the name of a tune.

**Amalek, Amalekites** (am′uh-lek, uh-mal′uh-kits). Amalek was a grandson of ESAU and a tribal chief of EDOM (Gen. 36:12, 15–16; 1 Chr. 1:36). The name is frequently applied to his descendants, the Amalekites, an ancient and nomadic people dwelling mainly in the NEGEV. They are first mentioned in the days of ABRAHAM (Gen. 14:7); later they became enemies of the Israelites (Exod. 17:8–16; Num. 14:45; Jdg. 3:13; 6:3, 33). During the monarchy, SAUL was commissioned to destroy them utterly but

The Amalekites roamed throughout a region known as the Desert of Zin. Z. Radovan/www.BibleLandPictures.com

failed to do so and spared their leader, AGAG (1 Sam. 15:8–9). The Amalekites are numbered among nations subdued by DAVID (2 Sam. 8:12; 1 Chr. 18:11).

**Amasa** (uh-may′suh). **(1)** A nephew of DAVID who was appointed captain of the Israelite army by ABSALOM when the latter attempted to overthrow David's rule in Israel (2 Sam. 17:25). After Absalom was defeated, David made Amasa captain of his army in place of JOAB (19:13), but later Joab assassinated him (20:8–10). **(2)** One of the princes of EPHRAIM who supported Oded the prophet in warning the Israelites not to take captives from JUDAH (2 Chr. 28:9–15).

**Amaziah** (am′uh-*zi*′uh). Son of Joash (JEHOASH) and his successor as king of JUDAH, reigning probably c. 796–767 BC (2 Ki. 14:1–20; 2 Chr. 25:1–28). Amaziah was quite successful against the Edomites but adopted their gods. Later he challenged the more powerful Jehoash, king of Israel, as a result of which he lost his kingdom.

**ambassador.** An official representative of a ruler or government. Ambassadors and envoys are mentioned throughout most of the biblical period (e.g., Num. 20:14; Jdg. 11:12; 2 Chr. 32:31; Isa. 30:4). In the NT the term is used only in a figurative sense of those who represent God (2 Cor. 5:20; Eph. 6:20).

**amen.** A Hebrew term used to express assent ("truly, verily"). In the OT it appears with doxologies (1 Chr. 16:36; Neh. 8:6; Ps. 41:13), with oaths (Neh. 5:13), etc. In the NT it can introduce a solemn saying of Jesus, always in the sense of "I tell you the truth" (Jn. 3:5). It is also used following a doxology (Rom. 11:36) or a benediction (15:33), as a title of God (Rev. 3:14), as an indication of agreement (1 Cor. 14:16), and in other contexts.

**amethyst.** A lovely violet or purple transparent variety of quartz included in the high priest's BREASTPIECE (Exod. 28:19; 39:12). One of the foundations of the new Jerusalem is decorated with this precious stone (Rev. 21:20).

**Ammon, Ammonites** (am′uhn, am′uh-*n*its). An ancient nation E of the JORDAN RIVER, N of MOAB; its inhabitants were descendants of Ben-Ammi, one of the sons of LOT (Gen. 19:38). They were closely related to the Moabites by ancestry and often appear in Scripture in united effort with them and as enemies of the Israelites (Deut 23:3–4; Jdg. 10–11; 1 Sam. 11:1–11; Ezek. 25:1–7; Amos 1:13–15). Although they were a nomadic people, they did have a few cities, their capital RABBAH (Rabbath-Ammon) being the most famous. Their chief idol was MOLECH (1 Ki. 11:7).

**Amnon** (am′non). Firstborn son of DAVID by AHINOAM (2 Sam. 3:2; 1 Chr. 3:1). He dishonored his half sister TAMAR and was subsequently slain (2 Sam. 13). See ABSALOM.

**Amon** (am′uhn). Son of MANASSEH and fifteenth king of JUDAH. The brief biblical accounts of Amon (2 Ki. 21:18–26 and 2 Chr. 33:20–25) describe him as an evil king who after only two years of reign (c. 642–640 BC) was slain by officials of his household. His son, however, was the illustrious King JOSIAH.

**Amorites** (am′uh-r*i*ts). A tribe of people who were descendants of CANAAN (Gen. 10:16) and apparently very wicked (15:16). It is believed that at one time their kingdom occupied the larger part of MESOPOTAMIA and SYRIA. Under the leadership of SIHON king of HESHBON, they subdued a large portion of the country of MOAB, where they settled (Num. 21:13, 26–31). JOSHUA defeated a league of five Amorite kings (Josh. 10).

**Amos, Book of** (ay′muhs). Amos was a shepherd who became a prophet and whose message is recorded in the book named after him. His ministry occurred in a time of great prosperity for the northern kingdom. This affluence was accompanied by social corruption, which he strongly denounced (Amos 2:6–8; 5:11–12). The style of his book, though simple, is picturesque, marked by striking illustrations taken from his rural surroundings.

**Amphipolis** (am-fip′uh-lis). A city of MACEDONIA, c. 33 mi. (53 km.) SW of PHILIPPI. PAUL passed through it on the way from Philippi to THESSALONICA (Acts 17:1).

**Anak, Anakim, Anakites** (ay′nak, an′uh-kim, an′uh-k*i*ts). Anak was a descendant of Arba, a Canaanite who possibly founded the city of Kiriath Arba, later known as HEBRON (Josh. 15:13). The descendants of Anak were the Anakites (some versions have "Anakim"), a tribe inhabiting PALESTINE in pre-Israelite times, with some relationship to the Nephilim or GIANTS (Num. 13:22, 33; cf. Gen. 6:4). See also REPHAIM (Deut. 2:11).

**Ananias** (an′uh-n*i*′uhs). **(1)** Husband of SAPPHIRA (Acts 5:1–11). He and his wife pretended to give to the church all they received from a sale of property but kept

## OVERVIEW OF AMOS

**AUTHOR:** Amos, a shepherd from TEKOA (near BETHLEHEM) who was called to serve as prophet, possibly for only a limited period of time.

**HISTORICAL SETTING:** Amos received his revelation about the year 760 BC, during the latter part of the prosperous reign of JEROBOAM II of ISRAEL. His ministry was directed primarily to the northern kingdom, making special reference to the region of SAMARIA and the city of BETHEL.

**PURPOSE:** To condemn the IDOLATRY prevalent in Israel and to challenge the social injustice of its wealthy inhabitants.

**CONTENTS:** The book begins with a general indictment of various nations (Amos 1–2), followed by an extensive condemnation of the northern kingdom of Israel (chs. 3–6) and by predictions of its destruction (chs. 7–9), although the prophecy ends with a promise of restoration (9:11–15).

Byzantine remains in Amphipolis. Todd Bolen/www.BiblePlaces.com

back part. When PETER denounced his deceit, Ananias fell down dead. **(2)** A disciple at DAMASCUS who, obeying a vision, was the means of healing the sight of Saul of Tarsus (PAUL) and of introducing him to the Christians of that city (Acts 9:10–19; 22:12–16). **(3)** A high priest before whom Paul was tried in JERUSALEM (Acts 23:1–5; also mentioned in 24:1).

**anathema** (uh-nath′uh-muh). This term, borrowed directly from Greek, occurs once in the KJV (1 Cor. 16:22) but not at all in most modern versions. The SEPTUAGINT uses the Greek term frequently (e.g., Lev. 27:28–29), referring to that which is devoted to God and withdrawn from common use; a person so devoted is doomed to death. The Greek word, usually translated "cursed" or the like, appears several times in the NT (Acts 23:14; Rom. 3:9; 1 Cor. 12:3; 16:22; Gal. 1:9).

**Anathoth** (an′uh-thoth). One of the forty-eight cities allotted to the Levites in the tribal territory of BENJAMIN (Josh. 21:18). Located some 2.5 mi. (4 km.) NE of JERUSALEM, Anathoth was the native place of ABIATHAR the priest (1 Ki. 2:26) and JEREMIAH the prophet (Jer. 1:1) and is mentioned several times in the OT (e.g., 2 Sam. 23:27; Isa. 10:30).

**Ancient of Days.** This elegant expression, meaning someone very old, occurs only in Dan. 7:9, 13, and 22, with reference to God. It was probably chosen to contrast the Lord and his kingdom with the temporary duration of the four successive kingdoms that are mentioned earlier in the chapter.

**Andrew** (an′dr*oo*). The brother of Simon PETER and one of the first disciples of Jesus. The name is Greek. Originally from BETHSAIDA in GALILEE (Jn. 1:44; 12:21), he was a fisherman who lived in CAPERNAUM with his brother (Mk. 1:29). Andrew was first a disciple of JOHN the Baptist (Jn. 1:25–42), but later Jesus called the two brothers to abandon their fishing and they became apostles (Matt. 4:18–19; 10:2; Mk. 3:18; Lk. 6:14; Acts 1:13). He is associated with the feeding of the five thousand (Jn. 6:6–9) and also with the request of the Greeks to see Jesus (12:22).

**Andronicus** (an-dron′uh-kuhs). An outstanding Christian at Rome to whom PAUL sent greetings (Rom. 16:7). The apostle calls him and JUNIAS "my relatives," though the Greek term may indicate simply fellow Jews (cf. 9:3).

**angel.** A supernatural, heavenly being. The English term is derived from Greek *angelos* and corresponds to Hebrew *mal'ak*, both meaning "messenger." Angels are created beings (Ps. 148:2–5; Col. 1:16) and are described as "spirits" (Heb. 1:14). Jesus said that they do not marry and do not die (Lk. 20:34–36). Their knowledge is limited (Matt. 24:36; 1 Pet. 1:12). Only one, MICHAEL, is expressly called an archangel in Scripture (Jude 9). The work of the angels is varied: they stand in the presence of God and worship him (Matt. 18:10; Heb. 1:6; Rev. 5:11); they also assist, protect, and deliver God's people (Gen. 19:11; Ps. 91:11; Dan. 3:28; 6:22; Acts 5:19). Some angels, however, rebelled against God's authority (see DEMON; SATAN).

**angel of the Lord.** This phrase (or "the angel of God") occurs frequently in the OT, and in almost every case the angel or messenger is regarded as deity and yet is distinguished from God (Gen. 16:7–14; 22:11–18; 31:11, 13; Exod. 3:2–5; Num. 22:22–35; Jdg. 6:11–23; 13:2–25; 1 Ki. 19:5–7; 1 Chr. 21:15–17). Evidently the Lord himself was adopting a visible form (and therefore a human appearance) for the sake of speaking with people. Many students of the Bible regard these appearances as Christophanies, manifestations of the Christ prior to the INCARNATION.

**anger.** A strong feeling of displeasure, often involving hostility. The Bible condemns anger because it encourages folly and evil (Ps. 37:8; Prov. 14:29; Matt. 5:22; 1 Tim. 2:8; Jas. 1:19–20). There is righteous anger, however, as when Jesus condemned the misuse of the TEMPLE (Jn. 2:12–17), the corruption of others (Mk. 9:42), and lack of compassion (3:5). It is possible to be angry without sinning (Eph. 4:26). The wrath of a just, pure, and holy God is dreadful to evildoers (Num. 11:1–10; Heb. 10:26–31), yet God is slow to anger, eager to forgive (Ps. 103:8–9), and so should we be (Eph. 4:31–32).

**Anna** (an′uh). A woman who lost her husband after seven years of marriage. She was a prophetess, and at the age of eighty-four, when the infant Jesus was brought into the TEMPLE to be dedicated, she recognized and proclaimed him as the MESSIAH (Lk. 2:36–38).

**Annas** (an′uhs). A HIGH PRIEST of the Jews from AD 6 to 15; he was father-in-law of CAIAPHAS, also a high priest (Jn. 18:13). When Jesus was arrested, he was led first to Annas (18:13) and only later was sent bound to Caiaphas (18:24). Annas is called the high priest in Acts 4:6.

**annunciation.** This term, though not found in Scripture, is used mainly with reference to the supernatural announcement made by the angel GABRIEL to MARY that she would conceive and give birth (Lk. 1:26–38).

**anoint.** To apply OIL to a person or thing. (1) Ordinary anointing with scented oils was common (Ruth 3:3; Ps. 23:5; 104:15; Prov. 27:9; Lk. 7:46). (2) There was also a special or sacred anointing, used to dedicate a thing or person to God (Gen. 28:18;

Exod. 30:22–29; 1 Sam. 9:16; 10:1; 1 Ki. 19:16). "The Lord's anointed" was the common term for a theocratic king (1 Sam. 12:3; Lam. 4:20) and could refer specifically to the coming MESSIAH; see also CHRIST. (3) Medical anointing, not necessarily with oil, was customary for the sick and wounded (Isa. 1:6; Mk. 6:13; Lk. 10:34; Jas. 5:14).

**antichrist.** A word meaning "against Christ" or "instead of Christ"; thus it may refer either to an enemy of CHRIST or to one who usurps Christ's name and rights. The word is found in only four verses (1 Jn. 2:18, 22; 4:3; 2 Jn. 7), but the idea appears elsewhere. For example, Jesus warned against the "false Christs" and the "false prophets" who would lead astray, if possible, even the elect (Matt. 24:24; Mk. 13:22). In 2 Thess. 2:1–12 PAUL gives us a very full description of a specific figure he calls "the man of lawlessness." The beast of Rev. 17:8 claims divine honor and makes war on God's people but is eventually destroyed by the Lord in a great battle (19:19–20).

**Antioch** (an′tee-ok). **(1)** Antioch of SYRIA was built in 301 BC on the Orontes River, 15 navigable mi. (24 km.) from the MEDITERRANEAN, and became a great commercial center. Antioch has an important place in the early history of Christianity. Many Christians, scattered at the death of STEPHEN, went there and founded the first GENTILE church (Acts 11:19–21). The disciples were called Christians first in Antioch (11:26), and the church in this city sent PAUL and BARNABAS out on their missionary work (13:1–3; cf. 14:26–27; 18:22). **(2)** Antioch of PISIDIA was a town in southern Asia Minor (modern Turkey) that became a part of the Roman province of GALATIA. Paul and Barnabas preached in the synagogue there on their first missionary journey (Acts 13:14–50; cf. also 14:21–23; 16:6; 18:23).

**Antipas** (an′tee-puhs). **(1)** A son of HEROD the Great who was made tetrarch of GALILEE and PEREA; he is simply called Herod in the NT (e.g., Lk. 3:1; 9:7; 13:31; 23:7–12). **(2)** A faithful Christian martyr in PERGAMUM (Rev. 2:13).

**anxiety.** See FEAR.

**Aphek** (ay′fek). The name of several towns in PALESTINE, including one on the Plain of SHARON near JOPPA (Josh. 12:18; 1 Sam. 4:1; 29:1) and another one E of the JORDAN where important battles were fought (1 Ki. 20:26–34; 2 Ki. 13:14–25).

**Apocalypse** (uh-pok′uh-lips′). Alternate name for the book of Revelation (see REVELATION, BOOK OF). The term *apocalyptic* refers to a religious point of view among Jewish groups that emphasized supposed revelations of the secret purposes of God, the end of the world, and the establishment of God's kingdom on earth.

**Apocrypha.** This term is applied to a group of books that are included as part of the OT in some editions of the Bible (e.g., in Roman Catholic versions). Although much valuable material is found in them, they are

These medieval ruins in Antioch of Pisidia possibly mark the site of the synagogue where Paul preached. www.HolyLandPhotos.org

not regarded as part of Scripture by most Protestants.

**Apollos** (uh-pol′uhs). A gifted and zealous preacher in the early Christian church (Acts 18:24–28; 19:1; 1 Cor. 1:12; 3:4–6, 22; 4:6; 16:12; Tit. 3:13). A native of ALEXANDRIA who had received the baptism associated with JOHN the Baptist, Apollos met AQUILA and PRISCILLA in EPHESUS and gained a fuller understanding of the GOSPEL. He then had a very effective ministry, especially in CORINTH.

**Apollyon.** See ABADDON.

**apostasy.** The abandonment of one's religion. The word is seldom found in English translations of the Bible, but it describes Israel's rebellion against God (Josh. 22:22; 2 Chr. 29:19; Jer. 2:19) as well as the act of falling away from Christian faith (1 Tim. 4:1; 2 Tim. 2:18), though many believe that this refers to those who had never truly believed (1 Jn. 1:19; cf. Jn. 15:6). PAUL applies the term to the coming of a time of great rebellion against God (2 Thess. 2:3).

**apostle.** This term, which derives from a Greek word meaning "one sent out," is applied once to CHRIST himself (Heb. 3:1), pointing to his role on earth as the ambassador of the Father. Usually, the word describes the twelve disciples whom Jesus chose to be with him and whom he commissioned and sent out to preach (Matt. 10:2; Mk. 3:14; 6:30; Lk. 6:13; 9:10; 11:49; 17:5; 22:14; 24:10). These men were the primary witnesses of the resurrection of Jesus, and their task was to proclaim the GOSPEL of God, establish churches, and teach sound doctrine (Acts 4:33; 5:12; 5:29; 8:1, 14–18). Since PAUL met the resurrected and glorified Jesus and was given a commission by him to be the messenger to the GENTILES, he too was regarded as an apostle (Rom. 1:1; Gal. 1:1). Sometimes the term is used in a more general way (e.g., Acts 14:4; Rom. 16:7).

**Apostolic Council.** See COUNCIL.

**Appius, Forum of** (ap′ee-uhs, for′uhm). A *forum* was the public square or marketplace of an ancient Roman city, and the Forum of Appius was a traveler's stop on the Appian Way, about 40 mi. (64 km.) S of ROME, where PAUL was met by Roman Christians on his way to the capital under guard (Acts 28:15).

**Aquila** (ak′wi-luh, uh-kwi′luh). A Jewish Christian whom PAUL found at CORINTH on his arrival from ATHENS (Acts 18:2, 18, 26; Rom. 16:3–4; 1 Cor. 16:19; 2 Tim. 4:19). Aquila and his wife PRISCILLA are always mentioned together. They received Paul into their home, where he remained for a year and a half. Their willingness to "risk their lives" for him earned the gratitude of all the churches. APOLLOS and many others were helped by their spiritual insight.

**Arab** (a′ruhb, air′uhb). See ARABIA.

**Arabah** (air′uh-buh). The great rift valley running S from the Sea of Galilee, including the JORDAN Valley and the DEAD SEA and extending all the way to the Gulf of Aqabah. In the KJV, the Hebrew word is rendered as the proper name "Arabah" only in Josh. 18:18 (elsewhere as "desert," "plain," "wilderness"). Modern translations more frequently take it as a proper name.

**Arabia** (uh-ray′bee-uh). A large and arid peninsula of SW Asia, bounded N by the Fertile Crescent, E by the Persian Gulf, SE and S by the Indian Ocean, SW and W by the Red Sea. Arabia or its inhabitants (Arabs, Arabians) are mentioned frequently in the OT (e.g., 1 Ki. 10:15; 2 Chr. 17:11; Isa. 21:13–17) and a few times in the NT (Acts 2:11; Gal. 1:17; 4:25).

**Arad** (a′rad, air′ad). A city in the NE NEGEV, some 17 mi. (27 km.) S of HEBRON. Arad

Aerial view of ancient Arad. The lower city (c. 2600 BC) is encompassed by a massive wall, while the Israelite fortress is situated on the upper area of the tell. © Baker Publishing Group

occupied an excellent strategic position and was a center of civilization from early times (Num. 21:1; 33:40; Josh. 12:14; Jdg. 1:16; in the first two passages, the KJV takes it as the name of a king).

**Aram, Aramean** (air′uhm, air′uh-mee′uhn). Aram was one of the five sons of SHEM (Gen. 10:22–23) and probably the ancestor of the Arameans. His name is also used for a country or region N of ISRAEL and extending eastward to MESOPOTAMIA (Aram is called SYRIA in the KJV and other versions). The Arameans (Syrians) established kingdoms and formed loose confederacies that frequently interacted with the Israelites, usually as enemies. The most important Aramean city was DAMASCUS. Prominent kings included several by the name (or title) of BEN-HADAD, as well as HADADEZER and REZON, who were rulers in ZOBAH.

**Aramaic** (air′uh-may′ik). A Semitic language closely related to HEBREW. Already in Gen. 31:47 Aramaic is mentioned as the language used by LABAN in contrast to JACOB's use of Hebrew. By the eighth century BC Aramaic had become the language of diplomacy (2 Ki. 18:26; Isa. 36:11), and it was adopted by the Jews during the Babylonian EXILE. Substantial sections in Ezra and Daniel are written in this language (Ezra 4:8–6:18; 7:12–26; Dan. 2:4–7:28). It was probably Jesus' mother tongue. Several Aramaic words occur in the NT, including ABBA and MARANATHA.

**Aram Naharaim** (air′uhm-nay-huh-ray′im). This name, usually rendered MESOPOTAMIA by the KJV, refers to the same general area as PADDAN ARAM, roughly between the rivers EUPHRATES and Habor (Gen. 24:10; Deut. 23:4; Jdg. 3:8–10; 1 Chr. 19:6).

**Ararat** (air′uh-rat). A region in Armenia, adjacent to Turkey (2 Ki. 19:37). The area is a mountainous tableland from which flow the TIGRIS, EUPHRATES, and other rivers. Its highest mountain (almost 17,000 ft. / 5,180 m.), called Mount Ararat, is now part of Turkey, and on that peak NOAH's ark is supposed to have rested (though the plural in Gen. 8:4 is indefinite: "On the mountains of Ararat").

**Araunah, Ornan** (uh-raw′nuh, or′nuhn). A Jebusite (see JEBUS) who owned the threshing floor on Mount MORIAH that DAVID purchased in order to erect an altar (2 Sam. 24:15–25; 1 Chr. 21:18–28 KJV).

**archangel.** A chief ANGEL (1 Thess 4:16; Jude 9). See MICHAEL.

**Archelaus** (ahr′kuh-lay′uhs). Son of HEROD the Great (Matt. 2:22); he succeeded his father as ruler of IDUMEA, SAMARIA, and JUDEA in 4 BC, but was deposed by the Roman government in AD 6.

**Archippus** (ahr-kip′uhs). A prominent Christian at COLOSSE; he was a close friend or relative of PHILEMON (Col. 4:17; Phlm. 2).

**Areopagus** (air′ee-op′uh-guhs). A Greek word meaning "hill of Ares" (god of war). Also known as "Mars' Hill" (Mars was the Roman god of war), the Areopagus is a large, irregular outcropping of limestone about 380 ft. (115 m.) high. It lies NW of the ACROPOLIS in ATHENS. Areopagus is also the name of the council that met on the hill, and PAUL was brought to this group to be examined regarding his teaching (Acts 17:19–22). DIONYSIUS the Areopagite, who became a Christian, was apparently a member of the court (17:34).

**Aretas** (air′uh-tuhs). A king of Nabatea (an Arabian kingdom) whose deputy sought to apprehend PAUL at DAMASCUS (2 Cor. 11:32; cf. Acts 9:24). The name (or title?) Aretas was borne by several rulers, and the king mentioned in the NT was Aretas IV.

**Ariel** (air′ee-uhl). A symbolical designation for JERUSALEM (Isa. 29:1–2, 7). The name may mean "God's hearth" or "God's lion."

**Arimathea** (air′uh-muh-thee′uh). The native town of JOSEPH, who obtained the body of Jesus and placed it in his own unused tomb (Matt. 27:57–60; Mk. 15:43; Lk. 23:50–53; Jn. 19:38). The location of Arimathea may have been some 20 mi. (32 km.) NW of JERUSALEM.

**Aristarchus** (air′is-tahr′kuhs). A Macedonian Christian from THESSALONICA. In EPHESUS, he and GAIUS were seized by the mob and rushed into the theater (Acts 19:29); later he accompanied PAUL to JERUSALEM (20:4) and was present also when the apostle left CAESAREA headed for ROME (see also Col. 4:10; Phlm. 24).

**ark.** (1) A vessel that God ordered NOAH to build for the purpose of preserving through the time of the FLOOD a remnant of the human race, together with two each of all animals (Gen. 6:14–16). The ark floated during the flood (7:11–8:3), then came to rest on the mountains of ARARAT (8:4). The ark of Noah is mentioned several times in the NT (Matt. 24:38; Lk. 17:27; Heb. 11:7; 1 Pet. 3:20). (2) The phrase "ark of bulrushes" is used by the KJV to describe the small basket made for the infant MOSES, in which he was floated on the NILE in order to escape detection by the Egyptians (Exod. 2:3). (3) The "ark of the covenant" (or "ark of the testimony") was a wooden chest overlaid with gold and resting in the TABERNACLE; it contained the tablets of the LAW, a gold jar of MANNA, and AARON's STAFF (Exod. 25:10–22; Deut. 10:2–5; Heb. 9:4). The ark was instrumental in the crossing of the JORDAN on dry land under JOSHUA (Josh. 3) and in the capture of JERICHO (4:7–11). In the days of ELI the ark was taken into battle against the PHILISTINES, who captured it but later returned it (1 Sam. 4–6). DAVID brought the ark to JERUSALEM (2 Sam. 6; 1 Chr. 13; 15), and it was later placed in SOLOMON's temple (1 Ki. 8:3–9). It was probably destroyed when the Babylonians captured Jerusalem.

**Armageddon** (ahr′muh-ged′uhn). Also Harmagedon. Probably meaning "mountain of Megiddo," this name is found only in Rev. 16:16 and refers to the final battleground between the forces of good and the forces of evil. The Valley of JEZREEL (Plain of Esdraelon) at the foot of Mount MEGIDDO was the scene of many decisive incidents in the history of Israel (e.g., Jdg. 5:19–20; 6:33; 1 Sam. 31; cf. 2 Sam. 4:4).

**Arnon** (ahr'nuhn). A river and valley that descend to the E side of the DEAD SEA; the river is dry most of the year. The Arnon served as the boundary between MOAB and the AMORITES in the time of MOSES (Num. 21:13; see also Jdg. 11:18–26; 2 Ki. 10:32–33).

**Aroer** (uh-roh'uhr). The name of several cities, including one E of the JORDAN on the N bank of the river ARNON about 14 mi. (23 km.) from the DEAD SEA. Initially it indicated the southern limit of the AMORITE kingdom of SIHON and was taken by Israel under MOSES (Deut. 2:36; 3:12; 4:48; Josh. 12:2; 13:7, 16; Jer. 48:18–20).

**Artaxerxes** (ahr'tuh-zuhrk'seez). The name of several Persian kings. The one mentioned in the Bible was Artaxerxes I Longimanus (464–424 BC), who reigned during the days of EZRA and NEHEMIAH and allowed their respective missions in JERUSALEM (Ezra 7:11–26; Neh. 2:1–8).

**Artemis** (ahr'tuh-mis). A goddess worshiped throughout the Greek world, identified as Diana by the Romans. Regarded as a hunter and as the nursing mother of nature, Artemis was the official goddess of EPHESUS. PAUL's preaching in that city caused a riot because it disrupted the business of the silversmiths who made shrines in her honor (Acts 19:24–35; "Diana" in KJV).

**Asa** (ay'suh). Third king of JUDAH, reigning from c. 910 to 869 BC (1 Ki. 15:9–24; 2 Chr. 14–16). He was the son of ABIJAH and grandson of REHOBOAM. Asa began his reign by deposing his wicked and powerful grandmother Maacah and by destroying the idols that his ancestors had worshiped. Later, however, he failed to trust in God and depended on political alliances. In the thirty-ninth year of his reign, he was taken with a severe disease of the feet and died two years later.

**Asahel** (as'uh-hel). DAVID's nephew (brother of JOAB and ABISHAI), noted for his bravery and fleetness. He became one of David's thirty mighty warriors but was killed by ABNER in battle (2 Sam. 2:18–23; 23:24; 1 Chr. 2:16; 27:7).

**Asaph** (ay'saf). A LEVITE appointed over the service of praise in the time of DAVID and SOLOMON (1 Chr. 16:5; 2 Chr. 5:12). He led the singing and sounded cymbals before the ark and apparently set up a school of music (Neh. 7:44). Twelve psalms are credited to Asaph (Ps. 50; 73–83).

**ascension of Christ.** The "going up" of Jesus to heaven after his RESURRECTION in order

Looking NE into the valley of the Arnon River. 

to sit at the right hand of the Father (Mk. 16:19; Lk. 24:51; Acts 1:9–11; Eph. 4:8–11; Heb. 1:3–4; 4:14; 6:19–20).

**Asenath** (as′uh-nath). Daughter of the Egyptian priest POTIPHERA. The PHARAOH gave her to JOSEPH as a wife, and she became the mother of EPHRAIM and MANASSEH (Gen. 41:45, 50; 46:20).

**Ashdod** (ash′dod). One of the five chief cities of the PHILISTINES: the other four were GAZA, ASHKELON, GATH, and EKRON. Ashdod was a center of DAGON worship, and when the Philistines thought to honor the ARK by placing it in their temple, God destroyed their idol (1 Sam. 5–6). The city is mentioned in various passages (e.g., Josh. 11:22; 2 Chr. 26:6; Isa. 20:1; Jer. 25:20; Amos 1:8). It is called Azotus in the NT (Acts 8:40).

**Asher** (ash′uhr). Son of JACOB (Gen 30:13) and ancestor of the Israelite tribe known by his name (Num. 1:13). The Asherites were given the territory along the Mediterranean in the NW corner of PALESTINE (Josh. 19:24–31).

Chapel of the Ascension on the Mount of Olives in Jerusalem.



**Asherah** (uh-shihr′uh). A Canaanite goddess (2 Ki. 23:7); the same Hebrew term (translated "grove" by KJV) can also refer to the sacred wooden poles associated with her cult (e.g., Exod. 34:13; Jdg. 6:25–30; 1 Ki. 14:13).

**Ashkelon** (ash′kuh-lon). One of the five chief cities of the PHILISTINES, situated on the MEDITERRANEAN sea coast about midway between ASHDOD and GAZA. Ashkelon was taken by the tribe of JUDAH shortly after the death of JOSHUA (Jdg. 1:18) but was retaken by the Philistines and denounced by the prophets (e.g., Jer 47:5; Amos 1:6–8).

**Ashtaroth** (ash′tuh-roth). A city E of the Sea of Galilee, home of OG king of BASHAN (Deut. 1:4; Josh. 9:10). The KJV and other versions also use the form Ashtaroth as the plural of ASHTORETH, the Canaanite goddess (e.g., Jdg. 2:13).

**Ashtoreth** (ash′tuh-reth). The OT Hebrew name of a Canaanite goddess otherwise known as Astarte (from Gk. sources) and corresponding to the Mesopotamian deity Ishtar (Jdg. 2:11–23; 1 Sam. 7:3–4; 1 Ki. 11:4–8; 2 Ki. 23:13–14).

**Asia** (ay′shuh). In the NT (e.g., Acts 2:9; 16:6; Rom. 16:5; Rev 1:4) this name always refers to a Roman province that comprised nearly one-third of the W end of Asia Minor (modern Turkey). This province was the richest part of the great peninsula. Its capital was EPHESUS.

**assembly.** See CONGREGATION.

**Asshur** (ash′uhr). Also Ashur and Assur. One of the three sons of SHEM (Gen. 10:22; 1 Chr. 1:17); his name was borne also by the people and territory of ASSYRIA (e.g., Gen. 2:14; Num. 24:22; most occurrences of the Heb. name are usually rendered "Assyria" or "Assyrians," e.g., 2 Ki. 15:19–20; Isa.

7:17–20; 19:23). Outside the Bible, Asshur is used also as the name of the Assyrian patron god and of the country's first capital city.

**assurance.** For Christian believers, FAITH in Jesus CHRIST and commitment to him carries with it assurance of salvation, confidence that they belong to God (Rom. 8:38–39; 1 Cor. 2:9–13; Col. 2:2; 1 Thess. 2:13; 2 Tim. 1:12; Heb. 10:22; cf. 6:11). There is also the internal witness of the HOLY SPIRIT bringing the knowledge that the believer is truly a child of God (Rom. 8:15–16) as well as the external testimony of a changed life (1 Jn. 2:3–5, 29; 3:9–14, 18–19; 4:7).

**Assyria** (uh-sir′ee-uh). A country in N MESOPOTAMIA with its capital first at ASSHUR, later at NINEVEH. Assyria was already a powerful political force by the time ISRAEL became a monarchy in the eleventh century BC, and by the ninth century it had developed into the dominant empire of the ancient Near East. In c. 733 BC the Assyrian king TIGLATH-PILESER III entered PALESTINE; his successor, SHALMANESER V, invaded the northern kingdom of Israel, and SAMARIA was captured in the year 721 (2 Ki. 17:3–6). Another Assyrian king, SENNACHERIB, nearly captured JERUSALEM in c. 700 (18:13–19:37). The empire then suffered decline, and Nineveh was taken by the Babylonians in 612. See BABYLONIA.

**astrology.** The observation of the sun, moon, planets, and stars for the purpose of determining the character of individuals and the course of events. The practice was common in BABYLONIA. Although the term *astrologer* appears several times in the English Bible (e.g., Dan. 2:2 NIV, but see marginal note), the only certain references to the practice are found in Isa. 47:13 and Jer. 10:2.

**Aswan** (as-wahn′). See SYENE.

Assyrian Empire.

A

**Athaliah** (ath'uh-li'uh). The wife of JEHORAM, king of JUDAH, and daughter of AHAB, king of ISRAEL (2 Ki. 8:18). Athaliah inherited the unscrupulous nature of her mother JEZEBEL and was responsible for introducing into Judah the worship of the Phoenician god, BAAL. After the death of her son AHAZIAH, Athaliah became the only woman to reign over Judah in OT times. She tried to exterminate the royal line, but in her seventh year she was assassinated (2 Ki. 11:1–20; 2 Chr. 22:10–23:21).

**Athens** (ath'inz). Chief city of GREECE (named after its patron goddess, Athene). Built around a rocky hill called the ACROPOLIS, the city is 4.5 mi. (7 km.) from the sea. PAUL visited Athens on his second missionary journey and spoke to an interested but somewhat disdainful audience (Acts 17).

**atonement.** A sacrificial act by which God restores the broken relationship between himself and sinful human beings. In the OT atonement was made by sacrificing animals (e.g., Exod. 29:36; Lev. 1:4). Although such offerings were made on a daily basis, the Day of Atonement (Yom Kippur) was a special event that took place only once a year to cover the sins of the people as a whole (Lev. 16; see SCAPEGOAT). According to the NT, animal SACRIFICES were only a shadow of the death of CHRIST, who alone can accomplish atonement (Rom. 3:25; Heb. 2:17; 7:23–28; 9:23–28). See PROPITIATION AND EXPIATION; RECONCILIATION.

**Augustus Caesar** (aw-guhs'tuhs see'zuhr). Augustus was the honorific title conferred in 27 BC on Octavian (Gaius Octavius, 63 BC to AD 14), the first of the Roman "emperors." Although he preserved the forms of a republic, he gradually assumed all the power into his hands. He is mentioned just once in the NT as the emperor under whose reign Jesus was born (Lk. 2:1). See CAESAR.

**avenger.** The Hebrew word *go'el* refers to the "next of kin" who was expected to protect

The Acropolis in Athens, with the Parthenon in the center.

a suffering relative (Ruth 3:12–13; 4:2–10) and can be applied to the Lord himself as the ultimate "Redeemer" (Isa. 43:14; see REDEMPTION). In addition, a *go'el* had the authority to exact the vengeance that the law demands (Num. 35:11–34). See VENGEANCE.

**ayin** (*i*'yin). The sixteenth letter of the Hebrew alphabet (ʻ transliterated as ʻ), used to begin each verse in Ps. 119:121–28.

**Azariah** (az'uh-r*i*'uh). The name of about thirty persons in the OT, including a king of JUDAH who is better known as UZZIAH (2 Ki. 14:21) and a companion of DANIEL who was renamed ABEDNEGO (Dan. 1:6–7).

**Azazel.** See SCAPEGOAT.

**Azekah** (uh-zee'kuh). A town in NW JUDAH some 15 mi. (24 km.) NW of HEBRON (Josh. 10:10–11); it was one of the last towns to fall to NEBUCHADNEZZAR before he attacked JERUSALEM (Jer. 34:7).

**Azotus.** See ASHDOD.

# B

**Baal** (bay′uhl, bah-ahl′). This Hebrew word originally meant "master" or "owner," but it became the proper name for the most significant god in the Canaanite religions. He was viewed as a storm deity who controlled the fertility of crops and livestock. The struggle between Baalism and the worship of the true God came to a head on Mount CARMEL when the prophet ELIJAH met the priests of Baal and had 450 of them killed (1 Ki. 16:32; 18:17–40), but this heathen worship continued to influence ISRAEL. Its plural form, Baals (or Baalim), may indicate different manifestations of the one Baal or the independent existence of distinct local gods.

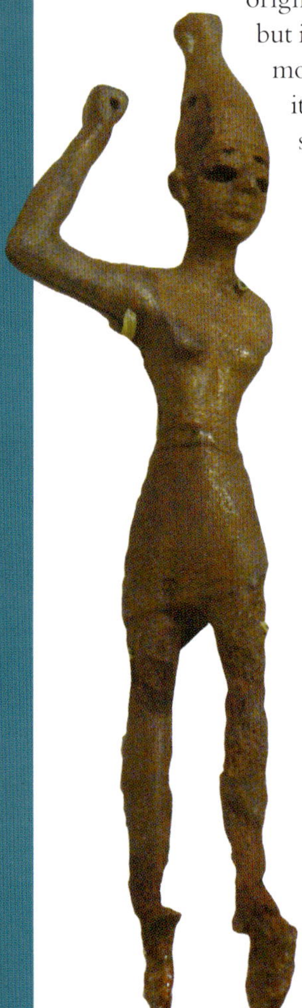

This ancient bronze statuette probably depicts the storm-god Baal.



**Baal-Berith** (bay′uhl-bi-rith′). A god worshiped by Israel after the death of GIDEON (Jdg. 8:33). ABIMELECH, Gideon's son, took seventy pieces of silver from the house of this god to hire followers in his time of rebellion (9:4).

**Baal Peor** (bay′uhl-pee′or). The "Baal of Peor" was a local deity worshiped by the Israelites while encamped at Shittim in MOAB (Num. 25:3–5). Their idolatry, involving immoral behavior with Moabite women, was considered a great sin (Num. 25:1–2; Ps. 106:28; Hos. 9:10). The same Hebrew name is used as a place name equivalent to Mount Peor (Deut. 4:3; Hos. 9:10).

**Baal Perazim** (bay′uhl-pi-ray′zim). Name given to a place a few miles SW of JERUSALEM where DAVID smote the PHILISTINES after he was made the king of ISRAEL (2 Sam. 5:20; 1 Chr. 14:11; cf. "Mount Perazim" in Isa. 28:21).

**Baal-Zebub** (bay′uhl-zee′buhb). The name (meaning "lord of the flies") under which BAAL was worshiped by the PHILISTINES of EKRON (2 Ki. 1:2, 3, 6, 16). See also BEELZEBUB.

**Baasha** (bay′uh-shuh). A man who became the third king of ISRAEL by assassinating NADAB son of JEROBOAM. He exterminated the house of Jeroboam and made TIRZAH his capital. During his reign of twenty-four years, he carried out a long war with ASA, king of Judah (1 Ki. 15–16).

**Babel, Tower of** (bay′buhl). An expression not found in the Bible, but commonly used for the structure built in the plain of SHINAR in ancient BABYLONIA (Gen. 11:1–9). Not long after the flood, the men of Shinar intended to build a tower that reached "to the heavens," but the Lord frustrated them by confusing their languages.

**Babylon** (bab′uh-luhn). Capital of the land of BABYLONIA, from which the land takes its

Facade of the Ishtar Gate from Babylon (restored version at the Pergamon Museum in Berlin). Paul Mannix/www.flickr.com

name. Babylon (meaning "the gate of the gods") was situated in central MESOPOTAMIA on the river EUPHRATES, some 50 mi. (80 km.) S of modern Baghdad, capital of Iraq. Being situated on an important caravan-trade route, it was in contact with all the most important cultural centers of the ancient Near East. The city was founded perhaps as early as 3000 BC and had a long and complicated history. Under NEBUCHADNEZZAR II (c. 605–562 BC) it attained the height of its splendor. The references to Babylon in the NT (1 Pet. 5:13; Rev. 14:8; etc.) are probably allusions to ROME.

**Babylonia** (bab´uh-loh´nee-uh). An ancient nation named after its capital city, BABYLON. It became a powerful kingdom (Old Babylonian empire) in the eighteenth century BC under Hammurabi but then declined in importance. The Neo-Babylonian empire arose in the eighth cent. BC and eventually defeated ASSYRIA. It was the Babylonians or Chaldeans who destroyed JERUSALEM in 586 and took many Jews captive. See CHALDEA.

**Bahurim** (buh-hyoor´im). A village in the territory of BENJAMIN, just NNE of the Mount of Olives (see OLIVES, MOUNT OF). It was the home of SHIMEI, who cursed DAVID, but some loyal supporters of the king lived there as well (2 Sam. 3:16; 16:5; 2 Sam. 17:18–20; 19:16).

**Balaam** (bay´luhm). A man from N MESOPOTAMIA who practiced divination and who was hired by BALAK, king of MOAB, to curse the Israelites; God prevented him from doing so and he blessed them instead (Num. 22:22–24:25; 31:8; 2 Pet. 2:15; Jude 11).

**Balak** (bay´lak). King of MOAB when Israel emerged from the wilderness to enter Canaan. Having seen what the Hebrews had done to the AMORITES, he attempted to prevent Israel's advance by hiring BALAAM to curse them (Num. 22–24).

B

**balance.** An instrument for weighing. The balances of the Hebrews consisted of a horizontal bar, with scales (trays) suspended from the ends of the bar, one for the object to be weighed, the other for the weight. The OT strongly condemns the use of "dishonest scales" (Mic. 6:11; cf. Lev. 19:36; Prov. 11:1).

**balm.** An aromatic resin (plant secretion) perhaps obtained in GILEAD (Gen. 37:25; Jer. 8:22; 46:11) and exported from PALESTINE. It was used as an ointment for healing wounds (Jer. 51:8).

**baptism.** Although this term can be used of water rituals in general, it usually refers to the Christian ceremony (or sacrament) of initiation whereby a person is received into the church. This observance was instituted by CHRIST (Matt. 28:18–20), and it indicates our identification with "the name of Jesus" (Acts 2:38), showing that we belong to him, but it has no magical saving power. The water symbolizes "the washing of rebirth" (Tit. 3:5) or cleansing from SIN (Acts 22:16; Eph. 5:26); it is closely linked with the saving work of the HOLY SPIRIT (Jn. 3:5; 1 Cor. 12:13) and with the human response of repentance and faith (Acts 2:38; 8:12). The ceremony pictures our death/burial to sin and RESURRECTION to new life (Rom. 6:4; Col. 2:12), our being clothed with Christ (Gal. 3:27), and our spiritual CIRCUMCISION (Col. 2:11). Christian groups have differed on whether immersion is the only proper form of baptism (some churches practice pouring or sprinkling) and on whether it is permissible to baptize infants (some churches believe that those baptized must be old enough to make an intelligent profession of faith).

**Barabbas** (buh-rab'uhs). A criminal who was chosen by the JERUSALEM mob, at the instigation of the chief priests, to be released instead of Jesus Christ (Matt. 27:16–26 and parallels). His personal name may have been JESUS (see TNIV and NRSV at 27:16–17).

**Barak** (bair'ak). An Israelite commander who, under DEBORAH, defeated the forces of JABIN, Canaanite king of HAZOR (Jdg. 4:1–24; Heb. 11:32).

**barbarian.** In English this term has a negative connotation, indicating that a person or culture is "uncivilized," lacking in refinement. The Greek word could have that sense too, but it primarily meant "foreign-speaking" or "foreign," that is, "non-Greek" (it appears in Acts 28:2, 4; Rom. 1:14; 1 Cor. 14:11; Col. 3:11).

**Bar-Jesus** (bahr-jee'zuhs). A "Jewish sorcerer and false prophet" at PAPHOS on CYPRUS who became temporarily blind when PAUL denounced him (Acts 13:6–11). The name means "Son of Joshua."

**Barnabas** (bahr'nuh-buhs). A Jewish Christian from CYPRUS who in the early days of the church sold a field and gave the proceeds to support the poorer members of the church in JERUSALEM (Acts 4:36–37). He was sent to oversee the Christian community in ANTIOCH of Syria (11:22–26), and later the church there commissioned him and Saul (PAUL) to embark on a missionary journey (chs. 13–14). Although the two men separated over a dispute (15:36–41; cf. Gal. 2:13), their mutual affection did not cease (1 Cor. 9:6; Col. 4:10).

**barrenness.** Infertility of land or of living beings; inability to bear children. To be a wife without motherhood has always been regarded in the E not merely as a matter of regret but also of reproach and humiliation (Gen. 18:12; 1 Sam. 1:10–17). The first mothers of the Hebrew race were by nature barren (Gen. 11:30; 25:21; 29:31), and therefore God's special intervention showed his favor to Israel. ISAIAH compared the nation of Israel with a barren woman who will sing because of the promise of children (Isa. 54:1), and PAUL appealed to that promise to illustrate the principle of freedom from the law (Gal. 4:27).

**Bartholomew** (bahr-thol′uh-my*oo*). One of the twelve apostles (Matt. 10:3; Mk. 3:18; Lk. 6:14; Acts 1:13). The Gospel of John never mentions Bartholomew, while the Synoptic Gospels and Acts never mention NATHANAEL (Jn. 1:45–46), and so many scholars believe that Bartholomew (Aramaic for "Son of Talmai") was Nathanael's surname.

**Bartimaeus** (bahr′tuh-mee′uhs). A blind man healed by Jesus as he went out from JERICHO (Mk. 10:46–52; similar accounts are given in Matt. 20:29–34 and Lk. 18:35–43).

**Baruch** (bair′uhk). A devoted friend of JEREMIAH who served as the prophet's secretary (Jer. 32:12; 36:4–32).

**Barzillai** (bahr-zil′*i*). An aged and wealthy man from GILEAD who, with others, brought provisions to DAVID and his army while they were fleeing from ABSALOM (2 Sam. 17:27; also mentioned in 19:31–39; 1 Ki. 2:7).

**Bashan** (bay′shuhn). The fertile tract of country on the E side of the upper JORDAN, adjacent to the Sea of Galilee. At one time it was ruled by the AMORITE king OG, but the entire district was assigned to the half tribe of MANASSEH (Deut. 3:13). Bashan is frequently mentioned in the OT (e.g., 1 Chr. 5:11; Ps. 22:12; Isa. 2:13; Ezek. 39:18).

**bath.** A Hebrew term referring to the standard liquid measure used in Israel (approximately 5–6 gallons).

**Bathsheba** (bath-shee′buh). Wife of URIAH the HITTITE, a soldier in DAVID's army. David committed adultery with her and she became pregnant; he then succeeded in having Uriah killed and married Bathsheba. Their child died, but she gave birth to other sons, including SOLOMON (2 Sam. 11–12). Many years later, with the help of the prophet NATHAN, she defeated the plot of ADONIJAH to usurp the kingdom and persuaded David to choose Solomon as his successor (1 Ki. 1:11–35).

**Beatitudes** (bee-at′uh-t*oo*ds). This term, which is not found in the Bible, refers to a state of blessedness and joy; it is applied most often to Jesus' initial declarations in the SERMON ON THE MOUNT (Matt. 5:3–11; cf. Lk. 6:20–22).

The so-called Mount of Beatitudes; on top of the hill sits the Church of Beatitudes.

**Beelzebub, Beelzebul** (bee-el′zi-buhb, -buhl). The first spelling links this name with BAAL-ZEBUB, but most Greek manuscripts of the NT spell it *Beelzebul* (origin and meaning unknown). He is described as "the prince of demons," possibly a reference to SATAN; Jesus was accused of casting out demons by the power of Beelzebul (Mk. 3:22; see also Matt. 10:25; 12:24–27; Lk. 11:18–19).

**Beersheba** (bee′uhr-shee′buh). The most southerly town of the Hebrews, hence the nation's practical boundary line; the familiar expression "from Dan to Beersheba" is used to designate the northern and southern extremities of the nation of ISRAEL (2 Sam. 3:10; 17:11; 24:2). The town figures in several important incidents (e.g., Gen. 21:14, 32; 22:19; 46:1; 1 Ki. 19:3).

Beersheba was the most southerly town in the nation of Israel.

**Belial** (bee′lee-uhl). A term that appears especially in the scornful phrase "sons of Belial" (e.g., Deut. 13:13; NIV "wicked men"). The Hebrew word is probably not a name but a term meaning "worthlessness." In the NT, Belial (Beliar) occurs once as the name of a figure (SATAN or ANTICHRIST) that stands opposed to Christ (2 Cor. 6:15).

**Belshazzar** (bel-shaz′uhr). King of BABYLON, known for the writing on the wall that appeared during a great banquet and that predicted his fall (Dan. 5; 7:1; 8:1).

**Belteshazzar** (bel′ti-shaz′uhr). The Babylonian name given to DANIEL (Dan. 1:7; 2:26; etc.).

**Benaiah** (bi-nay′yuh). The name of various men in the OT, especially a commander under DAVID (2 Sam. 8:18; 20:23). He is described as "a valiant fighter" and was put in charge of the king's bodyguard (2 Sam. 23:20–23; 1 Chr. 11:22–25; 27:5–6). Later he was among those chosen to make arrangements for the proclamation of SOLOMON as king (1 Ki. 1:32–40) and replaced JOAB as head of the army (2:35; 4:4).

**Ben-Ammi** (ben-am′*i*). See AMMON.

**Ben-Hadad** (ben-hay′dad). The name or title of three Aramean kings (see ARAM). **(1)** Ben-Hadad I, son of Tabrimmon and grandson of Hezion, ruled in DAMASCUS and was a contemporary with ASA, king of JUDAH, from 910 to 869 BC (1 Ki. 15:18–20). **(2)** Ben-Hadad II (1 Ki. 20:1–34; 2 Ki. 6:24; 8:7–9), probably the son of Ben-Hadad I, was contemporary with AHAB of ISRAEL (873–853 BC), against whom he waged war. **(3)** Ben-Hadad III (796–770 BC), son of the usurper HAZAEL, fought against JEHOAHAZ and JEHOASH of Israel (2 Ki. 13:3–7; 13:25; cf. Amos 1:4–5; Jer. 49:27).

**Benjamin** (ben′juh-muhn). Youngest son of the patriarch JACOB (Gen. 35:16–18). His mother RACHEL did not survive the difficulties of childbirth, and just before she died, she named the baby Ben-Oni ("son of my sorrow"), but Jacob gave him the name Benjamin ("son of my right hand"). He appears as a special object of his father's love (44:18–34). After the conquest of CANAAN, the tribe of Benjamin was assigned the portion of land between JUDAH on the S and EPHRAIM on the N (Josh. 18:11–28), thus occupying a strategic position. The civil war with Benjamin constitutes a sad and strange story (Jdg. 19–20). Important Benjamites include King SAUL (1 Sam. 9:1–2) and Saul of Tarsus (PAUL; Phil. 3:5).

**Berea** (bi-ree′uh). A populous city in SW MACEDONIA; the Bereans who heard PAUL preach welcomed his teaching (Acts 17:10–15; 20:4).

**Bernice** (buhr-nees′). Daughter of Herod AGRIPPA I; she was a widow who shared the household of her brother, Agrippa II (Acts 25:13, 23; 26:30).

**beth** (beth). The second letter of the Hebrew alphabet (ב, transliterated as *b*), used to begin each verse in Ps. 119:9–16. The word *beth* means "house" and is used as part of the name of many towns (e.g., Bethel means "house of God").

**Bethabara** (beth-ab′uh-ruh). See BETHANY #2.

**Bethany** (beth′uh-nee). **(1)** A village less than 2 mi. (3 km.) SE of JERUSALEM, on the E side of the Mount of Olives (see OLIVES, MOUNT OF) and on the road to JERICHO (Mk. 11:1; 14:3; Lk. 19:29; Jn. 11:11, 18). MARY, MARTHA, and LAZARUS lived in Bethany, as did Simon the Leper, and it was there that Lazarus was raised from the dead. The ASCENSION OF CHRIST took place near the town (Lk. 24:50–51). **(2)** A place E of the JORDAN where JOHN the Baptist ministered and where his confrontation with the delegation of priests and Levites from Jerusalem took place (Jn. 1:28, where the KJV has Bethabara). Its location is uncertain.

**Bethel** (beth′uhl). A town originally known as Luz, 12 mi. (19 km.) N of JERUSALEM (Gen. 28:19). ABRAHAM stopped near this spot on his way to the NEGEV and offered a sacrifice (12:8; 13:3). JACOB called Luz "Bethel," or "house of God," since God met him here (28:10–22; 35:1–7). The town became part of the tribe of BENJAMIN (Josh. 18:21–22). Much later, after the kingdom was divided, JEROBOAM chose Bethel as one of the two centers in which he set up golden calves (1 Ki. 12:26–30).

**Bethesda** (buh-thez′duh). A spring-fed pool at JERUSALEM, near the Sheep Gate and surrounded by five porches (Jn. 5:2; some

Remains of the Pool of Bethesda in Jerusalem.

Berthold Werner/Wikimedia Commons

versions have Beth-zatha). Sick people waited to step down into these waters, which were thought to have healing properties. Here Jesus healed a man who had been sick for thirty-eight years (5:1–16).

**Beth Horon** (beth-hor′uhn). The name of twin towns belonging to the tribe of EPHRAIM and on the boundary line with BENJAMIN (Josh. 16:3, 5). It was near these towns that JOSHUA commanded the sun and moon to stand still while he fought the AMORITE kings in his defense of the Gibeonites (10:10–13).

**Bethlehem** (beth′li-hem). A town 5 mi. (8 km.) SW of JERUSALEM on the main highway to HEBRON and EGYPT. In JACOB's time it was called EPHRATH and was the burial place of RACHEL (Gen. 35:16, 19; 48:7). Bethlehem was DAVID's hometown and was known as "the city of David" (Lk. 2:4, 11); here the MESSIAH was born (Matt. 2:1; Lk. 2:1–7). (A different town by the same name was in the N, within the tribal territory of ZEBULUN, Josh. 19:15.)

This excavated area may be the site of ancient Bethsaida. The N shore of the Sea of Galilee is visible at the top of the image.



**Beth Peor** (beth-pee′or). A city in MOAB that was assigned to the tribe of REUBEN (Josh. 13:20). Before entering the land of Canaan, the Israelites encamped in the valley near Beth Peor, and in that area God buried MOSES (Deut. 3:29; 4:46; 34:6). BAAL PEOR may have been the patron deity of this city (Num. 25:3, 5, 18).

**Bethphage** (beth′fuh-jee). A village on the Mount of Olives (see OLIVES, MOUNT OF) and near BETHANY. As Jesus approached this town on his way to JERUSALEM, he sent two of his disciples to procure a colt in preparation for the TRIUMPHAL ENTRY (Matt. 21:1; Mk. 11:1; Lk. 19:29).

**Bethsaida** (beth-say′uh-duh). A town on the N shore of the Sea of GALILEE; it was the home of ANDREW and PETER and of PHILIP (Jn. 1:44; 12:21). Bethsaida was the scene of the feeding of the 5,000 (Lk. 9:10–17) and here Jesus healed a blind man (Mk. 8:22–26).

**Beth Shan** (beth-shan′). Also Beth-shean. A town 14 mi. (23 km.) S of the Sea of GALILEE, where the PHILISTINES fastened SAUL's body to the city wall (1 Sam. 31:8–12).

**Beth Shemesh** (beth-sheh′mish). The name of several towns, the most prominent of which was on the northern boundary of JUDAH's tribal inheritance (Josh. 15:10), some 16 mi. (26 km.) W of JERUSALEM. When the ARK of the covenant was returned to Israel by the PHILISTINES, it was brought to Beth Shemesh (1 Sam. 6; other references to the town include 1 Ki. 4:9; 2 Ki. 14:8–14; 2 Chr. 25:17–24; 28:18).

**betrothal.** See WEDDING.

**Bible.** This English term, derived (through Latin) from Greek *biblion*, "book," refers to the collection of books recognized by the Christian church as God's revelation of himself and of his will to human beings. The names "Old Testament" and "New Testament" (or Old Covenant and New Covenant) have been used since the close of the second century AD to distinguish the Jewish and Christian Scriptures. The OT in our English Bibles is composed of thirty-nine books (the Roman Catholic Church and the Eastern Orthodox Churches recognize some additional books, which Protestants group under the name APOCRYPHA). The NT contains twenty-seven documents written by some of Christ's APOSTLES and their associates, who proclaimed God's new covenant. Most of the OT was written in the HEBREW language, spoken by the Israelites in CANAAN before the Babylonian captivity (most of Ezra 4–7 and Dan. 2–7 are written in ARAMAIC, a related language). The NT was composed in GREEK, the language of ordinary conversation in the Hellenistic world. See also INSPIRATION.

**Bildad** (bil′dad). One of the three friends of JOB who came to comfort him but who really added to his grief (Job 2:11; 8:1; 18:1; 25:1; 42:9). He is called a "Shuhite," which may mean that he was descended from a son of ABRAHAM and KETURAH named Shuah (Gen. 25:2).

**Bilhah** (bil′huh). A slave girl given by LABAN to his daughter RACHEL (Gen. 29:29); she also became a CONCUBINE of JACOB and bore him two sons, whom Rachel named DAN and NAPHTALI, thus claiming them as her own (Gen. 30:1–8; 35:25; 46:25). Bilhah later engaged in incest with REUBEN (35:22).

**birthright.** In ancient Israel, as in many other cultures, the FIRSTBORN son was given privileges above those of his younger brothers. The firstborn's birthright included a double portion of the inheritance (Deut. 21:15–17) and the privilege of priesthood (Exod. 13:1–2; 24:5), although in Israel God later set apart the tribe of LEVI instead of the firstborn for priestly service.

**bishop.** The KJV and other versions use this term to render Greek *episkopos*, which simply means "overseer." In the NT it evidently refers to the principal officer of the local church (what we now call a minister or pastor; see 1 Tim. 3:1–7). The title ELDER (or "presbyter") generally applied to the same officer. After the NT, the term *bishop* came to mean a minister (or priest) of higher rank, in charge of a group of churches.

**Bithynia** (bi-thin′ee-uh). A region in NW Asia Minor (modern Turkey). PAUL and his companions desired to enter Bithynia (Acts 16:6–10), but the HOLY SPIRIT was leading toward Europe, and so they could not enter. Eventually, the GOSPEL did reach this area (1 Pet. 1:1).

**bitter herbs, bitter water.** Israel was commanded at the Feast of Passover to eat bitter herbs with the roast lamb and UNLEAVENED BREAD; the observance was meant to symbolize the bitterness and agony of their Egyptian servitude (Exod. 12:8). The ceremony of the bitter water was a ritual test for a wife who was accused of being unfaithful (Num. 5:18–27).

**blasphemy.** The act of insulting or showing contempt for someone. To speak lightly or carelessly of God is an especially grievous sin (Exod. 20:7). In Israel the punishment for such blasphemy was death by stoning (Lev. 24:10–16). Execution was in the minds of those who charged Jesus with blasphemy (Matt. 9:3; 26:65; Lk. 5:31; Jn. 10:33); what Jesus said about himself would have been blasphemy against God were it not true. See also UNPARDONABLE SIN.

**bless.** The Bible states that God blesses nature (Gen. 1:22), mankind (1:28), the Sabbath (2:3), individuals (24:1), and whole nations (Ps. 33:12). Divine blessing is the assurance that God is conferring his grace. On the other hand, when godly men and women "bless" God, they adore him, worship him, and praise him (Ps. 103:1–2). When we "bless" God, we bring his glories before our mind and respond in worship and adoration; when we ask him to "bless" us, we invite him to call our needs to mind and respond in meeting them.

**blood.** Most Bible references to this bodily fluid reflect the practical truth that loss of blood leads to loss of vitality, and a draining away of the blood leads to DEATH (e.g., Gen. 9:4–6). The statement "Your blood be on your own head" (e.g., 2 Sam. 1:16) suggests that those who are guilty of murder will pay with their own life. Because blood is essential to physical life, ATONEMENT requires the shedding of blood (Lev. 17:11). See SACRIFICE.

**Boanerges** (boh′uh-nuhr′jeez). A surname interpreted as meaning "Sons of Thunder" and given by Jesus to JAMES and JOHN at the time they were chosen apostles (Mk. 3:17). Perhaps it referred to their fiery eloquence or to their passionate zeal.

**boast.** This term is used often by PAUL, especially in 2 Cor. 10–12 (e.g., 10:13–17). The idea of boasting may convey both a good sense (e.g., Ps. 44:8; 2 Cor. 7:14) and a bad sense (e.g., Ps. 10:3; Rom. 2:17; 2 Tim. 3:2). The fundamental biblical principle is expressed by God's declaration, "let him who boasts boast about this: / that he understands and knows me, / that I am the LORD" (Jer. 9:24; quoted in 1 Cor. 1:31).

**Boaz** (boh′az). A well-to-do Bethlehemite in the days of the judges who became an ancestor of Jesus by marrying RUTH the Moabitess (Ruth 2–4).

According to Deut. 28–31, the Israelites were instructed to remember God's covenant by proclaiming God's blessings from Mt. Gerizim (left ridge) and potential curses from Mt. Ebal (right ridge). (View to the W.) 

In ancient Mesopotamia, books were produced in the form of inscribed clay tablets like this one (19th cent. BC), which commemorates the building of the city of Ur.



**body of Christ.** The apostle PAUL uses this expression with reference to the CHURCH, that is, God's people, who are united to Christ in grace by faith and through baptism. Believers "form one body, and each member belongs to all the others" (Rom. 12:5) in submission to Christ, who is the Head (see 1 Cor. 12:12–27; Eph. 3:6; 4:11–16; 5:23). See UNITY.

**bond, bondage.** See SLAVE, SLAVERY.

**bone.** In the living body, bones form the strong framework, and the connotation is one of strength. Dry bones form a picture of hopeless DEATH (Ezek. 37:1–12). The Passover LAMB, without a broken bone (Exod. 12:46), was a type of the Lamb of God (Jn. 19:36).

**book.** The Bible makes frequent mention of written documents. Little is known of certain writings, such as the Book of Jasher (Josh. 10:13; 2 Sam. 1:18) and the Book of the Wars of the Lord (Num. 21:14). Of special importance is the Book of the Law (e.g., Deut. 29:21; Josh. 1:8; 2 Ki. 22:8), which sometimes may refer in general to all the commandments God gave through Moses but usually seems to be applied specifically to the book of DEUTERONOMY. The Bible mentions also "the book of life," a figure of speech referring to the heavenly record of those who belong to God (e.g., Phil. 4:3; Rev. 3:5; 20:12–15; cf. also Exod. 32:32–33).

**Booths, Feast of.** See FEASTS.

**booty.** Goods taken from a defeated enemy.

**bosom.** The human chest. In Scripture the term is generally used in an affectionate sense; for example, "the only Son, who is in the bosom of the Father" (Jn. 1:18 RSV); lambs are carried in God's bosom (Isa. 40:11 KJV); LAZARUS rested in ABRAHAM'S BOSOM (Lk. 16:22–23 KJV). It can be almost synonymous with "heart" as the center of one's life (cf. Ps. 35:13; Eccl. 7:9 KJV).

**bowels.** In the KJV this English word occurs thirty-six times and in three principal senses: (1) literally (2 Chr. 21:15–19; Acts 1:18); (2) as the generative parts of the body, whether male or female (Gen. 15:4; Ps. 71:6); and (3) as the seat of the emotions (e.g. Lam. 1:20 [NIV "heart"]; Phil. 1:8 [NIV "affection"]).

**Bozrah** (boz′ruh). An ancient city in the mountains of EDOM, strongly fortified and virtually impregnable (Gen. 36:33; Isa. 34:6; 63:1; Jer. 49:13, 22; Amos 1:12).

**brasen.** See BRONZE SEA; BRONZE SNAKE.

**bread.** The main source of food in the ancient world, generally baked from dough made

B

of wheat flour (the poorer people were more likely to use barley instead of wheat). The Hebrew and Greek words for *bread* in the Bible often refer to food in general (e.g., Gen. 3:19; Prov. 27:27; 2 Thess. 3:8). See also SHOWBREAD.

**breastpiece, breastplate.** An elaborately decorated square of linen worn on the breast as part of the robes of Israel's HIGH PRIEST (Exod. 28:15–30; 39:8–21; Lev. 8:8). It was fastened from the top to the shoulder of the EPHOD by gold cords, and by a blue lace from the lower corners to gold rings on the ephod.

**brimstone.** Modern Bible translations prefer the more common term *sulfur,* a yellow nonmetallic element that burns with a blue flame and forms a noxious gas. The biblical use of the term is generally connected with JUDGMENT, as when the Lord rained "brimstone and fire" on SODOM and GOMORRAH (Gen. 19:24 KJV; NIV "burning sulfur"; cf. also Isa. 34:9; Rev. 14:10).

**bronze sea.** Name given to a very large laver that SOLOMON placed in front of the TEMPLE for washing the SACRIFICES and the bodies of the priests (2 Ki. 25:13; 1 Chr. 18:8; Jer. 52:17; KJV "brasen sea"). It is also known as the "molten sea" (1 Ki. 7:23; 2 Chr. 4:2; NIV "Sea of cast metal").

**bronze snake.** According to Num. 21:4–9, the people of ISRAEL complained against God and MOSES because they had no bread or water. In judgment God sent venomous snakes against them. When the people confessed their sin, Moses made a snake of bronze and set it on a pole so that "anyone who is bitten can look at it and live." Centuries later it was regarded as an idol (2 Ki. 18:4; KJV "brasen serpent"; see also Jn. 3:15).

**burden.** That which is laid on an animal or person in order to be carried. When used figuratively, the word can refer to responsibility (Num. 11:11; Matt. 11:30) or to sorrow (Ps. 55:22 KJV; NIV "cares"). The KJV uses "burden" also in passages where the Hebrew word has the different meaning of "divine pronouncement, oracle" (e.g., Isa. 13:1).

**burial.** The act of placing a dead body in a TOMB, in the earth, or in the sea, generally with ceremonies. Partly because of God's declaration to ADAM, "For dust you are and to dust you will return" (Gen. 3:19), the people of ISRAEL almost always buried their dead. Because the land of CANAAN had so many caves, these places were very frequently used as places of burial.

**burning.** The burning of the SACRIFICE (Lev. 1–7) was a symbolic way of conveying the offering, and thus the commitment of the sacrificer, to God: as the sacrifice was consumed and the smoke and odor arose to heaven, it symbolized the entrance into the divine presence. Burning as a means of JUDGMENT has been literally carried out in history, and it will so be used again at the consummation of all things (Lev. 10:1–2; Josh. 6:24; 8:28; 1 Cor. 3:13; Heb. 12:29). Burning can also indicate zeal and passion, both in positive and in negative contexts (Lk. 24:32; Jn. 5:35; Rom. 1:27; 1 Cor. 7:9).

**burning bush.** A thorny bush that MOSES saw burning without being consumed and from which he heard the Lord speak (Exod. 3:2–3; Deut. 33:16; Mk. 12:26). The incident contains the first direct statement in the Bible linking HOLINESS with the very life of God and making fire the symbol of that holiness.

**burnt offering.** See SACRIFICE.

# C

**Caesar** (see′zuhr). Surname of the Julian family, whose most eminent member was Caius (Gaius) Julius Caesar, the great soldier, statesman, orator, and author (102–44 BC). Because the name was then taken as a title by each of the Roman emperors (e.g., AUGUSTUS, Lk. 2:1; TIBERIUS, 3:1), it came to be used as a symbol of the state in general (e.g., Matt. 22:17, 21; Jn. 19:12; Acts 25:8).

**Caesarea** (ses′uh-ree′uh). A city on the coast of the MEDITERRANEAN SEA, also known as Caesarea Maritima ("by the sea") to distinguish it from CAESAREA PHILIPPI. It was built by HEROD the Great at a vast cost and named in honor of his patron AUGUSTUS CAESAR. Caesarea was the home of CORNELIUS, in whose house PETER first preached to the GENTILES (Acts 10). It served also as the enforced residence of PAUL while he was a prisoner for two years, where he also preached before King AGRIPPA II (23:31–26:32).

**Caesarea Philippi** (ses′uh-ree′uh-fil′i-p*i*′). A town at the extreme N boundary of PALESTINE, about 30 mi. (50 km.) inland from TYRE, in the beautiful hill country on the southern slopes of Mount HERMON, probably near the scene of Jesus' TRANSFIGURATION. It was at a secluded spot in this area that PETER made his famous confession (Matt. 16:13–17; Mk. 8:27).

**Caesar's household.** A term referring to the imperial staff, composed of both slaves and freedmen (Phil. 4:22); it was more commonly applied to the imperial civil service at ROME but also throughout the empire, particularly in the imperial provinces.

**Caiaphas** (kay′uh-fuhs). Son-in-law of ANNAS and official HIGH PRIEST during the ministry and trial of Jesus (Matt. 26:3, 57; Lk. 3:2; Jn. 11:49; 18:13–14, 24, 28; Acts 4:6).

**Cain** (kayn). The first son of ADAM and EVE and a farmer by occupation. As an offering to God, he brought some of the fruits of

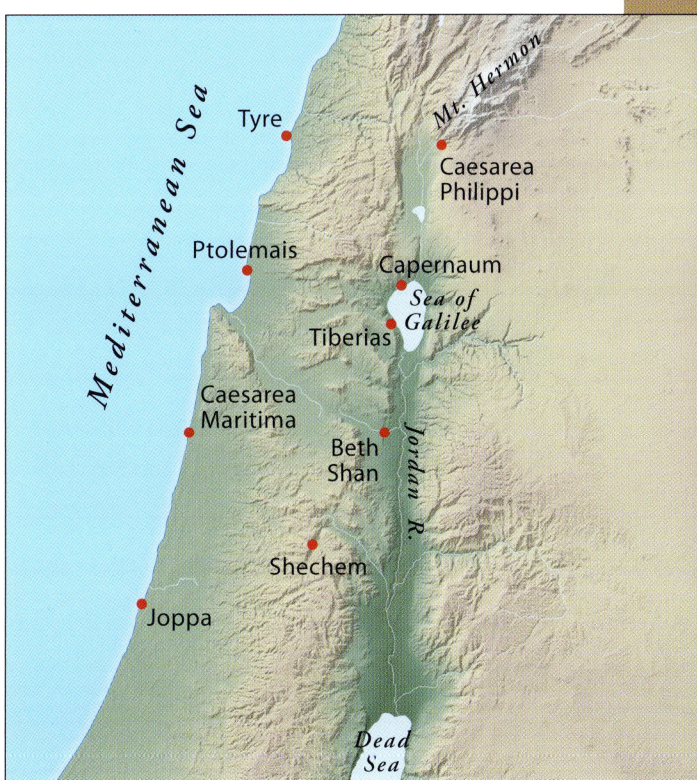

Caesarea Maritima and Caesarea Philippi.

the ground, while his brother brought an animal SACRIFICE. Angry when his offering was not received, he murdered his brother (Gen. 4; Heb. 11:4; 1 Jn. 3:12; Jude 11).

**Caleb** (kay′luhb). A leader of the tribe of JUDAH whom MOSES sent with eleven others to spy out the Promised Land (Num. 13:6). Most of the spies brought back a pessimistic report, but Caleb and JOSHUA encouraged the people to go up and take the land. Caleb lived to enter CANAAN forty years later and received HEBRON as his inheritance (Josh. 14:13–14). His son-in-law was OTHNIEL, the first of the "judges" (Jdg. 1:12–13).

**calendar.** The Hebrew calendar consisted of two concurrent systems based on lunar months: the sacred year, beginning in the spring with Nisan (the month when the EXODUS took place), and the civil year, beginning in the fall with Tishri. Important FEASTS were intricately woven into the sacred year.

One of the earliest Hebrew texts is this limestone inscription known as the Gezer Calendar (10th cent. BC), which lists the agricultural phases of the year.



**calf, golden.** Calf or bull WORSHIP was part of the religious life of most Semitic peoples. While MOSES was on the mountain receiving God's law, AARON made a golden image of a male calf in order that the people might worship the Lord under this form (Exod. 32:4). Centuries later, after the division of the kingdom, JEROBOAM set up two golden calves in Israel, one at BETHEL and one at DAN (1 Ki. 12:28–29), because he feared that his people might desert him if they continued to worship in JERUSALEM.

**call.** This term can have several meanings (e.g., "to summon," "to name"), but especially important is its use with reference to SALVATION (Heb. 3:1). God's call comes to people in all situations and occupations (1 Cor. 1:26; 7:20). Often a distinction is made between the universal call ("many are called, but few are chosen," Matt. 22:14 NRSV) and the effectual call ("those he called, he also justified," Rom. 8:30). Christians are therefore described as "called" in the special sense that they have responded to the divine invitation (e.g., Rom. 1:6–7; 1 Cor. 1:2, 24).

**Calneh, Calno** (kal′neh, kal′noh). TNIV Kalneh, Kalno. Calneh was a city founded by NIMROD in some unknown location in SHINAR (BABYLONIA, Gen. 10:10). It is probably different from the Calneh mentioned in Amos 6:2 (called Calno in Isa. 10:9), which apparently was located in the northern part of MESOPOTAMIA.

**Calvary.** See GOLGOTHA.

**Cana** (kay′nuh). A town in GALILEE, about 5 mi. (8 km.) NE of NAZARETH, mentioned only in the Gospel of John. Here Jesus performed his first miracle, converting the water to wine at a marriage feast (Jn. 2:1–11). It was here too that he announced to the nobleman from CAPERNAUM the healing of his apparently dying son (4:46). NATHANAEL came from Cana (21:2).

**Canaan, Canaanites** (kay′nuhn, kay′nuh-nits). Canaan was the fourth son of HAM, father of SIDON, and ancestor of many Canaanite people groups, such as the HITTITES, the JEBUSITES, and the AMORITES (Gen. 9:18; 10:6, 15–18). He received the curse from NOAH as a result of Ham's offense (9:22–27). In the Bible, the name is used almost always to designate the land W of JORDAN occupied by the Israelites at the time of the conquest. According to Jdg. 1:9–10, Canaanites lived throughout the land. They worshiped various gods, especially BAAL, sometimes associated with immoral practices.

**Canaanite, Simon the.** See CANANAEAN.

**Cananaean** (kay′nuh-nee′uhn). Surname given to SIMON, one of Jesus' disciples (NRSV and other versions of Matt. 10:4; Mk. 3:18; KJV "Canaanite"; NIV "the Zealot"). This name, which served to distinguish him from Simon PETER, comes from an ARAMAIC term meaning "zealot, enthusiast" (cf. Lk. 6:15; Acts 1:13; see ZEALOT).

**Candace** (kan′duh-see). TNIV Kandake. The title of the queen of ETHIOPIA, whose treasurer was baptized between JERUSALEM and GAZA by PHILIP the evangelist (Acts 8:26–27).

**candlestick.** See LAMPSTAND.

**canon.** The Greek word *kanôn* means "measuring rule" and more generally "rule" or "standard." In theology its chief application is to those books received as divinely authoritative and making up our BIBLE.

The books recognized by the church as inspired are known collectively as the Bible or as the canon of Scripture.

PhotoDisc

The Protestant canon includes thirty-nine books in the OT, twenty-seven in the NT. The Roman Catholic and Orthodox canons add seven books and some additional pieces in the OT (See APOCRYPHA). The Jews accept as authoritative the same books of the OT as do Protestants.

**Canticles.** See SONG OF SOLOMON.

**Capernaum** (kuh-puhr′nay-uhm). An important town on the NW shore of the Sea of Galilee where Jesus made his headquarters during his ministry in GALILEE (Matt. 4:13; Mk. 2:1). Jesus performed many striking miracles in the town, among them the healing of the centurion's palsied servant (Matt. 8:5–13), the paralytic who was lowered through a roof by four friends (Mk. 2:1–13), and a nobleman's son (Jn. 4:46–54). It was there that Jesus called MATTHEW to the apostleship as he was sitting at the tax collector's booth (Matt. 9:9–13).

**caph.** See KAPH.

Capernaum.

**Caphtor, Caphtorim, Caphtorite** (kaf′tor, kaf′tuh-rim, kaf′tuh-r*it*). The PHILISTINES are said to have come from a place named Caphtor (Jer. 47:4; Amos 9:7) and thus may have been related to the Caphtorites (Deut. 2:23). Many scholars believe that Caphtor is the island of CRETE.

**Cappadocia** (kap′uh-doh′shee-uh). A large inland region of Asia Minor (modern Turkey) between PONTUS to the N and CILICIA to the S. Cappadocian Jews who were converted on the Day of PENTECOST (Acts 2:9) must have taken the message of the GOSPEL back to their homeland (1 Pet. 1:1).

**captivity.** See EXILE.

**Carchemish** (kahr′kuh-mish). An ancient and important city of the HITTITES located on the W bank of the EUPHRATES. When the Assyrian king SARGON captured it in 717 BC, the Hittite empire fell with it (Isa. 10:9). Carchemish was the scene of a great victory by NEBUCHADNEZZAR over Pharaoh NECO in 605 (Jer. 46:2; 2 Chr. 35:20).

**Carmel** (kahr′muhl). **(1)** A city of the Maon district within the tribal territory of JUDAH, 7.5 mi. (12 km.) SE of HEBRON (Josh. 15:55). This town was the home of NABAL and ABIGAIL (1 Sam. 25:2–40). **(2)** Mount Carmel is a promontory jutting into the MEDITERRANEAN SEA just S of the modern city of Haifa and straight W of the Sea of Galilee. It is often used to illustrate a beautiful and fruitful place (Isa. 35:2). Here ELIJAH stood against 450 heathen prophets and defeated them (1 Ki. 18).

**carnal.** A term meaning "fleshly," that is, in the manner of the FLESH or belonging to the realm of the flesh, and thus opposite of that which is spiritual. The word is used frequently in the KJV and has two main references. (1) *Physical:* that which is earthly, material, temporary (Rom. 15:27; 1 Cor. 9:11; 2 Cor. 3:3; 10:4; Heb. 7:16). (2) *Ethical (moral):* pertaining to or characterized by the sinful human nature, hence weak and corrupt (Rom. 7:14; 8:5–8; 2 Cor. 1:12). Because in modern English the word *carnal* usually has a specific sexual meaning, the NIV uses various alternate renderings, such as "material," "human," "unspiritual," "worldly," and "sinful."

**Castor and Pollux** (kas′tuhr, pol′ukhs). In Greek mythology they were "sons of Zeus" (Gk. *Dioskouroi*) who were put in the sky in the constellation known as Gemini ("the Twins") and were considered deities favorable to sailors, a fact that explains why the ship in which PAUL sailed was named in their honor (Acts 28:11; NRSV "the Twin Brothers").

**Catholic Epistles.** Also *General Epistles.* A term applied to the letters of JAMES, PETER, JOHN, and JUDE. The word *catholic* means "universal" or "general" and was probably chosen because these epistles were addressed not to individual churches or persons but to

Remnants of ancient buildings and a rodeway at the harbor in Cenchrea.

www.HolyLandPhotos.org

a number of churches, thus to the church at large (2–3 John are personal but were joined with 1 John).

**Cenchrea** (sen′kree-uh). Also Cenchreae. A small village that served as the eastern harbor of CORINTH, about 7 mi. (11 km.) from the city. Ships (or their cargo) were dragged on sleds across the isthmus from Cenchrea to Lechaeum (the western harbor of Corinth) to avoid sailing the dangerous southern tip of the Peloponnesus. PAUL stopped here to have his head shaved in fulfillment of a vow (Acts 18:18). PHOEBE was from Cenchrea (Rom. 16:1).

**censer.** A shallow vessel used mainly to burn INCENSE (Num. 16:6–7).

**centurion.** A commander of one hundred soldiers in the Roman army (e.g., Matt. 8:5; 27:54; Acts 10:1; 22:25–26).

**Cephas** (see′fuhs). See PETER.

**chaff.** The refuse of the grain that has been threshed and winnowed. On a windy day the grain is tossed into the air and the chaff and the shorter pieces of straw are blown away. Chaff is used as a figure for godless people (Ps. 1:4; Isa. 17:13; Matt. 3:12).

**Chaldea** (kal-dee′uh). Also Chaldaea, Chaldee. The name of a district in S BABYLONIA, later applied to a dynasty that controlled all of Babylonia (Gen. 11:28; Ezek. 23:14–16).

**charity.** This term, which in present-day English means "almsgiving, benevolence," is used in the KJV (Epistles and Revelation) with its older meaning, LOVE (e.g., 1 Cor. 13:1).

**Charran.** See HARAN.

**chastisement.** This English term, which in modern English means "punishment" or "severe censure," is used by the KJV and other versions to translate Hebrew and Greek words that mean more broadly "discipline, admonition, correction, chastening" (e.g., Deut. 11:2; Job 5:17).

**Chebar.** See KEBAR.

**Chedorlaomer.** See KEDORLAOMER.

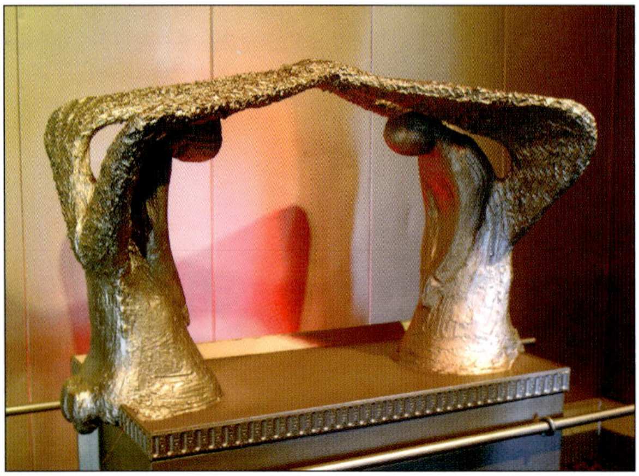

Artist's rendition of the cherubim that were placed on opposite ends of the ark of the covenant in the tabernacle. © Baker Publishing Group

**Chemosh** (kee'mosh). The god of MOAB (Num. 21:29; 1 Ki. 11:7, 33; 2 Ki. 23:13). He was worshiped also by the AMMONITES (Jdg. 11:24).

**Cherethim, Cherethite.** See KERETHITE.

**Cherith.** See KERITH.

**cherub, cherubim** (cher'uhb, cher'uh-bim). The term *cherubim* is the Hebrew plural form of *cherub*, which refers to a winged angelic creature (Ezek. 10). Cherubim (or cherubs) and a flaming sword were placed at the E of EDEN to guard the way to the tree of life after ADAM and EVE were expelled from the garden (Gen. 3:24; see TREE OF KNOWLEDGE, TREE OF LIFE). Images of cherubim were common in the TABERNACLE and the TEMPLE. In particular, two cherubim of beaten gold appeared on the mercy seat above the ARK of the covenant in the Most Holy Place (25:18–22; 37:7–9). See ANGEL; SERAPH.

**cheth.** See HETH.

**Chinnereth.** See KINNERETH.

**Chorazin.** See KORAZIN.

**Christ** (kr*i*st). This term is derived from the Greek word *christos*, meaning "anointed" (see ANOINT) and corresponding to MESSIAH. It is primarily a title applied to JESUS

The modern city of Nazareth, with a view of the Basilica of the Annunciation. Nazareth was a very small village when Jesus lived there. www.HolyLandPhotos.org

of Nazareth (Matt. 16:16), signifying that he was the promised deliverer (Isa. 61:1–3); in time it was used also as his personal name (Rom. 5:6).

**Christian.** Someone who gives allegiance to CHRIST. The followers of Jesus were formally called Christians first in ANTIOCH of Syria (Acts 11:26; cf. 26:28), and they gladly accepted this title (1 Pet. 4:16).

**Chronicles, Books of.** Two books that record the history of the Davidic kingdom. The account parallels that of 2 Samuel and 1–2 Kings, but it pays little attention to the northern kingdom of ISRAEL and provides a stronger theological interpretation.

**church.** This word translates the Greek noun *ekklēsia*, which means "assembly" (it is used in Acts 19:32 of the Ephesian crowd), but was applied both to local bodies of Christians (Acts 8:1; 1 Cor. 1:2) and to the redeemed people of God as a whole (the church universal, Matt. 16:18; Eph. 1:22). See BODY OF CHRIST.

**Cilicia** (suh lish'ee uh). A country in SE Asia Minor (modern Turkey), bounded on the N and W by the Taurus range and on the S by the MEDITERRANEAN SEA. Its chief city was TARSUS, the birthplace of PAUL (Acts 21:39). The GOSPEL reached Cilicia early (15:23), probably through Paul (9:30; Gal. 1:21).

**circumcision.** The surgical removal of the foreskin or prepuce, a covering of skin on the head of the male sexual organ. This custom has prevailed among many peoples in different parts of the world. Among the Hebrews the rite was instituted by God as the sign of the COVENANT between him and ABRAHAM (Gen. 17:9–14). This outward rite, to have any personal significance, was to be accompanied by a "circumcision of the heart," that is, spiritual purity and obedience to God

## OVERVIEW OF 1–2 CHRONICLES

**AUTHOR:** Unknown, though Jewish tradition attributed it (as well as Ezra and Nehemiah) to EZRA.

**HISTORICAL SETTING:** Chronicles treats approximately the same period covered by the books of 2 Samuel and 1–2 Kings, but from the perspective of someone living after the Babylonian EXILE, probably in the fifth century BC (some date Chronicles as late as 250 BC).

**PURPOSE:** To provide a historical-theological account of the Hebrew nation from the reign of DAVID to the fall of JERUSALEM, focusing almost exclusively on the southern kingdom of JUDAH and reminding the people of the glories of the Davidic dynasty, the importance of the TEMPLE for Jewish WORSHIP, and the divine principle of BLESSING and RETRIBUTION.

**CONTENTS:** After a genealogical background establishing the continuity of postexilic ISRAEL with the people of God (1 Chr. 1–9), the writer provides a narrative of the united Hebrew kingdom under David and SOLOMON, with emphasis on both the preparations for and the actual building of the temple (1 Chr. 10 to 2 Chr. 9); the last section traces the history of Judah after the division of the kingdom (2 Chr. 10–36).

The mountains of Cilicia.



(Lev. 26:41; Deut. 30:6; Ezek. 44:7; Rom. 2:25–29). In the early days of the Christian church, some argued for the necessity of circumcising GENTILES, but the apostles agreed with PAUL that the signs of the old covenant could not be forced on the children of the new covenant (Acts 15; Gal. 2:1–10). Those who depend not on themselves but on Christ are now the true circumcision (Phil. 3:3).

**cities, Levitical.** See LEVITICAL CITIES.

**cities of refuge.** Six cities, three E of the JORDAN (Bezer in Reuben, Ramoth Gilead in Gad, and Golan in Manasseh) and three to the W (Hebron in Judah, Shechem in Ephraim, and Kedesh in Naphtali), set apart by MOSES and JOSHUA as places of asylum. If someone guilty of unintentional killing reached a city of refuge before the avenger of blood could kill him, he was given protection until a fair trial could be held (Num. 35; Deut. 4:41–43; 19:1–13; Josh. 20).

**City of David.** Although this expression is applied to BETHLEHEM in Luke's nativity story (Lk. 2:4, 11; NIV "town of David"), the phrase refers primarily to ZION, that is, the Jebusite fortress that DAVID captured and made his royal residence (2 Sam. 5:7, 9, and frequently; see JEBUS).

**Claudius** (klaw′dee-uhs). The fourth Roman emperor (AD 41–54). Despite some physical disabilities, he ruled well for a number of years; the latter part of his reign, however, was marked by intrigue and suspicion. Claudius is mentioned in passing twice in the NT (Acts 11:28; 18:2).

**Claudius Lysias** (klaw′dee-uhs lis′ee-uhs). Commander of the Roman garrison in JERUSALEM at the time of PAUL's arrest (Acts 21:31–39; 22:23–30; 23:10–35; the name occurs only in 23:26; 24:22). Lysias was prepared to examine Paul by torture until he learned that he was a Roman citizen and therefore exempt from such treatment.

**Cleopas** (klee'oh-puhs). One of the two disciples whom Jesus joined on the road to EMMAUS during the afternoon of the day of his RESURRECTION (Lk. 24:13–32; the other disciple is not named). Some have thought he was the same as CLOPAS (Jn. 19:25), but there is no evidence for this view.

**Clopas** (kloh'puhs). The husband (or other relative) of a certain MARY, one of the women who stood at the foot of the cross when Jesus was crucified (Jn. 19:25; KJV Cleophas). She is probably the same as "Mary the mother of James and Joseph [Joses]" (Matt. 27:56; Mk. 15:40). If this JAMES is the same as the son of ALPHAEUS (Matt. 10:3), then Clopas would be the same as Alphaeus.

**cloud, pillar of.** A symbol of the presence and guidance of God in the forty-year wilderness journey of the Israelites from EGYPT to CANAAN (Exod. 13:21–22). At night it became fire. When God wanted Israel to rest in any place, the cloud rested on the TABERNACLE (29:42–43; 33:9–10).

**Colosse** (kuh-lah'see). Also Colossae. An ancient city of PHRYGIA, situated on the S bank of the Lycus River. It was about 11 mi. (18 km.) from LAODICEA. The church at Colosse was probably established on PAUL's third missionary journey, during his three years in EPHESUS, not by Paul himself (Col. 2:1) but by EPAPHRAS (1:7, 12–13). ARCHIPPUS also exercised a fruitful ministry there (4:17; Phlm. 2). PHILEMON was an active member of this church, and so also was ONESIMUS (Col. 4:9).

**Colossians, Epistle to the.** A letter of PAUL to the church in COLOSSE. It was written by the apostle when he was a prisoner (Col. 4:3, 10, 18), probably during his first imprisonment in ROME (Acts 28:30–31). In the few years since Paul had been in the province of ASIA, an insidious error had crept into the church at Colosse. The teaching attacked

Site of ancient Colosse.

C

by Paul is described in Col. 2:8, 16–23. He responds by presenting the countertruth that Jesus Christ is the image of the invisible God (1:15), in whom are hid all the treasures of WISDOM and KNOWLEDGE and in whom the fullness of the divine perfections find their perfect embodiment (1:19).

**Comforter.** See ADVOCATE; HOLY SPIRIT.

**commandment.** This word is used in the English Bible to translate a variety of Hebrew and Greek terms. The idea of authority conveyed by these words comes from the fact that God as sovereign Lord has a right to be obeyed. The instruction of Jesus is full of ethical teachings that have the force of divine commandments. In addition, the writings of John speak of a "new commandment" that emphasizes the substance and spiritual power of LOVE (Jn. 13:34–35; 1 Jn. 2:7–8; 2 Jn. 5).

**Commandments, Ten.** The central ethical teaching of the OT LAW (Exod. 20:1–17; Deut. 5:6–21). Also known as the *Decalogue*, these commands were received by MOSES directly from God on Mount SINAI. The Decalogue is specifically the gift of GRACE of God the Redeemer, given to his people not to bring them into bondage but because they have been brought out of bondage (Exod. 20:2). Various passages in the NT allude to the Ten Commandments (Matt. 19:18–19; Rom. 13:9; Jas. 2:11).

**Commission, Great.** The usual designation of Jesus' instructions to "make disciples of all nations" (Matt. 28:18–20; see also Acts 1:8).

**common.** This English term usually means "shared" (Tit. 1:4; Jude 3), but it is used also in the sense of "profane" Lev. 10:10; 1 Sam. 21:4–5) or "unclean" (Mk. 7:2, 5; Acts 10:14–15). See HOLINESS; UNCLEAN.

**communion.** See FELLOWSHIP; LORD'S SUPPER.

**compassion.** See KINDNESS; MERCY.

**concubine.** In the Bible this word refers to a woman lawfully united in MARRIAGE to a man in a relation inferior to that of the regular wife (Gen. 25:6; Exod. 21:7–11; Deut. 21:10–14; 2 Sam. 5:13). Their children were regarded as legitimate, although the children of the first wife were preferred in the distribution of the inheritance.

**concupiscence.** This English term is used in the KJV with reference to strong wrongful desires (Rom. 7:8, Col. 3:5; 1 Thess. 4:5). See LUST.

## OVERVIEW OF COLOSSIANS

**AUTHOR:** The apostle PAUL.

**HISTORICAL SETTING:** Probably written from ROME during the apostle's first imprisonment in that city (c. AD 61–63), but some scholars prefer an earlier date and alternate places (EPHESUS or CAESAREA). The letter may have been written in response to news about heretical influences in the church at COLOSSE.

**PURPOSE:** To oppose false teachings concerning ceremonial and ascetic practices by exalting CHRIST as the one who holds supremacy over all and in whom true wisdom is to be found.

**CONTENTS:** The preeminence of Christ over against human teachings (Col. 1–2) and the implications of this truth for Christian conduct (chs. 3–4).

**condemn, condemnation.** These terms involve the thought of declaring JUDGMENT against someone or treating a person as guilty. Christ prohibited wrongful judging: "Do not condemn, and you will not be condemned" (Lk. 6:37; cf. Rom. 2:1). God has rightfully judged and condemned men and women for their SIN in the past (2 Pet. 2:6), but he sent Jesus Christ not "to condemn the world, but to save the world through him" (Jn. 3:17).

**confession.** To confess is openly to acknowledge truth; occasionally it means to praise God by thankfully acknowledging him (Rom. 14:11; Heb. 13:15). Confession of SIN before God is a condition of FORGIVENESS. Christ taught the necessity of confessing offenses committed against other people (Matt. 5:24; Lk. 17:4).

**congregation.** A word used in Scripture most often to refer to the Hebrew people in a collective capacity, especially when viewed as an assembly summoned for a definite purpose (1 Ki. 8:65) or meeting on a festive occasion (Deut. 23:1). In the NT, the Greek word *ekklēsia* (see CHURCH) often refers to local congregations of Christians.

**Coniah** (koh-*ni*'uh). See JECONIAH and JEHOIACHIN.

**conscience.** A sense of what is morally right or wrong. The OT alludes to the conscience when, for example, it says that DAVID's "heart smote him" (1 Sam. 24:5 KJV; the NIV renders, "David was conscience-stricken"). As a result of accepting the gospel, people receive a purified, or perfected, conscience (Heb. 9:14; 10:22). PAUL described the universal existence of conscience as the internal moral witness found in all human beings (Rom. 2:14–16) and stressed that Christians should have a clear and good conscience (2 Cor. 1:12; 1 Tim. 1:5, 19; 3:9).

**consecration.** An act by which a person or thing is dedicated to the service and worship of God; sometimes a religious ceremony is involved (e.g., Lev. 8:10–12; 1 Ki. 8:64; Isa. 66:17). In the NT, the idea is conveyed by such verbs as "set apart" and "sanctify" (Jn. 10:36; 17:17; 1 Tim. 4:5). See DEDICATION; SANCTIFICATION.

**contentment.** The state of being content or satisfied. In the Bible it means having a settled disposition to regard God's gifts as sufficient and his assignments as appropriate (Lk. 3:14; Phil. 4:11; 1 Tim. 6:6, 8; Heb. 13:5).

**contrite.** An attitude of remorse for sin. God does not despise the "broken and contrite heart" (Ps. 51:17; 34:18); he is pleased with those who are "contrite and lowly in spirit" (Isa. 57:15).

**conversation.** This English term is used by the KJV in its archaic sense of "conduct" (e.g., Gal. 1:13; Heb. 13:7; 1 Pet. 1:15, 18).

**conversion.** See REPENTANCE.

**conviction.** This word often means "strong belief" but also can refer to an intense sense of guilt (Jn. 16:7–11).

**Corban** (kor'ban). A Hebrew term meaning "gift, offering"; in NT times it was applied to the dedication of property intended for the Lord's use. Jesus condemned this practice when used to sidestep the obligation to support one's parents by claiming that the property was the Lord's and could not be used for other purposes (Mk. 7:11; cf. Matt. 15:5).

**Core.** See KORAH.

**Corinth** (kor'inth). A city of GREECE on the narrow isthmus between the Peloponnesus and the mainland. Under the Romans, it became the capital of the province called ACHAIA. Much of the commerce between ROME and the E was brought to its harbors; ancient sailors dreaded making the voyage

This satellite image shows the modern canal that links the Gulf of Corinth (left) with the Saronic Gulf. NASA

round the southern capes of the Peloponnesus, and thus many of the smaller ships and their cargoes were hauled across the narrow isthmus on a track. In Roman times Corinth was a city of wealth, luxury, and immorality. PAUL visited Corinth for the first time on his second missionary journey (Acts 18). There is evidence that during Paul's stay in EPHESUS on his third journey, he paid a brief visit to Corinth (2 Cor. 12:14; 13:1; later he spent three months in Greece, probably Corinth, Acts 20:2–3).

**Corinthians, Letters to the.** Two letters that PAUL wrote to the church in CORINTH during his third missionary journey. He had previously written a letter to the Corinthians (now lost) in which he had warned against associating with immoral persons (1 Cor. 5:9). In reply Paul received a letter from the church (alluded to in 5:10; 7:1; 8:1) dealing with various problems; what we call First Corinthians was written largely in response to their letter, but also to address other issues that had come to Paul's attention (1:11). Second Corinthians was written by Paul later somewhere in MACEDONIA, where TITUS had met him with a report concerning the church at Corinth. This report was, on the whole, very encouraging, but the apostle had to deal with several matters in preparation for his visit to the city.

**Cornelius** (kor-neel′yuhs). The name of a Roman CENTURION, described as "devout and God-fearing," who was stationed in CAESAREA. After receiving a vision, he sent for Simon PETER, who preached the GOSPEL to him and his household. As a result the HOLY SPIRIT came upon a group of GENTILES for the first time (Acts 10).

**council.** A group of people meeting as an advisory, administrative, or legislative body. In the Bible, the most frequent use of this term, however, is in reference to the high court of the Jews, the SANHEDRIN (Matt. 26:59; Acts 5:21; here and in other passages the NIV translates "Sanhedrin"). The expression "Council of Jerusalem" (or "Apostolic Council") is applied to a meeting of delegates from the church in ANTIOCH with the apostles and elders in JERUSALEM to discuss whether GENTILE

## OVERVIEW OF 1 CORINTHIANS

**AUTHOR:** The apostle PAUL.

**HISTORICAL SETTING:** Written from EPHESUS during Paul's third missionary journey (c. AD 56) in response to (a) reports from members of Chloe's household (1 Cor. 1:11), and (b) a letter written by the Corinthian Christians themselves (7:1).

**PURPOSE:** To give instruction and directions concerning many problems faced by the church in CORINTH, including internal divisions, immorality, partaking of idol food, disorder in worship, and false teaching concerning the resurrection.

**CONTENTS:** After an introductory paragraph (1 Cor. 1:1–9), the apostle first addresses the problems reported by Chloe's household—quarrels within the Corinthian church (1:10–4:21) and moral and ethical issues (5:1–6:20); he then responds to the questions raised by the Corinthians' letter—about marriage and divorce (ch. 7), food offered to idols (chs. 8–10), worship (ch. 11), spiritual gifts (chs. 12–14), the resurrection (ch. 15), and the collection and other matters (ch. 16).

## OVERVIEW OF 2 CORINTHIANS

**AUTHOR:** The apostle PAUL.

**HISTORICAL SETTING:** Written from MACEDONIA during Paul's third missionary journey (c. AD 56) in response to a report brought by TITUS (2 Cor. 2:13; 7:6, 13).

**PURPOSE:** To commend the Corinthians for their positive response to Titus's mission; to help them understand the nature of Paul's ministry; to encourage them to participate in the collection for other Christians in need; and to admonish a rebellious group in the church.

**CONTENTS:** After an introductory paragraph (2 Cor. 1:1–11), Paul gives an account of his recent activities (1:12–2:13), leading to an explanation of his apostolic ministry (2:14–6:10) and to various appeals (6:11–7:16); he then urges them to fulfill their intention of contributing to the collection being raised for the poor in Jerusalem (chs. 8–9); finally, he vindicates his apostolic authority by rebuking some false teachers who are still causing problems in the Corinthian church (chs. 10–13).

The amphitheater of ancient Caesarea, the city where Cornelius was stationed. Michael Melford/National Geographic Stock

converts should be required to submit to the Mosaic LAW, especially CIRCUMCISION (Acts 15).

**counselor.** See HOLY SPIRIT.

**covenant.** A binding agreement or treaty. In the OT the corresponding Hebrew term, *berith*, can refer to a two-sided covenant between human parties who voluntarily accept the terms of the agreement (friendship, 1 Sam. 18:3–4; marriage, Mal. 2:14; political alliance, Josh. 9:15; Obad. 7) or to a one-sided disposition imposed by a superior party (Ezek. 17:12–14). God's covenant with his people is of the latter sort (Gen. 15:18; 17:7). A distinction also is made between the covenant made at SINAI and the new covenant established by Christ (Jer. 31:31–34; Heb. 8:6–13; 9:15). In the NT, the KJV (following the Latin Vulgate) sometimes uses the translation "testament" (e.g., Matt. 26:28; 2 Cor. 3:6), which led to the use of the terms "Old Testament" and "New Testament."

**covetousness.** An inordinate and envious desire to have what belongs to another. It is a SIN mentioned frequently in both OT and NT, considered the root of other serious evils (Exod. 20:17; Lk. 22:15).

**creation.** The Bible teaches clearly that the universe, including all matter ("the heavens and the earth"), had a beginning and came into existence out of nothing through the will of the eternal God (Gen. 1–2; Heb. 11:3). The length of the creative "days" of Gen. 1 is a matter of debate among Christians. Scripture also gives no specific statement as to how long ago the first day of creation began or when the sixth day ended. According to the NT, all things were made through Christ, the Word (Jn. 1:3; Col. 1:16; Heb. 1:2).

**creation (creature), new.** See REGENERATION.

**Crete** (kreet). A large island (c. 160 mi./260 km. long) in the eastern MEDITERRANEAN, SE of the Greek mainland (see GREECE). In the OT the KERETHITES (1 Sam. 30:14; Ezek. 25:16), related to the PHILISTINES, are thought to have come from Crete. In the NT a number of Cretans are represented as being present on the Day of PENTECOST (Acts 2:11). PAUL, on the way to ROME, sailed on a grain ship along the southern coast of Crete (27:12–13). Years later he left TITUS on the island to supervise the churches there (Tit. 1:5). The Cretans apparently had a poor reputation (1:12).

**crimson.** A vivid or deep red color, similar to SCARLET, used as a symbol for the spiritual stain of sin (Isa. 1:18).

**Crispus** (kris′puhs). A superintendent of the SYNAGOGUE in CORINTH and an early convert there with his family (Acts 18:8); he was one of the few Corinthians baptized by PAUL (1 Cor. 1:14).

**cross.** A wooden post with a crossbeam on top, used by the Romans and others as an instrument of barbarous torture and death. Because of the sacrificial death of the Savior on the cross, the term came to mean "Christ's crucifixion." The preaching of the cross is foolishness to the world (1 Cor. 1:17) but brings peace and salvation to sinners (Eph. 2:16; Col. 1:20; 2:14). Those who want to be Jesus' disciples must deny themselves and take up their cross (Lk. 9:23), that is, they must follow him regardless of the consequences, even if it means death. In a different sense, Christians have been crucified with Christ because they have died (broken their relationship) to sin (Rom. 6:6; Gal. 2:19–20; 5:24; 6:14).

**crucify.** To put to death on a CROSS.

**cubit.** A unit of measurement, based on the distance between the elbow and the fingertip, but standardized to approximately 18 inches (46 cm.).

**curse.** The expression of a wish that evil fall on someone; the opposite of *blessing* (see BLESS). On the divine level, to curse is to impose JUDGMENT (Gen. 3:14). The curse of BALAAM on ISRAEL turned to a blessing (Num. 24:10). After the Israelites reached the Promised Land, half of the tribes stood on Mount GERIZIM and half on Mount EBAL to utter blessings and curses respectively (Deut. 27:12–13; Josh. 8:33–34). Christ commanded those who would be his disciples to bless and not to curse (Lk. 6:28). PAUL represents the curse of the LAW as borne by Christ on the CROSS for the believer (Gal. 3:13). See also BLASPHEMY.

**Cush** (koosh). Also Kush. Oldest son of HAM and grandson of NOAH (Gen. 10:6–8). From him descended several tribes, including the southernmost people group known to the Hebrews, and so the name usually refers to a land lying to the S of EGYPT, in the upper NILE region (Nubia), and corresponding roughly to ETHIOPIA. At times the reference to Cush is merely one that implies a country lying as far off as possible (cf. Ezek. 29:10). Cushites are mentioned several times in the OT (e.g., Num. 12:1; 2 Sam. 18:21–23; Jer. 38:7–13).

God's creation includes deep space objects such as this unusual galaxy (ESO 510-G13) that seems to have a twisted structure. NASA

A medieval castle sits on top of this mountain in Saint Hilarion, Cyprus. J. Baylor Roberts/National Geographic Stock

**Cyprus** (*si*′pruhs). An island in the eastern part of the MEDITERRANEAN directly off the coast of SYRIA and CILICIA, about 150 mi. (240 km.) long and about 40 mi. (65 km.) across. Before NT times, a large colony of Jews settled there; they must have formed the nucleus of the Christian church ministered to by PAUL and his companions, who passed through the island from SALAMIS to PAPHOS (Acts 13:4–12). BARNABAS, who accompanied Paul on this first missionary journey, was a native of the island (4:36); with John Mark (see MARK, JOHN) he later returned to evangelize Cyprus after they had left Paul's company (15:36–39).

**Cyrene** (*si*-ree′nee). A city of LIBYA in N Africa, W of EGYPT. A native of Cyrene, Simon by name, was pressed by the Roman soldiers to carry the CROSS of Jesus (Lk. 23:26). Jews from this city were present in JERUSALEM on the day of PENTECOST (Acts 2:10; see also 6:9; 13:1).

**Cyrenius.** See QUIRINIUS.

**Cyrus** (*si*′ruhs). The name of several rulers of PERSIA, the most important being Cyrus II the Great (559–530 BC), son of Cambyses and founder of the Achaemenid empire, which overthrew the Babylonian empire and continued for two centuries to the time of ALEXANDER THE GREAT. Cyrus instituted a kindly policy of repatriation for captive peoples, including the Hebrews, whom he encouraged to return to Judea to rebuild their temple (2 Chr. 36:22–23; Ezra 1:1–6). Isaiah refers to Cyrus as "his [i.e., the Lord's] anointed" (Isa. 45:1).

# D

**Dagon** (day′gon). Chief god of the PHILISTINES (Jdg. 16:23) but possibly worshiped earlier by the Canaanites. When the Philistines captured the ARK of the covenant and set it beside an image of Dagon, the statue fell twice on its face and broke, and moreover the Lord afflicted the people with tumors (1 Sam. 5:1–7). It is uncertain whether Dagon was a sea (fish) god, an agricultural deity, or a storm god.

**daleth** (dah′leth). The fourth letter of the Hebrew alphabet (ד, transliterated as *d*), used to begin each verse in Ps. 119:25–32.

**Dalmanutha** (dal-muh-*noo*′thuh). A village near the W shore of the Sea of Galilee (only in Mk. 8:10). See GALILEE, SEA OF. Following the feeding of the 4,000, Jesus and his disciples came to this region, an area that must have been near (or the same as) MAGADAN (see Matt. 15:39).

**Dalmatia** (dal-may′shee-uh). A district in the southern part of ILLYRICUM to which TITUS went during PAUL's final imprisonment (2 Tim. 4:10).

**Damaris** (dam′uh-ris). One of Paul's converts at Mars' Hill in ATHENS (Acts 17:34; see AREOPAGUS). Beyond this we know nothing of her, though some have thought that she may have been a woman of high social rank.

**Damascus** (duh-mas′kuhs). A very important city NE of Mount HERMON; its name could be applied also to the general geographic region in S SYRIA (ARAM) where the city was located. By the time of ABRAHAM, it was already well enough known to be a landmark (Gen. 14:15). DAVID subjugated and ruled the city for a time (2 Sam. 8:5–6; 1 Chr. 18:3–6), but the Arameans of Damascus harassed Israel for many years (1 Ki. 11:23–25; 2 Ki. 10:32–33). See BEN-HADAD; HAZAEL. During NT days, Damascus was an important center, ruled by ARABIA under ARETAS (2 Cor. 11:32). It was while en route there to arrest the believers that PAUL was converted (Acts 9:1–18; see also 9:25; 2 Cor. 11:33).

**Dan** (dan). Son of JACOB through BILHAH (Gen. 30:6). The name is applied also to the tribe descended from him and to the

Archaeological remains of the city of Dan. 

## OVERVIEW OF DANIEL

**AUTHOR:** Daniel, a member of the Hebrew nobility who was taken into EXILE and rose to prominence in the Babylonian administration. The narrative of the first six chapters refers to Daniel in the third person without explicit claim of authorship, but the visions in the second part of the book are related in the first person (e.g., "I, Daniel," Dan. 8:1).

**HISTORICAL SETTING:** The sixth century BC in BABYLON and SUSA, though many scholars reject this traditional view and date the book to the second century BC.

**PURPOSE:** To encourage the believing community by stressing God's sovereignty over the oppressive nations of the world and his power to deliver those who trust him.

**CONTENTS:** Six narratives on the life of Daniel and his friends (Dan. 1–6), followed by four apocalyptic visions predicting God's victory over evil (chs. 7–12).

main tribal city. After the conquest of CANAAN, the Danites were given a fertile area lying by the Mediterranean Sea that was occupied by the PHILISTINES. SAMSON was a Danite (Jdg. 13:2, 24). Failure to conquer Philistia made the Danites move northward, where they conquered Leshem (Laish) and renamed it Dan (Josh. 19:47; Jdg. 18:1–29). The city was situated on the S base of Mount HERMON and was commonly used as a symbol of the extent of Israelite territory in the phrase, "from Dan to Beersheba" (Jdg. 20:1).

This relief may be a depiction of King Darius the Great (from the northern stairs of the Apadana or Audience Hall at Persepolis). © www.Livius.org

**Daniel** (dan′yuhl). The name of several individuals in the OT (see 1 Chr. 3:1; Ezra 8:2; Ezek. 14:14) but especially of a Hebrew nobleman who as a youth was taken captive to BABYLON and later became a high official there. The OT book attributed to him relates that, though pressured to adopt foreign practices, he maintained himself loyal to God's law (Dan. 1:1–16). He had the gifts of dream interpretation and prophecy and because of his wisdom King NEBUCHADNEZZAR "made him ruler over the entire province of Babylon" (2:48). During his long life he served under several other Babylonian and Persian kings; he also received important visions about the future.

**Darius** (duh-ri′uhs). **(1)** A ruler described as "Darius the Mede," otherwise unknown, is mentioned only twice in the Bible (Dan. 5:31; 9:1). **(2)** Darius I Hystaspes, also known as Darius the Great, was the fourth ruler of the Persian empire (521–486 BC); under his lenient reign, the Jews restored the walls of JERUSALEM and rebuilt the temple (Ezra 6:1–15). **(3)** Darius II Ochus, son of ARTAXERXES I, became the seventh ruler of the Persian empire (423–404 BC); it was probably during his reign that NEHEMIAH went to Jerusalem the second time and found that many abuses had arisen (Neh. 13:6–11; cf. 12:22).

**darkness.** Beyond its literal sense, the word is used metaphorically to indicate such concepts as mystery (e.g., Exod. 20:21; 2 Sam. 22:10; Matt. 10:27), ignorance (Job 37:19; Prov. 2:13; Jn. 12:35; 1 Thess. 5:1–8), evil (Prov. 4:19; Matt. 6:23; Rom. 13:12), eternal punishment (Matt. 22:13; 2 Pet. 2:4), and spiritual blindness (Isa. 9:2; Jn. 1:5; Eph. 5:8). Darkness, however, never holds sway where the Redeemer has come to shed his light (Col. 1:13).

**Dathan** (day'thuhn). One of the Israelites who joined the Levite KORAH in leading a rebellion against the leadership of MOSES and AARON (Num. 16:1, 12, 24–25, 27; 26:9).

**daughter.** The Hebrew word for "daughter," *bath*, can be used for female descendants in general; it also has such figurative usages as "village" (Num. 21:25 KJV mg.), "[beloved] offspring" in general (Jer. 9:1 KJV), and "city inhabitants" (Zech. 9:9).

**David** (day'vid). Second king of Israel (1 Sam. 16–1 Ki. 2:11; 1 Chr. 11–29). David ranks with MOSES as one of the most commanding figures in the OT. Born about 1040 BC, he was the youngest son of Jesse of Bethlehem (1 Sam. 16:10–11). When God rejected SAUL, the prophet SAMUEL sought out David and secretly anointed him as ISRAEL's next king; and God's Spirit came upon David from that time on (16:13). His adventurous life included numerous military victories, such as defeating GOLIATH, but also much pain, such as being persecuted by Saul and having to flee from his own son ABSALOM. David elevated JERUSALEM to be his religious capital by installing the ARK of the covenant in a tent there (2 Sam. 6). God's Spirit inspired David to compose many beautiful psalms, in some of which he spoke prophetically of his own descendant, the MESSIAH (e.g., Ps. 16 and 110 are cited in Acts 2:15–36). Jesus was known as the Son of David (e.g., Matt. 20:30–31; 21:9).

**Day of Atonement.** See ATONEMENT.

**day of the Lord (of God, of Christ).** A phrase referring to the end time, focusing on God's triumph over his foes and the deliverance of his people (Isa. 2:12–21; 13:6–13; Ezek. 30:1–9; Joel 3:14–21; Obad. 15–17). It includes the second coming of Christ, the final JUDGMENT, and the establishment of a new heaven and a new earth (1 Cor. 1:8; 5:5; 2 Cor. 1:14; Phil. 1:6, 10; 2:16; 1 Thess. 5:2; 2 Thess. 2:2). It can be called simply "that day" (Matt. 7:22) or "the Day" (1 Cor. 3:13). See ESCHATOLOGY.

In this important inscription from the 9th cent. BC, an Aramean king claims to have killed King Ahaziah of Judah, who is identified as belonging to the "House of David" (apparently the earliest occurrence of this expression outside the Bible).

The mineral salts of the Dead Sea are evident in this photo.

© Alex Gulevich/www.BigStockPhoto.com

View from inside Cave 1 in Qumran. Some of the most important documents among the Dead Sea Scrolls were discovered here.

Todd Bolen/www.BiblePlaces.com

**deacon.** An ordained officer in the Christian CHURCH. The specific responsibilities of deacons differ among denominations. The Greek noun *diakonos*, however, was a very common term meaning "servant, assistant, messenger." Because the related words *diakonia* ("service") and *diakoneō* ("to serve") are used in Acts 6:1–2, the seven men chosen to aid those in need (vv. 3–6) are usually identified as the original deacons, but the office of deacon probably developed later. PAUL refers to deacons along with BISHOPS ("overseers," Phil. 1:1); the qualifications for deacons are given in 1 Tim. 3:8–13.

**Dead Sea.** An extremely salty lake at the S end of the JORDAN RIVER, called in Scripture the Salt Sea (e.g., Gen. 14:3), the Sea of the Arabah (Deut. 3:17), and "the eastern sea" (Ezek. 47:18; Joel 2:20). It is 47 mi. (75 km.) long and has the earth's lowest surface, 1,290 ft. (393 m.) below sea level. The waters of the Jordan empty here and evaporate quickly because of the dry heat, resulting in salt concentration of about 25 percent, four times that of ocean water. Magnesium bromide prevents organic life.

**Dead Sea Scrolls.** The popular name given to a collection of manuscripts belonging originally to an ancient religious community living at a place now known as Khirbet Qumran, a short distance from the NW corner of the DEAD SEA. Many of these scrolls represent the oldest surviving copies of most books of the Hebrew OT. The rest of the scrolls provide insights into the Qumran community, which most scholars identify as ESSENE; they include commentaries on biblical books, hymns of praise, rules of conduct for its members, etc.

**death.** This term refers primarily to the end of physical life on earth but also to the absence of a spiritual communion with God. Both physical and spiritual death are the result of sin (Rom. 5:12; 6:23). The devil is said to hold the power of death, but Christ by his own death destroyed that power and freed believers from the fear of death (Heb. 2:14–15; see also Acts 2:24). And just as Christ was raised from the dead, so also those who believe in him are raised both from spiritual death (Jn. 5:24; Rom. 6:4) and from physical death (1 Cor. 15:12–22). Those who reject God are not only spiritually dead; they will also experience "the second death, the lake of fire" (Rev. 20:14).

**Debir** (dee′buhr). The name of several towns, especially one near HEBRON previously known as Kiriath Sepher (Josh. 10:38–39; 15:15). It was also the name of an AMORITE who was defeated by JOSHUA (Josh. 10:2).

**Deborah** (deb′uh-ruh). **(1)** The nurse of REBEKAH, wife of ISAAC (Gen. 35:8; cf. 24:59). **(2)** A prophetess who also served as one of the "judges" or leaders of Israel prior to the monarchy. She and BARAK defeated the forces of a powerful Canaanite king under the command of SISERA (Jdg. 4–5).

**Decalogue.** See COMMANDMENTS, TEN.

**Decapolis** (di-kap′uh-lis). This name was given to a large area mostly E of the JORDAN RIVER, where a league of "ten cities" (the meaning of the term) was constituted after the Romans conquered the region in the first century BC (the number of cities was later increased). They had their own coinage, courts, and army. Jesus drove the demons into swine near GADARA, one of these cities (Mk. 5:1–20), and became popular in the Decapolis (Matt. 4:24–25; Mk. 7:31–37).

**deceit, deception.** See LIE.

**decision, valley of.** See JEHOSHAPHAT, VALLEY OF.

**decree.** An official edict or a decision issued by a ruler (e.g., Esth. 9:32; Lk. 2:1). The term can refer also to God's commands (Exod. 15:25) and to his plans and decisions (Job 23:14; Ps. 2:7; 105:10). See ELECTION; PROVIDENCE.

**Dedan** (dee′duhn). The name of two different individuals (Gen. 10:7; 25:3); the second

The Decapolis.

D

of them probably gave his name to a territory in ARABIA that was later condemned by the prophets (Isa. 21:13; Jer. 25:23; 49:8; Ezek. 25:13; 38:13–14).

**dedication.** The act of setting apart or devoting someone or something to God for holy ends. Examples include the TABERNACLE (Num. 7), the TEMPLE (1 Ki. 8), and groups of people (1 Sam. 16:5). See also HOLINESS; NAZIRITE; SANCTIFICATION.

**Dedication, Feast of.** This phrase occurs once in the NT (Jn. 10:22). It refers to the Feast of Hanukkah, celebrated annually by the Jews for eight days in mid-December to commemorate the cleansing of the TEMPLE in Jerusalem after it had been desecrated by the Syrians in the second century BC (1 Macc. 4:52–59; 2 Macc. 10:5).

**deep, the.** This term translates a Hebrew word used with reference to the earth before it was fully formed (Gen. 1:2); elsewhere it can designate the RED SEA through which Israel passed (e.g., Isa. 51:10) and other bodies of water (Gen. 7:11; Ps. 107:26; Jon. 2:5). See also ABYSS.

**defile.** To make something or someone UNCLEAN. In the OT impurity is often ceremonial (e.g., Lev. 11:24), but it can also be religious (idolatry, Ezek. 37:23) and moral (murder, Isa. 59:3 KJV). In the NT ceremonial defilement recedes into the background (cf. Acts 10:15), so the emphasis falls on ethical behavior. An undefiled person or thing is one untainted with moral evil (KJV Ps. 119:1; Cant. 5:2; 6:9; Heb. 7:26; 13:4; Jas. 1:27; 1 Pet. 1:4). See HOLINESS.

**deity.** This English term can refer both to the true God and to a false god or goddess. It can also mean "divine nature" (Col. 2:9; KJV "Godhead").

**Delilah** (di-li′luh). A non-Israelite woman, probably a PHILISTINE, who persuaded SAMSON to reveal the source of his strength (Jdg. 16:4–20).

**Demas** (dee′muhs). A companion of PAUL first mentioned in the greetings he sent to the church in COLOSSE (Col. 4:14; Phlm. 24) but later marked for his desertion of the apostle (2 Tim. 4:10).

**Demetrius** (di-mee′tree-uhs). **(1)** A jeweler in EPHESUS who raised a mob against PAUL because the apostle's preaching had resulted in damage to the lucrative business of making silver shrines of the goddess ARTEMIS (Acts 19:23–27). **(2)** A disciple commended by JOHN the apostle in his letter to GAIUS (3 Jn. 12).

**demon.** A term synonymous with "evil spirit" (compare Matt. 17:18 with Mk. 9:25). Demons are apparently fallen angels under SATAN who oppose God. They can take control of some people to torment them, but Jesus showed his power over Satan by casting out demons (Matt. 4:24; 8:16).

**denarius.** A Roman silver coin; laborers normally received one denarius for a full day's work (cf. Matt. 20:1–16).

**deny.** When PETER "denied" Jesus (Matt. 26:34; NIV "disown"), he was refusing to admit any connection with the Lord. To "deny" the faith (1 Tim. 5:8) means to reject or contradict the gospel (see APOSTASY). But when Jesus tells his disciples to "deny themselves" (Matt. 16:24), he is instructing them to set aside their self-interests and give him full priority.

**Derbe** (duhr′bee). A city of Asia Minor (modern Turkey) in the SE corner of LYCAONIA, a region that was part of the Roman province of GALATIA. PAUL visited it more than once (Acts 14:20; 16:1).

**Deuteronomy** (d*oo*′tuh-ron′uh-mee). The fifth book of the Bible and traditionally one of the five books of MOSES (see PENTATEUCH). In sight of CANAAN, which he would not be allowed to enter, Moses gathered the hosts of Israel about him for his farewell addresses. These, along with several brief

D

## OVERVIEW OF DEUTERONOMY

**AUTHOR:** Although technically anonymous, most of the book consists of discourses attributed directly to MOSES.

**HISTORICAL SETTING:** The end of the wilderness wanderings, as a new generation of Israelites are camped E of the JORDAN ready to take possession of the Promised Land (c. 1400 or 1250 BC, depending on the date of the EXODUS).

**PURPOSE:** To exhort the people to renew their COVENANT with God, avoiding the sins of the previous generation and thus becoming spiritually prepared to conquer the land before them.

**CONTENTS:** Historical review of God's dealings with the Israelites (Deut. 1–4); extended exposition of the Ten Commandments (see COMMANDMENTS, TEN) and other laws (chs. 5–26); renewal of the covenant by affirming the curses and blessings (chs. 27–30); Moses' last words and death (chs. 31–34).

narrative passages, constitute the book of Deuteronomy. The name (first used by the SEPTUAGINT) means "second law," alluding to the fact that the book repeats many of the commandments so that the new generation of Israelites would renew the COVENANT made earlier at SINAI.

**devil.** Although in the KJV this word occurs often in the plural with reference to DEMONS (e.g., Lev. 17:7; Matt. 4:24), most versions use it only to translate the Greek term *diabolos* ("slanderer"), designating SATAN (e.g., Matt. 4:1; 13:39; Jn. 13:2; Rev. 2:10).

**Diana.** See ARTEMIS.

**Dibon** (d*i*′bon). **(1)** A Judean town toward the S, inhabited in the time of NEHEMIAH by members of the tribe of JUDAH (Neh. 11:25); it seems to be the same as Dimonah (Josh. 15:22). **(2)** A city in MOAB, E of the DEAD SEA and N of the ARNON River, given to the tribes of GAD and REUBEN (Num. 32:3, 34; Josh. 13:9; Jer. 48:22).

**Didymus** (did′uh-muhs). See THOMAS.

**Dinah** (d*i*′nuh). A daughter of JACOB who was violated by SHECHEM; two of Dinah's brothers, SIMEON and LEVI, took revenge by killing Shechem and all the men in his city (Gen. 30:21; 34:1–31; 46:15).

**Dionysius** (d*i*′uh-nish′ee-uhs). A convert of PAUL in ATHENS who was apparently a member of the council of the AREOPAGUS (Acts 17:34).

**Diotrephes** (d*i*-ot′ruh-feez). A church leader who abused his authority and opposed the instructions of JOHN the apostle (3 Jn. 9–10).

**disciple.** A student or follower. The word appears many times in the NT, almost always with reference to Jesus' followers; it implies the acceptance in mind and life of the views and practices of the teacher. Sometimes the word designates the twelve APOSTLES specifically (e.g., Matt. 10:1; 11:1); more often Christians in general are in view (Acts 6:1–2, 7; 9:36). Although Christian discipleship had many facets, it was summed up in a single concept—obedience to the LOVE command (Jn. 13:34–35).

**discipline.** See CHASTISEMENT.

Dor was an important harbor along the Mediterranean Sea.

Z. Radovan/www.BibleLandPictures.com

**dispensation.** This English term is used by the KJV four times to render the Greek word *oikonomia*, which means "management, commission, arrangement, plan" (1 Cor. 9:17; Eph. 1:10; 3:2; Col. 1:25). In modern theological use, *dispensation* refers to a period of time characterized by specific divine instructions; for instance, some refer to the period between Moses and Christ as the dispensation of the LAW.

**divination.** The practice of consulting supernatural beings or observing omens to gain information about the future and other matters removed from normal knowledge. Divination was severely condemned by MOSES (Deut. 18:10–11) and the prophets (Hos. 4:12; Ezek. 8:17).

**divinity.** The quality of being God. See TRINITY.

**divorce.** An act whereby a legal MARRIAGE is dissolved publicly and the participants are freed from further obligations of the matrimonial relationship. The OT provides for divorce in some cases (Deut. 24:1, probably referring to immorality), and EZRA required it of those Jews who had married foreign wives in BABYLONIA (Ezra 9:2; 10:3, 16–17). However, Malachi has strong words against divorce (Mal. 2:16), and Jesus asserted that God had allowed divorce only as a concession to the hardness of the human heart (Matt. 19:8). PAUL states that Christian spouses should not separate (1 Cor. 7:10–15).

**doctrine.** This term is used frequently by the KJV in the sense of "teaching" (e.g., Acts 2:42). In its modern use the word refers to what a person believes about God and salvation (e.g., 1 Tim. 1:10).

**Doeg** (doh'ig). An Edomite who served King SAUL as head shepherd and who killed numerous priests and their families (1 Sam. 21:7; 22:17–19).

**Dor** (dor). A fortified city on the coast of PALESTINE, S of Mount CARMEL, c. 8 mi. (13 km.) N of CAESAREA. The surrounding hilly area was known as Naphoth Dor (Josh. 11:2; 12:23; 1 Ki. 4:11; cf. Josh.

17:11). It was settled in very ancient times by PHOENICIA because of the abundance of shells along the coast that were the source of a rich purple dye.

**Dorcas** (dor′kuhs). A Christian woman of JOPPA who died and was raised from the dead by PETER (Acts 9:36–43). Her ARAMAIC name was Tabitha, which has the same meaning as Dorcas.

**Dothan** (doh′thuhn). A prominent town in the boundaries between the tribes of MANASSEH and ISSACHAR (c. 5 mi./8 km. S of the JEZREEL Valley), where JOSEPH was cast by his brothers into a dry well-pit (Gen. 37:24; see also 2 Ki. 6:13).

**dowry.** Money (or property) given by a bride to her husband at MARRIAGE. The word is used by the KJV several times in the OT, but the Hebrew word there refers to the compensation a husband pays to the bride's family for losing her services. It is thus better translated "marriage present" or "bride-price" (Gen. 34:12; Exod. 22:17; 1 Sam. 18:25).

**doxology.** An ascription of PRAISE or GLORY to God in song or prayer (from Gk. *doxa*, "glory, praise, honor"). Although the word itself does not occur in the Bible, many passages consist of doxologies (e.g., Ps. 41:13; 72:18–19; Lk. 2:14; 19:37–38; Heb. 13:20–21; Jude 24–25; Rev. 5:13).

**dragon.** This English term is used by some Bible versions in places where the NIV has the more general word "monster" (e.g., Job 7:12; Ps. 74:13; Isa. 27:1). In the book of Revelation it designates SATAN (Rev. 12:3–17; 13:1–11; 16:13; 20:2).

**dream.** In ancient times God sometimes spoke in dreams both to his people (e.g., Gen. 28:10–17; Num. 12:6) and to pagans (e.g., Gen. 20:3; 41:36; Dan. 2:1–45; 4:5–33). In the NT the only individuals said to have received meaningful dreams from God are JOSEPH the husband of MARY and the MAGI, in both cases before the ministry of Christ (Matt. 1:20; 2:12–13, 19, 22; note also PILATE's wife, 27:19). Many Christians believe that the fuller revelation through Christ makes special dreams unnecessary (cf. Heb. 1:1–2).

**drunkenness.** The Scriptures show that drunkenness was one of the major vices of antiquity, even among the Hebrews (e.g., Gen. 9:21; 19:33, 35; 1 Sam. 25:36; 2 Sam. 13:28). The prophets denounced intoxication as a great social evil (e.g., Isa. 28:7; Amos 4:1), and the NT also warns against it (e.g., Eph. 5:18; 1 Tim. 3:8).

**Drusilla** (dr*oo*-sil′uh). The youngest of the three daughters of Herod AGRIPPA I; she became the wife of the procurator FELIX (Acts 24:24–27).

**Dung Gate.** One of the gates of JERUSALEM in NEHEMIAH's day; it was located between the Valley Gate and the Fountain Gate (Neh. 2:13; 3:13–15; 12:31). Perhaps it is the same as the Potsherd Gate (Jer. 19:2; 2 Ki. 23:10).

# E

**earnest.** An adjective meaning "intense, serious, eager" (e.g., Rom. 8:19 KJV). As a noun it means "deposit, pledge"; used by the KJV in passages where the HOLY SPIRIT is portrayed as guaranteeing the Christian's future glory (2 Cor. 1:22; 5:5; Eph. 1:14).

**earth.** See WORLD.

**east.** Possibly because east is the direction in which the sun rises, it was the primary point of orientation for the Israelites and other ancient peoples. The gate of the TABERNACLE was on the east side (Exod. 38:13–14; see also Ezek. 43:2, 4). In PALESTINE, the "east wind" is the hot, dry, and sometimes destructive air that blows from the desert (Ezek. 19:12).

**Ebal, Mount** (ee'buhl). A mountain 3,077 ft. (938 m.) high, one of the highest points in the land of SAMARIA, near the city of SHECHEM. The Israelites were instructed to recite the blessings of the LAW from Mount GERIZIM and the curses from Mount Ebal (Deut. 27:4–26; Josh. 8:30–35).

**Ebenezer** (eb'uh-nee'zuhr). A name meaning "stone of help" and referring to a place where the Israelites were defeated twice by the PHILISTINES (1 Sam. 4:1–11; 5:1). This name was given by SAMUEL to the stone set

Rugged mountains in Edom.

Z. Radovan/www.BibleLandPictures.com

## OVERVIEW OF ECCLESIASTES

**AUTHOR:** "The Teacher [Preacher], son of David, king in Jerusalem" (Eccl. 1:1), apparently a reference to SOLOMON, but many (including some conservative scholars) believe that the book was written by a later, unknown sage.

**HISTORICAL SETTING:** If Ecclesiastes is the work of Solomon, it must have been composed during the last years of his life (c. 940 BC). Those who do not accept a Solomonic authorship date the book after the EXILE, some as late as the third century BC.

**PURPOSE:** To show that, apart from the fear of God, life has no meaning and leads to despair.

**CONTENTS:** After a prologue (Eccl. 1:1–11), the book seeks to demonstrate the meaninglessness of all earthly things (1:12–6:12), provides practical advice on various topics (7:1–12:7), and ends with an epilogue apparently written by someone other than "the Teacher" (12:8–14).



up by him to commemorate a later Israelite victory over the Philistines (7:12), but it is not certain whether the same place is meant.

**Ecclesiastes, Book of** (i-klee′zee-as′teez). One of the WISDOM books of the OT, known in Hebrew as Qoheleth (also Koheleth), which means "teacher" or "preacher." The name Ecclesiastes comes from the Greek translation (SEPTUAGINT) and means "a member of the assembly." There has been much debate about the author of the book, its character, and the interpretation of some of its statements, but its central theme is the meaninglessness of life without God, and the conclusion is clear: "Fear God and keep his commandments" (Eccl. 12:13).

**Eden** (ee′duhn). The region in which the Lord God planted a garden for the first man and woman. In it grew every tree that was pleasant to see and good for food, including the tree of life and the tree of the knowledge of good and evil (see TREE OF KNOWLEDGE, TREE OF LIFE). A river flowed out of Eden and divided into four streams (Gen. 2:8–14). ADAM and EVE lived there until they sinned by eating the forbidden fruit and were expelled from it (Gen. 2–3). Scripture writers mention Eden as an illustration of a delightful place (Isa. 51:3; Ezek. 28:13; 31:9, 16, 18; 36:35; Joel 2:3).

**edification.** The act of building up. This term is used figuratively to indicate the process of helping other Christians become strong and mature (Rom. 14:19; 1 Cor. 14:5; Eph. 4:12).

**Edom** (ee′duhm). A name that can refer to ESAU (Gen. 25:30), to the land of his descendants (32:3; 36:20–21, 30), or to the Edomites as a people (Num. 20:18–21; Amos 1:6, 11; Mal. 1:4). The country was also called Seir or Mount Seir (Gen. 32:3; Josh. 15:10), referring to a mountain and plateau area SE of the DEAD SEA. The Edomites were enemies of Israel for much of their history. See also IDUMEA.

**Edrei** (ed′ree-*i*). **(1)** A residence city of OG king of BASHAN (Deut. 1:4; 3:10; Josh. 12:4; 13:12); it was 30 mi. (50 km.) E of the JORDAN. **(2)** A fortified city allotted to the tribe of NAPHTALI in Upper GALILEE (Josh. 19:37).

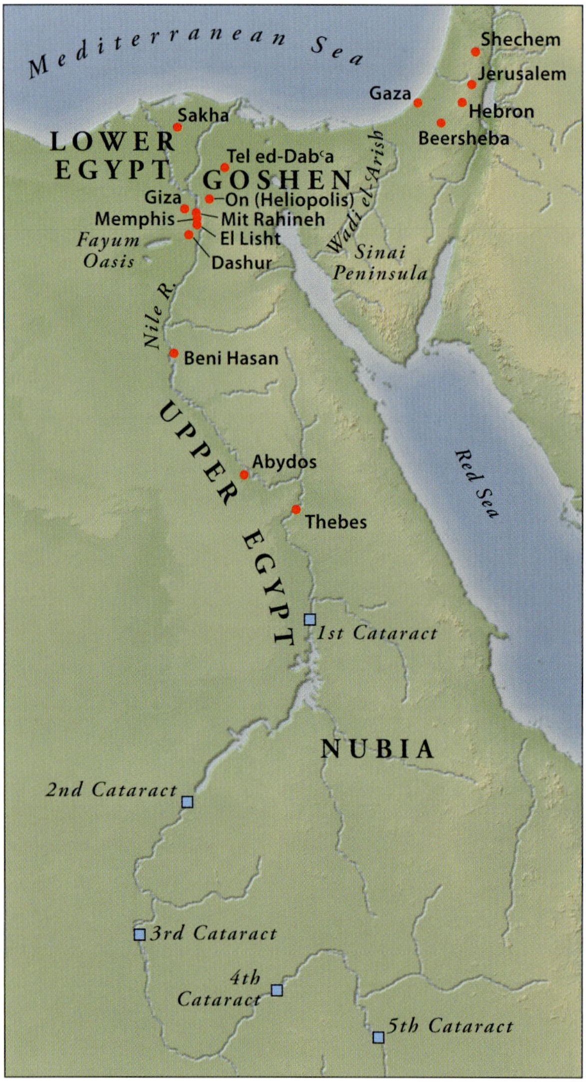


Egypt at the time of Abraham (Middle Kingdom Egypt).

**Eglon** (eg′lon). **(1)** An obese king of MOAB who dominated the Israelites for eighteen years; he was assassinated by the judge EHUD (Jdg. 3:12–22). **(2)** An AMORITE town whose king, DEBIR, joined four others against the Gibeonites; JOSHUA defeated the five kings and captured Eglon (Josh. 10:3, 5, 23, 34–37; 12:12).

**Egypt** (ee′jipt). A country in the NE corner of Africa, including the NILE delta and valley, with their flanking deserts. It was home to one of the most ancient civilizations of the world. During times of famine, both ABRAHAM and JACOB sojourned in Egypt (Gen. 12:10; 46:6). Jacob's descendants spent over four centuries there (Exod. 12:40) until they were delivered through MOSES (see EXODUS). The Bible contains many other references to Egypt (e.g., 1 Ki. 3:1; 2 Ki. 23:29; Isa. 19:12–25). See also MIZRAIM.

**Ehud** (ee′huhd). A left-handed Israelite hero who assassinated King EGLON and led a revolt against MOAB (Jdg. 3:15–31).

**Ekron** (ek′ruhn). The northernmost of the five chief cities of the PHILISTINES (1 Sam. 5:10; 6:16–17; 7:14).

**Elah, Valley of** (ee′luh). A valley about 18 mi. (29 km.) WSW of JERUSALEM where the combat between DAVID and GOLIATH took place (1 Sam. 17:2, 19; 21:9).

**Elam** (ee′luhm). The name of several persons in the OT, especially a son of SHEM (Gen. 10:22; 1 Chr. 1:17). He was probably the ancestor of the Elamites, who formed an ancient civilization near BABYLONIA. The country of Elam is mentioned as an enemy of Israel (e.g., Jer. 49:34–39). Elamites were present on the Day of PENTECOST (Acts 2:9).

**Elath, Eloth** (ee′lath, ee′loth). A town of strategic position on the northern end of the Gulf of Aqabah (also known as the Gulf of Elath, the NE arm of the RED SEA). The town is sometimes mentioned along with EZION GEBER (Deut. 2:8; 1 Ki. 9:26).

**elder.** In ISRAEL, the elders were adult men who gathered as a kind of council in every village and served as local rulers (Exod. 4:29; 1 Sam. 16:4). In NT times, when Christian churches came into being, elders were appointed for each congregation (Acts 14:23). The "elders" of Acts 20:17 are referred to as BISHOPS in v. 28 (NIV "overseers"). They were required to be blameless in their lives and obedient to the truth in their faith (1 Tim. 3:1–7; Tit. 1:6–9).

**Elead** (el′ee-uhd) Son (or possibly grandson) of EPHRAIM; he and Ezer (prob. his brother), while raiding the livestock in GATH, were killed by the men of the city (1 Chr. 7:21).

**Eleazar** (el′ee-ay′zuhr). The name of several men, but especially a son of AARON (Exod. 6:23). After Aaron's death, Eleazar succeeded his father in the high priestly office (Num. 20:25–28; Deut. 10:6). With JOSHUA, he divided the land of PALESTINE by lot (Josh. 14:1; 17:4).

**election.** The act of choosing. God chose the Israelites as his people not because of their qualities but because of his love and promises (Deut. 7:6–8). Jesus said that "many are invited, but few are chosen" (Matt. 22:14; cf. 1 Cor. 1:27–28; Eph. 1:4; Jas. 2:5; 1 Pet. 1:2). Those who belong to God are called "the elect" (Mk. 13:20; Col. 3:12 KJV). "God's purpose in election" is firm (Rom. 9:11). This doctrine does not mean, however, that God violates the human will or forces a person's choice (Deut. 30:19; Isa. 66:3; Rev. 22:17).

**Eli** (ee′l*i*). A descendant of AARON who served as both judge and HIGH PRIEST in ISRAEL. He lost control of his sons, who led immoral lives (1 Sam. 2:12–17). Young SAMUEL was trained under him (1:25–28; 3:1). Eli died of a fall when he heard that the ARK of the covenant had been taken by the PHILISTINES (4:18).

**Eli, Eli, lama sabachthani.** See ELOI, ELOI, LAMA SABACHTHANI.

**Eliakim** (i-l*i*′uh-kim). **(1)** The birth name of King JEHOIAKIM. **(2)** Son of HILKIAH and palace administrator under King HEZEKIAH; he was among those who negotiated with the besieging Assyrian army (2 Ki. 18:18–19:7; Isa. 22:20–24; 36:3–37:7).

The ancient town of Elath was located in this area. Todd Bolen/www.BiblePlaces.com

This Russian painting (c. 1600) depicts Elijah in the desert and then taken up to heaven as Elisha watches.
Mark Gallery, London, UK/The Bridgeman Art Library International

**Elias** (i-l*i*′uhs). See ELIJAH.

**Eliezer** (el′ee-ee′zuhr). An important servant in the household of ABRAHAM who was due to receive the family inheritance if the latter had no sons (Gen. 15:2–3). He was most likely the unnamed but devout servant of Gen. 24 who was sent to get a wife for ISAAC from among Abraham's people. Other OT men were named Eliezer, including the second son of MOSES by ZIPPORAH (Exod. 18:4; 1 Chr. 23:15).

**Elihu** (i-l*i*′hy*oo*). The name of several men in the OT, including a friend of JOB who became angry with him and his other friends; in his long speech he insisted that suffering has a disciplinary purpose (Job 32:2–37:24).

**Elijah** (i-l*i*′juh). KJV NT Elias. The name of several men in the OT but especially the famous ninth-century prophet who served in the northern kingdom in the reigns of AHAB and his son AHAZIAH (1 Ki. 17:1–2 Ki. 2:12). He courageously confronted the prophets of BAAL and showed the power of the God he trusted (1 Ki. 18:20–40). Instead of dying, he was taken up to heaven in a whirlwind (2 Ki. 2:11).

**Elimelech** (i-lim′uh-lek). TNIV Elimelek. The husband of NAOMI (Ruth 1:2–3; 2:1, 3; 4:3, 9).

**Eliphaz** (el′i-faz). An Edomite friend of JOB who showed some kindness but also accused him of sinning (Job 2:11; chs. 4–5; 15; 22).

**Elisha** (i-l*i*′shuh). KJV NT Eliseus. A prophet who succeeded ELIJAH (1 Ki. 19:16–21; 2 Ki. 2:9–15). Elisha had a long ministry under four kings of Israel, and during this time he performed many miracles, such as raising a boy from the dead (2 Ki. 4:37) and healing NAAMAN from his leprosy (5:1–14).

**Elizabeth** (i-liz′uh-buhth). KJV Elisabeth. Relative of MARY and mother of JOHN the Baptist (Lk. 1:5–45, 57–63).

**Elkanah** (el-kay′nuh). A common name, especially among LEVITES, including the father of the prophet SAMUEL (1 Sam. 1:1–23).

**Elohim** (el′oh-him). The most frequent Hebrew word for GOD, occurring over 2,200 times in the OT (e.g., Gen. 1:1). This term is plural in form (probably indicating majesty), but is usually singular in construction. A different but related term is *El*, which often appears in compounds (e.g., Bethel means "house of God").

**Eloi, Eloi, lama sabachthani** (ee′loh-*i* ee′loh-*i* lah′muh suh-bak′thuh-n*i*). An ARAMAIC phrase meaning, "My God, my God, why have you forsaken me?" It comes from Ps. 22:1 and was quoted by Jesus on the cross (Matt. 27:46 [KJV Eli]; Mk. 15:34).

**Eloth.** See ELATH, ELOTH.

**Elul** (ee′luhl). The sixth month (August-September) in the Jewish CALENDAR (Neh. 6:15).

**Elymas** (el′uh-muhs). Another name (or title) for BAR-JESUS.

**Emmanuel.** See IMMANUEL.

**Emmaus** (i-may′uhs). A village near JERUSALEM to which two disciples were going when the risen Jesus appeared to them (Lk. 24:7–35).

**Endor** (en′dor). A town near the river KISHON where BARAK defeated the forces of the Canaanite king JABIN (Josh. 17:11; Ps. 83:9–10). Here King SAUL sought the help of a medium (see FAMILIAR SPIRIT) shortly before his final battle (1 Sam. 28:7).

**En Gedi** (en-ged′*i*). A spring with associated streams on the W side of the DEAD SEA where DAVID hid when fleeing from SAUL (1 Sam. 23:29; 24:1; cf. Josh. 15:62; 2 Chr. 20:2; Ezek. 47:10).

**Enoch** (ee′nuhk). **(1)** Son of CAIN, who named a city after him (Gen. 4:17–18). **(2)** Father of METHUSELAH. Because he "walked with God," he was taken to heaven without dying (Gen. 5:18–24; Heb. 11:5; Jude 14–15).

**envy.** A feeling of displeasure and ill will because of another's advantages or possessions. The OT warns against the temptation of becoming envious of evil persons when they seem to prosper in spite of their wrongdoing (Ps. 37:1; 73:2, 3; Prov. 3:31; 23:17; 24:1, 19). Envy led to the crucifixion of Jesus (Matt. 27:18), and it is listed by Jesus and by Paul as a serious SIN (Mk. 7:22; Rom. 1:29; Gal. 5:21).

**Epaphras** (ep′uh-fras). A native of COLOSSE and founder of the Colossian church; he was highly regarded by PAUL (Col. 1:7–8; 4:12–13; Phlm. 23).

**Epaphroditus** (i-paf′ruh-d*i*′tuhs). A member of the church at PHILIPPI who brought a gift to PAUL when the apostle was imprisoned (Phil. 2:25–30; 4:18).

**ephah** (ee′fuh). A unit of dry measure equivalent to about 22 liters (almost two-thirds of a bushel).

Water springs in the canyon at En Gedi.



**Ephesians, Letter to the.** One of the richest and most profound of PAUL's letters, written while the apostle was a prisoner in ROME and sent to the church in EPHESUS and probably to several other churches near that city. Ephesians sets forth the wealth of the believer in union with Christ and emphasizes the nature of the CHURCH as the BODY OF CHRIST.

**Ephesus** (ef′uh-suhs). A major city on the W coast of Asia Minor (modern Turkey) and a center for the worship of the goddess ARTEMIS. PAUL spent more than two years ministering in Ephesus (Acts 19). The

## OVERVIEW OF EPHESIANS

**AUTHOR:** The apostle PAUL, though some argue that the letter consists of Pauline material brought together and edited by one or more of his disciples.

**HISTORICAL SETTING:** Probably written from ROME during the apostle's first imprisonment in that city (c. AD 61–63; those who believe that someone other than Paul was the author date the letter two or three decades later). Ephesians may have been addressed to several churches in and around EPHESUS in the aftermath of the problems that occasioned the writing of COLOSSIANS.

**PURPOSE:** To expound on the blessings enjoyed by the CHURCH, to stress the unity of the BODY OF CHRIST, and to encourage believers to walk in the ways of CHRIST.

**CONTENTS:** A doctrinal section that focuses on our standing in Christ (Eph. 1–3), followed by a practical section on righteous Christian living (chs. 4–6).



church in that city is rebuked in Revelation (Rev. 2:1–7).

**ephod** (ee′fod). A sacred vest worn primarily by the HIGH PRIEST; on each shoulderpiece was an onyx stone engraved with six names of the tribes of Israel (Exod. 28:6–14; 39:2–7). In the time of the JUDGES, the ephod was misused as an object of idolatrous worship by GIDEON (Jdg. 8:27). DAVID used it to find out God's will (1 Sam. 23:6, 9; 30:7–8). See URIM AND THUMMIM.

This great ampitheater in Ephesus could seat 25,000 spectators.
© William D. Mounce

**ephphatha** (ef′uh-thuh). A HEBREW or ARAMAIC word meaning, "Be opened"; it was used by Jesus to heal a deaf mute (Mk. 7:34).

**Ephraim** (ee′fray-im). **(1)** The younger of two sons born to JOSEPH; his older brother was MANASSEH (Gen. 41:50–52; 46:20). He was also the ancestor of the tribe that bears his name. Instead of one tribe of Joseph, the Hebrews recognized the descendants of Ephraim and Manassah as two distinct tribes. The Ephraimites received the central hill country of PALESTINE. Because of their influence, the name Ephraim sometimes denotes the whole northern kingdom of ISRAEL (Isa. 7:2, 5, 9, 17; Hos. 9:3–16). **(2)** The name of a town about 13 mi. (21 km.) NNE of JERUSALEM (Jn. 11:54; perhaps also 2 Sam. 13:23, but this may be a reference to the tribal territory of Ephraim).

**Ephrath, Ephrathah** (ef′rath, ef′ruh-thuh). A city or area associated with (and at some point absorbed into) BETHLEHEM (Gen. 35:16–20; 48:7; Mic. 5:2). DAVID's father, JESSE, is identified as an Ephrathite (1 Sam. 17:12).

**Epicurean** (ep′i-kyoo-ree′uhn). A prominent philosophical school in the Greco-Roman period (Acts 17:18). They followed the philosophy of Epicurus (341–270 BC), who taught that the chief purpose of human beings is to achieve happiness through a life of pleasure, by which he meant the avoidance of pain and the pursuit of knowledge.

**epistle.** A literary composition in the form of a letter. Since the "epistles" of the NT are real pieces of correspondence (not intended as published literary works), it is better to use the term LETTER.

**Erastus** (i-ras′tuhs). **(1)** A helper of PAUL (Acts 19:22; probably the same person who is mentioned in 2 Tim. 4:20). **(2)** A man described as "director of public works" in CORINTH (Rom. 16:23; Romans was written from Corinth).

**Esaias.** See ISAIAH.

**Esarhaddon** (ee′suhr-had′uhn). Son of SENNACHERIB and king of ASSYRIA (2 Ki. 19:36–37; 2 Chr. 32:21; Isa. 37:37–38). He ruled from 681 to 669 BC, and his main achievement was the conquest of EGYPT in 671.

**Esau** (ee′saw). Son of ISAAC and REBEKAH, also named EDOM. He sold his BIRTHRIGHT to his twin brother JACOB (Gen. 25:25–34) and later failed to receive his father's blessing because of Jacob's trickery (ch. 27; see also chs. 33; 36; Mal. 1:2–3; Rom. 9:10–13; Heb. 12:16–17). The Edomites descended from him.

**eschatology.** The doctrine of the last things; it includes the study of such important events as the second coming of Jesus Christ, the MILLENNIUM, the JUDGMENT of the world, the RESURRECTION of the dead, and the creation of the new heaven and earth.

**Essenes** (es′eens). A Jewish religious group that flourished between the 2nd cent. BC and the 1st cent. AD. Although not mentioned by the NT writers, the Essenes formed an important school of thought in the time of CHRIST. They lived a simple life of sharing everything in common and practiced strict rules of conduct. Most scholars think that the DEAD SEA SCROLLS were produced by them.

**Esther, Book of** (es′tuhr). The last of the historical books of the OT. Esther was a

Watchtower in the hill country of Ephraim. Todd Bolen/www.BiblePlaces.com

## OVERVIEW OF ESTHER

**AUTHOR:** Unknown.

**HISTORICAL SETTING:** The book was probably written in PERSIA sometime between 450 and 350 BC.

**PURPOSE:** To provide a historical-theological account of the origin of the Feast of PURIM and thus to encourage the Jewish people of the DISPERSION in the midst of their suffering.

**CONTENTS:** The rejection of VASHTI and the selection of Esther (Esth. 1–2); the plot of HAMAN (chs. 3–4); the triumph of MORDECAI (chs. 5–7); the vindication of the Jews (chs. 8–10).

Jewish woman whose Hebrew name was Hadassah (Esth. 2:7). Her cousin MORDECAI, who was a minor official of the palace, reared her as his own daughter. XERXES (Ahasuerus), the Persian king, had divorced his wife. When he sought a new queen from among the maidens of the realm, he chose Esther. When the Jews in the empire were faced with destruction, she was able to save them. In her honor the book of Esther is read every year at the Feast of PURIM.

**eternal.** This word—and its synonyms "everlasting," "forever"—sometimes refer simply to a long time (e.g., Gen. 17:8; 2 Sam. 7:16). When applied to God, his words, and his acts, however, it clearly signifies the eternal and everlasting in the literal and absolute sense of the term. In the NT, its most common use is in the phrase "eternal life," which mingles future and present: it indicates not only endless duration, but also divine quality (Matt. 25:46; Jn. 3:16; 17:3).

**Ethiopia** (ee'thee-oh'pee-uh). A country referred to also as Nubia, located S of EGYPT, in what is now N Sudan (Ps. 68:31; Isa. 20:3–5; Ezek. 30:4–5; modern Ethiopia lies farther S and E). See also CUSH.

**Eunice** (yoo'nis). The mother of TIMOTHY and a woman of sincere faith (2 Tim. 1:5). She was Jewish, but her husband was a GENTILE (Acts 16:1). Eunice and her mother LOIS were faithful in teaching the Scriptures to Timothy (2 Tim. 3:15).

**eunuch.** A castrated man. In the Bible the term usually refers to a male officer in the court or household of a ruler; such officials were sometimes, but not always, emasculated (Gen. 37:36; 40:2; 1 Ki. 22:9; 2 Ki. 8:6; 1 Chr. 28:1; Jer. 52:25). In some passages the term is used in the literal sense (Deut. 23:1; Isa. 56:4; Matt. 19:12).

**Euodia** (yoo-oh'dee-uh). A Christian woman in PHILIPPI whom PAUL asked to be reconciled to SYNTYCHE (Phil. 4:2). The cause of their disagreement is unknown.

**Euphrates** (yoo-fray'teez). The longest river of W Asia (c. 1,780 mi./2,865 km.). It rises in the mountains of ARMENIA in modern Turkey, swings in a wide bow in SYRIA, and heads SE in MESOPOTAMIA; eventually it joins the TIGRIS and empties into the Persian Gulf (see Gen. 2:14; Deut. 11:24; 2 Sam. 8:3). In the OT the Euphrates is sometimes referred to as "the River" (Isa. 8:7) or "the great river" (Gen. 15:18; cf. Rev. 9:14; 16:12).

**Eutychus** (*yoo*′tuh-kuhs). A young man at TROAS who fell from a window seat during a prolonged discourse by PAUL late in the evening. He died from the fall, but came back to life when the apostle put his arms around him (Acts 20:7–12; cf. ELIJAH in 1 Ki. 17:21 and ELISHA in 2 Ki. 4:34).

**evangelist.** A preacher of the GOSPEL (from Greek *euangelion*, "good news"). The APOSTLES did evangelistic work (Acts 8:25; 14:7; 1 Cor. 1:17), and TIMOTHY was instructed to "do the work of an evangelist" (2 Tim. 4:5). The term also designates a particular class of ministry (Eph. 4:11), and PHILIP is called "the evangelist" (Acts 21:8). In later usage, the word was applied to the authors of the four Gospels.

**Eve** (eev). The first WOMAN, who was deceived by the serpent. This name was given to her by ADAM after the FALL (Gen. 3:20). PAUL twice refers to Eve in his letters (2 Cor. 11:3; 1 Tim. 2:13).

**everlasting.** See ETERNAL.

**evil.** Although this noun sometimes means "calamity," indicating suffering or misfortune (Deut. 31:17 KJV), it more often refers to what is morally bad (e.g., "the tree of the knowledge of good and evil," Gen. 2:9); as an adjective, *evil* almost always has a moral sense (6:5). SATAN is described as "the evil one" (Jn. 17:15; 1 Jn. 5:18–19). Christians are told, "Hate what is evil" (Rom. 12:9).

**evil spirits.** See DEMONS.

**ewe.** A female sheep, sometimes used in SACRIFICES (Gen. 21:28; Lev. 14:10).

**exalt.** This verb means either "to praise, glorify, extol" (Ps. 34:3) or "to raise in rank or power" (Matt. 23:12). At his RESURRECTION and ASCENSION, Christ was exalted "to the highest place" (Phil. 2:9; cf. Acts 2:33; Heb. 7:26).

**exhort.** To encourage strongly, urge, warn (Lk. 3:18). The author of Hebrews called his letter a "word of exhortation" (Heb. 13:22).

The Euphrates River.

Possible route of the exodus.

**exile.** In the Bible this term usually refers to the period of time in the sixth century BC during which the southern kingdom (JUDAH) was taken captive to BABYLON (1 Chr. 5:41). Under the Persian king CYRUS, the Jews were allowed to return home (Ezra 1:1–4). Earlier, in the year 722, the northern kingdom (ISRAEL) had been exiled to ASSYRIA (2 Ki. 17:6).

**Exodus, Book of.** The second book of the Bible. The title is derived from the Greek word *exodos*, meaning "a going out," and referring to the departure of the Hebrew people from EGYPT and so their deliverance from slavery. The book is attributed to Moses and covers the history of the Israelites from the events surrounding the exodus to the giving of the LAW at SINAI.

**exorcism.** The act of expelling an evil spirit from a person (see DEMON).

**expanse.** See FIRMAMENT.

**expiation.** See PROPITIATION AND EXPIATION.

**Ezekiel, Book of.** The third book among the Major Prophets of the OT. Ezekiel was born of a priestly family (Ezek. 1:3) and was taken into EXILE in BABYLON in 597 BC, probably early in life. He was a younger contemporary of the prophet JEREMIAH and probably a somewhat older contemporary of DANIEL, who also as a young man was taken to Babylon. Ezekiel was a powerful preacher who used vivid figures and symbolic actions to clothe his message. His call to the prophetic work is described in chs. 1–3, which describe his vision of the divine glory. The first major part of the book pronounces judgment against JUDAH and predicts the destruction of JERUSALEM. In the next section he prophesies judgment against foreign nations. The restoration of Israel is promised in the last section of the book, which includes a description of the future temple.

## OVERVIEW OF EXODUS

**AUTHOR:** Anonymous, but comments elsewhere in the Bible seem to support the traditional view that MOSES is responsible for the PENTATEUCH as a whole.

**HISTORICAL SETTING:** The initial composition of the book must have taken place during the wilderness wanderings (either late in the fifteenth cent. or early in the thirteenth cent. BC).

**PURPOSE:** To provide a historical-theological account of the life of Moses, the deliverance of the Israelites from slavery in Egypt, the establishment of the COVENANT at Sinai, and the building of the TABERNACLE.

**CONTENTS:** Birth, earthly life, and calling of Moses (Exod. 1–4); confrontation with PHARAOH, leading to the plagues, the institution of the Passover, and the exodus (chs. 5–15); from the crossing of the RED SEA to the establishment of the covenant (chs. 16–24); instructions for the building and operation of the tabernacle (chs. 25–31); Israel's sin and restoration, followed by the construction of the tabernacle (chs. 32–40).

## OVERVIEW OF EZEKIEL

**AUTHOR:** The priest-prophet Ezekiel.

**HISTORICAL SETTING:** Ezekiel received his visions while in exile in Babylon from c. 593 to c. 571 BC.

**PURPOSE:** To impress on the Hebrew exiles the truth that their captivity and the destruction of the nation were the result of their faithlessness, to bring them to repentance, and to assure them that God will yet restore them.

**CONTENTS:** Oracles against JUDAH (Ezek. 1–24); oracles against pagan nations (chs. 25–32); promises of restoration (chs. 33–39); visions of the future temple (chs. 40–48).

**Ezion Geber** (ee'zee-uhn-gay'buhr). A city located on the N end of the Gulf of Aqabah (the NE arm of the RED SEA), banked on the E by the hills of EDOM and on the W by those of PALESTINE. The city's period of greatest prosperity was in the time of SOLOMON, who there built a fleet of ships that sailed between Ezion Geber and OPHIR, a source of gold (1 Ki. 9:26–28; 2 Chr. 8:17–18).

**Ezra, Book of.** One of the historical books of the OT. It is so named because its principal character is Ezra, the famous Jewish priest and scribe who in c. 458 BC traveled from BABYLON to JERUSALEM to carry out a religious reform (he later worked with

Some scholars believe that Pharaoh's Island was the site of Ezion Geber. Todd Bolen/www.BiblePlaces.com

NEHEMIAH also). The book of Ezra continues the narrative after Chronicles and records the return of the Jewish exiles and the rebuilding of the TEMPLE, thus covering a period of almost eighty years (from c. 536 to 458). The book shows how God fulfilled his promise to restore his exiled people to their own land.

## OVERVIEW OF EZRA

**AUTHOR:** Anonymous, though Jewish tradition attributed it (as well as Chronicles and Nehemiah) to the priest Ezra.

**HISTORICAL SETTING:** The book was written possibly c. 430–400 BC in postexilic JUDEA under Persian jurisdiction.

**PURPOSE:** To provide a historical-theological account of the restoration of Israel through the return of Hebrew exiles from Babylon to Jerusalem, and to encourage the people to lead a life of repentance from sin and obedience to the law.

**CONTENTS:** The first part describes the return of Jewish exiles under ZERUBBABEL and JESHUA (Ezra 1–2), leading to the restoration of worship through the rebuilding of the temple (chs. 3–6); the second part details the return of additional exiles under Ezra (chs. 7–8), leading to the restoration of the community (chs. 9–10).

# F

**fable.** A fictitious narrative or legend (e.g., 1 Tim. 1:4 KJV). In a more specific sense, the word refers to a story in which animals and inanimate objects are made to act and speak as if they were human beings (Jdg. 9:7–15; 2 Ki. 14:9).

**face.** In a figurative sense, the Bible speaks of the face of God (Num. 6:25–26) and of Christ (2 Cor. 4:6) to indicate the divine presence or glory. Falling on one's face before someone else can symbolize humility (Ruth 2:10). To cover the face expressed mourning (Exod. 3:6).

**faith.** Belief, trust, loyalty. Faith is not merely an intellectual assent to doctrines or acceptance of divine commands, but utter confidence in the FAITHFULNESS of God, personal commitment to him, and a consequent loving obedience to his will. Faith in the person of Christ is foundational to the GOSPEL, for God's RIGHTEOUSNESS comes only to those who believe (Jn. 1:12–13; 3:15–18; Rom. 1:16–17; 3:25–31; 5:1; Eph. 2:10). The word *faith* can mean also "Christian teaching" (Jude 3). Unbelief is usually a sign of disobedience and leads to judgment (Matt. 17:17; Rom. 11:20; Heb. 3:12, 19).

**faithfulness.** When used of God, faithfulness refers to his absolute reliability and also to his steadfast love and loyalty toward his people (Exod. 34:6; Deut. 7:9). He is faithful in keeping his promises and is therefore worthy of trust (Heb. 10:23; cf. 6:17–18). God expects faithfulness from his people, that is, commitment, dependability, and PERSEVERANCE (Lev. 25:18; Rev. 2:10).

**fall, the.** A term used with reference to the first SIN of ADAM and EVE, who through disobedience lost the state of integrity and bliss in which God had created them and therefore brought a curse upon themselves and their descendants (Gen. 3:1–24; Rom. 5:12–21).

**false.** Not genuine; untrue. The Ten Commandments forbid giving "false testimony" (Exod. 20:16). The Bible warns of "false prophets" and "false apostles" who teach lies and lead people astray (Matt. 7:15; 2 Pet. 2:1; 2 Cor. 11:13). See LIE; COMMANDMENTS, TEN.

**familiar spirit.** This phrase is used by the KJV to render a Hebrew word that modern versions usually translate as "medium," that is, someone who claims to communicate with the dead (Deut. 18:11; 1 Sam. 28:7–9).

**family.** The fundamental unit of human society. The Bible places emphasis on the household as the focus of God's saving work (Gen. 7:1; 18:19; Jn. 4:53; Acts 16:31–33). Because believers are God's children (Jn. 1:12–13; Gal. 4:6–7), they belong to a spiritual family (Gal. 6:10; 1 Pet. 4:17).

**famine.** An acute and prolonged food shortage. In ancient times in PALESTINE and EGYPT, famines were common because of drought, storms, and insects that destroyed crops (Gen. 12:10; 41:56; Ruth 1:1; 1 Ki. 18:2; Acts 11:28).

**farthing.** A former British coin of very little value (used by KJV in Matt. 5:26; 10:29; Mk. 12:42; NIV "penny").

**fasting.** The practice of going without food, especially for religious purposes, as an indication of grief or of an urgent need to depend on God. The only fast required by the OT law was that of the Day of ATONEMENT (Lev. 16:29–31), but the Bible frequently mentions the practice (e.g., 1 Sam. 7:6; Jer. 36:9; Matt. 6:16–18; Lk. 2:37; Acts 13:2–3).

**father.** The Scriptures many times set forth the character and duties of an ideal father (e.g., Deut. 4:9; 6:7; 31:13; Prov. 22:6; Isa. 28:9). The term *father* can be used figuratively of a spiritual ancestor, whether good or bad (e.g., ABRAHAM, Rom. 4:11; the devil, Jn. 8:44); it can also refer to a revered superior (1 Sam. 10:12; 1 Jn. 2:13). Our supreme Father is God, both because he is the Creator (Jas. 1:17) and because he gives us spiritual life (Rom. 8:15).

**fear.** Many biblical passages assure God's people that they need not be afraid (Gen. 15:1; Exod. 14:13; Deut. 1:21; Ps. 23:4; Isa. 41:10; Matt. 10:31; Heb. 13:6). On the other hand, we are told to fear God, which means not only to be afraid of his judgment if we are rebellious (Matt. 10:28; Heb. 12:28–29) but more important, to respect, reverence, serve, and obey him (Deut. 10:12; Job 28:28; Prov. 8:13; 2 Cor. 7:1 [KJV]). The fear of the Lord is the foundation of WISDOM and true KNOWLEDGE (Job 28:28; Prov. 1:7).

**feasts.** Sacred festivals held an important place in Jewish religion. Six feasts were prescribed by the law: (1) The weekly SABBATH was fundamental (Exod. 20:8–11; Lev. 23:3). (2) The PASSOVER (or Feast of Unleavened Bread) in the spring season was the first of all the annual feasts, and historically and religiously it was the most important of all (23:4–8). (3) The Feast of PENTECOST (Feast of Weeks, Feast of Harvest) was celebrated seven weeks after Passover (23:15–21). (4) The Feast of Trumpets or New Moon (*Rosh Hashannah*) in early fall began the civil year (23:23–25). (5) Ten days later was the Day of ATONEMENT, when the high priest made confession of all the sins of the community (23:26–32). (6) The Feast of Tabernacles (Booths, Ingathering) began five days later, marking the completion of the harvest (23:33–43). See also DEDICATION, FEAST OF; PURIM.

**feet, washing of.** See FOOTWASHING.

**Felix** (fee′liks). A Roman procurator or GOVERNOR of JUDEA who held PAUL prisoner for two years (Acts 23:24–25:14).

**fellowship.** Close association, companionship, communion. In the Bible the word indicates participation, belonging, enjoying a common spirit (Acts 2:42; 1 Cor. 1:9; Phil. 1:5; 1 Jn. 1:3).

**Festus, Porcius** (fes′tuhs, por′shuhs). Roman procurator or GOVERNOR who succeeded FELIX in the province of JUDEA (Acts 24:27–26:32). Festus evidently knew that PAUL was a good man (25:25), but he was unable to understand Paul's reasoning with King AGRIPPA II and thought that Paul had gone mad with much study (26:24).

**fiery serpent.** This expression is used by the KJV with reference to the poisonous desert vipers that attacked the Hebrews in the wilderness as they journeyed around MOAB (Num. 21:6, 8; Deut. 8:15).

**fillet.** This term is used by the KJV with reference to the "bands" (NIV) or rings binding the pillars of the TABERNACLE (Exod. 36:38; 38:10–12, 17, 19).

**fire.** When the priesthood was instituted, God sent fire from heaven to consume the first offering to show his acceptance (Lev. 9:24). This fire was to be kept burning continually (6:9). An invalid offering described as "unauthorized fire" resulted in a fiery judgment from God (10:1, 9–10). The final destiny of the enemies of God is the "fiery lake" (Rev. 19:20; 20:10, 14). This world will someday be consumed by fire (2 Pet. 3:7–12).

**firmament.** Traditional (KJV) rendering of a difficult Hebrew word used only with reference to the sky (e.g., Gen. 1:6–8, 14–17, 20; Ps. 19:1; 150:1; Ezek. 1:22–26; 10:1; Dan. 12:3). Modern versions use such renderings as "expanse" (NIV), "vault" (TNIV), and "dome" (NRSV).

**firstborn.** Because the firstborn sons of the Israelites were preserved at the time of the first Passover (see FEASTS), every firstborn male of humans and animals became consecrated to God (Exod. 13:2; 34:19 [KJV "firstling"]). Among the Israelites the firstborn son possessed special privileges: he succeeded his father as the head of the house and received as his share of the inheritance a double portion. For that reason, sometimes the meaning of the term is figurative, denoting priority or supremacy. Israel was God's "firstborn son" (Exod. 4:22; Jer. 31:9). Christ is the "firstborn" because he has preeminent position over others in relation to him (Rom. 8:29; Col. 1:15; Heb. 1:6).

**firstfruits.** To show their thankfulness for God's goodness in providing a HARVEST, the Israelites brought as an offering a portion of the fruits that ripened first (Exod. 23:19; Lev. 23:10, 17). In a figurative sense, Jesus is the firstfruits of all who die in faith; that is, the RESURRECTION of believers is made possible and is guaranteed by his resurrection (1 Cor. 15:20).

**firstling.** See FIRSTBORN.

**Fish Gate.** An entrance on the N wall of JERUSALEM (2 Chr. 33:14; Neh. 3:3; Neh. 12:39; Zeph. 1:10). There may have been a fish market nearby.

**flagon.** A large vessel used for holding liquors. The KJV uses this term several times to translate a Hebrew word that really means "raisin cake" (2 Sam. 6:19; 1 Chr. 16:3; Cant. 2:5; Hos. 3:1).

**flesh.** This term, which refers to soft parts of the body, is used often in the Bible in figurative ways. The phrase "every living thing of all flesh" (Gen. 6:19 KJV) means simply "all living creatures" (NIV). PAUL uses the word in a special way to refer to the human nature deprived of the Spirit of God and dominated by SIN; in these passages the NIV uses such renderings as "unspiritual" (Col. 2:18), "world" (2 Cor. 10:2), "human effort" (Gal. 3:3), and especially "sinful nature" (Rom. 8:3–13; Gal. 5:13–24). See CARNAL.

**flock.** A group of sheep under the care of a shepherd, sometimes including goats also (Gen. 27:9). Figuratively, ISRAEL and the CHURCH are counted as flocks, and God is the Good Shepherd (Isa. 40:11; Matt. 26:31; Lk. 12:32; 1 Pet. 5:2–3).

**flood, the.** The great deluge that occurred during the days of NOAH, recorded in Gen. 6–9. The NT compares this event with the destruction of SODOM and GOMORRAH (Lk. 17:27–29; 2 Pet. 2:5–6) and with the JUDGMENT at the second coming of the Lord (Matt. 24:39).

**follow.** See DISCIPLE.

**food.** Because nutritive material is vital for life (Gen. 1:29–30; 9:3–4), food in the Bible is a figure of spiritual sustenance. Christians should "crave pure spiritual milk" (1 Pet. 2:2) and be able to eat solid food (1 Cor. 3:1–2).

F

This clay tablet (c. 1635 BC) contains one version of the Babylonian flood story. Todd Bolen/www.BiblePlaces.com

**foolishness, folly.** The opposite of WISDOM (Eccl. 2:13). In the Bible foolishness has less to do with mental ability than with spiritual sensitivity (Ps. 14:1; Prov. 10:18; 15:5). PAUL says that the preaching of the CROSS is "foolishness" to the lost (1 Cor. 1:18).

**footwashing.** In biblical times guests ordinarily were offered water for washing the feet, a necessity when wearing sandals on dusty roads (Gen. 18:4; 24:32; Jdg. 19:21). As a special act of affection or HUMILITY, the host or hostess might even wash a guest's feet (1 Sam. 25:41; Lk. 7:36–44). At the Last Supper the Lord washed the feet of the disciples, an act that symbolized not only humility but also spiritual cleansing (Jn. 13:4–10; cf. 1 Tim. 5:10). Some Christian groups believe footwashing is an ordinance that should be followed today.

**forbearance.** See PATIENCE.

**foreigner.** See STRANGER.

**foreknowledge.** Because God knows everything (see OMNISCIENCE), the future is not hidden from him; thus with him there is no uncertainty, and he can reveal things that have yet to happen. Foreknowledge is closely related to foreordination and ELECTION (Isa. 46:10; Acts 2:23; 1 Pet. 1:2). Moreover, to say that God knows his people (Amos 3:2 KJV) means not simply that he has intellectual awareness of them but that he loves them (see KNOWLEDGE); therefore, for God to have foreknown them (Rom. 8:29; 11:2) indicates that he set his affection on them beforehand and chose them (cf. Deut. 7:6–8).

**foreskin.** The prepuce, a fold of skin that covers the glans of the penis. See CIRCUMCISION.

**forgiveness.** The act of pardoning or setting aside punishment and resentment for an offense. On the basis of Christ's atoning death (see ATONEMENT), God forgives the sins of those who repent and believe (see FAITH; REPENTANCE). Christ himself claimed to have the power to forgive sins (Mk. 2:7; Lk. 5:21; 7:49). Just as God has forgiven us, so we must forgive others without setting limits (Matt. 5:23–24; 6:12; Lk. 17:3; Col. 1:14; 3:13). An unforgiving spirit is one of the most serious of sins (Matt. 18:34–35).

**fornication.** This English term, which generally refers to sexual intercourse between persons not married to each other, is used by the KJV and other versions a few times in the OT (e.g., Ezek. 16:26) but primarily in the NT to render the Greek noun *porneia* (usually translated "sexual immorality" in the NIV, e.g., Gal. 5:19; Eph. 5:3). Because the Greek term can be applied to various situations, its meaning must be determined by the context of each passage.

**foundation.** The basis on which something stands or is supported. The word is used of the CREATION, when God "laid the earth's foundation" (Job 38:4; Ps. 78:69). CHRIST is the foundation of the CHURCH (1 Cor. 3:11), and God's "solid foundation" stands firm and immovable (2 Tim. 2:19).

**frankincense.** A clear yellow resin obtained from certain trees of the *Boswellia* genus, native to northern India and Arabia (NIV "incense"). It is used in perfumes, as a medicine, and as INCENSE in religious rites (Exod. 30:34–38; Lev. 2:1, 15–16). It was one of the gifts brought to Jesus by the MAGI (Matt. 2:11, 15).

**freewill offering.** See SACRIFICE.

**fruit.** The fruits most often mentioned in Scripture are the grape, pomegranate, fig, olive, and apple, all of which are grown today. The word *fruit* is often used metaphorically (e.g., "the fruit of your womb," Deut. 7:13); the fruit of the HOLY SPIRIT consists of the Christian virtues (Gal. 5:22–23). See FIRSTFRUITS.

# G

**Gaal** (gay'uhl). Leader of a revolt against ABIMELECH, son of GIDEON (Jdg. 9:26–41).

**Gaash** (gay'ash). A name used to identify a mountain and its ravines in the hill country of EPHRAIM (Josh. 24:30; Jdg. 2:9; 2 Sam. 23:30; 1 Chr. 11:32).

**Gabbatha** (gab'uh-thuh). The ARAMAIC (KJV "Hebrew") name for "the Stone Pavement," where PILATE judged Jesus (Jn. 19:13). It may have been in the palace of HEROD in the W part of JERUSALEM or in the fortress of Antonia in the E.

**Gabriel** (gay'bree-uhl). An ANGEL mentioned four times in Scripture, each time bringing an important message: interpreting visions to DANIEL (Dan. 8:16–17; 9:21–22); announcing the birth of JOHN the Baptist to ZECHARIAH (Lk. 1:11–20); and announcing the birth of Jesus to MARY (1:26–38).

Remains of the ancient city of Gadara.



**Gad** (gad). **(1)** Seventh son of JACOB and ancestor of the tribe that bore his name (Gen. 30:9–11; 46:16; Num. 1:24–25). The tribes of Gad and REUBEN and the half tribe of MANASSEH had "very large herds and flocks" (32:1), so they requested of MOSES the rich pasture lands E of JORDAN for their possession (Josh. 18:7). **(2)** A seer or prophet of King DAVID who performed various duties (1 Sam. 22:5; 24:11–17; 2 Sam. 24:18; 1 Chr. 29:29; 2 Chr. 29:25). **(3)** The name of a Semitic god of good fortune, mentioned with MENI (Isa. 65:11; modern versions usually render these two names respectively as "Fortune" and "Destiny").

**Gadara, Gadarene** (gad'uh-ruh, gad'uh-reen). Gadara was a city of TRANSJORDAN, about 6 mi. (10 km.) SE of the southern end of the Sea of Galilee, and one of the cities of the DECAPOLIS. Its inhabitants, the Gadarenes, were predominantly non-Jewish. The only NT reference to them is the account of the healing of two demoniacs and the drowning of the swine in the Sea of Galilee (Matt. 8:28; KJV "Gergesenes"). The parallel passages use the term GERASENES (Mk. 5:1; Lk. 8:26; KJV "Gadarenes"), probably because the area designations overlapped; Gadara was the chief city of the immediate area, whereas Gerasa may have referred both to a city and to the wider region.

**Gaius** (gay'yuhs). **(1)** A Christian from MACEDONIA who was a travel companion of PAUL (Acts 19:29). **(2)** A Christian from DERBE, listed among those waiting for Paul at TROAS (Acts 20:4). **(3)** A Christian in CORINTH who was baptized by Paul and who provided hospitality for him (Rom. 16:23; 1 Cor. 1:14, 17). **(4)** The addressee of John's third epistle (3 Jn. 1).

**Galatia** (guh-lay'shuh). This name was applied in NT times to **(1)** a broad territory in north-central Asia Minor; and **(2)** a Roman PROVINCE established in 25 BC that covered a smaller region in the southern part of that territory. The cities of ANTIOCH, ICONIUM, LYSTRA, and DERBE, evangelized by PAUL on his first missionary journey (Acts 13–14), were in the province of Galatia. The name occurs in Acts 16:6; 18:23; 1 Cor. 16:1; Gal. 1:2; 2 Tim. 4:10; 1 Pet. 1:1.

Cities visited by the apostle Paul in Galatia.



## OVERVIEW OF GALATIANS

**AUTHOR:** The apostle PAUL.

**HISTORICAL SETTING:** Disputed. According to one view, Paul was writing to churches in the northern region of GALATIA during his third journey (c. AD 55), probably from EPHESUS. According to others, the letter was written from Syrian ANTIOCH to communities in the Roman province of southern Galatia prior to the Jerusalem Council of Acts 15 (AD 49), making Galatians the earliest Pauline letter known. A third view accepts that the addressees were South Galatians but dates the letter after the council. In any case, this epistle was motivated by the Galatians' error in accepting the JUDAIZERS' doctrine, namely, that GENTILES must be circumcised and submit to the Mosaic LAW if they want to be part of the people of God.

**PURPOSE:** To counter the message of the false teachers by demonstrating the truth of the GOSPEL of GRACE, including its implications for Christian conduct.

**CONTENTS:** After an introductory paragraph (Gal. 1:1–10), the apostle defends his authority (1:11–2:21), expounds the doctrine of JUSTIFICATION by FAITH (3:1–4:31), clarifies the nature of Christian liberty (5:1–6:10), and ends with some forceful statements (6:11–18).

**Galatians, Letter to the** (guh-lay′shuhnz). A letter addressed by the apostle PAUL to the Christian churches in GALATIA. It is a short but very important document, containing his passionate polemic against the perversion of the GOSPEL of God's GRACE. It remains as the abiding monument of the liberation of Christianity from the shackles of legalism. Certain Jewish teachers, though acknowledging Jesus as MESSIAH, were obscuring the simplicity of the gospel of free grace with their insistence on CIRCUMCISION and obedience to the Mosaic LAW (Gal. 2:16; 3:2–3; 4:10, 21; 5:2–4; 6:12). Paul realized clearly that this teaching neutralized the truth of Christ's all-sufficiency for SALVATION and destroyed the message of JUSTIFICATION by FAITH. By means of this letter Paul sought to save his converts from this fatal mixing of law and grace.

**Galilee** (gal′uh-lee). A region in N PALESTINE about 30 mi. (50 km.) wide, between the JORDAN RIVER on the E and the MEDITERRANEAN Sea on the W; it measures approximately 50 mi. (80 km.) N to S. An imaginary E–W line from the Plain of ACCO to the N end of the Sea of Galilee divided the country into Upper and Lower Galilee. "Galilee of the Gentiles" (Matt. 4:15) refers chiefly to Upper Galilee, which is separated from LEBANON by the Leontes River. Galilee was the territory of the tribes of ASHER and NAPHTALI. The land was luxurious and productive. Significant cities in Galilee included NAZARETH, where Jesus lived as a child and young man; CAPERNAUM, which served as headquarters during his ministry; and TIBERIAS, which became the capital under Herod ANTIPAS. Galileans were easily distinguishable to their fellow Jews by their speech (Mk. 14:70; Lk. 22:59).

**Galilee, Sea of.** This well-known freshwater lake is also called the Sea of KINNERETH

Aerial view of the Sea of Galilee (looking N).

(Num. 34:11), the Lake of GENNESARET (Lk. 5:1), and the Sea of TIBERIAS (Jn. 6:1; 21:10). Located some 60 mi. (100 km.) N of JERUSALEM, its bed is but a lower depression of the JORDAN Valley. The Jordan River enters the Sea of Galilee at its N end and flows out of its S end, a distance of 13 mi. (21 km.). The greatest width of the sea is 8 mi. (13 km.). On its shores Jesus called his first disciples, who were fishermen (Mk. 1:16–20). The lake was the scene of the calming of the storm (4:35–41) and of Jesus walking on the tempestuous water (6:45–53).

**gall.** Another term for *bile* (a bitter secretion of the liver) but used by the KJV with reference to a poisonous herb (e.g., Deut. 29:18). Most versions use it for the substance given to Jesus on the CROSS (Matt. 27:34). The word also has a figurative sense, indicating a harsh, bitter experience or attitude (e.g., Lam. 3:19; Acts 8:23).

**Gallio** (gal′ee-oh). The PROCONSUL of ACHAIA in AD 51–52 (or 52–53), with residence at CORINTH. His indifference to the accusations of the Jews against PAUL amounted to a legal decision that the preaching of the GOSPEL was not subversive of Roman authority (Acts 18:12–17).

**Gamaliel** (guh-may′lee-uhl). **(1)** The leader of the tribe of MANASSEH in the wilderness (Num. 2:20). **(2)** A famous Jewish rabbi who advised moderation in the treatment of the apostles and who had earlier been PAUL's teacher (Acts 5:34; 22:3).

**gate.** The entrance to enclosed buildings, grounds, or cities. It was at the gates of a city that the people of the ancient Near East went for legal business, conversation, bargaining, and news. The usual gateway consisted of double doors plated with metal (Ps. 107:16; Isa. 45:2). As the weakest points in a city's walls, the gates were often the object of enemy attack (Jdg. 5:8; 1 Sam. 23:7; Ezek. 21:15, 22) and therefore were flanked by towers (2 Chr. 26:9).

**Gath** (gath). One of the five great PHILISTINE cities, the others being ASHDOD, GAZA, ASHKELON, and EKRON (Josh. 13:3; 1 Sam. 6:17). Its people were the Gittites, including GOLIATH and other giants (2 Sam. 21:19–22). DAVID fled from SAUL to Gath on two occasions (21:10–15; 27:2–6).

**Gaza** (gay′zuh, gah′zuh). The southernmost of the five chief cities of the PHILISTINES in SW PALESTINE. SAMSON perished there while destroying his captors (Jdg. 16:1, 21). SOLOMON ruled over it (1 Ki. 4:24), but it was HEZEKIAH who gave the decisive blow to the Philistines (2 Ki. 18:8). PHILIP met the Ethiopian eunuch on "the road—the desert road—that goes down from Jerusalem to Gaza" (Acts 8:26).

**Geba** (gee′buh). A city about 6 mi. (10 km.) NNE of JERUSALEM in the territory of the tribe of BENJAMIN (Josh. 18:24; KJV "Gaba"); it was assigned to the LEVITES (21:17). Geba was the site of conflict with the PHILISTINES (1 Sam. 13:3). It is mentioned also elsewhere (e.g., 1 Ki. 15:22; 2 Ki. 23:8).

**Gedaliah** (ged′uh-*li*′uh). The name of several men in the OT, including the governor of JUDAH after the fall of JERUSALEM; he ruled for only two months in MIZPAH before he was assassinated (2 Ki. 25:22–26; Jer. 40:6–41:18).

**Gehazi** (gi-hay′z*i*). The servant of the prophet ELISHA (2 Ki. 4:12–15, 25–36; 5:20–27; 8:4–5). Although Gehazi had positive qualities, he was also guilty of greed and was punished with leprosy (5:26–27).

**Gehenna** (gi-hen′uh). In the Greek NT this name, which means "Valley of Hinnom," refers to the final place of punishment of the ungodly and is usually translated HELL (e.g., Matt. 5:22; Lk. 12:5). See HINNOM, VALLEY OF.

**genealogy.** A list of ancestors or descendants, compiled usually to show family identity, the right of inheritance, or succession to an office. Because genealogies were important for the Hebrew people, the Bible includes many of them (e.g., Gen. 5; 1 Chr. 1–9; Matt. 1). Sometimes they could be misused (1 Tim. 1:4).

**General Epistles.** See CATHOLIC EPISTLES.

**generation.** A group of persons who happened to be born about the same time or who belong to the same stage in the line of descent. The average length of a generation is often assumed to be forty years, for in the wilderness a whole generation (all Israelites over twenty) died within that time (Deut. 2:14). Many times Jesus spoke of the faithless and perverse generation that opposed him (Matt. 17:17).

**Genesis, Book of.** The first book of the Bible. Tradition (which includes some biblical statements) ascribes Genesis to MOSES, though many scholars believe that the book is composed of several documents that were written over several centuries and then put together after the EXILE (see PENTATEUCH). Much of the book is concerned with "beginnings" (the Gk. word *genesis* means "origin"), including the CREATION of the world, the FALL into sin, the FLOOD, and the choosing of ABRAHAM, but the larger portion consists of the history of Abraham, ISAAC, JACOB, and JOSEPH. Genesis provides the theological foundation for the rest of the Bible, setting forth important doctrines, such as the goodness of creation (Gen. 1–2), the character and growth of SIN (chs. 3–11), FAITH (e.g., 15:6), and PROVIDENCE (e.g., 50:20).

**Gennesaret** (gi-nes′uh-ret). A small plain located on the NW side of the Sea of Galilee between CAPERNAUM and Magdala (see MAGDALENE); here Jesus landed when he crossed the lake after feeding the 5,000 (Matt. 14:34; Mk. 6:53). The name probably derives from KINNERETH, a town on that plain. See also GALILEE, SEA OF.

**Gentile.** A non-Jewish person. The English term *Gentiles* is used primarily in the

## OVERVIEW OF GENESIS

**AUTHOR:** Anonymous, but comments elsewhere in the Bible seem to support the traditional view that MOSES is responsible for the PENTATEUCH as a whole.

**HISTORICAL SETTING:** The initial composition of the book must have taken place during the wilderness wanderings (either late in the fifteenth or early in the thirteenth cent. BC; those who reject Moses' authorship usually date the book after the EXILE, while acknowledging that much of the material is several centuries earlier).

**PURPOSE:** To provide a historical-theological account of the long period from the CREATION to the time of JOSEPH, with emphasis on God's choosing of Abram (ABRAHAM) and his descendants; to provide those fundamental truths about God on which the rest of the Bible is built.

**CONTENTS:** From the creation to Abraham's settling in HARAN (Gen. 1–11); God's COVENANT with Abraham (12:1–25:18); God's dealings with ISAAC and JACOB (25:19–36:43); God's preservation of Joseph (chs. 37–50).

Mt. Gerizim (left) and Mt. Ebal (looking W). www.HolyLandPhotos.org

NT to translate a Greek term that means "nations." In the OT the nation of Israel was supposed to have only limited relations with other peoples. Over time the separation between Jew and Gentile became stricter and increasingly hostile, but the GOSPEL ultimately broke down "the middle wall of partition" between the two (Rom. 1:16; 1 Cor. 1:24; Gal. 3:28; Eph. 2:14; Col. 3:11).

**Gerar** (gee′rahr). A town and probably also a district S of GAZA and SW of the southern border of CANAAN near the MEDITERRANEAN SEA (Gen. 10:19; 20:1–2; 26:1, 6–11; 2 Chr. 14:13–14). See ABIMELECH.

**Gerasene** (ger′uh-seen). An inhabitant of Gerasa, one of the cities of the DECAPOLIS in TRANSJORDAN, situated about 35 mi. (55 km.) SE of the S end of the Sea of Galilee (Mk. 5:1; Lk. 8:26, 37). See GADARA, GADARENE.

**Gergesene.** See GADARA, GADARENE.

**Gerizim** (ger′uh-zim). A mountain of SAMARIA, now known as Jebel et-Tur, 2,850 ft. (870 m.) high, SW of Mount EBAL. MOSES commanded that when the Israelites came into the Promised Land, the blessing for keeping the LAW should be spoken from Mount Gerizim and the curse for not obeying it from Mount Ebal (Deut. 11:29; 27:4–26), six tribes standing on the slopes of each peak (27:11–14). Mount Gerizim is mentioned also in Jdg. 9:7–21, and it was the mountain to which the Samaritan woman referred as the place where her people worshiped (Jn. 4:20–21).

**Gershom** (guhr′shuhm). Firstborn son of MOSES (Exod. 2:22 [cf. 4:24–26]; 18:3). See also GERSHON.

**Gershon** (guhr′shuhn). Son of LEVI and grandson of JACOB (Gen. 46:11; in the Heb. text of Chronicles, this name almost always appears as Gershom). Gershon's descendants became an important family of LEVITES who "were responsible for the care of the tabernacle and tent" (Num. 3:25; see also 1 Chr. 15:7; 16:4–5).

**Gethsemane** (geth-sem′uh-nee). The place of Jesus' agony and arrest (Matt. 26:36; Mk. 14:32). Without giving the name, Luke says that the place was one to which Jesus customarily went and that it was on the Mount of Olives (Lk. 22:39; see OLIVES, MOUNT OF), while John identifies it as a garden or (olive) grove across the KIDRON Valley from JERUSALEM (Jn. 18:1).

**Gezer** (gee′zuhr). A major city about 18 mi. (29 km.) NW of JERUSALEM, between the Sorek and Aijalon valleys. Its king was defeated by JOSHUA (Josh. 12:12; cf. 10:33), but its Canaanite inhabitants were not driven out (16:10; see also 1 Ki. 9:15–17).

**ghost.** This English term, which in modern usage refers specifically to the disembodied soul of a dead person, is frequently used by the KJV with the meaning SPIRIT, especially with reference to the HOLY SPIRIT.

**giant.** A term used by the KJV in Gen. 6:4 (and elsewhere), but the NIV and other modern versions have "Nephilim," a Hebrew word that possibly means "fallen ones." Nephilim were found in CANAAN when the spies went through the land (Num. 13:33). See also ANAK; GOLIATH; REPHAIM.

**Gibeah** (gib′ee-uh). The name of several locations in PALESTINE ("Gibeah" means simply "hill"), the most important of which was Gibeah of BENJAMIN (1 Sam. 13:15), also known as Gibeah of SAUL (11:4). This city, a few miles N of JERUSALEM, is frequently mentioned in the OT (e.g., Jdg. 19:12–20:37; 1 Sam. 10:26; 22:6; Isa. 10:29; Hos. 5:8; 9:9).

**Gibeon** (gib′ee-uhn). An important city in the hill country of BENJAMIN, about 6 mi. (10 km.) NW of JERUSALEM. JOSHUA was deceived by the ambassadors of Gibeon into making a treaty with them (Josh. 9–10). The city is mentioned elsewhere (e.g., 2 Sam. 2:12–13; 20:8–10; 1 Ki. 3:4–5; Jer. 41:11–16).

Gibeon village in the mid-20th century.

Library of Congress, LC-DIG-matpc-22851

The mountainous region of Gilead. Z. Radovan/www.BibleLandPictures.com

**Gideon** (gid′ee-uhn). One of the great JUDGES (leaders) of Israel (Jdg. 6–8; also called Jerub-Baal and Jerub-Besheth). After receiving a supernatural call from God, he summoned the Israelites to war against the Midianites. He was instructed by the Lord to reduce the size of his army, and a relatively small band defeated the enemy.

**gifts, spiritual.** Specific abilities that the HOLY SPIRIT grants to believers for the benefit of the CHURCH as a whole (Rom. 1:11; 12:6–8; 1 Cor. 12:1–11, 28–30; 14:1). PAUL told the Corinthians to diligently seek these gifts, but he pointed out that "the most excellent way" (12:31) was an emphasis on FAITH, HOPE, and LOVE, among which love is the greatest gift (13:13).

**Gihon** (g*i*′hon). **(1)** One of the four headwaters into which the river in EDEN separated (Gen. 2:10–14). **(2)** A noted spring near JERUSALEM where SOLOMON was anointed to succeed DAVID (1 Ki. 1:32–40; see also 2 Chr. 32:27–30).

**Gilboa, Mount** (gil-boh′uh). A mountain or range of mountains on the border between SAMARIA and GALILEE, some 17 mi. (27 km.) SW of the Sea of Galilee. The last battle and the death of SAUL and his three sons took place on this western slope (1 Sam. 31; 2 Sam. 1; 21:12; 1 Chr. 10:1–8).

**Gilead** (gil′ee-uhd). The name of several persons in the OT, especially the son of MAKIR (and grandson of MANASSEH, Num. 26:29–30). There is no doubt a connection between him and the land of Gilead, a large mountainous region E of the JORDAN that is frequently mentioned in Scripture (e.g., Gen. 31:21–25; Num. 32:40; Josh. 22:9; Jdg. 10:3; 2 Ki. 10:33). In NT times the area was known as PEREA.

**Gilgal** (gil′gal). **(1)** A town in the tribal territory of EPHRAIM, not far from BETHEL (2 Ki. 2:1; 4:38). **(2)** A region of uncertain location (Josh. 12:23). **(3)** A town or region on the NE boundary of the tribe of JUDAH (Josh. 15:7). **(4)** The Gilgal most frequently mentioned in the Bible is a site "on the eastern border of Jericho" where the Israelites camped soon after entering the Promised Land (Josh. 4:19). There they built a monument of twelve stones (v. 20), the rite of CIRCUMCISION was performed (5:8), and the Passover was celebrated (5:10; see also 10:7–9; 1 Sam. 7:16; 11:14–15).

**gimel** (gim'uhl). The third letter of the Hebrew alphabet (ג, transliterated as *g*), used to begin each verse in Ps. 119:17–24.

G

**Gittite** (git'*i*t). An inhabitant of GATH.

**glean.** To gather the grain left behind by the reapers. The OT LAW allowed for gleaning by the poor (Lev. 19:9–10; 23:22), a practice beautifully illustrated in the story of RUTH and BOAZ (Ruth 2:3, 7–8). The concept is used metaphorically by the prophets (Isa. 17:5–6; Jer. 6:9; Mic. 7:1).

**glory.** Great honor or praise; used especially of God's majestic splendor. It may indicate the presence of God in the fullness of his attributes (Exod. 33:19–34:8; Isa. 6:3; Lk. 2:9). Chiefly, the word refers to the REVELATION of God in Christ (Jn. 1:14; 2:11; Heb. 1:3; 2 Pet. 1:16–17). To glorify God means to acknowledge his greatness and to praise him for it (Ps. 34:3; Lk. 1:46). But for God to glorify his people means that he will transform them to an exalted state (Rom. 8:30; Phil. 3:20).

**gluttony.** Excessive eating (or drinking), a fault condemned in Scripture (Prov. 23:20–21).

**gnashing the teeth.** An expression that can indicate the hatred and scorn of enemies (Job 16:9; Ps. 35:16; Acts 7:54) but used often by Jesus to describe the suffering of those excluded from heaven (e.g., Matt. 8:12; 13:42; Lk. 13:28; see HELL).

**Gnosticism** (nos'tuh-siz'uhm). Derived from the Greek word *gnōsis*, meaning "knowledge," this term refers primarily to a religious movement that developed after NT times within Christianity but was condemned as a HERESY by the church. Gnosticism involved a complicated system of myths, and it taught that matter (the world, the body) is evil; only those who have a spark of pure spirit can achieve full KNOWLEDGE and be brought to God. The NT criticizes certain claims to knowledge and WISDOM that may have been the roots of later Gnosticism (1 Tim. 6:20–21; cf. also 1 Cor. 1:18–31; 8:1; Col. 2:20–23). The Gnostics also denied the real humanity of Jesus, and this error is condemned in 1 Jn. 4:2–3; 2 Jn. 7 (see INCARNATION).

**God.** The Bible does not contain a formal definition of this term, yet God's personal being and attributes are displayed throughout. He is eternal, infinite, and holy; he is a spirit without a body or other material limitations; he knows all things and can do all things; he is just, merciful, and faithful; he created all things and preserves them; he is both Judge and Savior. For biblical references, see the relevant articles (e.g., CREATION; ETERNAL; HOLINESS; JUSTICE; OMNIPOTENCE; SALVATION). See also ELOHIM; HOLY SPIRIT; JEHOVAH; JESUS; TRINITY. On false gods, see IDOLATRY.

**godliness.** Devotion toward God, including the proper conduct that springs from a right relationship with him (1 Tim. 2:2; 6:11; 2 Pet. 1:3).

**Gog** (gog). In prophecy, a prince from the land of MAGOG who leads ungodly armies against God's people (Ezek. 38:2–23; 39:1–16; Rev. 20:7–9).

**Golgotha** (gol'guh-thuh). The ARAMAIC name of the "Place of the Skull," an area near JERUSALEM where Jesus was crucified (Matt. 27:33; Mk. 15:22; Jn. 19:17). Luke does not use this Semitic word but only its corresponding Greek term for "skull" (Lk. 23:33), which the Latin version (Vulgate) in turn translates with Latin *calvaria*, thus KJV "Calvary."

**Goliath** (guh-lī'uhth). A PHILISTINE warrior, giant in size, who defied the army of King SAUL but was killed by young DAVID with a single stone (1 Sam. 17).

**Gomer** (goh'muhr). **(1)** Son of JAPHETH and grandson of NOAH (Gen. 10:2–3). **(2)** A nation that possibly descended from (1) and that was prophesied to attack Israel (Ezek. 38:6). **(3)** Wife of the prophet HOSEA (Hos. 1:3–8).

**Gomorrah** (guh-mor'uh). A city located probably at the S end of the DEAD SEA, destroyed by God because of its sin (Gen. 18–19). SODOM and Gomorrah became bywords for the judgment of God (e.g., Isa. 1:9–10; Jer. 23:14; Amos 4:11; Matt. 10:15; 2 Pet. 2:6; Jude 7).

**good.** God is the source of all goodness, and thus there is no good apart from him (Mk. 10:18). The world he created was "very good" (Gen. 1:31). The "good" deeds of sinful human beings have no merit before God (cf. Isa. 64:6), but believers have been "created in Christ Jesus to do good works" (Eph. 2:10; cf. Matt. 5:16; 1 Tim. 6:18; Heb. 10:24; 1 Pet. 2:12).

**Goshen** (goh'shuhn). The name of several places mentioned in the Bible, especially a region in EGYPT where JACOB and his family settled (Gen. 45:10; 47:4–6); it was closely linked with the land and city of RAMESES (Raamses), on the eastern side of the NILE delta (47:11).

**gospel.** Translation of the Greek word *euangelion*, "good news," referring to the Christian message of REDEMPTION proclaimed by Jesus and his apostles (Matt. 24:14; Rom. 1:1–2). This English term is used also to designate the four NT accounts of the life of Christ. See MATTHEW; MARK; LUKE; JOHN.

**government.** The control and administration of public policy. The ancient nation of ISRAEL was unique in that it was organized as a theocracy (direct rule by God). All human authority, however, is derived from God and is ultimately under his control (Rom. 13:1–7). The laws of the state are to be obeyed unless they conflict with divine LAW (Acts 5:29).

**governor.** A general term for various kinds of rulers. In the NT it usually refers to one of the Roman officials in charge of the province of JUDEA (e.g., PILATE, Matt. 27:2; FELIX, Acts 23:24).

**grace.** Although this word can refer to charm and loveliness or to kindness in general, the Bible uses it primarily of God's goodwill to those who do not deserve it, that is, his *unmerited* favor bestowed on sinners because of the work of Jesus Christ (Eph. 2:4–5). Christ is "full of grace and truth" (Jn. 1:14) and makes possible the gracious gift of SALVATION (Rom. 5:15–17; Tit. 2:11). Grace is also regarded as the sustaining influence enabling the believer to persevere in the Christian life (Acts 11:23; 2 Cor. 9:14).

**grave.** See TOMB.

**Grecian** (gree'shuhn). An inhabitant of GREECE (Joel 3:6 KJV) or a speaker of the GREEK LANGUAGE (Acts 6:1; 9:29). See HELLENISM.

**Greece** (grees). A geographical area or country in SE Europe; it occupies a peninsula that is separated from Italy on the W by the Adriatic Sea and from Asia Minor on the E by the Aegean Sea. The OT refers to it as JAVAN (Isa. 66:19 KJV). In NT times its most important cities included ATHENS and CORINTH, both in the province of ACHAIA.

**Greek language.** The language of GREECE, spoken continuously from very ancient times until the present day. It was the instrument of a great literature in classical times (sixth to fourth centuries BC). As a result of the conquests of ALEXANDER the Great, Greek developed into a form known as the Koine (common dialect), which became the primary language of commerce and

G

The Greek language continued to be used widely even during the Roman period. © Willam D. Mounce

diplomacy even into Roman times. For that reason, the NT books were written in Koine Greek, which reflects the colloquial or spoken language rather than the more sophisticated literary form.

**guilt.** This term can refer to a personal sense of wrongdoing, but in the Bible it usually indicates the actual deserving of PUNISHMENT because of a breach of conduct. Jesus stressed the importance of a right heart attitude in distinction from outwardly correct acts and taught that there are degrees of guilt, depending on a person's knowledge and motive (Lk. 11:29–32; 12:47–48; 23:34). However, the LAW makes everyone guilty before God (Rom. 3:19).

# H

**Habakkuk, Book of** (huh-bak′uhk). The eighth book of the Minor Prophets. Of the man Habakkuk nothing is known outside of the book itself, which was probably written soon after 605 BC, during the reign of King JEHOIAKIM. In the first two chapters the prophet expresses confusion and asks for divine enlightenment. Why are the wicked in JUDAH not punished? God answers that he is about to send the Babylonians to judge the Hebrews (Hab. 1:2–11). This response plunges Habakkuk into a greater perplexity: How can a righteous God use the godless Babylonians to punish his people? God's answer is that the proud conquerors will themselves be punished (1:12–2:20). The Babylonians are puffed up with self-sufficient pride, but in this hour of national calamity the righteous will live by the constancy of their trust in God (2:4). This truth naturally becomes important to the NT writers and is quoted in Rom. 1:17; Gal. 3:11; and Heb. 10:38. The second answer to Habakkuk concludes with a series of woes against the Babylonians (Hab. 2:5–20). The third chapter is a prayer in which the prophet describes the divine revelation in terms of a story (3:2–15) and concludes that, no matter what happens, he will trust in God (3:16–19).

**Hadad** (hay′dad). The name of several men in the OT, especially an Edomite prince who was an adversary of SOLOMON (1 Ki. 11:14–22, 25). Hadad (or Adad) was also the name of a popular deity in CANAAN, SYRIA, and MESOPOTAMIA; though not mentioned in the Bible, his influence is reflected in such personal names as BEN-HADAD and HADADEZER.

## OVERVIEW OF HABAKKUK

**AUTHOR:** The prophet Habakkuk.

**HISTORICAL SETTING:** The book was written during the final decline of the southern kingdom of Judah, probably after the rise of the Babylonian king NEBUCHADNEZZAR (605 BC) but before the fall of JERUSALEM (586 BC).

**PURPOSE:** To show God's perspective in the midst of evil and suffering and thus to encourage the righteous to remain faithful.

**CONTENTS:** Habakkuk's first question and God's reply (Hab. 1:1–11); Habakkuk's second question and God's reply (1:12–2:20); Habakkuk's prayer (ch. 3).

**Hadadezer** (hay′dad-ee′zuhr). KJV Hadarezer. King of ZOBAH in ARAM (SYRIA), defeated by DAVID on several occasions (2 Sam. 8:3–8; 10:5–14; 10:15–18).

**Hades** (hay′deez). In Greek mythology, the god that ruled the world of the dead, but the term was then applied to the underworld itself (e.g., Matt. 16:18 [TNIV "death"]; Acts 2:27 [NIV "grave"]; Rev. 20:13). The word is often translated HELL; see also GEHENNA; SHEOL.

**Hagar** (hay′gahr). An Egyptian woman who was SARAH's servant and who bore ISHMAEL to ABRAHAM (Gen. 16). Eventually Sarah herself had a son, ISAAC (21:1–3). The contrast between Sarah/Isaac and Hagar/Ishmael served to represent the difference between the slavery of the LAW and the freedom of GRACE (Gal. 4:21–31; KJV "Agar").

**Haggai, Book of** (hag′*i*). The tenth book of the Minor Prophets. The prophet Haggai lived soon after the Babylonian EXILE and was contemporary with ZECHARIAH (cf. Hag. 1:1 with Zech. 1:1). After the Israelites returned from the captivity, the foundation for the second TEMPLE was laid, but then they were compelled to cease building for some years. Haggai's mission was to rebuke the Jews and to encourage them in rebuilding the temple. Within a few months the whole situation changed from defeat and discouragement to victory.

**Hagiographa** (hag′ee-og′ruh-fuh). A term meaning "Sacred Writings" and applied to the third division of the Hebrew Bible (the first two being the Law and the Prophets). Also known simply as the Writings (or Ketubim), this section consists of the following books: Psalms, Proverbs, Job, Song of Solomon, Ruth, Lamentations, Ecclesiastes, Esther, Daniel, Ezra, Nehemiah, and 1–2 Chronicles.

**Hakeldamah.** See AKELDAMA.

**half tribe of Manasseh.** See MANASSEH.

**hallelujah** (hal′uh-*loo*′yuh). This expression consists of two Hebrew words, and English versions of the OT translate it as "Praise the LORD" (e.g., Ps. 106:1). The corresponding Greek term in the NT is usually transliterated "hallelujah" (KJV "alleluia"; e.g., Rev. 19:1). Its use is limited altogether to songs of praise, appearing only in Psalms and Revelation.

**hallow.** To render or treat as holy; to sanctify or consecrate. This English term is com-

## OVERVIEW OF HAGGAI

**AUTHOR:** The prophet Haggai.

**HISTORICAL SETTING:** Postexilic JERUSALEM during the second year of the Persian king DARIUS I (520 BC), at a time when the Jewish returnees had ceased to rebuild the TEMPLE (cf. ZECHARIAH, BOOK OF).

**PURPOSE:** To admonish the Israelites for failing to construct the temple.

**CONTENTS:** The book records the following four messages (delivered on four different days during a three-month period): the need to complete rebuilding the temple (Hag. 1:1–15); the promise of God's presence (2:1–9); blessings for a defiled people (2:10–19); the final victory (2:20–23).

mon in the KJV but rare in modern versions; the NIV uses it only in the LORD'S PRAYER (Matt. 6:9; Lk. 11:1). See CONSECRATION; DEDICATION; HOLINESS; SANCTIFICATION.

**Ham** (ham). Son of NOAH and brother of SHEM and JAPHETH (Gen. 5:32). Ham had four sons: CUSH (linked to ETHIOPIA), MIZRAIM (EGYPT), PUT, and CANAAN (Gen. 10:6; cf. Ps. 78:51; 105:23, 27). He is therefore identified as the ancestor of the Egyptians and of other people groups in NE Africa and Palestine. Because Ham was disrespectful to Noah, his son Canaan was cursed (Gen. 9:20–25).

**Haman** (hay'muhn). Prime minister of PERSIA under XERXES (Ahasuerus). MORDECAI, the cousin of ESTHER, would not pay him honor, so he determined in revenge to kill not only Mordecai but also all the Jews in the Persian empire (Esth. 3:1–9). Through the intervention of Esther, however, Haman died on the very gallows he had prepared for Mordecai (7:10), and the Jewish people were saved.

**Hamath** (hay'math). A very ancient and important city in SYRIA (ARAM), c. 120 mi. (190 km.) N of DAMASCUS. The king of Hamath had dealings with DAVID (2 Sam. 8:9); later the city was under the control of SOLOMON (2 Chr. 8:4; see also 2 Ki. 14:28; Jer. 39:5).

**Hananiah** (han'uh-n*i*'uh). The name of over a dozen persons in the OT, including a companion of DANIEL who was renamed SHADRACH (Dan. 1:6–7).

**Hannah** (han'uh). The mother of the prophet SAMUEL (1 Sam. 1). Humiliated and despondent because she could not bear children, she prayed for a son and vowed to give him to the Lord. God heard her prayer and Samuel was born. Hannah's song of praise (2:1–10) shows that she was a deeply spiritual woman.

**Hanukkah** (hah'nuh-kuh). A Hebrew word meaning "dedication"; it is the name of an important Jewish feast. See DEDICATION, FEAST OF.

**Haran** (hair'uhn). The name of several OT figures, including the brother of ABRAHAM (Gen. 11:26–28). A different Hebrew word, but also spelled Haran (or Harran or Charran) in English, was the name of an important city of MESOPOTAMIA to which Terah (Abraham's father) emigrated with his family (11:31; see also 12:4–5; 27:43; 29:4; 2 Ki. 19:12; Isa. 37:12; Ezek. 27:23).

**hardening, spiritual.** The SIN of stubborn human resistance to God is often described with the expression "to harden the heart." Of special interest are the statements that God hardened PHARAOH's heart (Exod. 7:3; 10:1; 14:4) and that Pharaoh hardened his own heart (Exod. 9:34–35; 13:15; cf. Rom. 9:17–18). Refusal to obey or to be thankful characterizes the hardened heart, and ISRAEL is portrayed as a prime example of this condition (2 Ki. 17:14; Neh. 9:16–17; Ps. 95:8; Eph. 4:18; Heb. 3:8).

**harvest.** The process of gathering crops. The economy of the Israelites was strictly agricultural, and thus harvest time was a very significant event for them. The barley reaping (Ruth 1:22) came in April–May; the wheat harvest (Gen. 30:14) was about six weeks later, in June–July; and the ingathering of the fruits of trees or vines took place in September–October. Important feasts were associated with these seasons. Harvest became a symbol for the final stage of the KINGDOM OF GOD (Mk. 4:20, 29; 2 Cor. 9:10; Gal. 6:9), which includes JUDGMENT on the ungodly (Joel 3:13; Rev. 14:15).

**hate, hatred.** An intense dislike, anger, or hostility. The Bible emphatically condemns hatred (Lev. 19:17; Matt. 5:43; Gal. 5:20).

The city of Hazor was built on this mound. Mt. Hermon is in the background. www.HolyLandPhotos.org

However, God hates evil (e.g., IDOLATRY, Deut. 12:31), and we are commanded to do the same (Rom. 12:9). When Jesus said that his disciples should hate their close relatives (Lk. 14:26), he clearly meant that even those nearest and dearest to us must be given second place to our loyalty and affection for Jesus. See LOVE.

**Hazael** (hay′zay-uhl). One of the most powerful of the kings of ARAM (SYRIA), ruling from c. 843 to c. 796 BC. ELIJAH was told to anoint Hazael (1 Ki. 19:15–17). Later, during the ministry of ELISHA, Hazael took the throne by murdering BEN-HADAD (2 Ki. 8:7–15) and became a fierce enemy of Israel (8:28–29; 9:14–15; 10:32–33; 12:17–18; 13:3, 22–25).

**Hazor** (hay′zor). The name of several places, but especially of a very large Canaanite city some 10 mi. (16 km.) N of the Sea of Galilee. Its king, JABIN, led a coalition of forces against the Israelites, but JOSHUA defeated them soundly and burned Hazor (Josh. 11:1–13). Nearly two centuries later, another Jabin reigning at Hazor was reckoned as king of CANAAN, but God used DEBORAH and BARAK to subdue and destroy him (Jdg. 4).

**he (letter)** (hay). The fifth letter in the Hebrew alphabet (ה, transliterated as *h*), used to begin each verse in Ps. 119:33–40.

**heap of stones.** The act of raising a heap of stones could be a symbol and reminder of a shameful act (e.g., Josh. 7:26) or of a COVENANT made between two persons (Gen. 31:46–52) or of God's JUDGMENT upon a sinful city or family (Job 15:28; Isa. 37:26; Jer. 9:11; Hos. 12:11).

**heart.** Aside from some literal references to the physical organ, this term in the Bible usually refers to the "inner person," the seat of mental functions (the "mind"), or the center of spiritual life (see SOUL). The heart is viewed as the fountain of SIN (Gen.

6:5; Deut. 29:17; Jer. 17:9; Matt. 12:34) but also as the focus of God's saving work (Ps. 51:12; Jer. 31:33; Ezek. 36:26; Rom. 2:29; Eph. 1:18).

**heathen.** This term is frequently used by the KJV to render Hebrew and Greek words that more properly mean "nation(s)" (e.g., Lev. 25:44; Acts 4:25). Many contexts, however, do indicate the sense "pagan," that is, someone who does not acknowledge the true God (e.g., Matt. 6:7). See GENTILE.

**heaven.** Although sometimes this word means simply "sky" (e.g., Gen. 1:1; 14:19), more often it refers to the abode of God (Gen. 28:17; Ps. 80:14; Isa. 66:1; Matt. 5:12) and of the good angels (Matt. 24:36), the place where the redeemed will someday be (Matt. 5:12; 6:20; Eph. 3:15). The expression "new heaven(s) and a new earth" describes the final, perfected state of the created universe (Isa. 65:17; 66:22; 2 Pet. 3:13; Rev. 21:1). See also KINGDOM OF GOD.

**Hebrew.** In the Bible, this name is first applied to ABRAHAM (Gen. 14:13) and then to his descendants (39:14; 43:32), especially the members of the nation of ISRAEL (Exod. 1:15–16; see also JEW). The name was later applied also to the language of the Israelites. Hebrew was one of several Canaanite dialects (others were Moabite and Phoenician; cf. Isa. 19:18) and a member of the larger language family called Semitic. With the exception of a few passages written in ARAMAIC, Hebrew is the language of the OT.

**Hebrews, Letter to the.** The longest of the non-Pauline letters in the NT. The writer of Hebrews did not identify himself, and thus there has been much discussion since the second century as to who wrote this document; suggestions include PAUL, BARNABAS, APOLLOS, and others, but the arguments are inconclusive. The whole letter has a highly polished Greek style, unlike Paul's usual manner of writing. Its first readers were Jewish Christians who spoke and wrote Greek; they possibly lived somewhere in Italy (Heb. 13:24). These Christians were suffering opposition (12:4) and were considering going

## OVERVIEW OF HEBREWS

**AUTHOR:** Anonymous (some parts of the early church attributed it to PAUL; suggestions include BARNABAS, APOLLOS, and others).

**HISTORICAL SETTING:** Addressed to Hebrew Christians (possibly living in or near ROME) who were suffering persecution and who were tempted to return to JUDAISM, thus abandoning the uniqueness of CHRIST and his priestly ministry. The letter was probably written shortly before AD 70, but some date it later.

**PURPOSE:** To prevent the apostasy of the readers by establishing the superiority of Christ over the old COVENANT.

**CONTENTS:** The superiority of Christ over the ANGELS (Heb. 1–2), over MOSES and JOSHUA (chs. 3–4), and over the Aaronic priesthood (chs. 5–7); the obsolescence of the old covenant (chs. 8:1–10:18); perseverance in faith (10:19–12:29); various exhortations and greetings (ch. 13).

back to JUDAISM, so the writer's first main task is to make clear the preeminence of Christ over the ANGELS, MOSES, and the OT priesthood. Christ is the only PRIEST we need (7:23–28), and so the readers are exhorted to persevere in their FAITH (10:23–25).

**Hebron** (hee'bruhn). **(1)** Son of KOHATH, uncle of MOSES, and ancestor of a Levitical clan (Exod. 6:18; Num. 3:19, 27; 1 Chr. 6:2, 18; 15:9; 23:12, 19; 24:23). **(2)** A descendant of CALEB (1 Chr. 2:42–43). **(3)** An ancient city located about 20 mi. (32 km.) SSW of JERUSALEM in the hills of JUDEA. Hebron, near MAMRE, was a camping place for ABRAHAM (Gen. 13:18). Later it was conquered by Caleb (Josh. 14:6–15; 15:14–19). DAVID made Hebron his capital city for seven and a half years before moving to JERUSALEM (2 Sam. 5:3–5).

**hell.** This English word is used by the KJV in the OT to render Hebrew SHEOL (e.g., Deut. 32:22); in the NT it renders Greek HADES (e.g., Matt. 11:23) and GEHENNA (e.g., Matt. 5:2). The NIV and other modern versions use it almost exclusively as a translation of this last term. The existence of hell is clearly taught in Scripture as both a *place* of the wicked dead and a *condition* of punishment for unredeemed sinners. It is described as eternal punishment (Matt. 25:46), eternal fire (Matt. 18:8, Jude 7), everlasting chains (Jude 6), outer darkness (Matt. 8:12), and second death (Rev. 21:8).

**Hellenism.** The civilization and culture of ancient GREECE; especially, the dissemination and adoption of Greek thought, customs, and lifestyle, often fusing with non-Greek culture. In the NT the term *Hellenists* refers to Jewish people whose language was Greek (NRSV Acts 6:1; 9:29; NIV "Grecian Jews"; TNIV "Hellenistic Jews"). They were probably Jews from other countries who had returned to PALESTINE.

**Helper.** See HOLY SPIRIT.

**Heman** (hee'man). The name of several men in the OT, but especially a prophet-musician whom DAVID appointed to lead in the musical services (1 Chr. 6:33; 15:17, 19; 16:41–42; 25:1–6).

**heresy.** A false teaching or opinion (2 Pet. 2:1).

**heritage.** See INHERITANCE.

**Hermon** (huhr'muhn). A mountain ridge on the northern boundary of PALESTINE (Deut. 3:8–9; Josh. 11:17; Ps. 89:12). Hermon is awe-inspiring; it has three peaks, two of them rising over 9,000 ft. (2,740 m.). Many believe that Jesus' TRANSFIGURATION (Mk. 9:2) took place on its slopes, for he was at CAESAREA PHILIPPI just S of the mountain only a week before (8:27).

**Herod** (her'uhd). The name of several rulers in Jewish PALESTINE during the period of Roman domination. The ones who are called by that name in the NT are the following: **(1)** Herod the Great, who was made king by the Romans in 37 BC and died in 4 BC (Matt. 2:1–19; Lk. 1:5; 3:1). **(2)** Herod Antipas, who was tetrarch of GALILEE and PEREA from 4 BC to AD 39 (Lk. 3:1; 9:7; 13:31; 23:7–12). **(3)** Herod Agrippa I, who ruled AD 37–44 (Acts 12; his first two years he ruled only some northern regions). See also AGRIPPA; ARCHELAUS; PHILIP.

**Herodians** (hi-roh'dee-uhnz). A political group whose members supported HEROD's dynasty; they cooperated with the PHARISEES on at least two different occasions in opposition to Jesus (Mk. 3:6; 12:13). Like the SADDUCEES, they may have had pro-Roman sympathies.

**Herodias** (hi-roh'dee-uhs). A granddaughter of HEROD the Great who married her uncle PHILIP; she then divorced him and married Philip's brother, Herod ANTIPAS. Because

JOHN the Baptist reproved Antipas for his unlawful marriage, Herodias secured John's death by a sordid scheme (Mk. 6:14–29).

**Heshbon** (hesh′bon). A city about 15 mi. (24 km.) ENE of the N tip of the DEAD SEA. Originally part of MOAB, it was captured by the AMORITE king SIHON, who made it his capital. Later Heshbon was taken by the Israelites and then rebuilt by the tribe of REUBEN (Num. 21:25–30; 32:37; Deut. 2:24–30). Subsequently it must have been retaken by the Moabites (Isa. 15:4; 16:8–9; Jer. 48:2, 34, 45; 49:3).

**heth (letter)** (hayth). Also *het* and *cheth*. The eighth letter of the Hebrew alphabet (ח, transliterated as *ch* or, better, *ḥ*, used to begin each verse in Ps. 119:57–64.

**Hezekiah** (hez′uh-k*i*′uh). The name of several men in the OT, but especially a godly king of JUDAH c. 716–687 BC (2 Ki. 18–20; 2 Chr. 29:1–32; Isa. 36–39). One of his first acts was the ritual cleansing and reopening of the TEMPLE, which his father Ahaz had left closed and desecrated. Hezekiah almost died from a serious illness, but God granted him a fifteen-year extension of life. During his reign, the Assyrian king SENNACHERIB was intent on destroying JERUSALEM, but God saved the city by sending a sudden plague that in one night killed 185,000 soldiers.

**high places.** Because the Canaanites and other ancient peoples believed that their gods lived in the heights, they often built altars and shrines on the top of hills and other elevated spots. The Israelites were commanded to destroy such high places (Num. 33:52), but throughout the history of the nation they often lapsed into idolatry and made use of high places (e.g., 1 Ki. 14:22–23; 15:14; 2 Ki. 16:2–4).

**high priest.** The head of the Hebrew priesthood. He alone was allowed into the HOLY OF HOLIES in the TABERNACLE once a year to make ATONEMENT for the sins of the people (Lev. 16). Jesus is the eternal high priest of Christians (Heb. 4:14; 7:26–28; 9:7–14). See also AARON; PRIEST.

**Hilkiah** (hil-k*i*′uh). The name of several men in the OT, but especially a HIGH PRIEST who helped King JOSIAH in his religious reforms and who found the BOOK of the Law in the temple (2 Ki. 22:4–14; 2 Chr. 34:9–22).

**hin.** A liquid measure equivalent to about one gallon (Exod. 29:40; Ezek. 4:11).

**Hinnom, Valley of (Ben)** (hin′uhm). A valley running southward on the W side of JERUSALEM until it joins the Valley of the KIDRON. It was a part of the boundary between JUDAH on the S (Josh. 15:8) and BENJAMIN on the N (18:16). This valley seems to have been a dumping ground and a place for burning (see also GEHENNA; TOPHETH).

**Hiram, Huram** (h*i*′ruhm, hyoor′uhm). **(1)** A king of TYRE who helped build the palaces of DAVID and SOLOMON as well as the TEMPLE by sending wood, gold, and skilled

In this aerial view of Jerusalem, the Hinnom Valley can be seen along the bottom and left of the image. Ted Spiegel/National Geographic Stock

H

This Egyptian painting depicts Pharaoh Ramses II defeating the Hittites.





laborers to JERUSALEM (2 Sam. 5:11; 1 Ki. 5:1–14). **(2)** A craftsman skilled in bronze; he was sent by King Hiram to make many of the furnishings of the temple (1 Ki. 7:13–45). To avoid confusion, the NIV uses "Hiram" for #1 and "Huram" for #2; in the Hebrew text, however, both forms are used for both individuals.

**Hittite** (hit′t*i*t). In the OT the term is applied to two distinct ethnic groups. One of them lived in PALESTINE from the time of ABRAHAM to the period of the conquest (Gen. 23:3–20; Josh. 12:8). During the Israelite monarchy, however, the term refers to the "neo-Hittite" peoples and kingdoms of N SYRIA (1 Ki. 10:29; 11:1), who in previous centuries had come from Asia Minor. URIAH the Hittite (2 Sam. 11:3) probably belonged to the latter group.

**Hivite** (hiv′*i*t). One of the names appearing in the lists of peoples dispossessed by the Israelites (e.g., Exod. 3:8, Deut. 7:1). In the Table of Nations, the Hivites are included as descendants of CANAAN (Gen. 10:17). Possibly they were closely related to the HORITES.

**holiness.** The state or quality of being morally pure and separate from evil. The adjective *holy* is a distinctly religious term. It refers primarily to God himself and his Son (Exod. 15:11; Isa. 6:3; Lk. 1:35; Jn. 17:11; Acts 3:14), but also to what has been sanctified by God, such as the TABERNACLE (Exod. 40:9), JERUSALEM (Isa. 48:2), and especially his people (Lev. 19:2; 1 Cor. 3:16–17; 1 Pet. 2:9).

**Holy of Holies, Holy Place.** In the description of the TABERNACLE (Exod. 26:33; Heb. 9:2–7), a distinction is made between the Holy Place and the Holy of Holies (NIV, "Most Holy Place"). In the former, which was accessible to the priests generally, were found the table of SHOWBREAD, the golden LAMPSTAND, and the golden altar of INCENSE. Only the HIGH PRIEST, and only once a year, was allowed to enter the Most Holy Place, which contained the ARK of the covenant.

**Holy Spirit.** The third person of the TRINITY (the KJV usually renders "Holy Ghost"). Although the OT contains many references to God's Spirit (e.g., Gen. 1:2; Exod. 31:3; 1 Sam. 10:10; Ps. 51:11), it is only in the NT that his distinct personality becomes clear (e.g., Matt. 28:19; Lk. 4:1; Jn. 16:7–15; Acts 1:16; Rom. 8:26–27; 1 Cor. 2:10–13). Jesus refers to the Holy Spirit with a Greek word (*paraklētos*) that can be translated "advocate," "counselor," "comforter," or "helper" (Jn. 14:16–17, 26).

Although the Spirit has always been active, he was poured out in a special way on the day of PENTECOST to constitute believers as a unified body, the CHURCH, and to empower them as witnesses of Christ (Acts 1:8; 2:1–21; 1 Cor. 12:13). The Holy Spirit is the guarantee of our future INHERITANCE (2 Cor. 1:22; Eph. 1:13–14).

**homer.** A dry measure equivalent to about 220 liters (Lev. 27:16).

**honesty.** See LIE; TRUTH.

**honor.** To regard with respect; to show esteem for someone. God should be honored not simply with our words, but also with our hearts, deeds, and substance (Isa. 29:13; Prov. 3:9). All people are to "honor the Son just as they honor the Father" (Jn. 5:23). The fifth commandment requires us to honor our parents (Exod. 20:12; Eph. 6:2–3). PETER exhorted his readers to honor everyone, especially "the king" (i.e., the emperor, 1 Pet. 2:17).

**hope.** This English word usually refers to a strong desire or expectation (e.g., Ruth 1:12; Job 6:11; Acts 16:19; Rom. 15:24). The more common use in the Bible, however, is stronger: it implies trust and is therefore very similar to FAITH. We are not to place our hope or trust in riches or in human beings, but rather in God (Job 13:15; 31:24–28; Ps. 42:5; Jer. 14:8; Matt. 12:21; Acts 23:6; Rom. 5:2–5; 8:24–25; 1 Tim. 6:17; Heb. 6:19).

**Hophni** (hof′n*i*). Son of the high priest ELI. Hophni and his brother PHINEHAS were greedy and immoral priests who were judged by God (1 Sam. 1:3; 2:12–17, 22, 27–34; 4:10–11).

**Hor** (hor). A mountain on the border of the land of EDOM where AARON died (Num. 20:22–29; 33:37–39; a different Mount Hor in northern PALESTINE is mentioned in Deut. 10:6).

**Horeb** (hor′eb). See SINAI, MOUNT.

**Horite** (hor′*i*t). The Horites were a people group who lived in EDOM (Gen. 14:6; 36:20–30; Deut. 2:12, 22 [KJV "Horims"]). It is uncertain whether they were connected with other tribes, such as the HIVITES or the Hurrians (the latter are mentioned in nonbiblical documents).

**horn.** This term is often used in the Bible as a symbol of power, victory, and salvation (e.g., 1 Sam. 2:1; Ps. 18:2; 89:17; Jer. 48:25; Lk. 1:69). The "horns" of the altar were four protrusions at the corners of a hewn stone ALTAR (Exod. 27:2); a person seeking sanctuary might catch hold of the horns of the altar in the temple (1 Ki. 1:50–51; 2:28–34).

**hosanna** (hoh-zan′uh). A Hebrew (or ARAMAIC) term meaning "Save, please," but used as a joyous acclamation, an ascription of praise to God (Matt. 21:9; Mk. 11:9–10; Jn. 12:13).

**Hosea, Book of** (hoh-zay′uh). First book of the Minor Prophets. Hosea exercised his prophetic ministry in the northern kingdom of ISRAEL, toward the end of the prosperous reign of JEROBOAM II (c. 786–746

Artistic representation of the prophet Hosea.

Orthodox Church in America, www.oca.org

BC). Unfortunately, the religious life of the Israelites had degenerated to the point of becoming identified with the shameless immoral worship of the pagan Canaanite deities. It was Hosea's primary duty to recall wayward Israel to its obligations under the COVENANT. He stressed that Israel was really God's bride (Hos. 2:7, 16, 19) and employed his MARRIAGE as a metaphor to demonstrate the voluntary association of the bride with her divine lover. The behavior of his wife, Gomer, was a clear picture of wayward Israel in its relationship with God and showed the unending faithfulness of the Almighty. The remainder of the prophecy (Hos. 4–14) is an indictment of Israel delivered at various times.

**Hoshea** (hoh-shee'uh). Original name of JOSHUA son of Nun before MOSES changed it (Num. 13:8, 16; KJV "Oshea"). It was also the name of several other men, especially the last king of ISRAEL, who ruled for nine years (732–724 BC) during a time of social and moral upheaval (2 Ki. 15:30; 17:1–6; 18:1, 9–10).

**hospitality.** A gracious disposition toward guests or the practice of providing generously for them. Although the word occurs only a few times in the Bible (e.g., Rom. 12:13; 1 Pet. 4:9), the idea appears frequently (e.g., Gen. 14:17–19; 18:1–8; Jdg. 13:2–23; 2 Ki. 4:8–10; Lk. 10:38–42; Acts 16:14–15).

**host.** In addition to the sense "someone who entertains guests," this word often means "multitude, army." The phrase "host of heaven" is found in the KJV where the NIV uses a variety of translations, such as "heavenly array" (Deut. 4:19) and "starry hosts" (2 Ki. 17:16). Sometimes it refers to angelic beings (1 Ki. 22:19). The expression "LORD of hosts" may refer to the angelic armies (e.g., 1 Sam. 17:45) or be a more general allusion to God's power (the NIV translates "LORD Almighty," e.g., Ps. 24:10).

**house.** The Hebrew and Greek words for "house" include a wide variety of meanings. They may refer to a household or FAMILY (Exod. 2:1), one's descendants (Lk.

## OVERVIEW OF HOSEA

**AUTHOR:** The prophet Hosea son of Beeri.

**HISTORICAL SETTING:** Hosea began his ministry in the northern kingdom of ISRAEL c. 750 BC, during the last years of King JEROBOAM II, and was still active at the beginning of the reign of HEZEKIAH, king of JUDAH, c. 715. He thus witnessed the final decline of the northern kingdom, which came to an end in 722.

**PURPOSE:** To show that Israel, by repudiating the Sinaitic COVENANT, had become a faithless wife, committing spiritual adultery against her divine spouse; and to bring the nation to repentance.

**CONTENTS:** Using his marriage as an illustration, Hosea depicts the relations of Israel with her God (Hos. 1–3); he then denounces the immorality and idolatry of the nation (chs. 4–8), prophesies its destruction (chs. 9–13), and urges the people to return to the Lord so that they may enjoy future blessings (ch. 14).

1:33), a royal dynasty (2 Sam. 7:11–12), a nomad tent (Gen. 14:13–14), a building in a city (19:2–11), the TABERNACLE or TEMPLE as the house of God (Exod. 23:19; 2 Sam. 7:5–7), or the human body (2 Cor. 5:1).

**Huldah** (huhl′duh). A prophetess who had a word from the Lord for King JOSIAH (2 Ki. 22:14–20).

**humanity.** The Bible often uses the generic term *man* with reference to the human race generally. As Creator, God made the human species, male and female, in the image and likeness of himself (Gen. 1:26–27; Ps. 8:5). This means, among other things, that we have the capacity for spiritual communion with our Creator. SIN, however, has seriously damaged and restricted this potential. As a result, men and women show signs of being both God's special creation and sinful creatures—capable of great heroism, public service, and personal kindness, but also of self-centeredness, pride, and cruelty (Mk. 7:20–23; Rom. 7:14–25). The eternal Son of God became Man, the "last Adam," in order to provide SALVATION from SIN (Rom. 5:14–19; 1 Cor. 15:45).

**humility.** Freedom from PRIDE, thus lowliness, meekness, modesty, mildness. God humbles people to bring them to obedience (Deut. 8:2). To humble ourselves is a condition of God's favor (2 Chr. 7:14) and his supreme requirement (Mic. 6:8). Jesus made humility the cornerstone of character (Matt. 5:3, 5; 18:4; 23:12; Lk. 14:11; 18:14). The apostles emphasized its importance (Rom. 12:10; 1 Cor. 13:4–6; Phil. 2:3–4; 1 Pet. 5:5–6).

Reconstruction of a house in Canaan dated during the period of the Israelite judges (c. 1100 BC). 

**Huram** (hyoor′uhm). See HIRAM.

**Hushai** (hoosh′*i*). A prominent man who was DAVID's adviser and "friend" (2 Sam. 15:32–37; 16:15–17:16).

**hypocrite.** A person who pretends to be something that he or she is not, especially by simulating virtue or piety. Some PHARISEES were guilty of this sin, and Jesus denounced it sternly (Matt. 6:2, 5; 7:5; 15:7; 23:18–28).

**hyssop.** A plant (possibly the marjoram) that was used to sprinkle blood or water for ceremonial purposes (Exod. 12:22; Num. 19:18).

# I

**Ichabod** (ik′uh-bod). This name, which probably means "inglorious," was given to the son of PHINEHAS (one of ELI's two evil sons) by his mother when she bore him on her deathbed after the "glory" (the ARK of the covenant) was taken from Israel (1 Sam. 4:21–22).

**Iconium** (*i*-koh′nee-uhm). An important city of Asia Minor (modern Turkey) that PAUL and BARNABAS visited after they had been expelled from ANTIOCH in PISIDIA (Acts 13:51–14:5; cf. 2 Tim. 3:11). Paul revisited it later (Acts 16:2).

**Iddo** (id′oh). The name of several men in the OT, especially a seer or prophet who received visions concerning SOLOMON and JEROBOAM (2 Chr. 9:29) and produced historical writings (12:15; 13:22). His writings served as a source for the material in the books of CHRONICLES.

**idleness.** The Scriptures criticize the idle or lazy person when the situation demands effort and work (e.g., Prov. 31:27; 19:15; 1 Thess. 5:14; 1 Tim. 5:13) as well as the busy person who speaks "idle words" (KJV), that is, who uses careless language (Matt. 12:36). God calls for purposeful work (not meaningless busyness) and also for purposeful rest (Exod. 20:8–11).

**idolatry.** This term refers to the WORSHIP of idols, i.e., false gods and images of them (Lev. 19:4; 1 Sam. 12:21; Ps. 106:38; 1 Thess. 1:9), but also to the worship of the true God by means of images (Exod. 20:4); in a derived sense it can refer to blind or excessive devotion to something or someone (Col. 3:5). The Bible views idolatry as the most heinous of crimes. The relation between God and his covenant people is often represented as a MARRIAGE bond (Isa. 54:5; Jer. 3:14), and the worship of false gods was regarded as religious prostitution. The penalty was death (Exod. 22:20; Deut. 13:6–10). The God of ISRAEL was a jealous God who brooked no rivals.

**Idumea** (id′y*oo*-mee′uh). Also Idumaea. A region in southern PALESTINE from which crowds came to follow Jesus (Mk. 3:8). The name derives from the fact that this area was occupied by Edomites (see EDOM) after the destruction of JERUSALEM in 586 BC. During the intertestamental period they were forced to adopt the Jewish religion; HEROD the Great was an Idumean but formally regarded as a Jew.

**Illyricum** (i-lihr′i-kuhm). A Roman PROVINCE in the western portion of the Balkan peninsula N of GREECE; PAUL took the gospel as far as Illyricum (Rom. 15:19).

**image.** See IDOLATRY.

**image of God.** See HUMANITY.

**Immanuel** (i-man′y*oo*-uhl). Also Emmanuel. A name meaning "God is with us," given to the child born of the virgin (Isa. 7:14; 8:8 [cf. 8:10]; Matt. 1:23). Because Jesus became God incarnate (see INCARNATION) and lived among human beings (Jn. 1:14), he truly fulfilled the Immanuel prophecy.

**immorality.** See FORNICATION.

**immortality.** Only God is truly immortal, not subject to DEATH (Rom. 1:23; 1 Tim. 1:17; 6:16), but he grants immortality to those who believe (Rom. 2:7; 1 Cor. 15:53–54). See ETERNAL; RESURRECTION.

**imputation.** The act of attributing something to a person. The SIN of ADAM was imputed to his posterity, but the RIGHTEOUSNESS of Christ is imputed to those who believe (Rom. 5:19; see JUSTIFICATION). In addition, our sin was imputed to Christ, i.e., he was treated and punished as though he had been a sinner (2 Cor. 5:21).

**incarnation.** This term means "being in flesh" and refers to the humiliation of the Son of God, who took on a human body, indeed became fully human, so that he could live among us, die for us, and redeem us (Jn. 1:14; Rom. 8:3; Phil. 2:5–11; Col. 2:9; 1 Tim. 3:16). See TRINITY.

**incense.** Material from spices, burned to make a fragrant smoke; the word is often used for the fragrance itself. The TABERNACLE had a special altar for burning incense, an important part of Hebrew WORSHIP (Exod. 30:1–10, 34–38). The rising smoke represented the PRAYER of God's people (Ps. 141:2; Lk. 1:10; Rev. 8:3–5).

**inheritance.** Something received from an ancestor through a legal will or TESTAMENT (Prov. 19:14; Lk. 12:13). In the Bible, the term has special significance, indicating (1) the gift of the land of CANAAN by God to ABRAHAM and his descendants (Exod. 32:13; Deut. 12:9–10; 1 Ki. 8:36); (2) the spiritual blessings that God gives to his people (Ps. 16:6; Mk. 10:17; 1 Cor. 6:9–10; Col. 3:24; 1 Pet. 1:4); (3) the people of God as his own possession (Ps. 33:12; Isa. 19:25; Zech. 2:12; cf. Eph. 1:14).

Bronze figurines of Canaanite deities.

Erich Lessing/Art Resource, NY

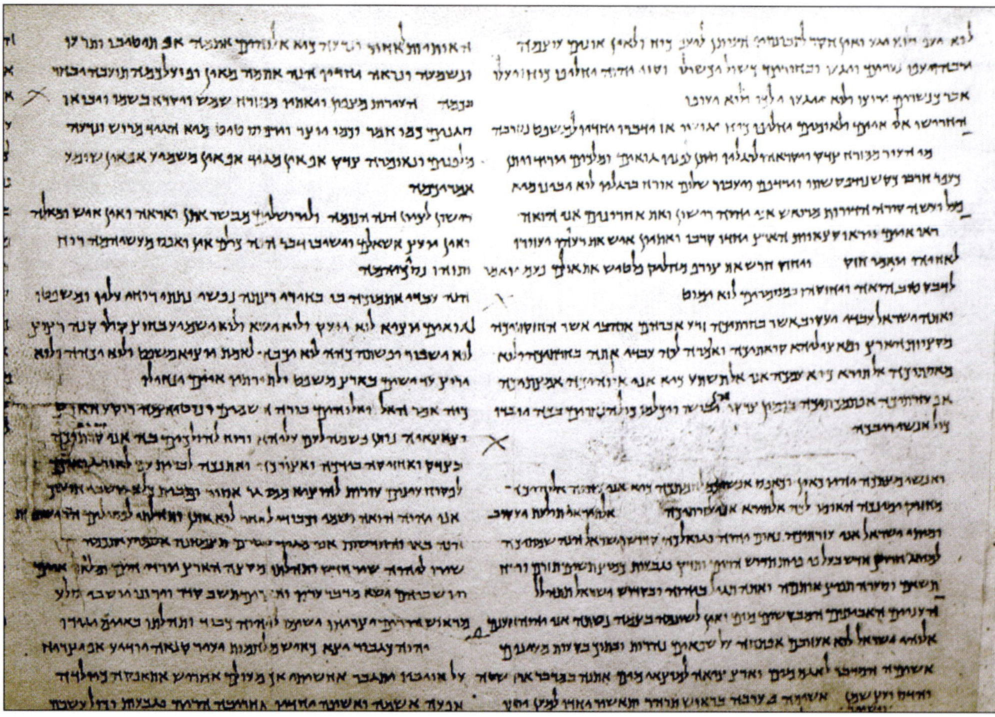

Facsimile of the Great Isaiah Scroll (2nd cent. BC).





**iniquity.** Wickedness (Ps. 25:11); an act of SIN (Isa. 59:2).

**inspiration.** Although this term can refer to anything that influences or motivates a person, in Christian theology it means the supernatural work of the HOLY SPIRIT whereby divine truth is communicated, especially in its written form, the BIBLE. When the KJV says that Scripture is "given by inspiration of God" (2 Tim. 3:16), it translates one Greek word, *theopneustos*, which literally means "God-breathed" (so NIV). The OT speaks of the power of God's breath as something that can bring both life and judgment (Gen. 2:7; Exod. 15:10; Ps. 28:15; 33:6; Isa. 11:4). Thus 2 Tim. 3:16 asserts that the Bible has its ultimate origin in God. The same idea is taught with different language in 2 Pet. 1:19–21 and other passages.

**intercession.** The act of pleading on behalf of someone else (1 Tim. 2:11). See PRAYER.

**Isaac** (*i'*zik). Son of ABRAHAM and SARAH, half brother of ISHMAEL, husband of REBEKAH, and father of ESAU and JACOB. His birth must be regarded as a miracle (Gen. 17:15–19; 21:1–7). When he was a young man, God ordered Abraham to offer him as a SACRIFICE, but his life was spared (22:1–19). Several other events in his life are recorded (chs. 23–27), and the NT mentions him frequently (especially Rom. 9:7–10; Gal. 4:21–31; Heb. 11:17–20).

**Isaiah, Book of** (*i*-zay*'*yuh). KJV NT Esaias. The first and largest book among the Major Prophets. Isaiah had a long ministry that covered at least part of the reigns of four kings of JUDAH (Isa. 1:1, c. 740–700 BC). It began with a dramatic vision and call the year King UZZIAH died (ch. 6); especially significant were his interactions with kings AHAZ (7:1–17) and HEZEKIAH (chs. 36–39). The book of Isaiah contains some of the most important OT prophecies about the MESSIAH (e.g., 7:14; 9:6–7; 11:1–10; 40:1–5; 42:1–4; 52:13–53:12; 61:1–3; the last one cited by Jesus in Lk. 4:16–21). It also includes oracles against many nations. Isaiah is preeminently the prophet of REDEMPTION, emphasizing the greatness and majesty of God, his HOLINESS and hatred of SIN and the folly of IDOLATRY, his GRACE and MERCY and LOVE, and the blessed rewards of OBEDIENCE. The NT writers quote Isaiah by name over twenty times, slightly more than all the other writing prophets taken together, and there are many more allusions and quotations where his name is not given.

**Iscariot.** See JUDAS.

**Ish-Bosheth** (ish-boh′shith). Son of SAUL who was made king over Israel by ABNER in repudiation of DAVID's claim to the throne; after two years he was assassinated (2 Sam. 2:8–4:12; NRSV "Ishbaal"; cf. "Esh-Baal" in 1 Chr. 8:33; 9:39).

**Ishmael** (ish′may-uhl). The name of several men in the OT but primarily of ABRAHAM's son by HAGAR, who was SARAH's Egyptian maid (Gen. 16). His birth created conflicts in Abraham's household, and eventually Hagar and her child were dismissed; Ishmael grew up in the Desert of PARAN (21:9–21). He had many descendants, thought to be the ancestors of the Arab peoples (25:12–18; cf. 37:25–28; Jdg. 8:24).

**Israel** (iz′ray-uhl). This name is used in Scripture to designate: **(1)** an individual man, the son of ISAAC (Gen. 38:28; see JACOB); **(2)** his descendants, the twelve tribes of the Hebrews (Exod. 3:16); or **(3)** only the ten northern tribes, led by the tribe of EPHRAIM, as opposed to the south-

## OVERVIEW OF ISAIAH

**AUTHOR:** The prophet Isaiah, son of Amoz, though some scholars attribute parts of the book (esp. Isa. 40–66) to unknown authors living at the time of the EXILE.

**HISTORICAL SETTING:** Ministering in the southern kingdom of JUDAH, Isaiah began his prophetic work toward the end of the reign of King UZZIAH (c. 740 BC) and continued his service during the reigns of JOTHAM, AHAZ, and HEZEKIAH.

**PURPOSE:** To denounce the nation for its flagrant violations of the divine COVENANT, but also to bring hope by prophesying the coming of the MESSIAH, the SERVANT OF THE LORD.

**CONTENTS:** The book begins with a harsh condemnation of Judah (Isa. 1–5), followed by an account of the prophet's commission (ch. 6) and the so-called "book of Immanuel" (chs. 7–12); it then moves to a condemnation of surrounding nations (chs. 13–23), followed by an apocalyptic vision (chs. 24–27) and by further prophecies of judgment and blessing (chs. 28–35). After a historical account of events in Hezekiah's reign (chs. 36–39), the book proclaims comfort to the exiles in Babylon (chs. 40–48), discloses God's plan for his Servant (chs. 49–55), and promises the future purification of his people (chs. 56–66).

ern kingdom, under the tribe of JUDAH (1 Ki. 12:20–21).

**Issachar** (is'uh-kahr). The ninth son of JACOB and the fifth of LEAH (Gen. 30:17–18; 35:23). Almost nothing is known of his personal history. The tribe that descended from Issachar consisted of five great clans (Num. 26:23–24). The territory allotted to the tribe in Canaan lay S of ZEBULUN and NAPHTALI and N of MANASSEH.

**Ithamar** (ith'uh-mahr). Youngest son of AARON and ELISHEBA (Exod. 6:23). Together with his father and brothers, Ithamar was consecrated to the priesthood (Exod. 28:1), and during the wilderness wanderings he was leader over all the LEVITES (38:21).

# J

**Jabbok** (jab'uhk). A river on the E side of the JORDAN RIVER, about 60 mi. (96 km.) in length, mentioned in connection with JACOB (Gen. 32:22). It served as a physical and political boundary between the two parts of GILEAD (Deut. 3:16; Josh. 12:2–6).

**Jabesh Gilead** (jay'bish-gil'ee-uhd). An important city in the area E of the JORDAN RIVER given to the half tribe of MANASSEH (Jdg. 21:8–15; 1 Sam. 11:1–15; 31:1–13; 2 Sam. 2:4–6).

**Jabin** (jay'bin). The name of two different kings of HAZOR (Josh. 11:1–12; Jdg. 4:2, 17, 23–24).

**Jacob** (jay'kuhb). Son of ISAAC and REBEKAH, younger twin brother of ESAU, and husband of LEAH and RACHEL. He later was called ISRAEL (Gen. 32:28; 49:2) and through his twelve sons became the ancestor of the Israelites. The Bible gives much attention to his life, including his birth (25:21–26), his rivalry with Esau (25:27–34; ch. 27), God's promises to him (28:10–22), his dealings with his father-in-law LABAN (chs. 29–31), his wrestling with God (32:22–32), and other incidents. After he moved to EGYPT, and shortly before his death, he uttered a remarkable prophecy regarding all his

The Jabbok River valley looking W.

sons (ch. 49). He is mentioned a number of times in the NT, especially in Rom. 9:10–13 and Heb. 11:20–21.

**Jairus** (jay-*i*′ruhs). A SYNAGOGUE official whose dead daughter Jesus raised to life (Mk. 5:22; Lk. 8:41).

**James** (jaymz). **(1)** A son of ZEBEDEE; he was one of the original twelve disciples and brother of the apostle JOHN (Mk. 1:19–20; 3:17). The two of them, along with PETER, are often found at the center of important events, such as the raising of JAIRUS's daughter (5:37), the TRANSFIGURATION (Mk. 9:2), and Jesus' agony in the Garden of GETHSEMANE (14:33). His early martyrdom (c. AD 41) is recorded in Acts 12:1–2. **(2)** A half brother of Jesus who was not a believer until after the resurrection; during the 40s he became the leader of the church in JERUSALEM (cf. Acts 15:13–21; 21:18; Gal. 2:9); he was probably the author of the epistle of James. **(3)** A son of ALPHAEUS who was one of the twelve disciples (Mk. 3:18). **(4)** A certain "James the younger" (Mk. 15:40; KJV "the less") may be the same as the son of Zebedee or the son of Alphaeus, but he is probably a different person. **(5)** The father of the disciple JUDAS (not Iscariot, Lk. 6:16; KJV "brother").

**James, Letter of.** The first of the CATHOLIC EPISTLES of the NT. The author, who identifies himself as "James, a servant of God and of the Lord Jesus Christ" (Jas. 1:1), was probably the half brother of the Lord; see JAMES #2. The letter has a strongly Jewish flavor and has affinities with the SERMON ON THE MOUNT; it seems to have been addressed to Jewish Christians living in various parts of the Roman empire. The object of the author was to rebuke and correct the error and sins into which his readers had fallen and to encourage them in the heavy trials through which they were going. He places much emphasis on authentic FAITH (1:22–27; 2:14–26).

**Japheth** (jay′fith). One of the three sons of NOAH (Gen. 5:32). The blessing that Noah pronounced on him (9:27) suggests that his descendants would be greatly multiplied, and the so-called Table of Nations in Gen. 10 indicates that Japheth became the ancestor of a wide-ranging family of peoples,

## OVERVIEW OF JAMES

**AUTHOR:** James, the half brother of Jesus.

**HISTORICAL SETTING:** The letter must have been written prior to AD 62, the year of James's martyrdom (some date it as early as AD 44, making it the first NT book to be written). It was probably addressed to Jewish Christians who lived in the Dispersion (unless Jas. 1:1 is to be taken figuratively); they were undergoing trials as well as experiencing spiritual failures.

**PURPOSE:** To stress the need for "wisdom from above" (Jas. 3:17) and for works of obedience that demonstrate the genuineness of saving FAITH.

**CONTENTS:** Wisdom amid trials and temptations (Jas. 1:1–18); being doers of the word and not merely hearers (1:19–2:26); dangers of the tongue, quarrels, and slander (3:1–4:12); depending on God and enduring with patience and prayer (4:13–5:20).

The ancient city of Jebus was located on the V-shaped ridge descending S into the valley in front of what is now known as the temple mount. (To the right of the ridge is the Kidron Valley.) © Baker Publishing Group

whose homes lay to the N and W of PALESTINE (10:1–5).

**Javan** (jay′vuhn). Son of JAPHETH (Gen. 10:2). The name corresponds to Ionia, and it is used by the OT prophets to denote the descendants of Javan in Ionia proper (W coast of Asia Minor) but also in GREECE and MACEDONIA; thus the NIV renders the name "Greece" or "Greeks" in these books (e.g., Isa. 66:19; Ezek. 27:13; Dan. 8:21).

**Jazer** (jay′zuhr). An AMORITE city in GILEAD that was captured by the Israelites and given to the tribe of GAD (Num. 21:32 [KJV "Jaazer"]; Josh. 13:25; see also 2 Sam. 24:5; Isa. 16:9; Jer. 48:32).

**jealousy.** Ardor or zeal for something or someone. When jealousy reflects concern for God's honor and glory, it is proper and good; God himself can be described as "jealous" (Exod. 34:14). There is also such a thing as "a godly jealousy" for others (2 Cor. 11:2). However, the term usually has a negative sense, indicating excessive regard for one's own self, as well as possessiveness, rivalry, and ill will toward others because of their good fortune (Gen. 37:34; 1 Sam. 18:6–9; Lk. 15:25–30; Acts 5:17; 7:9). As such, it is condemned in Scripture (Rom. 13:13; 1 Cor. 3:3; Gal. 5:20).

**Jebus** (jee′buhs). The name by which JERUSALEM was known before its Canaanite inhabitants, the Jebusites, were dislodged by DAVID and JOAB (Gen. 10:16; Josh. 15:8, 63; 2 Sam. 5:1–9).

**Jeconiah** (jek′uh-ni′uh). Alternate name of JEHOIACHIN, king of Judah (1 Chr. 3:16–17).

**Jedidiah** (jed′uh-di′uh). This name, meaning "beloved of Yahweh [the LORD]," was given by God to SOLOMON when he was born (2 Sam. 12:25).

**Jeduthun** (ji-dyoo′thuhn). A Levitical musician and "royal seer" in the time of DAVID (1 Chr. 16:41–42; 25:1–6; 2 Chr. 5:12; 35:15). The name "Jeduthun" in the titles of several psalms (Ps. 39; 62; 77) possibly refers to him.

**Jehoahaz** (ji-hoh′uh-haz). **(1)** Son of JEHU and king of ISRAEL from c. 814 to c. 797 BC (2 Ki. 10:35; 13:1–9). Although Jehoahaz practiced IDOLATRY, he invoked the name of the Lord in desperation, and his prayer was answered (13:4–5). **(2)** Son of JOSIAH and king of JUDAH for three months in 609 BC (2 Ki. 23:30–34; 2 Chr. 36:1–4). He was also known as Shallum (1 Chr. 3:15; Jer. 22:11). **(3)** Another name for another king of Judah. See AHAZIAH #2.

**Jehoash, Joash** (ji-hoh′ash, joh′ash). The name of several men in the OT, especially two kings. **(1)** Son of AHAZIAH and king of JUDAH from 835 to c. 796 BC (2 Ki. 11:1–12:21; 2 Chr. 22:10–24:27; in the NIV he is always called by the shorter form, Joash). As an infant, he was saved from Queen ATHALIAH, who massacred the royal family. When he was seven years old, the priest JEHOIADA crowned him before the people. Later Joash turned to pagan worship. **(2)** Son of JEHOAHAZ and king of ISRAEL approximately from 798 to 782 BC (2 Ki. 13:10–25; 14:8–16; 2 Chr. 25:17–24; in the NIV he is always called by the longer form, Jehoash). He inflicted three defeats on BEN-HADAD III that marked the beginning of Israel's political revival.

**Jehoiachin** (ji-hoi′uh-kin). Son of JEHOIAKIM and last king of JUDAH before the EXILE in 597 BC (2 Ki. 24:6–15; 25:27–30). Also known as Jeconiah and Coniah, he reigned in JERUSALEM three months and ten days (2 Chr. 36:9). He displayed contempt for the Word of God by cutting up and burning the prophecies of JEREMIAH (Jer. 36:23, 32). NEBUCHADNEZZAR took him to BABYLON, where he remained a captive the rest of his life.

**Jehoiada** (ji-hoi′uh-duh). The name of several men in the OT, but especially of a very influential HIGH PRIEST in JERUSALEM who organized the coup that ousted ATHALIAH and set Joash (JEHOASH) on the throne; he was for many years the young king's trusted adviser (2 Ki. 11–12; 2 Chr. 23–24).

**Jehoiakim** (ji-hoi′uh-kim). Son of JOSIAH and king of JUDAH from 607 to 597 BC (2 Ki. 23:34–24:6). His birth name was Eliakim, but Pharaoh NECO changed it and appointed him king in JERUSALEM. Jehoiakim was an oppressive and thoroughly godless ruler (cf. Jer. 26:21–23; 36:20–32).

**Jehoram, Joram** (ji-hoh′ruhm, jor′uhm). **(1)** Son of AHAB and king of the northern kingdom of ISRAEL; usually called Joram (2 Ki. 1:17; 3:1–27; 8:16; 9:14–27; 2 Chr. 22:5–7). Early in his reign he was joined by JUDAH (under JEHOSHAPHAT) and EDOM in a war against MOAB that almost ended in disaster. He was a weak king who practiced IDOLATRY. Both he and his mother JEZEBEL were killed by the rampaging JEHU, who also exterminated all members of the family and all officials of the BAAL cult. **(2)** Son of JEHOSHAPHAT and king of the southern kingdom of Judah; sometimes called Joram (2 Ki. 8:16–19; 2 Chr. 21). He married ATHALIAH, daughter of Ahab, and followed her pagan worship. After living to see God's judgment on all his sons save one, he died of a terrible disease.

**Jehoshaphat** (ji-hosh′uh-fat). The name of several men in the OT, especially a son of ASA who was the fourth king of the southern kingdom of JUDAH (1 Ki. 22; 2 Chr. 17–20). He began his reign c. 871 BC and ruled for twenty-five years. Jehoshaphat was outstanding for godliness: he removed pagan worship and fostered the religious education of the people (2 Chr. 17:6–9), though he made a great mistake in associating with the wicked King AHAB of the northern kingdom.

**Jehovah** (ji-hoh′vuh). Traditional English rendering of the divine name *YHWH* (e.g.,

This section of the famous Black Obelisk shows King Jehu prostrate as he brings tribute to the Assyrian king Shalmaneser III (859-824 BC).
Todd Bolen/www.BiblePlaces.com



Exod. 6:3 KJV), which originally may have been pronounced *Yahweh* (the letter *y* in Heb. names is usually represented in English with *j*). Because Jewish tradition does not allow the pronunciation of this name, in public reading it is regularly substituted with *Adonai*, "my Lord"; to indicate such a reading, Hebrew copies of the Bible preserve the consonants of *YHWH* but insert the vowels of *Adonai*. This practice misled translators to create the hybrid form *Jehovah*, which never existed in Hebrew. Most versions render the name with small caps as "the LORD."

**Jehu** (jee'hy*oo*, jay'h*oo*). The name of several men in the OT, especially a king of ISRAEL who reigned c. 841–814 BC (1 Ki. 19:16–17; 2 Ki. 9–10). An impetuous and violent man, Jehu was used of God to execute judgment on the royal house of AHAB and to exterminate the worship of BAAL, but he continued the practice of calf worship (2 Ki. 10:29).

**Jephthah** (jef'thuh). A warrior from GILEAD who as a judge delivered ISRAEL from the Ammonites (see AMMON), sacrificed his daughter to fulfill a vow to God, and defeated the Ephraimites (Jdg. 11:1–12:7).

**Jeremiah** (jer'uh-m*i*'uh). The name of several men in the OT, especially a prophet in the southern kingdom of JUDAH. See JEREMIAH, BOOK OF.

**Jeremiah, Book of.** The second book among the Major Prophets. Jeremiah was born into a priestly family and was called to prophesy in the thirteenth year of King JOSIAH (c. 626 BC). His ministry continued through the reigns of four additional kings, a period of unrest and decline; he saw the final destruction of JERUSALEM in 586 and died a few years later in Egypt. He preached a message of judgment but also spoke of the hope of a new COVENANT (Jer. 31:31–34). Because his book is full of autobiographical sections, Jeremiah's personality, with his strong emotions, can be understood more clearly than that of any other prophet. He also had a penetrating understanding of the spiritual condition of his people and emphasized the inner spiritual character of true religion.

**Jericho** (jer'uh-koh). One of the oldest cities in the world, located 5 mi. (8 km.) W of the JORDAN and 7 mi. (11 km.) N of the DEAD SEA, some 800 ft. (245 m.) below sea level.

## OVERVIEW OF JEREMIAH

**AUTHOR:** The priest-prophet Jeremiah, son of Hilkiah.

**HISTORICAL SETTING:** Although Jeremiah was apparently called to be a prophet in the thirteenth year of JOSIAH's reign (c. 626 BC, Jer. 1:2), in the wake of a great revival, most of his prophecies came subsequently, during the period of decline that led to the destruction of JERUSALEM (586). The book as a whole may have been put together by Jeremiah himself near the end of his life while an exile in EGYPT (c. 580).

**PURPOSE:** To warn of judgment against JUDAH because of IDOLATRY, to urge REPENTANCE upon the people, and to assure them of future restoration.

**CONTENTS:** Jeremiah's call (Jer. 1); denunciation of Judah's sins (chs. 2–25); reactions to the prophecies (chs. 26–29); future restoration (chs. 30–33); prediction, fulfillment, and aftermath of the fall of Jerusalem (chs. 34–45); oracles against foreign nations (chs. 46–51); summary of the fall of Jerusalem and its aftermath (ch. 52).



Jericho was captured by JOSHUA and the invading Hebrews as the opening wedge of their campaign to take CANAAN (Josh. 2; 6). Some centuries later it was rebuilt (1 Ki. 16:34; cf. 2 Ki. 2:4–5). The Jericho of NT times was on a nearby site, and Jesus passed through it on a number of occasions (Matt. 20:29–34; Mk. 10:46–52; Lk. 19:1–10); he also mentioned it in the parable of the Good Samaritan (Lk. 10:29–37).

The foreground of this image shows the OT site of Jericho.



**Jeroboam** (jer′uh-boh′uhm). The name of two Israelite kings. **(1)** Jeroboam I had been an official under SOLOMON, and when the kingdom was split in 930 BC he founded the northern kingdom of ISRAEL (1 Ki. 11:26–40; 12:1–20). Afraid that if his people went annually to JERUSALEM to worship it would not be long before they would be won back to the house of David, he set up a golden calf in each of the two extremities of his kingdom—DAN in the N and BETHEL in the S—thus leading the people into idolatrous worship (12:26–33). Jeroboam reigned for twenty-two years, but his rule was a political and religious calamity. **(2)** Jeroboam II, son of King JEHOASH, began to rule in SAMARIA c. 790 BC and reigned forty-one years (2 Ki. 14:23–29). He followed the example of Jeroboam I in keeping up the idolatrous worship of the golden calves, but his reign outwardly flourished. The prophet AMOS denounced the corruption that prevailed

Aerial view of Jerusalem, with the temple mount in the foreground.



in the land during this time (Amos 1:2; 6:1–7; 7:9).

**Jerub-Baal** (ji'ruhb-bay'uhl). The name given to GIDEON when he destroyed his father's BAAL altar (Jdg. 6:32).

**Jerusalem** (ji-roo'suh-luhm). The capital of the Hebrew nation and the most important city in biblical history—the place where God chose "to put his Name" (1 Ki. 14:21). It never occupied a large area, but was centrally located, being 34 mi. (55 km.) E of the MEDITERRANEAN and only 17 mi. (27 km.) W of the JORDAN RIVER, at an elevation of c. 2,550 ft. (780 m.) above sea level. The old city rests on three hills. The SE hill was the original city of the Jebusites (see JEBUS), taken by DAVID and later called ZION. The N hill is the one on which SOLOMON built the great TEMPLE. Between them is a minor elevation (see OPHEL). When the kingdom was divided in 930 BC, Jerusalem remained the capital of the southern kingdom of JUDAH and expanded westward. It was destroyed by the Babylonians in 586, then rebuilt after 538 by the Jewish exiles who were allowed to return. Jerusalem played a significant role in the life and ministry of Jesus (Lk. 2:22–52; 9:51; Jn. 2:13–25; 5:1–2; 7:2; 10:21); it was in and near the city that he spent the final week of his life (Matt. 26:1–27:66). The church came into existence in Jerusalem (Acts 2; cf. 1:4, 8), and some of the most important events in early Christianity took place there (chs. 3–7; 15; 21–23; Gal. 2:1–10). The heavenly city is called the "new Jerusalem" (Rev. 3:12; 21:2; cf. Gal. 4:26; Heb. 12:22).

**Jeshua** (jesh'yoo-uh). See JOSHUA.

**Jesse** (jes'ee). Father of King DAVID (1 Sam. 16) and ancestor of the MESSIAH (Isa. 11:1, 10; Rom. 15:12).

**Jesus** (jee'zuhs). Greek form of the Hebrew name JOSHUA (Acts 7:45; Heb. 4:8), which means "Yahweh is salvation." Although a common name (cf. Matt. 27:16–17 TNIV, NRSV; Col. 4:11), it was given new significance because of Jesus CHRIST (or MESSIAH), often identified as Jesus of NAZARETH (e.g., Matt. 26:71; Mk. 1:24; Jn. 1:45; Acts 2:22). The four Gospels recount his life, death, and RESURRECTION. He was born around the year 5 BC in BETHLEHEM (Matt. 2:1; Lk. 2:4–7) but grew up in Nazareth (Matt. 2:23; Lk. 2:39), and most of his ministry, which began when he was about thirty (Lk. 3:23), took place in the territory of GALILEE, with headquarters in the city of CAPERNAUM (Matt. 4:13). He preached REPENTANCE and the coming of the KINGDOM OF GOD (Mk. 1:15). The sick and demon-possessed came to him to be healed (Matt. 4:23–24). At the end of his short ministry (two and a half or three and a half years), he was crucified during the feast of PASSOVER in JERUSALEM, but after three days rose from the dead (Matt. 27–28), and forty days later he ascended to heaven (Acts 1:3, 9–11).

**Jethro** (jeth'roh). Priest of MIDIAN and father-in-law of MOSES (Exod. 3:1; 4:18; 18:1–12, 27; also called Reuel, 2:18).

**Jew** (j*oo*). This name originally denoted one belonging to the tribe of JUDAH (2 Ki. 16:6; 25:25), but later it was applied to any Hebrew who returned from the EXILE and settled in JUDEA. As these exiles were the main historical representatives of ancient ISRAEL, the term *Jews* came finally to comprehend all of the Hebrew race throughout the world (Esth. 2:5; Matt. 2:2).

**Jezebel** (jez'uh-bel). Daughter of Ethbaal king of SIDON (in PHOENICIA), wife of AHAB king of ISRAEL, and mother of ATHALIAH queen of JUDAH (1 Ki. 16:31; 18:4; 21:5–25; 2 Ki. 9:7–37). She tried to impose the worship of BAAL on Israel, even if it meant killing the prophets of the Lord. Jezebel's name became symbolic of APOSTASY and is used in the NT with reference to an immoral false prophetess (Rev. 2:20–22).

**Jezreel** (jez'ree-uhl). The name of two individuals (1 Chr. 4:3; Hos. 1:4–5), of two towns (one S in JUDAH, Josh. 15:56; the other N in ISSACHAR, 19:18), and especially of an important valley that divides the hills of GALILEE on the N from those of SAMARIA on the S (Josh. 17:6). Several passes enter into the Valley of Jezreel, making it easy to access and valuable for commerce and military operations. Many towns were situated in it, including the city of Jezreel in Issachar mentioned above, where King AHAB built a palace (1 Ki. 21:2; cf. 2 Ki. 8:29); also important was MEGIDDO, which guarded one of the main entrances. This plain was the scene of some of the most important battles in Bible history (Jdg. 4; 1 Sam. 31; 2 Ki. 23:29). Later it became known as Esdraelon.

**Joab** (joh'ab). The name of several men in the OT, but especially of a great warrior who became DAVID's commander in chief (2 Sam. 8:16) and who figures prominently in the biblical narrative (e.g., 2:12–32; 3:22–30; 10:6–14; 14:1–33; 18:1–19:7; 20:4–22). Joab's mother was ZERUIAH (David's sister or half sister), and his brothers were the celebrated soldiers ABISHAI and ASAHEL (1 Chr. 2:16). Joab was very influential in David's reign but could also be cruel and treacherous (1 Ki. 2:5). Because he presented a threat to the reign of SOLOMON, the new king had him executed (2:28–35).

**Joash.** See JEHOASH.

**Job, Book of** (johb). One of the poetic books of the Bible, named after its main character, a godly man who was grievously tempted by SATAN but who refused to speak against God (Job 1:1–2:10). Most of the book is a discussion of suffering between Job and his

Job's wealth was measured by the livestock he owned.



friends, but in the end God reveals himself (chs. 38–41) and Job becomes prosperous again (ch. 42). Although the events seem to belong to the early patriarchal period, the book must have been written much later, possibly during the time of King SOLOMON.

The dialogue form of the writing is paralleled to an extent in Egyptian and Babylonian wisdom poetry, but it is distinctive in blending exquisite lyric and dramatic qualities within a narrative framework. The book does not reveal the why of the

## OVERVIEW OF JOB

**AUTHOR:** Anonymous. Possibly written by an otherwise unknown sage during the period of development of Wisdom Literature (i.e., the reign of SOLOMON or sometime after).

**HISTORICAL SETTING:** The story takes place in UZ, an uncertain desert region E of PALESTINE; the time appears to be roughly contemporary to that of the Hebrew PATRIARCHS, that is, early in the second millennium BC.

**PURPOSE:** To examine the value of conventional wisdom in dealing with the question, Why do the righteous suffer?

**CONTENTS:** SATAN tests Job, leading to an initial lament (Job 1–3); Job's friends debate the matter in three cycles of speeches (chs. 4–14; 15–21; 22–31), followed by ELIHU's discourse (chs. 32–37); God pronounces his own verdict (chs. 38–41), resulting in Job's repentance and restoration (ch. 42).

## OVERVIEW OF JOEL

**AUTHOR:** The prophet Joel, son of Pethuel.

**HISTORICAL SETTING:** Disputed, with proposals ranging from the late ninth to the third century BC; many recent scholars prefer dates between 600 and 400 BC.

**PURPOSE:** To warn the nation of JUDAH about the coming DAY OF THE LORD and to lead the people to REPENTANCE so they can enjoy the future blessings.

**CONTENTS:** The Lord's judgment on Judah (Joel 1:1–2:17); the Lord's pity on his people (2:18–32); the Lord's judgment on foreign nations and future blessings on his people (3:1–21).



particular sufferings of Job or any other believer, but it does present the servants of God with a framework for hope.

**Joel** (joh′uhl). The name of over a dozen men in the OT, but especially of a writing prophet. See JOEL, BOOK OF.

**Joel, Book of.** Second book among the Minor Prophets. No indication is given about the date either of the ministry of the prophet Joel or of the writing of the book, but a time shortly before the Babylonian EXILE is possible. The occasion was a devastating locust plague, and the prophet, after describing the resulting chaos, urges the nation to repent of its sins. The locust invasion, however, provided Joel with a catalyst for his message that a greater day of judgment, known as the DAY OF THE LORD, would come if God's people did not repent. This frequent theme of OT prophecy is here presented with emphasis on the outpouring of the Spirit of God that will begin that day (Joel 2:28–29; quoted by PETER in his sermon on the day of PENTECOST, Acts 2:14–21).

**John** (jon). **(1)** A son of ZEBEDEE; he was one of the original twelve disciples and brother of the apostle JAMES (Mk. 1:19–20; 3:17). John is thought to be the author of the gospel and epistles that bear his name, and also of the book of Revelation. He is probably "the disciple whom Jesus loved," a description found only in his gospel (Jn. 13:23; 19:26; 20:2; 21:7, 20). John, his brother James, and PETER were the three most prominent disciples (e.g., Matt. 17:1; Mk. 14:33). The early chapters of Acts focus on Peter and John (Acts 3–4; 8:14–25); PAUL refers to them, along with James, brother of Jesus, as "pillars" of the church (Gal. 2:9). **(2)** John the Baptist was the son of ZECHARIAH and ELIZABETH (Lk. 1:5–25, 57–80). As forerunner of the MESSIAH, he prepared the way for Jesus by preaching REPENTANCE and baptizing those who received his message (3:1–18). Soon after baptizing Jesus, John was arrested by Herod ANTIPAS and eventually decapitated (Mk. 6:14–29). Jesus spoke very highly of him (Matt. 11:7–15). **(3)** An early disciple better known as Mark. See MARK, JOHN. **(4)** The father of ANDREW and PETER (Jn. 1:42; 21:15–17; the KJV has "Jona" and "Jonas" respectively). **(5)** A relative of the high priests ANNAS and CAIAPHAS (Acts 4:6).

**John, Gospel of.** Also known as the "fourth gospel," this book gives a more theological description of Jesus than the Synoptic Gospels (MATTHEW, MARK, and LUKE). According to early Christian tradition, it was written by JOHN the apostle in EPHESUS sometime toward the close of the first century AD. The author says he wrote the book "that you may believe that Jesus is the Christ, the Son of God, and that by believing you may have life in his name" (Jn. 20:31). He introduces Jesus as the Word who is God, who created all things, and who took on human nature to save the world (Jn. 1:1–3, 12–14). The Gospel of John includes longer discourses by Jesus (e.g., 5:19–47; 6:35–51; 8:12–59; chs. 14–16), and about half of the book (chs. 13–21) is devoted to the last twenty-four hours of Jesus' life and to his resurrection.

**John, Letters of.** Three anonymous books from among the CATHOLIC EPISTLES in the NT that traditionally have been ascribed to JOHN the apostle. These letters suggest that an early form of GNOSTICISM was already in existence. The purpose of 1 John is to warn the readers against false teachers who are trying to mislead them and to exhort them to hold fast to the Christian faith they have received, fulfilling conscientiously the duties, especially brotherly LOVE, that flow from it. The letters we call 2 and 3 John are similar in words, style, ideas, and character to 1 John and must have been written by the same author, who refers to himself simply as "the elder." Both are very brief, containing just the number of words that could conveniently be written on one sheet. Second John is addressed to "the chosen lady and her children" (2 Jn. 1), probably a reference to a church and its members. Third John is addressed to Gaius, "my dear friend" (3 Jn. 1), who is commended for walking in the truth and being hospitable to evangelists sent, whereas a certain Diotrephes is censured for his overbearing conduct.

**Jonah, Book of.** Fifth book among the Minor Prophets. According to 2 Ki. 14:25, Jonah, son of Amittai, predicted the restoration of the land of ISRAEL to its ancient boundaries during the reign of JEROBOAM II in the eighth century BC. While the author of the book of Jonah is not identified, the likelihood is that the prophet himself wrote it not long after the events took place, in the latter part of Jeroboam's reign. In con-

## OVERVIEW OF GOSPEL OF JOHN

**AUTHOR:** Anonymous, but traditionally attributed to JOHN the apostle, son of Zebedee.

**HISTORICAL SETTING:** Covers the life of CHRIST from his baptism to his resurrection. According to early Christian writers, the book was written c. AD 90 from EPHESUS.

**PURPOSE:** To evoke FAITH in Jesus as the Christ (Jn. 20:30–31); possibly also to supplement the other Gospels by providing information not found in them and by presenting a different, more theological, perspective.

**CONTENTS:** After a prologue and introduction (Jn. 1), the author shows how Jesus revealed his glory to the world, only to be rejected (chs. 2–12); he then devotes the second half of the book to the last hours of Jesus' life, his death, and his resurrection (chs. 13–21).

J

## OVERVIEW OF 1 JOHN

**AUTHOR:** Anonymous, but traditionally attributed to JOHN the apostle, son of Zebedee.

**HISTORICAL SETTING:** Probably written toward the end of the first century, at a time when an incipient form of GNOSTICISM was influencing the Christian communities of Asia Minor.

**PURPOSE:** To counteract false teaching concerning CHRIST and the Christian life.

**CONTENTS:** Fellowship with God (1 Jn. 1:1–2:2); obeying Jesus' commandments and loving one another (2:3–3:24); acknowledging that Jesus is the Christ who has come in the flesh (ch. 4); victory and assurance (ch. 5).

## OVERVIEW OF 2–3 JOHN

**AUTHOR:** "The elder," traditionally understood to be JOHN the apostle, son of Zebedee.

**HISTORICAL SETTING:** Probably written toward the end of the first century, and addressed respectively to an unnamed woman (2 John) and to a Christian leader named Gaius (3 John).

**PURPOSE:** To warn against falsehood and to encourage hospitality to the true ministers of the gospel.

**CONTENTS:** Walking in the truth and avoiding false teachers (2 John). Commendation of Gaius, warning about Diotrephes, and encouragement to do what is good (3 John).

## OVERVIEW OF JONAH

**AUTHOR:** Anonymous, but probably composed by the main character of the book, the prophet Jonah, son of Amittai.

**HISTORICAL SETTING:** The events described take place during the height of the Assyrian empire, in the reign of JEROBOAM II of ISRAEL (c. 750 BC). The book was probably written soon after the events.

**PURPOSE:** To point out the stubbornness and excessive nationalism of the Israelites and to stress God's compassion for those outside Israel.

**CONTENTS:** Jonah flees from God's call (Jon. 1), prays in the belly of the fish (ch. 2), preaches in NINEVEH (ch. 3), and sulks before God (ch. 4).

trast to the other Minor Prophets, Jonah is mainly occupied with a narrative, describing the prophet's call to preach at NINEVEH, his disobedience, his experience in the belly of the fish, and the events in Nineveh. The purpose of the book is primarily to teach that God's gracious purposes are not limited to Israel but extend to the GENTILE world.

**Jonathan** (jon'uh-thun). The name of over a dozen men in the OT, but especially the firstborn son of King SAUL and heir apparent to the throne of ISRAEL (1 Sam. 14:49). Jonathan had great military qualities (see 13:1–2; 14:1–14) but is best remembered as the unselfish and loyal friend of DAVID (18:1–4; 19:1–7). Jonathan died with his father and brothers on Mount GILBOA in battle against the PHILISTINES (31:2).

**Joppa** (jop'uh). A coastal city c. 35 mi. (56 km.) NW of JERUSALEM; it served as the seaport for the Israelite capital (2 Chr. 2:16; Ezra 3:7; Jon. 1:3). In NT times PETER ministered there (Acts 9:36–43). The modern city, Jaffa, is a suburb of Tel Aviv.

**Joram** (jor'uhm). See JEHORAM.

**Jordan River** (jor'duhn). The major river of PALESTINE, which begins at Mount HERMON in the N, flows through the Sea of GALILEE, and ends at the DEAD SEA in the S. The distance from the Sea of Galilee to the Dead Sea is about 70 mi. (110 km.), but the river itself, because of its serpentine path, is 200 mi. (320 km.) long. The most significant single event relating to the Jordan River was its miraculous crossing by the Israelites on their way to conquer the land (Josh. 3). It was here also that Jesus was baptized by JOHN the Baptist (Matt. 3:13–17).

**Joseph** (joh'sif). The name of about a dozen men in the Bible, the most significant of whom are the following: **(1)** Son of JACOB and RACHEL (Gen. 30:22–24). He was the eleventh of Jacob's twelve sons, but the firstborn of Rachel. Joseph's life is the major focus of Gen. 37–50 (cf. Ps. 105:17–22; Acts 7:9–14; Heb. 11:22). Jealous of him, his brothers sold him into slavery. Although a man of integrity, he

Jesus may have been baptized near this area of the Jordan River. © Dario Bajurin/www.BigStockPhoto.com

J

## OVERVIEW OF JOSHUA

**AUTHOR:** Unknown.

**HISTORICAL SETTING:** Covers the period from the commissioning of Joshua to his death (either c. 1400–1380 or c. 1250–1230 BC, depending on the date of the EXODUS). Some believe that the book was written by an eyewitness (perhaps AARON's grandson PHINEHAS, Josh. 24:33) within a generation after the events it relates; others date its composition centuries later.

**PURPOSE:** To provide a historical-theological account of the conquest of CANAAN and the distribution of the land among the Israelite tribes; to show the fulfillment of God's promises and to encourage faithfulness to the COVENANT.

**CONTENTS:** Preparing to conquer the land (Josh. 1–5); the fall of JERICHO and AI (chs. 6–8); victory in the southern and northern territories (chs. 9–12); allotment of the land (chs. 13–22); covenant renewal and death of Joshua (chs. 23–24).



was put in prison, but because of his gift of dream interpretation, he became the second most powerful man in EGYPT and made it possible for his family to settle there. **(2)** Husband of MARY, mother of Jesus (Matt. 1:16). He was a carpenter (13:55) and "a righteous man" (1:19), and he received revelations in dreams in connection with the birth and early childhood of Jesus (1:19–25; 2:13–15, 19–21). **(3)** A rich man from the town of ARIMATHEA who was a Jewish official and who became a disciple of Jesus. After the crucifixion, he buried Jesus in his own new tomb (Matt. 27:57–60; Mk. 15:43–46; Lk. 23:50–53; Jn. 19:38–40).

**Joshua** (josh′*yoo*-uh). The name of several men in the OT, but especially the following: **(1)** The commander of the Israelites during the conquest of CANAAN. He first served in the wilderness as MOSES' assistant (Exod. 17:9–14; 24:13; 32:17); he and CALEB were the only two spies who believed the Israelites should move into Canaan (Num. 14:6–9, 30). When Moses died, Joshua succeeded him (Josh. 1:1–9), leading the nation across the JORDAN (ch. 3), conquering most of the land, and distributing it to the Israelite tribes. See JOSHUA, BOOK OF. **(2)** A high priest at the time of the return from BABYLON. He and ZERUBBABEL were exhorted to further the work of rebuilding the temple (Hag. 1:14; 2:2, 4). Joshua figures in the great prophecies regarding the "Branch" (Zech. 3; 6:11–13). In EZRA and NEHEMIAH he is called Jeshua (e.g., Ezra 3:2; Neh. 12:26).

**Joshua, Book of.** The first of the historical books of the OT. It relates the appointment of JOSHUA as successor to MOSES, the conquest of CANAAN, and the allotment of the land to the Israelite tribes. The author of the book is not identified, and the time of writing is uncertain (probably during the time of the JUDGES). The narrative begins with Joshua's inauguration (Josh. 1), the story of the JERICHO spies (ch. 2), the crossing of the JORDAN (ch. 3), and some ceremonies (chs. 4–5). The description of the conquest moves from the center to the S and then to the N (chs. 6–12). Israel's settlement includes the territorial apportionments at GILGAL (chs. 13–17) and SHILOH (chs. 18–19), including CITIES OF REFUGE and LEVITICAL CITIES (chs. 20–22). The account demonstrates how God "gave Israel all the land he had sworn to give their forefathers" (21:43).

**Josiah** (joh-*si*'uh). Son of AMON and king of JUDAH (2 Ki. 22–23; 2 Chr. 34–35). When palace officials murdered his father in 640 BC (2 Ki. 21:23), the eight-year-old succeeded him. Josiah's reign on the Davidic throne for thirty-one years was the last surge of political independence and religious revival before the disintegration of the southern kingdom that ended with the destruction of JERUSALEM in 586 BC. In the course of renovating the TEMPLE (622 BC), the Book of the Law was recovered, an event that gave greater impetus to the reformation movement (22:8–13). Josiah's leadership ranks him with JEHOSHAPHAT and HEZEKIAH (Josiah's great-grandfather) as an outstanding righteous ruler.

**jot** (jot). See YOD.

**Jotham** (joh'thuhm). **(1)** Youngest son of GIDEON (Jerub-Baal, Jdg. 9:5–21). **(2)** A descendant of JUDAH (1 Chr. 2:47); **(3)** Son of UZZIAH (Azariah) and king of the southern kingdom of JUDAH (2 Ki. 15:32–38; 2 Chr. 26:21–27:9). When his father was struck with leprosy, Jotham acted as coregent (c. 750 BC), and ten years later he became sole ruler upon Uzziah's death (c. 740), apparently about the time ISAIAH began his great ministry (Isa. 6:1). He enjoyed military victories and was a great builder.

**joy.** In the OT, feasting or offering SACRIFICE (Deut. 12:12; Isa. 56:7), celebration of HARVEST or victory (1 Sam. 18:6; Joel 1:16), and enjoying prosperity or personal triumph (Ps. 31:7; Isa. 61:3–4) are all occasions of joy. In the NT, the word is often found in connection with SALVATION (1 Pet. 1:6) but sometimes with suffering. When reviled or persecuted or lied about, the Christian is to "rejoice and be glad," knowing that this is traditionally part of the believer's portion (Matt. 5:11–12). Joy comes from the HOLY SPIRIT (Gal. 5:22).

**Jubilee.** According to Lev. 25, every fiftieth year in Israel was to be announced as a Jubilee Year. Three essential features characterized this year: (1) liberty was proclaimed to all Israelites who were in bondage to any of their countrymen; (2) there was to be a return of ancestral possessions to those who had been compelled to sell them because of poverty; (3) the land was to remain fallow, giving rest to the ground.

**Judah** (*joo*'duh). The name of several persons in the OT, but especially the fourth son of JACOB; his mother was LEAH (Gen. 29:35). In spite of some disgraceful actions (ch. 38), he seems to have enjoyed leadership among his brothers (37:26–28; 43:3; 46:28). Judah's descendants became a very important Hebrew tribe, from whom the

The beginning of the Jubilee Year was marked by the sounding of the shofar.

MESSIAH was to come (cf. 49:8–12; Heb. 7:14; Rev. 5:5). After the conquest of CANAAN, the tribe of Judah received a large territory S of JERUSALEM and played a significant role during the united kingdom under SAUL, DAVID, and SOLOMON. When Solomon died, the nation was divided into the northern kingdom of ISRAEL (consisting of ten tribes) and the southern kingdom of Judah (the remaining two tribes). The kingdom of Judah preserved the Davidic line in Jerusalem, but the city was destroyed by the Babylonians in 586 BC. When the exiles returned after 538, the area was a Persian province named JUDEA.

**Judaism.** Although this term can be used broadly of the Hebrew culture as a whole, it often refers to the religion of the Jews subsequent to the OT period (see Gal. 1:13–14 [KJV "the Jews' religion"]; cf. also 2:14). Postbiblical Judaism is based not only on the Hebrew Scriptures but also on important rabbinic writings, especially the Talmud.

**Judas** (*joo*′duhs). Greek form of Hebrew JUDAH; after the EXILE, it became a very common name. **(1)** Judas the Galilean, a Jewish rebel (Acts 5:37). **(2)** Judas the half brother of Jesus (Matt. 13:55; Mk. 6:3); he was probably the author of the letter of JUDE. **(3)** Judas the son (according to some, brother) of James, included among the twelve apostles (Lk. 6:16; Acts 1:13; Jn. 14:22); he may have been the same as THADDAEUS (Matt. 10:3; Mk. 3:18). **(4)** Judas Iscariot (possibly meaning "man of Kerioth"), the disciple who betrayed Jesus (Matt. 10:4). He was appointed treasurer for the disciples and apparently was greedy (Jn. 12:6; 13:29). He sold the Lord for thirty pieces of silver, betrayed him with a kiss, then in remorse threw down the money before the chief priests and elders (Matt. 27:3–10) and went out and committed suicide. **(5)** Judas of Damascus, an early Christian disciple (Acts 9:11). **(6)** Judas Barsabbas, a leader of the church in JERUSALEM (Acts 15:22, 27, 30–32); he was perhaps a brother of Joseph Barsabbas Justus (1:25).

**Jude, Letter of.** The last among the CATHOLIC EPISTLES. The opening verse describes the author as "Jude, a servant of Jesus Christ and a brother of James," probably the same person as JUDAS, brother of James and Jesus (Matt. 13:55; Mk. 6:3). In this letter, which is very similar to 2 Pet. 2, the author urges his readers "to contend for the faith that was once for all entrusted to the saints" (Jude 3) because of serious false teaching that threatens the churches from within. Using the most striking images (rainless clouds, blighted trees, wandering stars), Jude warns against those who pretend to piety but are rotten at heart and leave the trace of the mire behind them. He also exhorts Christians to continued perseverance.

**Judea** (joo-*dee*′uh). Also Judaea. Name used for the southern part of PALESTINE, especially after the end of the kingdom of JUDAH. Under the Persian empire, Judea was a district administered by a governor who was usually a Jew (Hag. 1:14; 2:2). Under Rome, it was first ruled by HEROD the Great, then briefly by his son ARCHELAUS, and then by Roman governors (except for a few years under Herod AGRIPPA I).

**Judges, Book of.** The seventh book of the OT. The book takes its name from the title of those who ruled Israel during the period from JOSHUA to SAMUEL; in this context the term really means "leader" or "ruler." The principal function of the Hebrew "judges" during this period was that of military deliverers. The book makes no clear claim to authorship or date of composition. The purposes of the book of Judges are (1) to bridge in some manner the historical gap between the death of Joshua and the inauguration of the monarchy; (2) to show the moral and political degradation of a people who neglected their religious heritage and compromised their faith with the surrounding paganism; (3) to show the need of the people for the unity and leadership

## OVERVIEW OF JUDE

**AUTHOR:** Jude, brother of JAMES (prob. referring to the half brother of Jesus).

**HISTORICAL SETTING:** The date, place of writing, and destination are unknown, but the addressees (possibly Jewish Christians of the Dispersion) were being challenged by heretical and immoral people. Some scholars speculate that the letter was written in the early 60s; others prefer a date near the end of the century.

**PURPOSE:** To urge the readers "to contend for the faith" (Jude 1), opposing false doctrine and immorality.

**CONTENTS:** After the introduction (Jude 1–4), the bulk of this brief letter consists of a denunciation of the false teachers (vv. 5–19), followed by positive exhortations and a doxology (vv. 20–25).

## OVERVIEW OF JUDGES

**AUTHOR:** Unknown.

**HISTORICAL SETTING:** Covers the period from the death of JOSHUA (c. 1380 or 1230 BC, depending on the date of the EXODUS) to the generation that preceded the monarchy (c. 1050 BC). The book itself may have been composed soon after the end of that period (a Jewish tradition attributed it to SAMUEL), but many scholars date it several centuries later.

**PURPOSE:** To provide a historical-theological account of the chaotic times following the Israelite occupation of CANAAN, and thus to show the nation's need for the centralized rule of a king.

**CONTENTS:** After a prologue (Jdg. 1:1–2:5) and a summary of the cycles of sin and deliverance (2:5–3:6), the book describes the work of twelve "judges" or leaders, with emphasis on DEBORAH, GIDEON, JEPHTHAH, and SAMSON (3:7–16:31), followed by an account of two shocking stories of religious and moral degeneration (chs. 17–21).

by a strong central government in the person of a king.

**judgment.** This term can refer to a human opinion or legal decision, but more often it indicates either a calamity regarded as sent by God for PUNISHMENT or a sentence of God as the Judge of all (e.g., Exod. 12:12; Ps. 76:8; Isa. 66:16). Judgment is an aspect of the deliverance of believers (Lk. 18:1–8; 2 Thess. 1:5–10; Rev. 6:10). God will entrust the final judgment to his Son at his appearance in glory (Matt. 3:11–12; Jn. 5:22; Rom. 2:16). Although Christians are free from condemnation (Rom. 8:1), they will "appear before the judgment seat of Christ, that each one may receive what is due him for the things done while in the body, whether good or bad" (2 Cor. 5:10; cf. Rom. 14:10; 1 Cor. 3:13–15).

**Jupiter.** See ZEUS.

**just, justice.** See RIGHTEOUSNESS.

**justification.** In Christian theology this term refers to an act of God as Judge by which he declares the sinner absolved from SIN, released from its penalty, and restored as righteous. On the basis of Christ's sacrificial death (see ATONEMENT), those who exercise FAITH receive the RIGHTEOUSNESS of Christ and so are placed by God in a right relationship with himself (see IMPUTATION). The doctrine is set forth in PAUL's letters, especially Rom. 3:21–26; 4:6–8; 5:18–19; 8:33–34; 2 Cor. 5:19–21; Gal. 3:6–14; Phil. 3:8–9.

# K

**Kadesh Barnea** (kay´dish-bahr′nee-uh). Also known simply as Kadesh; a site in the N of SINAI, c. 50 mi. (80 km.) SW of BEERSHEBA. Shortly after the EXODUS, the Israelites camped in this wilderness area (Deut. 1:19), where MIRIAM died (Num. 20:1), and there they stayed "many days" (Deut. 1:46). After the conquest of CANAAN, Kadesh Barnea was regarded as the S border of Judah (Josh. 15:3).

**kaph** (kaf). The eleventh letter of the Hebrew alphabet (כ, transliterated as *k*), used to begin each verse in Ps. 119:81–88.

**Kebar** (kee′bahr). Also Chebar. An artificial watercourse in BABYLON; NEBUCHADNEZZAR settled a colony of Jewish exiles on its banks, and EZEKIEL saw his earlier visions as he ministered here (Ezek. 1:1, 3, etc.).

**Kedar** (kee′duhr). Son of ISHMAEL and grandson of ABRAHAM (Gen. 25:13; 1 Chr. 1:29); probably the ancestor of an Arabian tribe mentioned in the OT (e.g., Ps. 120:5; Isa. 42:11; Jer. 49:28–29).

**Kedesh** (kee′dish). The name of several cities, the most prominent of which was in GALILEE, within the tribal territory of NAPHTALI; it became one of the CITIES OF REFUGE and was also one of the LEVITICAL CITIES (Josh. 12:22; 19:37; 20:7).

**Kedorlaomer**. Also Chedorlaomer. King of ELAM and leader of a coalition that sacked SODOM and GOMORRAH when these cities revolted after a period of submission; the coalition was defeated by ABRAHAM (Gen. 14:1–7).

**Keilah** (kee-*i*′luh). A town allotted to the tribe of JUDAH, c. 17 mi. (27 km.) SW of JERUSALEM (Josh. 15:44). DAVID led a daring expedition to Keilah to deliver it from attacks by the PHILISTINES (1 Sam. 23:1–13).

**Kenite** (ken′*i*t). Clan or tribal name of some loosely related groups in S PALESTINE and SINAI (Gen. 15:19; Num. 24:21–22; 1 Sam. 15:6); the meaning of the name suggests that they were known as metalworkers. MOSES' father-in-law is identified as a Kenite in Jdg. 1:16.

**Kerethite** (ker′uh-th*i*t). Also Cherethite. The name of a people group (possibly related to the PHILISTINES) that may have come to PALESTINE from CRETE; DAVID chose his personal guard from the Kerethites and the PELETHITES (1 Sam. 30:14; 2 Sam. 8:18; etc.).

Region S of Hebron where the Kenites lived. 

This stone slab depicts the Assyrian king Ashurbanipal (7th cent. BC). 

**Keturah** (ki-ty*oo*′ruh). Wife of ABRAHAM, apparently after the death of SARAH (Gen. 25:1, 4; called a CONCUBINE in 1 Chr. 1:32–33).

**Kidron** (kid′ruhn). A valley E of JERUSALEM c. 3 mi. (5 km.) in length, lying between the walls of the city and the Mount of Olives (see OLIVES, MOUNT OF). See 2 Sam. 15:23; 1 Ki. 2:37; 2 Ki. 23:4; Jn. 18:1 [KJV Cedron]). During the short wet season in the winter, a torrent would run through it.

**kindness.** Generosity, friendliness, good will, tenderness; the word can also refer to a particular instance of kind behavior. Kindness is both an attribute of God (Tit. 3:4) and a characteristic of true LOVE (1 Cor. 13:4). God's kindness is great (Joel 2:13; Jon. 4:2) and everlasting (Isa. 54:8, 10). God's people are exhorted to possess this trait (Col. 3:12; 2 Pet. 1:7). See also GOOD; GRACE; LOVING-KINDNESS; MERCY.

## OVERVIEW OF 1–2 KINGS

**AUTHOR:** Unknown.

**HISTORICAL SETTING:** Covers the period from the death of DAVID (c. 970 BC) to the fall of JERUSALEM (586 BC). The work was probably completed during the period of Babylonian EXILE, around the middle of the sixth century BC.

**PURPOSE:** To provide a historical-theological account of the reign of SOLOMON, the division of the kingdom, and the decline of both ISRAEL and JUDAH; to show that the exile was a righteous divine judgment; and to bring the nation back to REPENTANCE.

**CONTENTS:** The transition from David to Solomon (1 Ki. 1:1–2:12); consolidation of Solomon's rule and evidence of his wisdom (1 Ki. 2:13–4:34); the building of the TEMPLE (1 Ki. 5:1–9:25); international involvements and decline of Solomon's reign (1 Ki. 9:26–11:43); division of the kingdom—REHOBOAM and JEROBOAM (1 Ki. 12–14); various kings of Judah and Israel, with emphasis on King AHAB and the prophet ELIJAH (1 Ki. 15:1–2 Ki. 1:18); decline and fall of Israel, with emphasis on the prophet ELISHA, and with attention to the kings of Judah (2 Ki. 2:1–17:41); from HEZEKIAH of Judah to the exile (2 Ki. 18:1–25:30).

**king.** A male ruler of a city, tribe, or nation; usually a hereditary position. In the ancient Near East, kings came to be regarded as divine beings. After the Israelites conquered CANAAN, they had no king for a long period (Jdg. 17:6), but toward the end of SAMUEL's judgeship, the nation demanded a king "such as all the other nations have" (1 Sam. 8:5; cf. Deut. 17:14–15). The first kings were SAUL (1 Sam. 12–31), DAVID (2 Sam. 1 to 1 Ki. 1), and SOLOMON (1 Ki. 1–11); then the kingdom was divided (see ISRAEL; JUDAH). The prophets speak of a messianic king (Isa. 32:1; Jer. 23:5; Zech. 9:9), and the Lord himself is identified as the King (Isa. 33:22; Jer. 10:7; Zech. 14:9). The NT describes Jesus as "king of the Jews" (Matt. 2:2) and as "King of kings" (Rev. 17:14; 19:16). See also KINGDOM OF GOD.

**kingdom of God (of heaven).** This phrase refers primarily not to a realm or territory but to the divine reign or rule (kingship). Although some biblical passages speak of people "entering" the kingdom of God or the like (e.g., Matt. 21:31; Col. 1:13), the emphasis is on a dynamic force manifested in Christ to destroy his (spiritual) enemies and to bring to men and women the blessings of God's reign. Jesus claimed that his ability to cast out DEMONS was evidence that the kingdom of God had come among people to break SATAN's power (Matt. 12:28–29; cf. 1 Cor. 15:24–26). The nature of God's kingdom is illustrated by many of Jesus' PARABLES (especially in Matt. 13).

**Kings, Books of.** These books cover almost four hundred years of Israelite kings, from SOLOMON in the tenth century BC to JEHOIACHIN in the sixth. They thus provide a sequel to the books of SAMUEL, which cover the reigns of SAUL and DAVID. Though regarded as "historical books" in the English Bible, the books of Samuel and Kings possess an essentially prophetic character, employing the events of past history as a vehicle for contemporary preaching (cf. Dan. 9:6). Thus, the author of Kings drove home lessons, born of previous disasters, because the Israelites "had not obeyed the LORD their God" (2 Ki. 18:12).

King's highway.

**king's highway.** An important road running N–S from DAMASCUS to the Gulf of Aqabah; it was located E of the DEAD SEA and the JORDAN Valley. MOSES requested permission to use this route for passing through foreign territories, promising to keep strictly to the highway (Num. 20:17; 21:22; cf. Deut. 2:27).

K

**Kinnereth** (kin'uh-reth). Also Chinnereth. **(1)** A fortified town on the NW shore of the Sea of GALILEE, within the tribal territory of NAPHTALI (Josh. 19:35). The small plain in that area is referred to as GENNESARET in the NT (Matt. 14:34; Mk. 6:53). **(2)** The Sea of Kinnereth is an old name applied to the Sea of Galilee (Num. 34:11). See GALILEE, SEA OF.

**Kiriath Jearim** (kihr'ee-ath-jee'uh-rim). KJV Kirjath-jearim. A city of the Gibeonites that was later on the border between the tribes of JUDAH and BENJAMIN (Josh. 9:17; 15:9), 8.5 mi. (13.5 km.) WNW of JERUSALEM. When the ARK of the covenant was returned by the PHILISTINES, the people of BETH SHEMESH brought it to Kiriath Jearim (1 Sam. 6:21; 7:1–2); it remained there twenty years until DAVID brought it up to Jerusalem (1 Chr. 13:5–6; 2 Chr. 1:4).

**Kish** (kish). The name of several men in the OT, especially the father of Israel's first king, SAUL (1 Sam. 9:1–3).

**Kishon** (ki'shon). A river that drains the Valley of JEZREEL E to NW; it is mentioned in connection with DEBORAH (Jdg. 4:7, 13; 5:21; Ps. 83:9) and ELIJAH (1 Ki. 18:40).

**knowledge.** Truth or information acquired through experience and education. The Bible frequently commends knowledge and WISDOM (1 Sam. 2:3; Ps. 14:4; 119:66; Prov. 8:10; Isa. 53:11; Jn. 8:32; 1 Cor. 13:12; Col. 1:9; 1 Jn. 5:20). The verb *to know* can be used in special senses. When Ps. 1:6 says that "the LORD knows the way of the righteous, but the way of the wicked will perish" (RSV), the word is used to indicate approval (cf. NIV "watches over"). Similarly, when Amos 3:2 says, "You only have I known of all the families of the earth" (RSV), the prophet is not denying that God knew the Egyptians and Canaanites; here the verb means "to choose, elect" (cf. NIV). See also GNOSTICISM; TREE OF KNOWLEDGE; WISDOM.

**Kohath** (koh'hath). Second son of LEVI (Gen. 46:11; Exod. 6:16) and grandfather of MOSES (6:18–20). His descendants, the Kohathites, were the most prominent of the Levitical families (Num. 3:30–31; 7:9; Josh. 21:4–5; 1 Chr. 23:13–20; 24:20–25; 2 Chr. 20:19; 29:12–19).

**Korah** (kor'uh). The name of several men in the OT, especially a grandson of KOHATH (Exod. 6:21, 24). Korah, with 250 leaders of the congregation, rose up against MOSES and AARON, charging them with exalting themselves above the assembly of the Lord (Num. 16:1–3). Judgment fell upon Korah and others because of their rebellion (16:20–35; cf. Jude 11 [KJV Core]).

**Korazin** (kor-ay'zin). Also Chorazin. A town situated near the Sea of GALILEE, mentioned in the Bible in only one context, when Jesus denounced its inhabitants for their sin (Matt. 11:21 = Lk. 10:13).

# L

**Laban** (lay′buhn). The nephew of ABRAHAM and brother of REBEKAH (Gen. 24:29; cf. v. 15). Laban had two daughters, LEAH and RACHEL, and through his trickery both of them became wives of JACOB, Rebekah's son (29:16–28). Laban evidently took advantage of Jacob in other ways as well (cf. 31:41), but they settled their differences through a covenant (31:44–54).

**Lachish** (lay′kish). A town in the western foothills of JUDAH, some 30 mi. (50 km.) SW of JERUSALEM (Josh. 10:31–32; 15:39). Lachish is mentioned a number of times in the OT (e.g., 2 Ki. 14:19; 18:14; 2 Chr. 25:27); it was one of the last towns to fall to NEBUCHADNEZZAR (Jer. 34:7). Archaeologists have discovered letters written on broken pieces of pottery (ostraca) shortly before its destruction.

**Laish** (lay′ish). See DAN.

The Lachish Letters, written on broken pieces of pottery, shed light on the unsettled conditions in Judah when the Babylonians attacked the country in 586 BC.

Doug Bookman/www.BiblePlaces.com

**lamb.** The principal animal of SACRIFICE among the Jews, being the offering each morning and each evening (Exod. 29:38–42) and especially at the Passover (see FEASTS). The lamb represented innocence and gentleness (Ps. 23; Isa. 11:6; 40:11), and it became a symbol of the suffering of the MESSIAH (Isa. 53:7; Acts 8:32). Jesus was called the Lamb of God by JOHN the Baptist (Jn. 1:29, 36) because he was sacrificed for the sins of the world (cf. 1 Cor. 5:7). Jesus is frequently called the Lamb in Revelation (e.g., Rev. 5:6, 12–13; 7:9–10; 15:3; 19:7–9; 22:1).

**Lamech** (lay′mik). **(1)** Son of METHUSHAEL and descendant of CAIN; he was an arrogant man and the first polygamist (Gen. 4:18–24). **(2)** Son of METHUSELAH, descendant of SETH, and father of NOAH (Gen. 5:25–31).

**lamed** (lah′mid). The twelfth letter of the Hebrew alphabet (ל, transliterated as *l*), used to begin each verse in Ps. 119:89–96.

**Lamentations, Book of.** A short book consisting of five poems that bemoan the desolation that had overtaken JERUSALEM in 586 BC. The author makes poignant confession of SIN on behalf of the people and their leaders, acknowledges complete submission to the divine will, and prays that God will once again favor and restore his people. Although in the Hebrew no person's name was attached to the book, the authorship was uniformly ascribed by the ancients to JEREMIAH.

**lampstand.** The Hebrew word *menorah*, although rendered "candlestick" in the

## OVERVIEW OF LAMENTATIONS

**AUTHOR:** Anonymous, though traditionally attributed to the prophet JEREMIAH.

**HISTORICAL SETTING:** Probably written during the Babylonian EXILE, thus sometime between the fall of JERUSALEM (586 BC) and the fall of BABYLON to the Persians (538 BC).

**PURPOSE:** To express deep sorrow over the end of the theocracy and the destruction of Jerusalem and the TEMPLE; to urge confession for sin and REPENTANCE.

**CONTENTS:** The book consists of five poems: Zion's devastation (Lam. 1); the anger of the Lord (ch. 2); despair and consolation (ch. 3); horrors of the destruction (ch. 4); prayer for restoration (ch. 5).

KJV, refers to an object that did not have candles but rather seven branches holding seven olive-oil lamps made of gold (described in Exod. 25:31–40). In the TEMPLE that SOLOMON built, ten lampstands of gold were placed in front of the Most Holy Place (1 Ki. 7:49). In the book of Revelation, seven lampstands represent the seven churches (e.g., Rev. 1:20).

**Land, Holy.** See PALESTINE.

**Laodicea**. A wealthy city in the province of ASIA. The Christian church in this city evidently had a close connection with the one in COLOSSE (Col. 2:1; 4:13–16). It is one of the seven churches mentioned in Revelation (Rev. 1:4; 3:14).

**lasciviousness.** This English term, meaning "lust, overt sexual desire," is used by the KJV in a number of passages (e.g., 2 Cor. 12:21; NIV "debauchery"; NRSV "licentiousness").

**Last Supper.** See LORD'S SUPPER.

**Latin.** The official language of the Roman empire (see ROME). The inscription on the CROSS of Christ was written in Latin, GREEK, and HEBREW or ARAMAIC (Jn. 19:20). Many Latin names, such as PAUL (*Paulus*), are found in the NT.

**law.** This English term most commonly means "a rule of conduct" or "commandment" (see COMMANDMENTS, TEN), and it often refers specifically to the COVENANT established by God through MOSES at SINAI. More generally, it can refer to the PENTATEUCH, the first five books of the OT. But the primary Hebrew word for "law," *torah*, has an even broader meaning, namely, "guidance, instruction, teaching," whether human (Prov. 1:8b) or divine (Isa. 1:10; cf. TNIV and NRSV).

**lawyer.** An expert in the law (e.g., Matt. 22:35 KJV). See SCRIBE.

**laying on of hands.** A ceremony used for various purposes. It can symbolize (1) the bestowal of authority (Num. 27:18; Acts 6:6); (2) the substitution of an animal for a person's guilt (Exod. 29:10); or (3) the reception of a blessing or a gift (Matt. 19:13; Acts 8:17).

**Lazarus** (laz'uh-ruhs). **(1)** The brother of MARTHA and MARY, who lived in BETHANY and who was raised from death by Jesus (Jn. 11:1–12:19). **(2)** The name of a beggar in a parable of Jesus (Lk. 16:19–31).

**Leah** (lee'uh). Eldest daughter of LABAN and first wife of JACOB (Gen. 29:16). Leah is described as "tender eyed" (29:17 KJV), which may mean that she did not have a positive appearance (cf. NIV "weak"). She gave birth to REUBEN, SIMEON, LEVI, JUDAH, ISSACHAR, ZEBULUN, and DINAH (29:31–35; 30:17–21).

**leaven.** A general term for substances that produce fermentation and cause dough to rise; it usually refers to yeast (the term used consistently by the NIV). Bread made in haste without allowing it to rise is the UNLEAVENED BREAD often mentioned in Scripture, especially in connection with the EXODUS and Passover (Exod. 12:11–15, 39; Deut. 16:3). Leaven is used as a symbol of power, either good or evil (Matt. 16:6, 11–12; 13:33; Lk. 13:21; 1 Cor. 5:6–8).

**Lebanon** (leb'uh-nuhn). A mountainous region in PHOENICIA just inland from the coast (Josh. 9:1; Jdg. 3:3). Its area corresponds roughly to that of the modern state of Lebanon. Ancient Lebanon was heavily forested with varieties of budding foliage (Ps. 72:16; Isa. 29:17; Nah. 1:4) and, above all, the great cedars of Lebanon (1 Ki. 4:33; Cant. 3:6–9). King SOLOMON contracted with HIRAM of TYRE for the use of Lebanon's cedars in the Jerusalem TEMPLE (1 Ki. 5:6–18).

**Lebbaeus** (li-bee'uhs). See THADDAEUS.

**Lebo Hamath** (lee'boh-hay'muth). A place on the S border of the territory controlled by HAMATH, regarded in the OT as the ideal N border of the Promised Land of Israel (Num. 34:7–8; 1 Ki. 8:65; 2 Ki. 14:25; Ezek. 47:15–20). The KJV renders it "the entrance of Hamath," but Lebo Hamath was probably the actual name of a particular region or city.

**lees.** A term used by the KJV and other versions for the dregs that settle at the bottom of wine jars and wineskins (Isa. 25:6 [NIV "aged wine"]; Jer. 48:11; Zeph. 1:12).

**legion.** The major unit in the Roman army, consisting of several thousand soldiers. In the NT the word, representing a vast number, is used only in the Gospels and with reference to ANGELS and DEMONS (Matt. 26:53; Mk. 5:9, 15; Lk. 8:30).

**Lemuel** (lem'yoo-uhl). A king who wrote Prov. 31, passing on his mother's teachings on various topics. Nothing else is known about him.

**leper, leprosy.** The KJV (see especially Lev. 13) uses this English term to translate a Hebrew word that refers to various diseases of the skin (including some that required isolation), but probably not the affliction that today we call *leprosy*, also known as Hansen's disease. It is uncertain whether this disease is meant in the NT references to leprosy (e.g., Mk. 1:40–42).

**Leshem** (lee'shem). See DAN.

**letter.** (1) A written message. In OT times (e.g., 2 Chr. 30:1; Neh. 2:7–9) an official communication was usually written on a small tablet with a clay envelope. Even before NT times, however, it also became common to use the stalk from a PAPYRUS plant (2 Jn. 12,

This small clay tablet is one of the famous Tell el-Amarna letters (c. 1350 BC), which provide much information about the social and political situation in Canaan. © Kim Walton

L

Reconstruction of the altar of incense, an important element of Hebrew worship. Todd Bolen/www.BiblePlaces.com

usually translated "paper"). See also EPISTLE. (2) A unit of the alphabet, that is, a written character (Gal. 6:11). (3) In Rom. 2:27–29, "letter" (KJV) refers to the written LAW.

**Levi** (lee′vi). The name of two ancestors of Jesus (Lk. 3:24, 29) and of the following prominent men: **(1)** Third son of JACOB and LEAH and ancestor of the tribe bearing his name (Gen. 29:34; 35:23; Exod. 1:2; 1 Chr. 2:1). His sons were GERSHON, KOHATH, and MERARI. See LEVITE; LEVITICAL CITIES. **(2)** A TAX COLLECTOR (publican) who later became one of the twelve apostles (Mk. 2:14–17; Lk. 5:27–32). See MATTHEW.

**Leviathan** (li-vi′uh-thuhn). The name of a sea creature used only in poetic imagery. In Job 41:1 and Ps. 104:26, it possibly refers to a crocodile. Elsewhere it seems to symbolize chaotic or evil forces (Job 3:8; Ps. 74:14; Isa. 27:1). See also RAHAB.

**Levite** (lee′vit). The name given to the descendants of LEVI son of JACOB. Within the tribe of Levi, AARON and his descendants were chosen to be PRIESTS. Because non-Aaronic Levites were assigned as priestly assistants (Num. 3:6–10; cf. also vv. 45–51), the name *Levite* took on an additional sense roughly equivalent to "minister." The tribe of Levi was not given a portion of the Promised Land. See LEVITICAL CITIES.

**Levitical cities.** Because the tribe of LEVI did not receive any part of the land of CANAAN as an INHERITANCE (Num. 18:20; Deut. 10:8–9), forty-eight cities, four each from the other tribes, were allotted to the LEVITES (Num. 35:1–8; Josh. 21). They also received the TITHES of Israelites for their support (Num. 18:21; Deut. 18:1–2). Thirteen of the cities, all within the tribe of JUDAH, were given to the PRIESTS (Josh. 21:4), and another six were CITIES OF REFUGE.

**Leviticus, Book of** (li-vit′i-kuhs). The third book of the Bible, one of the five books of MOSES (the PENTATEUCH or TORAH). Leviticus is closely associated with EXODUS and NUMBERS but differs from them in that the historical element is subordinate to legal and ritual considerations. The book is intended primarily to instruct the PRIESTS in the conduct of WORSHIP and the regulating of social life. The first seven chapters give the detailed sacrificial procedures showing how the various kinds of burnt offerings, the meal offering, the sin and guilt offerings, and other SACRIFICES avail for the removal of sin and defilement under the COVENANT. Other topics treated in the book include the consecration of AARON and the priesthood, the ritual of the Day of ATONEMENT, the consecration of seasons, and others. Human SIN, substitutionary atonement, and divine HOLINESS are prominent themes throughout Leviticus.

**Libya** (lib′ee-uh). A country in N AFRICA just W of EGYPT. Libyans (KJV "Lubim") are mentioned several times in the OT (2 Chr. 12:3; 16:8; Nah. 3:9), and visitors from "the parts of Libya near Cyrene" were present in JERUSALEM at PENTECOST (Acts 2:10). See CYRENE.

**lie.** A false or misleading statement intended to deceive someone. Since God is TRUTH and truthful, he cannot lie as humans do (Num. 23:19). In the LAW of Moses there are laws against bearing false witness (Exod. 20:16) and perjury (Lev. 19:12), and there is the general command, "Do not lie" (19:11). Referring to IDOLATRY, PAUL says that the people of the world "exchanged the truth of God for a lie" (Rom. 1:25). Within the churches there are those who make God a liar by claiming they are not sinners (1 Jn. 1:10). The source of lies is the DEVIL (Jn. 8:44; Acts 5:3). Christians must not lie to one another (Eph. 4:25; Col. 3:9). See TRUTH.

**life.** The Bible often speaks of physical or natural life, whether animal (Gen. 1:20; 6:17; Rev. 8:9) or human (Lev. 17:14; Matt. 2:20; Lk. 12:22). The unlawful taking of human life is prohibited (Gen. 9:5; Exod. 20:13; Lev. 24:17). But the primary concern of the Scriptures is ETERNAL life for the human race. It is the gift of God, mediated through FAITH in Jesus CHRIST (Jn. 3:36; 5:24; Rom. 6:23; 1 Jn. 5:11–12). It involves the impartation of a new nature (2 Pet. 1:3–4) and is not interrupted by physical death (1 Thess. 5:10).

**life, book of.** This figurative NT expression (Rev. 3:5; 13:8; 21:27; cf. also Phil. 4:3) is based on OT references to God's book in which were written the names of the righteous (Exod. 32:32; Ps. 69:28). To be in the book of life is ground for the certainty of SALVATION. Not to be found in the book of life (Rev. 17:8; 20:15) means separation from God and perdition.

**life, tree of.** See TREE OF KNOWLEDGE, TREE OF LIFE.

**light.** God is the creator of light and watches over the orderly succession of light and DARKNESS (Gen. 1:3–5; Ps. 104:20; Isa. 45:6–7; Amos 4:13). TRUTH and LAW give the light of knowledge (Ps. 19:8; 139:11–12). God is described as "the Father of the heavenly lights" (Jas. 1:17), he who

L

## OVERVIEW OF LEVITICUS

**AUTHOR:** Anonymous, but comments elsewhere in the Bible seem to support the traditional view that MOSES is responsible for the PENTATEUCH as a whole.

**HISTORICAL SETTING:** The initial composition of the book must have taken place during the wilderness wanderings (either late in the fifteenth or early in the thirteenth cent. BC).

**PURPOSE:** To provide details of the laws that were to govern God's people, with emphasis on sacrificial requirements and ritual cleanness; to impress upon the people the need for HOLINESS.

**CONTENTS:** The laws of SACRIFICE (Lev. 1–7); the consecration of the PRIESTS (chs. 8–10); ceremonial purity (chs. 11–16); the ways of holiness (chs. 17–27).

dwells in light (Exod. 13:21; Ps. 104:2; 1 Tim. 6:16). Conversion is spoken of as enlightenment (Heb. 6:4; 10:32). Believers are "people of the light" (Lk. 16:8; 1 Thess. 5:5) and the "light of the world" (Matt. 5:14). In the new age there will be no more night (Rev. 21:23).

**Lod, Lydda** (lod, lid′uh). Lod, situated c. 11 mi. (18 km.) SE of JOPPA, was one of the towns to which the Jews returned after the EXILE (Ezra 2:33; Neh. 7:37; 11:35). After the OT period it came to be known as Lydda; PETER cured a man with palsy there (Acts 9:32–35).

**Logos** (loh′gohs). See WORD.

**loins.** The part of the body between the ribs and the hip bones, but the word can refer also to the lower abdomen and the reproductive organs. In some passages where the KJV uses this term, modern English would prefer "waist" (e.g., 2 Ki. 1:8; Jer. 13:1; Matt. 3:4). Since long garments were normally worn loose, to gird up the loins (by tucking the robe under a belt) signified preparation for vigorous action (Exod. 12:11; 1 Ki. 18:46; Job 38:3; Prov. 31:17; Lk. 12:35; 1 Pet. 1:13). To have the loins girded with truth indicates strength in attachment to truth (Eph. 6:14; cf. Isa. 11:5).

**Lois** (loh′is). The grandmother of TIMOTHY, a woman of unpretending faith; she was probably the mother of Timothy's mother, EUNICE (2 Tim. 1:5).

**lord.** As a title of men, *lord* can mean simply "master" or "sir," but it is especially applied to governmental, religious, and military officials. For its use as a divine title in the OT, see JEHOVAH. In the NT it is the supreme title given to CHRIST. "Jesus is Lord" was perhaps the earliest creedal statement formulated and recited by the early Christians (Rom. 10:9; 1 Cor. 12:3; 16:22; Phil. 2:9–11). By that title they intended to identify Jesus with the God of the OT. This intent is seen most clearly in those NT passages where OT texts originally referring to Yahweh are now boldly quoted as referring to Jesus (Rom. 10:13; Heb. 1:10; 1 Pet. 2:3; 3:15).

**Lord's Prayer.** The traditional name given to the prayer Jesus taught his disciples, as recorded in Matt. 6:9–13 and, more briefly, in Lk. 11:2–4. It directs believers, as members of God's family, reverently to pray to a personal heavenly Father, to place his interests first, and then to pray for their own needs.

**Lord's Supper.** This expression is found only once in the NT (1 Cor. 11:20); it is also called the "Lord's table" (10:21), while the expression "breaking of bread," which occurs several times in Acts, probably also refers to the Lord's Supper. The institution of this ceremony is described in four passages (Matt. 26:26–29; Mk. 14:22–25; Lk. 22:15–20; 1 Cor. 11:23–25). Believers continue to celebrate the Lord's Supper (1) in remembrance of Jesus' atoning death and (2) in expectation of the arrival of the kingdom of God in its fullness.

**Lot** (lot). Son of HARAN and nephew of ABRAHAM (Gen. 11:27). Lot followed Abraham in his journeys from MESOPOTAMIA to CANAAN, thence to EGYPT, and back again to Canaan (12:5, 10; 13:1). Because of a conflict between their herdsmen, Abraham suggested that his nephew choose another place, and Lot chose the country in the environs of a sinful city, SODOM (13:5–13). This fatal choice determined his subsequent destiny (cf. 14:12), including the destruction of his wife, who was turned into a pillar of salt (ch. 19). Nevertheless, the NT describes him as "a righteous man" (2 Pet. 2:7–8).

**lots.** Objects (such as stones of various sizes) used for making a choice. The casting of lots is often mentioned in the OT as a means of determining the will of God (e.g., Lev. 16:7–10, 21–22; Josh. 7:14; 14:2; 1 Sam. 14:42; 1 Chr. 25:7–8; Neh. 10:34; once in the NT, Acts 1:26), but the specific method used is not clearly defined. See also PURIM; URIM AND THUMMIM.

**love.** Love is presented in Scripture as the very nature of God (1 Jn. 4:8, 16) and the greatest of the Christian virtues (1 Cor. 13:13). It is described positively with such concepts as patience, kindness, protection, and trust; negatively, by saying that love, for example, is not envious, boastful, self-seeking, or easily angered (13:4–7). Jesus taught that it is essential in our relationship to God and to others (Matt. 22:37–40; Mk. 12:28–31; Jn. 13:34–35). Love is the fulfillment of the LAW, for its sense of obligation and desire for the welfare of the one loved impels it to carry out the demands of the law (Rom. 13:8–10). Love found its supreme expression in Jesus' self-sacrifice on Calvary (1 Jn. 4:10).

**love feast.** See AGAPE.

**lovingkindness.** This term, rarely found in modern versions, is used often by the KJV, especially in the Psalms, to render a Hebrew word that refers to God's faithful, kind, and merciful LOVE (NRSV "steadfast love"; e.g., Ps. 17:7; 26:3; 89:33).

**Lubim.** See LIBYA.

**Lucifer** (*loo*'si-fuhr). KJV rendering of a Hebrew word that occurs only once in reference to the proud king of BABYLON (Isa. 14:12). The Latin word *lucifer* means "light-bringing" and is applied to the MORNING STAR, that is, Venus. Some early Christians associated this OT passage with Lk. 10:18 (cf. also 2 Cor. 11:14), applied the name to SATAN, and this usage became common.

**Lucius** (*loo*'shuhs). **(1)** A Christian from CYRENE, named third among the five "prophets and teachers" in the church at ANTIOCH of Syria (Acts 13:1). **(2)** A Christian who sent greetings to the church in ROME (Rom. 16:21); he and two others are described as "relatives" of PAUL (NIV) or as his "compatriots" (NRSV margin; TNIV "fellow Jews").

**Lud** (luhd). See LYDIA #2.

**Luke** (*look*). An early Christian worker who was a physician and a companion of the apostle PAUL (Col. 4:14; Phlm. 24; 2 Tim. 4:11). According to very ancient tradition, Luke was a GENTILE who composed the third gospel (see LUKE, GOSPEL OF) and the ACTS OF THE APOSTLES. If so, we learn some details about him from four passages in Acts (the so-called "we sections") where he writes in the first person (Acts 16:10–17; 20:5–15; 21:1–18; 27:1–28:16). He was no doubt a man of education and culture who probably knew MARY, mother of Jesus (she is the focus of Lk. 1–2). He seems to have had a close association with the city of PHILIPPI in MACEDONIA (some think he was the Macedonian who appeared to Paul in a vision, Acts 16:9).

**Luke, Gospel of.** The longest of the GOSPELS; it is the first of a two-volume work, the second being the ACTS OF THE APOSTLES (cf. Lk. 1:1–4 with Acts 1:1–2). It is unique among the Gospels in several respects. Luke alone gives information about the annunciation and birth of JOHN the Baptist, the annunciation to MARY, various details surrounding the birth of Jesus, and Jesus' childhood (Lk. 1–2). Many well-known PARABLES—e.g., the good Samaritan, the prodigal son, the unjust steward, the Pharisee and the publican—are found only in Luke. His work is characterized by a higher literary style and by greater historical interest. He gives emphasis to those social groups that were often despised or belittled, such as women,

## OVERVIEW OF LUKE

**AUTHOR:** Anonymous, but traditionally attributed to LUKE the physician.

**HISTORICAL SETTING:** Covers the period from the annunciation of JOHN the Baptist to the ASCENSION OF CHRIST. The book was probably written in ROME c. AD 60, but some date it to the 70s or even later.

**PURPOSE:** To provide a full and orderly historical-theological account of the life of CHRIST that will reassure the reader concerning the certainty of the GOSPEL (Lk. 1:3–4), focusing on such themes as the universality of SALVATION (offered even to Gentiles and tax collectors), the HOLY SPIRIT, and PRAYER.

**CONTENTS:** The nativity stories and Jesus' childhood (Lk. 1–2); the baptism and temptation, leading to ministry in GALILEE (3:1–9:50); journey to JERUSALEM, with much unique material, especially a number of PARABLES found only in this gospel (9:51–19:27); ministry in Jerusalem, leading to Jesus' death, resurrection, and ascension (19:28–24:53).



GENTILES, and TAX COLLECTORS (he alone tells the story of ZACCHAEUS, 19:1–10).

**lust.** This term refers to an intense desire, most often with a negative connotation and used especially of unrestrained sexual craving (e.g., Col. 3:5 NIV; 1 Thess. 4:5).

**Luz** (luhz). **(1)** The earlier Canaanite name of the city better known as BETHEL (Gen.

The mound where Lystra was situated. www.HolyLandPhotos.org

28:19; 35:6). **(2)** A town built in the land of the HITTITES, the location of which is unknown (Jdg. 1:26).

**LXX.** Abbreviation for SEPTUAGINT.

**Lycaonia** (lik′uh-oh′nee-uh). A region in south central Asia Minor (modern Turkey) that under the Romans became part of GALATIA. Its leading cities were LYSTRA and DERBE. Its inhabitants thought that PAUL and BARNABAS were gods (Acts 14:6–18).

**Lydda.** See LOD.

**Lydia** (lid′ee-uh). **(1)** A businesswoman from THYATIRA; she lived in PHILIPPI and was PAUL's first convert there (Acts 16:12–15). Her home apparently became the meeting place of the local church (16:40). **(2)** A large territory in NW Asia Minor (modern Turkey) whose capital was SARDIS. A son of SHEM named Lud was probably the ancestor of the Lydians (Gen. 10:22; see also Isa. 66:19; Ezek. 27:10; 30:5). Most of the churches addressed in Rev. 2–3 were in this region.

**Lysias.** See CLAUDIUS LYSIAS.

**Lystra** (lis′truh). A town in the central region of S Asia Minor (modern Turkey), part of the district of LYCAONIA, and the home of TIMOTHY (Acts 14:6, 8, 21; 16:1–2; 2 Tim. 3:11). PAUL and BARNABAS healed a lame man there, leading the inhabitants to think that they were gods.

# M

**Macedonia** (mas'uh-doh'nee-uh). Also Macedon. A region in the Balkan Peninsula that encompasses much of what is now northern GREECE. The ancient country of the Macedonians (an ethnic group closely related to the Greeks) is best known for its king, ALEXANDER the Great. In NT times it was a Roman senatorial PROVINCE, and the apostle PAUL brought the gospel to several of its cities, such as PHILIPPI (Acts 16:9–40), THESSALONICA (17:1–9), and BEREA (17:10–14). Macedonia is mentioned in various passages (e.g., 19:21–22; 20:1–3; Rom. 15:26; 1 Cor. 16:5; 2 Cor. 8:1; Phil. 4:15; 1 Thess. 1:7–8).

**Machir.** See MAKIR.

**Magdalene** (mag'duh-leen). An inhabitant of Magdala, which was probably a town on the SW shore of the Sea of Galilee, near TIBERIAS (the town is mentioned in Matt. 15:39 KJV, but modern versions here have "Magadan"). See MARY #5.

**Magi** (may'j*i*). Originally this term referred to a class of religious officials in PERSIA who had great interest in ASTROLOGY and the interpretation of DREAMS. Some believe, however, that the Magi mentioned in Matt. 2:1–12 (KJV "wise men") may have come from ARABIA (the old Arabian caravan routes entered Palestine "from the East").

**magistrate.** An official with administrative or judicial responsibilities. The magistrates in PHILIPPI (Acts 16:20–22, 35–38) were the primary civic leaders of this Roman colony and probably had broad political powers.

**Magog** (may'gog). Son of JAPHETH (Gen. 10:2). In Ezek. 38:2 and 39:6, the name is applied to his descendants (or to their land), whose chief ruler was GOG. Possibly they lived in Asia Minor (modern Turkey), and they seem to represent northern nations who in the "latter days" come against ISRAEL in battle and experience God's wrath in defeat (38:14–16; cf. Rev. 20:8).

**Mahanaim** (may'huh-nay'im). Name given by JACOB to a site E of the JORDAN (Gen. 32:2). It became an important city in GILEAD, on the boundary between the tribes of GAD and MANASSEH (Josh. 13:26, 30). After the death of SAUL, Mahanaim was made the capital of ISRAEL for a short time (2 Sam. 2:8)

**Makir** (may'kihr). Also Machir. **(1)** Son of MANASSEH and grandson of JOSEPH (Gen. 50:23). Makir's son Gilead gave his name to (or was named for?) the area E of the JORDAN that his family inhabited (Num. 27:1; 32:39–40). In addition, BASHAN was allotted to the Makirites because they were "great soldiers" (Josh. 17:1). **(2)** A man in whose house MEPHIBOSHETH the son of JONATHAN stayed (2 Sam. 9:4–5). He subsequently helped DAVID when the latter went into exile (17:27–29).

**Malachi, Book of** (mal'uh-k*i*). The last book among the twelve Minor Prophets. It was written after the return of the Israelites from EXILE, after the rebuilding of

## OVERVIEW OF MALACHI

**AUTHOR:** The prophet Malachi.

**HISTORICAL SETTING:** The postexilic period in JERUSALEM, after the rebuilding of the TEMPLE (516 BC). Most scholars date the book to c. 450 BC.

**PURPOSE:** To condemn the negligence of the priests and the faithlessness of the people, and to announce "the great and dreadful day of the LORD" (Mal. 4:5).

**CONTENTS:** After reminding the Israelites of their privileges (Mal. 1:1–5), God denounces the failures of the priests (1:6–2:9) and the unfaithfulness of the people (2:10–3:18), concluding with a warning about the coming of the DAY OF THE LORD (ch. 4).

the TEMPLE had been completed and SACRIFICES were being offered (Mal. 1:7–10; 3:8). Malachi ministered during a time of moral and religious decline. Mixed marriages (2:10–12), the failure to pay tithes (3:8–10), and the offering of blemished sacrifices (1:6–14) are conditions not unlike those referred to in the days of EZRA and NEHEMIAH (cf. Ezra 7; Neh. 13); it would seem that Malachi's prophecy was given at about that time, or possibly shortly thereafter—about the middle or end of the fifth century BC. There are two principal themes in the book: the SIN and APOSTASY of the people of ISRAEL, emphasized in Mal. 1–2, and the JUDGMENT that will come on the faithless and the blessing in store for those who repent, emphasized in chs. 3–4.

**Malchus** (mal'kuhs). A servant of the high priest (CAIAPHAS); Simon PETER struck him with a sword and cut off his right ear when Jesus was arrested (Jn. 18:10; cf. Matt. 26:51; Mk. 14:47; Lk. 22:50–51).

**malice.** An evil desire to do harm to someone (e.g., Ps. 41:5); it is an attitude that Christians must put away (Eph. 4:31; 1 Pet. 2:1).

**Malta** (mawl'tuh). A Mediterranean island c. 90 mi. (145 km.) S of Sicily; here PAUL was shipwrecked on his journey to ROME (Acts 28:1; KJV "Melita").

**mammon** (mam'uhn). An ARAMAIC term found in the KJV in Matt. 6:24; Lk. 16:9, 11, 13. The NIV and other modern translations, instead of using this transliteration, render the word as "wealth" or "money."

**Mamre** (mam'ree). An AMORITE who apparently resided near HEBRON (Gen. 14:13, 24). The expression "the great trees of Mamre the Amorite" (14:13) suggests that he owned the place that came to be known by his name. ABRAHAM lived for some time in the town or district known as Mamre, which apparently was part of HEBRON (13:18; 18:1). He also bought a field in nearby Machpelah, where he buried SARAH (23:17–20).

**man.** See HUMANITY.

**Manasseh** (muh-nas'uh). **(1)** The older of two sons born to JOSEPH (Gen. 41:50–51; 46:20). When Joseph brought his sons EPHRAIM and Manasseh to his father for his blessing, JACOB adopted them as his own, placing them on an equality with his own sons as progenitors of separate tribes (48:1–5). Manasseh's ARAMEAN concubine gave birth to MAKIR, whose descendants

M

The Jezreel Valley in the tribal territory of Manasseh.





became the tribe of Manasseh (1 Chr. 7:14). Before the Israelites crossed over the JORDAN RIVER into CANAAN, half the tribe of Manasseh, along with the tribes of REUBEN and GAD, chose land E of the river, and MOSES assigned it to them (Num. 32:33). The Manassites conquered GILEAD and lived there. The rest of the tribe was given ten portions of land W of the Jordan. **(2)** Son of HEZEKIAH and king of JUDAH from c. 696 to 641 BC (2 Ki. 21:1–18; 2 Chr. 33:1–20). Manasseh was only twelve years of age when he succeeded his father as king, and his reign of fifty-five years was the longest in Judah's history. According to the account in 2 Ki. 23:26–27, his was the most immoral reign of all the kings and was the reason for the ultimate collapse of the southern kingdom. Eventually he was arrested and deported by the Assyrians, and during his imprisonment he repented of his sins and was restored to his kingdom (2 Chr. 33:12–13).

**mandrake.** A plant native to the Mediterranean countries, sometimes called the "love apple." It was thought to have magical and medicinal powers and to promote fertility (Gen. 30:14–16; Cant. 7:13).

**manger.** A receptacle for feeding livestock. Most English versions use it to indicate the place where the baby Jesus was laid (Lk. 2:7, 12, 16), though some think the Greek word here has the broader meaning "stable."

**manna** (man′uh). Miraculous food that resembled "thin flakes like frost" and "tasted like wafers made with honey" (Exod. 16:14–15, 31). It was provided by God for the Israelites in the wilderness on a daily basis, but on the sixth day they were to take twice as much so that it would last them through the SABBATH (16:16–30).

## OVERVIEW OF MARK

**AUTHOR:** Anonymous, but traditionally attributed to John Mark.

**HISTORICAL SETTING:** Covers the period from the baptism to the resurrection of CHRIST. The book was probably written in ROME, and if it served as a literary source for Matthew and Luke, it may have been completed in the 50s, but many date it to the 60s or even later.

**PURPOSE:** To provide a brief historical-theological account of the ministry of Christ that focuses on his activity as evidence that he is the Son of God.

**CONTENTS:** After a short introduction (Mk. 1:1–13), the book focuses on Jesus' Galilean ministry, characterized by both popularity and growing opposition (1:14–9:50), followed by the briefer period in Perea and Judea (ch. 10), and then by passion week (chs. 11–15) and the resurrection (ch. 16).

Some manna was kept in a jar in the TABERNACLE (16:32–34; cf. Heb. 9:4). This miracle was part of God's testing (Deut. 8:2–4; cf. Matt. 4:4). Jesus alluded to the manna when he claimed to be "bread from heaven" (Jn. 6:31–35, 41, 48–51, 58; cf. Rev. 2:17).

**Manoah** (muh-noh'uh). The father of SAMSON (Jdg. 13:2–25).

**maranatha** (mair'uh-nath'uh). An ARAMAIC phrase occurring only in 1 Cor. 16:22 and meaning either "Our Lord has come" or, more probably, "Our Lord, come!" (cf. Rev. 22:20).

**Mark, Gospel of.** The second book of the NT. It is the shortest of the four Gospels, containing relatively little of the teachings of Jesus (a few parables [Mk. 4], with only one long discourse [ch. 13]), and nothing at all about his birth and childhood. According to early Christian tradition, the book was written by John Mark (see MARK, JOHN), who sought to preserve the preaching of PETER. It is probably the earliest of the Gospels, and conservative scholars commonly hold to a date in the 50s. Mark seems to write primarily for GENTILES living in ROME, for he uses a number of Latin words and at several points explains Jewish customs. The narrative moves quickly from one event to the next, includes vivid details, and gives picturesque descriptions.

**Mark, John** (mahrk, jon). Son of a Christian woman named Mary (Acts 12:12), cousin of BARNABAS (Col. 4:10), assistant to PAUL and Barnabas, and traditionally the author of the second gospel (see MARK, GOSPEL OF). John was his Jewish name, Mark (Marcus) his Roman surname. There may be a self-allusion in Mk. 14:51–52, but the first definite reference to John Mark is Acts 12:12. Later, he accompanied Barnabas and Saul (Paul) on their missionary journey as "their helper" (13:5; cf. 12:25). Because Mark abandoned them (13:13), Paul refused to take him on a subsequent journey; instead, Mark went with Barnabas to CYPRUS (15:36–39). Evidently, Paul and Mark later reconciled (Col. 4:20; Phlm. 24; 2 Tim. 4:11). PETER refers to him as "my son Mark" (1 Pet. 5:13).

**marriage.** The formal and lawful union of a man and a woman as husband and wife so that they become one, thus laying the

M

foundation for a family. Marriage was instituted by God himself (Gen. 2:18–25; Matt. 19:4–6) and illustrates the relationship between Christ and the CHURCH (Eph. 5:22–33). See also ADULTERY; CONCUBINE; DIVORCE; FAMILY; POLYGAMY.

**Mars′ Hill.** See AREOPAGUS.

**Martha** (mahr′thuh). The sister of MARY and LAZARUS, all three being among the special friends of Jesus (Jn. 11:5). Their home was in BETHANY, very near JERUSALEM (11:1). Martha seemed devoted to serve others (12:2), but at least on one occasion this good quality disturbed her peace of mind (Lk. 10:38–42). Her faith came to expression when Lazarus died (Jn. 11:20–27).

**Mary** (mair′ee). Greek form of the Hebrew name MIRIAM. At least six women of this name are mentioned in the NT. **(1)** The mother of Jesus. She receives special attention in Luke's version of the nativity story (Lk. 1:26–56; 2:1–35). She is mentioned also in several other passages (e.g., Matt. 12:46–50; Lk. 2:48–51; Jn. 2:1–11; 19:26–27; Acts 1:14). **(2)** The mother of John Mark (Acts 12:12; see MARK, JOHN). **(3)** The sister of LAZARUS and MARTHA, from BETHANY (Jn. 11:1; cf. also vv. 28–32). She loved to listen to Jesus as he taught (Lk. 10:38–42), and on one occasion she showed her devotion by pouring expensive perfume on him (Jn. 12:1–8; cf. Matt. 26:6–10; Mk. 14:3–9). **(4)** The mother of JAMES the younger and of Joseph/Joses (Matt. 27:56; 28:1 ["the other Mary"]; Mk. 15:40, 47). She may be the same Mary who is identified as "the wife of Clopas" (Jn. 19:25), but some believe she

The feeding of the five thousand, a miracle related in Matt. 14:13-21, is depicted in this illumination (from the Codex de Predis, 15th cent.).

## OVERVIEW OF MATTHEW

**AUTHOR:** Anonymous, but traditionally attributed to the apostle Matthew/Levi.

**HISTORICAL SETTING:** Covers the period from the baptism to the resurrection of CHRIST. The book was probably written in ANTIOCH of Syria in the late 60s, but some date it to the 70s or even later.

**PURPOSE:** To provide a full historical-theological account of the ministry of CHRIST that focuses on his discourses; to show that Jesus is the fulfillment of the OT; to encourage Jewish Christians who are suffering persecution and are tempted to be lax in their discipleship.

**CONTENTS:** Genealogy and nativity story (Matt. 1–2); the beginning of the Galilean ministry, followed by the SERMON ON THE MOUNT (chs. 3–7); the miracles of Jesus, followed by a discourse on mission (chs. 8–10); growing opposition, followed by the PARABLES of the KINGDOM (chs. 11–13); final stage of the Galilean ministry, followed by a discourse on HUMILITY (chs. 14–18); ministry in Perea and Judea, followed by a denunciation of Jewish leaders and by the Olivet Discourse (chs. 19–25); Jesus' passion, death, and resurrection (chs. 26–28).

M

is a different person. **(5)** Mary Magdalene, so called after the name of her native city, Magdala (see MAGDALENE). Jesus had driven seven DEMONS out of her (Lk. 8:2). There is no evidence that she was a prostitute. This Mary is mentioned more often than most of the other believing women, and usually first (Matt. 27:56, 61; 28:1; Mk. 15:40, 47; 16:1; Lk. 24:10; Jn. 19:25; 20:1–2, 11–18). **(6)** An early Christian who "worked very hard" for the church in Rome (Rom. 16:6).

**maskil** (mas′kil). A musical or poetic term found in the title of fourteen psalms, beginning with Ps. 32 (KJV "Maschil"); it possibly means "meditation" or "skillful poem."

**Massah** (mas′uh). A place in the Desert of SINAI where the Israelites quarreled and tested God because of their thirst; this place was also given the name Meribah (Exod. 17:1–7; the Meribah of Num. 20:1–13 seems to be a different location). Both names appear elsewhere (e.g., Deut. 33:8). See REPHIDIM.

**master.** See RABBI; TEACHING.

**Matthew** (math′yoo). A Jewish tax collector or revenue officer of CAPERNAUM, called to be a disciple of Jesus (Matt. 9:9; 10:3; Mk. 3:18; Lk. 6:15; Acts 1:13), identified with LEVI son of ALPHAEUS (Mk. 2:14; Lk. 5:27–29), and traditionally thought to be the author of the first gospel. See MATTHEW, GOSPEL OF.

**Matthew, Gospel of.** The first book of the NT. According to very early tradition, it was written by one of Jesus' twelve disciples, MATTHEW, probably in ANTIOCH of Syria. Many scholars believe that Matthew made use of (and thus is later than) the Gospel of Mark but that he composed the book shortly before the destruction of JERUSALEM in AD 70. Matthew devotes much more attention to Jesus' teaching than Mark does, and the whole of his gospel is woven around five great discourses: (1) Matt. 5–7; (2) ch. 10; (3) ch. 13; (4) ch. 18; (5) chs. 24–25. He also emphasizes such themes as the kingship of Jesus (2:2; 27:11), the CHURCH and its discipline (16:18; 18:17), and the fulfillment of the OT (2:15; 5:17).

**Matthias** (muh-thi′uhs). The name of the "twelfth apostle," chosen through the casting of LOTS to take the place of JUDAS Iscariot, the traitor (Acts 1:16–26).

**Medes.** See MEDIA.

**Media** (mee′dee-uh). The home of the Medes, an ancient Indo-European people of NW Iran who were absorbed by the rise of PERSIA in the 7th cent. BC. They are mentioned often in Scripture (e.g., 2 Ki. 17:8; Ezra 6:2; Esth. 1:3; Isa. 21:2; Jer. 51:1; Dan. 5:28; Acts 2:9).

**mediator.** One who acts as intermediary between parties, especially when RECONCILIATION is needed. MOSES is described as a mediator, communicating God's LAW to the Israelites (Gal. 3:19–20), but the term is applied primarily to Christ (1 Tim. 2:5; Heb. 8:6; 9:15; 12:24). All people are alienated from God because of their SIN, but Jesus took on human form (see INCARNATION) so that he might die for sinners and bring them back to God.

**meditate.** To think about carefully and deeply, ponder, reflect on. The Lord commanded JOSHUA to meditate on the Book of the Law "day and night" (Josh. 1:8; cf. Ps. 1:2; 119:97). The godly meditate also on God and his works (Ps. 19:14; 77:12; 119:27; 145:5).

**Mediterranean Sea.** The great body of water that separates Africa from Europe; among the Hebrews and others it became known simply as "the Great Sea" or simply "the Sea," marking the western end of the Promised Land (Num. 34:6). PAUL's missionary tours and his travel to ROME (Acts 13–28) took him across the eastern half of the Mediterranean.

**medium.** See DIVINATION; FAMILIAR SPIRIT.

**meekness.** Mildness and gentleness of character, a quality often commended in Scripture. The word does not imply a

Megiddo lies at a key crossroads on what served as an international highway.

weak nature. Meekness is characteristic of Jesus (Matt. 11:29; 2 Cor. 10:1), who pronounced a blessing on the meek, "for they will inherit the earth" (Matt. 5:5).

**Megiddo** (mi-gid′oh). A major city of Palestine, with a strategic location in the JEZREEL Plain. Its king was defeated by JOSHUA during the conquest of the land (Josh. 12:21). The city became especially important during the time of SOLOMON (1 Ki. 9:15; cf. 2 Ki. 23:29–30; Zech. 12:11). See also ARMAGEDDON.

**Melchizedek** (mel-kiz′uh-dek). A priest-king mentioned in three biblical books (Gen. 14:18–20; Ps. 110:4; Heb. 5:6–11; 6:20–7:28). Melchizedek presented ABRAHAM with bread and wine and blessed him; then Abraham gave him "a tenth of everything." Christ is said to be not a Levitical PRIEST but a priest belonging to the order of Melchizedek.

**Melita.** See MALTA.

**mem** (maym). The thirteenth letter of the Hebrew alphabet (מ, transliterated as *m*), used to begin each verse in Ps. 119:97–104.

**Memphis** (mem′fis). KJV Noph (except. Hos. 9:6). A city of EGYPT, on the W bank of the NILE, some 13 mi. (21 km.) S of Cairo. Memphis is mentioned only in the Prophets, who sometimes spoke judgment against it (e.g., Jer. 46:13, 19; Ezek. 30:13, 16).

**Menahem** (men′uh-hem). One of the last kings of Israel (2 Ki. 15:14–22). He began his reign of ten years by killing his predecessor SHALLUM. The biblical historian states, "He did evil in the eyes of the LORD" (v. 18).

**mene, mene, tekel, parsin (upharsin)** (mee′nee, mee′nee, tek′uhl, pahr′sin, *yoo*-fahr′sin). An inscription that appeared on the wall of the palace of BELSHAZZAR at BABYLON (Dan. 5:25–28). The words may refer to weights ("Mina, mina, shekel, and half-shekels")

Tiglath-Pileser III (relief from Nimrud, c. 728 BC). Menahem king of Judah was forced to pay tribute to this Assyrian conqueror.
Todd Bolen/www.BiblePlaces.com

or they may be proverbial ("Counted, counted, weighed, and assessed"). DANIEL interpreted them to mean that the king had "been weighed on the scales and found wanting" and that he would lose his kingdom to the Medes and Persians.

**Mephibosheth** (mi-fib′oh-sheth). **(1)** Son of SAUL by his concubine RIZPAH (2 Sam. 21:8). **(2)** Son of JONATHAN and grandson of Saul (2 Sam. 4:4; 9:6–13; called Merib-Baal in 1 Chr. 8:34; 9:40).

**Merari** (mi-rah′r*i*). Third son of LEVI and ancestor of the Merarites, an important Levitical family (Gen. 46:11; Exod. 6:16; Num. 3:36–37; 1 Chr. 6:16).

**mercy.** Compassion or leniency shown to another, especially an offender. In this sense, mercy has special reference to God's act of FORGIVENESS (Deut. 13:17; Neh. 9:31; Ps. 51:1; Lk. 1:50; Rom. 11:30–32; Tit. 3:5). In a more general sense, mercy is the compassion that causes one to help the weak, the sick, or the poor. Showing mercy is one of the cardinal virtues of a true Christian (Matt. 5:7; Rom. 12:8; Jas. 2:1–13; 3:17). See also LOVE; LOVINGKINDNESS.

M

This satellite image of the area known as Mesopotamia shows Lake Tharthar in Iraq (lower right), with the Euphrates River below it and the Tigris River above it. NASA, earth.jsc.nasa.gov

M

**mercy seat.** KJV rendering of a Hebrew term that refers to the cover on the ARK of the covenant (Exod. 25:17–22).

**Meribah** (mer′i-bah). See MASSAH.

**Merib-Baal** (mer′ib-bay′uhl). See MEPHIBOSHETH #2.

**Meshach** (mee′shak). A pagan name given to Mishael, one of DANIEL's companions taken by NEBUCHADNEZZAR to be trained in his palace as counselors to the king (Dan. 1:3–7). See ABEDNEGO.

**Mesopotamia** (mes′uh-puh-tay′mee-uh). A name meaning "between rivers" and referring to the land around and between the TIGRIS and EUPHRATES Rivers (e.g., Gen. 24:10 KJV, where NIV has "Aram Naharaim"; cf. also Acts 2:9; 7:2).

**Messiah** (muh-s*i*′uh). A Hebrew word (*meshiach*) meaning "anointed one" (Dan. 9:25–26 KJV; Jn. 1:41; 4:25). The corresponding Greek word is *christos* (CHRIST), and such versions as the NRSV and TNIV use *Messiah* in many NT passages where the term *christos* seems to function as a title rather than as a name (e.g., Matt. 1:1; Mk. 14:61; Lk. 2:11; Jn. 1:20; Acts 2:31; Rom. 9:5; Rev. 11:15). See ANOINT.

**Methuselah** (mi-th*oo*′suh-luh). Son of ENOCH, descendant of SETH, and grandfather of NOAH (Gen. 5:21–22, 25–27); he is said to have lived 969 years, longer than anyone else (Gen. 5:27).

**Micah** (m*i*′kuh). The name of various individuals in the OT, two of whom were prominent. **(1)** An Ephraimite who set up an idolatrous shrine and whose idols were used by the Danites when they resettled in LAISH (Jdg. 17–18). **(2)** A writing prophet from JUDAH. See MICAH, BOOK OF.

**Micah, Book of.** Sixth book among the Minor Prophets. Micah was a contemporary of ISAIAH and a native of Moresheth Gath, a town in JUDAH that was probably close to the PHILISTINE city of GATH. The book predicts the fall of SAMARIA, which occurred in 722 BC, but concerns more especially the sins and dangers of JERUSALEM in the days of HEZEKIAH around 700. The message varies between strong condemnation for present sins and God's purpose of ultimate blessing for his people. One of the book's best-known passages is the messianic hope of Mic. 5:2, where the mention of BETHLEHEM Ephrathah identifies the MESSIAH as of DAVID's line. The book closes with the prophet's declaration of faith in the ultimate fulfillment of God's COVENANT of blessing for ABRAHAM.

**Micaiah** (mi-kay'yuh). The name of several persons in the OT, especially a courageous prophet who confronted King AHAB in SAMARIA and predicted his death in battle (1 Ki. 22:8–26; 2 Chr. 18:7–25).

**Michael** (m*i*'kay-uhl, m*i*'kuhl). The name of ten different men in the OT, but also of a prominent ANGEL who is described as "the great prince" who protects ISRAEL (Dan. 12:1; cf. 10:13, 21) and as an archangel (Jude 9; cf. Rev. 12:7; 1 Thess. 4:16).

**Michal** (m*i*'kuhl). Younger daughter of King SAUL (1 Sam. 14:49). She was given to DAVID as a wife after he killed two hundred PHILISTINES (18:20–27; see also 19:11–17; 2 Sam. 6:16–23).

**Midian** (mid'ee-uhn). Son of ABRAHAM and KETURAH (Gen. 25:1–2) and ancestor of a people group that lived E and SE of CANAAN (cf. 25:6). Traders in the caravan that bought JOSEPH are called "Midianites" (37:36), and MOSES' father-in-law, JETHRO, was a priest in Midian (Exod. 3:1). Later the Midianites caused problems among the Hebrews (Num. 22:4–18; 31:1–11; Jdg. 6:1–6).

**Milcom** (mil'kuhm). See MOLECH.

**millennium.** A term meaning "one thousand years." The phrase *the millennium* is used to identify the period described in Rev. 20:1–6. The view known as premillennialism teaches that Jesus returns before the millennium to establish a literal one-thousand-year reign on earth.

## OVERVIEW OF MICAH

**AUTHOR:** The prophet Micah from the Judahite town of MORESHETH GATH.

**HISTORICAL SETTING:** A contemporary of ISAIAH, Micah received his revelations during the last decades of the eighth century BC and the early years of the seventh. Thus he lived through the decline and fall of the northern kingdom of ISRAEL and prophesied during the reigns of JOTHAM, AHAZ, and HEZEKIAH, kings of JUDAH (Mic. 1:1). The composition of the book should probably be dated prior to the death of Hezekiah (c. 687 BC or perhaps ten years earlier).

**PURPOSE:** To denounce the sin and predict the destruction of both Israel and Judah but also to announce the hope of messianic salvation.

**CONTENTS:** Condemnation of SAMARIA and JERUSALEM (Mic. 1–3), followed by promises of restoration (chs. 4–5); God's complaints against Israel (6:1–7:7), followed by a psalm of hope and praise (7:8–20).

M

Another interpretation, postmillennialism, holds that Jesus returns after a long period of spiritual prosperity. According to amillennialism, the passage refers to the present period, when Christ rules over the CHURCH and SATAN is unable to prevent the GOSPEL from reaching pagan nations.

**Millo** (mil′oh). A fortification near JERUSALEM, constructed by SOLOMON with forced labor (1 Ki. 9:15, 24; 11:27). The NIV translates the Hebrew term as a common noun, "supporting terraces" (TNIV simply "terraces").

**minister.** In a religious sense, this term as a noun usually refers to someone who serves the church in an official capacity (cf. Col. 1:7; 4:7; 1 Tim. 4:6). As a verb it can mean both "to perform an official religious function" (e.g., Exod. 28:43; Heb. 13:10) and more generally "to provide service, give aid" (e.g., Matt. 25:44 KJV; NIV "help"). See also BISHOP; CHURCH; DEACON; ELDER; WORSHIP.

**miracles.** Extraordinary events that manifest God's intervention in nature and in human affairs. The majority of the miracles recorded in the Bible fall into three great epochs: (1) the time of MOSES and JOSHUA; (2) the ministry of ELIJAH and ELISHA; (3) the NT period. The purpose of miracles is revelation, confirmation, and edification (Jn. 20:31; Heb. 2:3–4).

**Miriam** (mihr′ee-uhm). The sister of MOSES and AARON (Num. 26:59). She protected the baby Moses when his mother placed him in a basket in the river (Exod. 2:3–8). Miriam, identified as a prophetess, led the Israelite women in celebrating the EXODUS (15:20–21). Later she was punished for criticizing Moses (Num. 12).

**Mishael** (mish′ay-uhl). See MESHACH.

**Mizpah, Mizpeh** (miz′puh, miz′peh). The name of several places, the most important of which was a town allotted to the tribe of BENJAMIN, c. 7.5 mi. (12 km.) NNW of JERUSALEM (Josh. 18:26). Mizpah played a prominent role in the days of the judges (Jdg. 11:11; 20:1; 21:1–8) and was closely associated with SAMUEL (1 Sam. 7:5–16). Much later it became the headquarters of GEDALIAH, governor of JUDAH (2 Ki. 25:22–25; Jer. 40:5–12).

**Mizraim** (miz-ray′im). A son of HAM (Gen. 10:6, 13). In the Hebrew Bible, Mizraim is the usual name for EGYPT and its people.

**Mnason** (nay′suhn). An early Christian, originally from CYPRUS, in whose home PAUL and his companions stayed (Acts 21:16).

**Moab** (moh′ab). An ancient nation lying E of the DEAD SEA and occupying the plateau between the rivers ARNON and ZERED. It was bounded on the S by EDOM. The Moabites descended from LOT through an incestuous union (Gen. 19:30–38), and

The famous Moabite Stone mentions conflict between King Mesha of Moab and the dynasty of Omri of Israel.

The hill of Moreh. Todd Bolen/www.BiblePlaces.com

they were constant enemies of the Israelites (Num. 22:1–21; Deut. 23:3–4; Jdg. 3:12–14; 1 Sam. 14:47; 2 Sam. 8:2; 2 Ki. 1:1; 2 Ki. 3:4–27; Isa. 15–16; Jer. 48; Amos 2:1–3).

**Molech** (moh′lek). TNIV Molek. A heathen god, especially of the AMMONITES, whose worship was sternly forbidden by God (Lev. 18:21; 20:1–5). Molech was apparently known also as Milcom (1 Ki. 11:5 KJV, NRSV). The prophets condemned this cult (Jer. 32:35; Zeph. 1:5).

**month.** See CALENDAR.

**Mordecai** (mor′duh-k*i*). A man from the tribe of BENJAMIN who lived in SUSA during the rule of the Persians (Esth. 2:5) and who was the guardian of his cousin ESTHER (2:7). Mordecai played a very prominent role in the story recorded in the book of Esther, and eventually he succeeded HAMAN as chief minister of the king (8:1–2).

**Moreh** (mor′eh). **(1)** A place near SHECHEM where God revealed himself to ABRAHAM (Gen. 12:6; cf. Deut. 11:30). **(2)** A hill at the E end of the Valley of JEZREEL where the Midianites were camping when they were attacked by GIDEON (Jdg. 7:1).

**Moriah** (muh-r*i*′uh). **(1)** The region to which God instructed ABRAHAM to go so that he might offer up ISAAC on one of its mountains (Gen. 22:2). **(2)** The rocky hilltop of JERUSALEM N of the City of David (see ZION) where God appeared to DAVID and where the TEMPLE was built (2 Chr. 3:1). Some have thought that this place is the same as #1.

**morning star.** This term is applied to Venus (occasionally to other bright planets)

## Moses

Artistic representation of Moses receiving the tablets of the law (from a 13th-cent. manuscript known as the Psalter of Ingeburg of Denmark).

Musee Conde, Chantilly, France/Giraudon/The Bridgeman Art Library International



because it is often visible in the eastern sky before sunrise (Isa. 14:12 [KJV LUCIFER]; see also 2 Pet. 1:19; Rev. 2:28; 22:16).

**Moses** (moh′zis). The national hero who delivered the Israelites from Egyptian slavery, gave them God's LAW, established them as an independent nation, and prepared them for entrance into CANAAN. Born in the land of EGYPT at a time when Hebrew boys were being killed, Moses was brought up by PHARAOH's daughter (Exod. 2:1–10). At age forty he killed an Egyptian and fled to MIDIAN, where he married ZIPPORAH, daughter of JETHRO, a priest (2:11–22). Forty years later he received God's call to bring the Hebrews out of Egypt (ch. 3; see EXODUS). During an additional forty years, he led the Israelites through the wilderness, but he died without entering the Promised Land (Deut. 34).

**Most Holy Place.** See HOLY OF HOLIES.

**Mount Hermon.** See HERMON (follow this same pattern of cross-referencing for other mountains that have proper names).

**mourning.** Ceremonies for expressing grief at the death of a relative or on any unhappy occasion are referred to frequently in the Bible. When bad news was received or when sudden calamity came, it was customary to tear the clothes (2 Sam. 1:2) and to sprinkle earth or ashes on the head (Josh. 7:6). Hair cloth ("sackcloth") was adopted as clothing in times of grief (Isa. 22:12). A death in the household set in motion an elaborate ritual of mourning that lasted a week or more.

**murder.** The crime of unlawfully killing a human being (Exod. 20:13). According to Hebrew LAW, the agreeing testimony of at least two persons was necessary for a murder conviction (Num. 35:30; Deut. 17:6). The right of asylum in a holy place was not granted a murderer; he was dragged away even from the horns of the altar (Exod. 21:14; 1 Ki. 2:28–34). No ransom could be accepted for a murderer (Num. 35:21). Jesus expanded the law against murder to include the intention of the heart manifested in ANGER (Matt. 5:21–22).

**myrrh.** A yellow to reddish-brown gum resin obtained from a number of small, thorny trees. It is used as a spice, medicine, or cosmetic (e.g., Cant. 5:5; Matt. 2:11; Mk. 15:23; Jn. 19:39).

**myrtle.** A small evergreen shrub with fragrant flowers, considered a symbol of peace and prosperity (Isa. 55:13). Myrtle boughs were used in constructing the booths for the Feast of Tabernacles (Neh. 8:15; Zech. 1:7–8).

**Mysia** (mis'ee-uh). A region in NW Asia Minor (modern Turkey) traversed by PAUL in the course of his second journey (Acts 16:7–8), but no pause was made there save at TROAS.

**mystery.** In the NT this term refers to the counsel of God, unknown to human beings except by REVELATION, especially concerning his saving works and ultimate purposes in history. PAUL uses it to denote the divine truth once hidden but now revealed in the GOSPEL (Rom. 16:25–26; Eph. 1:9; 3:3–6; Col. 1:26; 4:3). Christianity has no secret doctrines, as did the ancient mystery religions, which involved a private initiation ceremony and a ritual hidden from outsiders.

M

# N

**Naaman** (nay'uh-muhn). The Aramean commander (see ARAM) who was cured of a skin disease by ELISHA (2 Ki. 5; see LEPER). Although at first reluctant to obey the prophet's instructions, Naaman later relented, washed himself seven times in the river JORDAN, and was healed. He also recognized the unique greatness of Israel's God. Jesus referred to this miracle (Lk. 4:27).

**Nabal** (nay'buhl). A wealthy but unpleasant man who insulted DAVID when the latter asked for remuneration after protecting Nabal's flocks and shepherds. His wife, ABIGAIL, made amends by bringing food to David and his men. Soon after, Nabal died, and Abigail became David's wife (1 Sam. 25).

**Naboth** (nay'both). The owner of a vineyard desired by King AHAB because it lay near

This triptych by Cornelis Engelbrechtsen (1468-1533) depicts Naaman washing in the Jordan River.

Kunsthistorisches Museum, Vienna, Austria/The Bridgeman Art Library International

## OVERVIEW OF NAHUM

**AUTHOR:** The prophet Nahum, an Elkoshite.

**HISTORICAL SETTING:** The focus of Nahum's prophecy is the nation of ASSYRIA prior to its fall (612 BC). The book was probably written sometime between 650 and 630 BC.

**PURPOSE:** To announce the coming destruction of NINEVEH and thus to bring comfort to God's people.

**CONTENTS:** After a psalm of praise to God (Nah. 1:1–11), the book promises deliverance to JUDAH (1:12–15) and proclaims judgments on Nineveh (chs. 2–3).

his alternate royal palace in JEZREEL (1 Ki. 21:1–29). Naboth refused to sell it because it was part of his paternal INHERITANCE (cf. Num. 36:7–9). Ahab's wife JEZEBEL forced the issue and Naboth was stoned to death.

**Nadab** (nay′dab). The name of several men in the OT, two of whom were prominent. **(1)** The eldest son of AARON (Exod. 6:23; 9–11; 28:1). As a priest, Nadab, along with his brother ABIHU, sinned in offering "unholy" (NIV "unauthorized") fire before the Lord, though the exact nature of the sin is not clear. They were immediately consumed in death by fire from the Lord (Lev. 10:1–2; Num. 3:4). **(2)** Son of JEROBOAM I and king of ISRAEL for less than two years, c. 910–909 BC (1 Ki. 15:25–31). Nadab was killed by BAASHA, who succeeded him.

**Nahash** (nay′hash). King of AMMON, defeated by King SAUL (1 Sam. 11:1–11; it is uncertain whether the same person is referred to in 2 Sam. 10:1–2 and 17:25).

**Nahor** (nay′hor). The name of ABRAHAM's grandfather (Gen. 11:22–25) and also of his brother (11:26–29). The phrase "the town of Nahor" (24:10) means either "the town called Nahor" or "the town where Nahor had lived," i.e., HARAN.

**Nahum, Book of.** The seventh book among the Minor Prophets. This short book is largely a poem, a literary masterpiece, predicting the downfall of NINEVEH, the capital of ASSYRIA. Perhaps it was during the reign of JOSIAH (639–608 BC) that Nahum prophesied the overthrow of the mighty nation that had so oppressed the Jews. The book has two parts: first, a poem concerning the greatness of God (Nah. 1:2–15), then another and longer poem detailing the overthrow of Nineveh (2:1–3:19). The impassioned expressions of Nahum can be better understood when we remember that the cruelty of the Assyrians was almost beyond belief. Their policy seems to have been one of calculated terror.

**Nain** (nayn). A town in GALILEE where Jesus brought back to life the son of a widow (Lk. 7:11–17). Nain was located c. 6.5 mi. (10.5 km.) SE of NAZARETH, on the N slope of Mount MOREH. It is intriguing that on the S side of the same hill lies the OT town of SHUNEM, where ELISHA also restored a child to life (2 Ki. 4:8–37).

**name.** In Bible times names had greater significance than they usually have today. A name was given only by a person in a position of authority (Gen. 2:19; 2 Ki. 23:34) and could signify that the person named was appointed to a particular position, function, or relationship (Gen. 35:18; 2 Sam. 12:25). The name given was often

N

determined by some circumstance at the time of birth (Gen. 19:22); sometimes the name expressed a hope or a prophecy (Isa. 8:1–4; Hos. 1:4). A person and his or her name were practically equivalent, so that to remove the name was to extinguish the person (Num. 27:4; Deut. 7:24). To forget God's name is to depart from him (Jer. 23:27). To pray in the name of Jesus (Jn. 14:13–14) is to pray as his representatives on earth—in his Spirit and with his aim—and implies the closest union with Christ.

**Naomi** (nay-oh′mee). The mother-in-law of RUTH. Naomi and her family, who were originally from BETHLEHEM, moved to MOAB because of a famine (Ruth 1:1–2). After her husband and sons died, she returned to Bethlehem with Ruth. In her depression she said she should no longer be called Naomi, "pleasant," but now more appropriately MARA, "bitter" (1:20). Through her advice, Ruth was married to BOAZ (3:1–6).

**Naphtali** (naf′tuh-l*i*). Sixth son of JACOB, and his second by BILHAH, the handmaid of RACHEL (Gen. 29:29). The tribe that descended from him was of moderate size (Num. 1:43). After the conquest of CANAAN, Naphtali was allotted the fertile scenic area just W of the Sea of Galilee, reaching the lake's lower limits almost up to a point opposite Mount HERMON. The chief cities of Naphtali were HAZOR, KINNERETH, and KEDESH.

**Nathan** (nay′thuhn). The name of several men in the OT, the most prominent of whom are the following: **(1)** A son of DAVID and BATHSHEBA; he was an older brother of SOLOMON (2 Sam. 5:14; 1 Chr. 3:5; 14:4; Lk. 3:31). **(2)** A prophet at the royal court in JERUSALEM during the reign of David and the early years of Solomon. David consulted him regarding the building of the TEMPLE (2 Sam. 7; 1 Chr. 17). Later Nathan rebuked David for adultery with Bathsheba (2 Sam. 12:1–25). When ADONIJAH sought to supplant his aged father David as king, Nathan intervened through Bathsheba to secure the succession for her son Solomon (1 Ki. 1:8–53).

View of Nazareth as it looked early in the 20th cent.

Library of Congress, LC-DIG-matpc-09027

Modern Kavala, site of ancient Neapolis. © Panagiotis Karapanagiotis/www.BigStockPhoto.com



**Nathanael** (nuh-than'ay-uhl). A disciple of Jesus, mentioned only in Jn. 1:45–51; 21:2. Jesus praised him as a man of integrity (1:47). Many have thought that Nathanael was the same person as BARTHOLOMEW.

**nations.** See GENTILE.

**Nazarene** (naz'uh-reen). An inhabitant of NAZARETH; the term is used in the NT specifically to identify Jesus (e.g., Mk. 14:67), though in one passage "the Nazarene sect" refers to the Christian church (Acts 24:5).

**Nazareth** (naz'uh-rith). A small town in GALILEE, about halfway between Mount CARMEL and the S end of the Sea of GALILEE. It was the home of Mary and Joseph, and here Jesus spent most of his life (Matt. 2:23; Lk. 1:26; 2:4; Jn. 1:46). After Jesus began his ministry, he visited the SYNAGOGUE in Nazareth and the people there rejected his message (Lk. 4:16–30; cf. Mk. 6:1–6a).

**Nazirite** (naz'uh-r*it*). KJV Nazarite. A member of a Hebrew religious class that was specially dedicated to God (Num. 6:1–21). Being a Nazirite involved (1) a renunciation of all products of the vine, including grapes; (2) prohibition of the use of the razor, allowing the hair to grow; and (3) avoidance of contact with a dead body. Usually this dedication was only temporary, but sometimes it was for life, as in the case of SAMSON, SAMUEL, and JOHN the Baptist.

**Neapolis** (nee-ap'uh-lis). A town on the N shore of the Aegean Sea (modern Kavala in Greece). It was the first point in Europe touched by PAUL and his companions when they came from TROAS (Acts 16:11). From here it was an easy journey to PHILIPPI (about 10 mi./16 km. inland).

**Nebo** (nee'boh). **(1)** The name of a Babylonian deity mentioned only in Isaiah's taunt song on the downfall of BABYLON (Isa. 46:1). **(2)** A mountain E of the JORDAN from which MOSES viewed the Promised

Land (Deut. 32:49; 34:1). **(3)** A town in MOAB near this mountain (Num. 32:3).

**Nebuchadnezzar** (neb′uh-kuhd-nez′uhr). Also Nebuchadrezzar. King of BABYLON (605–562 BC) who destroyed JERUSALEM and carried away the people of JUDAH as captives (2 Ki. 24). He is mentioned frequently in Jeremiah and figures prominently in the book of DANIEL (esp. Dan. 2–4).

**Neco** (nee′koh). The second king (or PHARAOH) of the 26th dynasty of EGYPT (ruled 610–595 BC). He defeated JOSIAH at the battle of MEGIDDO (2 Ki. 23:29; 2 Chr. 35:20–24).

**necromancy.** The practice of conjuring the spirits of the dead to inquire about the future. The Mosaic LAW sternly forbade such a practice (Deut. 18:10–11). The most familiar case in the Bible is that of King SAUL and the medium of ENDOR (1 Sam. 28:7–25). See also DIVINATION.

**Negev** (neg′ev). Also Negeb. The name of the southern, desert region of PALESTINE (Gen. 12:9; Num. 13:17; Deut. 1:7); thus the term acquired the additional meaning "south" (e.g., Gen. 13:14; the Heb. term is usually so rendered in the KJV). The Negev was considered to be the tribal territory of JUDAH, but some of it was allotted to SIMEON (Josh. 15:20–32; 19:1–9).

**Nehemiah, Book of.** One of the last historical books of the OT, recounting the history and reforms of a Hebrew man named Nehemiah who became the governor of JUDEA from 444 to about 420 BC. Nehemiah's great work of restoring the wall of JERUSALEM depended basically on securing permission from the Persian king. The actual building of the wall was parceled out among different leaders. Nehemiah's reform involved the teaching of Moses' LAW by Ezra and others at the Feast of Tabernacles (as commanded in Deut. 31:10). This led to the great prayer of confession of Neh. 9, and a covenant was solemnly sealed to walk in the law of the Lord as given by Moses (10:29).

**Nephilim.** See GIANT.

**Nero** (nihr′oh). The fifth emperor of ROME (AD 54–68). Although not mentioned by

## OVERVIEW OF NEHEMIAH

**AUTHOR:** Most of the narrative is written in the first person by Nehemiah himself, but Jewish tradition attributed the composition of the book as a whole (as well as Chronicles and Ezra) to the priest EZRA.

**HISTORICAL SETTING:** The book was written possibly c. 430–400 BC and deals with postexilic JUDEA under Persian jurisdiction.

**PURPOSE:** To recount the reforms of Nehemiah as governor in JERUSALEM, particularly in rebuilding the wall of the city, and thus to encourage the returnees to continue the work of restoration.

**CONTENTS:** Nehemiah secures permission to travel to Jerusalem (Neh. 1:1–2:8); the wall of the city is rebuilt, and more exiles return (2:9–7:73a); the COVENANT is renewed and the wall is dedicated (7:73b–12:47); Nehemiah brings reforms to the community (ch. 13).

This papyrus fragment ($P^{37}$, from the 3rd or 4th cent. AD) contains the text of Matt. 26:19-52.

Image digitally reproduced with the permission of the Papyrology Collection, Graduate Library, University of Michigan

name in the NT, Nero was the emperor before whom PAUL had to appear on probably two different occasions (cf. Acts 25:10–11; 2 Tim. 4:16–17). According to early Christian tradition, both Paul and PETER suffered martyrdom under Nero.

**Nethinim** (neth′in-im). The KJV uses the transliteration *Nethinims* (*Nethinim* itself is a plural form in Hebrew) to represent a term that modern versions render with "temple servants" (e.g., 1 Chr. 9:2; Ezra 2:43; 8:20).

**new birth.** See REGENERATION.

**New Testament.** A collection of twenty-seven documents that make up the second part of the sacred Scriptures of the Christian church, the first part being called by contrast the OLD TESTAMENT. The word *testament* here represents a Greek word (*diathēkē*) that is better translated COVENANT. The new covenant is the new order inaugurated by the death and resurrection of Jesus (Lk. 22:20; cf. Jer. 31:31–34; 2 Cor. 3:14; Heb. 8:13). The foundational documents of this new order are accordingly known as "the books of the new covenant (testament)." See separate articles for each of the NT books.

**Nicodemus** (nik′uh-dee′muhs). A leading PHARISEE and member of the SANHEDRIN to whom Jesus announced the necessity of a new birth (Jn. 3:1–14; see REGENERATION). Later, Nicodemus objected to the way other Jewish leaders were accusing Jesus (7:50–51). He also assisted JOSEPH of Arimathea in the burial of Jesus' body (19:38–40).

**Nicolaitan** (nik′uh-lay′uh-tuhn). Name given to a heretical group in the early church, mentioned only twice in the book of Revelation (Rev. 2:6, 15–16). The specific nature of their teaching is unknown, but they were judged by the author of Revelation to be most dangerous.

**Niger** (ni′guhr). The surname of Simeon, one of the five "prophets and teachers" listed as ministering in the church at ANTIOCH of Syria (Acts 13:1). Because the name means "black," suggesting he was African in origin, some have thought that he was the same as Simon of CYRENE (Lk. 23:26).

**Nile** (nil). The main river in Africa, covering some 4,160 mi. (6,700 km.) from its sources near the equator to its delta on the MEDITERRANEAN. The Nile fostered in EGYPT one of the oldest and most long-lived civilizations of the world. It is mentioned often in the OT (e.g., Gen. 41:1; Exod. 2:3; 4:9; Isa. 19:7–8; Ezek. 29:3; the KJV translates simply "the river").

**Nimrod** (nim′rod). Son of CUSH and grandson of HAM; an early warrior and hunter

N

This satellite photo of Egypt shows the Nile River, including its delta. On the right is the end of the NW arm of the Red Sea.

NASA, earth.jsc.nasa.gov

The book of Numbers relates the wanderings of the Israelites in the wilderness.

who founded a kingdom in MESOPOTAMIA (Gen. 10:6–12; 1 Chr. 1:10). His rule included great cities, including BABYLON and NINEVEH.

**Nineveh** (nin′uh-vuh). One of the most ancient cities of the world, founded by NIMROD (Gen. 10:11–12) and enduring till 612 BC. Nineveh lay on the banks of the TIGRIS and was for many years the capital of ASSYRIA. The city figures prominently in the books of JONAH and NAHUM.

**Nisan** (n*i*′san, nee′sahn). See ABIB.

**Noah** (noh′uh). KJV NT Noe. Son of LAMECH and descendant of SETH (Gen. 5:28–29). Noah was uniquely righteous in the midst of a very corrupt generation (6:5–9; cf. Heb. 11:7; 2 Pet. 2:5). God warned him that the world would be destroyed by water and gave him instructions to build an ark that would save his family (Gen. 6:13–22; cf. 1 Pet. 3:10). See FLOOD, THE. His sons, SHEM, HAM, and

## OVERVIEW OF NUMBERS

**AUTHOR:** Anonymous, but comments elsewhere in the Bible seem to support the traditional view that MOSES is responsible for the PENTATEUCH as a whole.

**HISTORICAL SETTING:** The initial composition of the book must have taken place at the end of the wilderness wanderings.

**PURPOSE:** To provide a historical-theological account of the Israelite wanderings beginning with their departure from SINAI, stressing their unfaithfulness in the wilderness, and ending with their arrival in the plains of MOAB; to encourage the new generation to remain faithful to God and thus to prepare themselves to conquer the Promised Land.

**CONTENTS:** Organization of the people for their march into the wilderness (Num. 1–4); sanctification of the people and beginning of their march (chs. 5–10); complaints and rebellion of the people (chs. 11–19); events during the last stage of the wanderings (chs. 20–25); preparation of the new generation to possess the Promised Land (chs. 26–36).

JAPHETH, became the ancestors of the surviving human race.

**Nob** (nob). A "town of the priests," just NE of JERUSALEM, to which DAVID fled when he was being pursued by SAUL (1 Sam. 22). Because the high priest AHIMELECH protected David, Saul slew eighty-five of the priests and put the city to the sword.

**Noph.** See MEMPHIS.

**Numbers, Book of.** The fourth book of the Bible and traditionally one of the five books of MOSES (the PENTATEUCH or TORAH). The English title, derived from the SEPTUAGINT, is based on the censuses of Num. 4 and 26. Most of the book, however, relates events that took place during the time that the Israelites were in the wilderness. Important incidents include the sending of the spies into CANAAN with the subsequent failure of the nation to trust God (chs. 13–14) as well as the story of BALAAM (chs. 22–24).

**nun (letter)** (noon). The thirteenth letter of the Hebrew alphabet (נ, transliterated as *n*), used to begin each verse in Ps. 119:105–112.

**Nun (person)** (nuhn). The father of JOSHUA (Exod. 33:11; Num. 11:28; 13:8).

**Nympha** (nim′fuh). A Christian woman in whose house the believers had meetings and to whom PAUL sent greetings (Col. 4:15). Apparently she lived in LAODICEA and was a woman of means. Some believe that the name is masculine and thus refers to a man (cf. KJV "Nymphas").

# O

**oath.** An appeal to God to witness the truth of a statement or of the binding character of a promise (Gen. 21:23; 31:53; Gal. 1:20; Heb. 6:16). Oaths played a very important part not only in legal and state affairs but also in the dealings of everyday life. By the time of Christ the OT law regarding oaths (Exod. 22:11) was often abused, and our Lord therefore condemned indiscriminate and light taking of oaths (Matt. 5:33–37).

**Obadiah** (oh′buh-d*i*′uh). The name of about a dozen men in the OT, the most prominent of whom are the following: **(1)** An official of King AHAB who was in charge of the palace and who risked his life to save a hundred of the prophets when they were being hunted by JEZEBEL (1 Ki. 18:3–16). **(2)** A prophet (Obad. 1). See OBADIAH, BOOK OF.

**Obadiah, Book of.** The shortest OT book, fourth among the Minor Prophets. It is directed against EDOM, a nation that was very hostile to the Hebrews. If Obad. 11 refers to the time when the Edomites and others rebelled against King JEHORAM of JUDAH in the ninth century BC (2 Ki. 8:20–22), the book probably would be dated quite early; but if the reference is to other events (cf. Ps. 137:7; 2 Chr. 36:20; Ezek. 25:13–14), the prophecy would be late, subsequent to 586 BC. The first section of the book (Obad. 1–9) is very similar to a section in JEREMIAH (Jer. 49:7–22), so perhaps one of these prophets made use of the other. Obadiah prophesies the destruction of Edom on the DAY OF THE LORD (Obad. 15–18) and predicts that as a result Israel will greatly enlarge its borders (vv. 19–21).

## OVERVIEW OF OBADIAH

**AUTHOR:** The prophet Obadiah.

**HISTORICAL SETTING:** Uncertain. The prophecy may have taken place as early as the ninth century BC or as late as the sixth.

**PURPOSE:** To denounce the nation of EDOM, predicting its destruction and thus reassuring the nation of JUDAH that God will bring deliverance.

**CONTENTS:** The book consists of a series of condemnatory statements against the Edomites (Obad. 1–16) followed by a promise that the Hebrew nation will experience triumph (vv. 17–21).

**Obed** (oh'bid). The name of several men in the OT, including the son of BOAZ and RUTH (Ruth 4:17, 21–22; Matt. 1:5; Lk. 3:32).

**Obed-Edom** (oh'bid-ee'duhm). The name of several men in the OT, the most prominent of whom are the following: **(1)** A "Gittite" (perhaps a PHILISTINE from GATH) in whose house King DAVID deposited the ARK of the covenant after the death of UZZAH (2 Sam. 6:10–12; 1 Chr. 13:13–14; 15:25). **(2)** Son of JEDUTHUN (1 Chr. 16:38). He was a LEVITE who may have served both as a gatekeeper for the ark (15:18, 24) and as a musician (15:21; 16:5). Some think he is the same as #1.

**obedience.** The Bible enjoins obedience to parents (Eph. 6:1; Col. 3:20; 1 Tim. 3:4), teachers (Prov. 5:12–13), husbands (Eph. 5:21–22, 24; Tit. 2:5), masters (Eph. 6:4; Col. 3:22; Tit. 2:9; 1 Pet. 2:18), and governmental authorities (Rom. 13:1–2, 5; Tit. 3:1; 1 Pet. 2:13). Supremely, however, we must obey God (Gen. 26:5; Eph. 5:24; Heb. 5:9; 12:9; Jas. 4:7). When there is a clear conflict regarding obedience to authority, Christians are to obey God, not human beings (Acts 5:29).

**offense.** This noun is used by the KJV (with the spelling *offence*) a number of times in its older sense, "stumbling" (e.g., Matt. 16:23; 1 Pet. 2:8).

**offerings.** See SACRIFICE.

**Og** (og). An AMORITE who was king of BASHAN and whose territory E of the JORDAN included part of GILEAD. The kingdom had two royal cities, EDREI and ASHTAROTH (Josh. 13:12). The account of his war with ISRAEL, after the defeat of SIHON, is given in Num. 21:33–35 and Deut. 3:1–12 and referred to elsewhere (e.g., Deut. 31:4; Josh. 2:10; Neh. 9:2; Ps. 135:11).

**oil.** In the Bible the reference is almost always to olive oil. The olives were sometimes beaten (Lev. 24:2), sometimes trodden (Mic. 6:15), but generally crushed in a mill designed for that purpose. Olive oil was not only a prime article of food, bread being dipped in it, but it was also used for cooking, for anointing, and for lighting. See ANOINT; OINTMENTS AND PERFUMES.

**ointments and perfumes.** The use of perfume in the form of ointment is very ancient and often mentioned in the Bible (e.g., Esth. 2:12; Ps. 104:15; Prov. 7:17; 27:9; Isa. 57:9). Anointing an honored guest was a courtesy a host performed (Lk. 7:46; Jn. 12:3).

**Old Testament.** This name, in Christian terminology, refers to the collection of books that constitute the Hebrew Bible (see also NEW TESTAMENT). In the English versions it consists of thirty-nine books: the five books of MOSES (PENTATEUCH), twelve historical books, five poetical books, and seventeen prophetical books. In the Hebrew Bible, the books are organized differently, and some of them are combined so that the total number of books is twenty-four. See separate articles for each of the OT books.

A beam press, used to extract oil from olives.

Jerusalem and the temple mount, with the Mount of Olives in the background.





**Olives, Mount of.** Also known as Olivet, this flattened and rounded ridge runs N to S and has four identifiable summits. Its name is derived from the olive groves that covered it in ancient times. It forms the highest level of the range of hills to the E of JERUSALEM (Ezek. 11:23; Zech. 14:4), rising c. 250 ft. (75 m.) higher than the TEMPLE mount and 2,600 ft. (790 m.) above sea level; hence it had great tactical significance. The Mount of Olives was the route of DAVID's flight from ABSALOM in the time of the palace rebellion (2 Sam. 15:30; 16:1, 13) but also of Christ's approach on Palm Sunday (Lk. 19:37). The town of BETHANY was located just E of the ridge.

**omega** (oh-meg′uh). The last letter of the Greek alphabet. See ALPHA AND OMEGA.

**omer.** A unit of dry measure equivalent to about two quarts.

**omnipotence.** The attribute of God by virtue of which he is able to do whatever he wills. God's will, however, is "limited" by his nature, and he therefore cannot do anything contrary to his nature as God, such as to ignore SIN, to sin, or to do something absurd or self-contradictory. Although the word *omnipotence* is not found in the Bible, the Scriptures clearly teach this doctrine (e.g., Job 42:2; Jer. 32:17; Matt. 19:26; Lk. 1:37; Rev. 19:6).

**omnipresence.** The attribute of God by virtue of which he fills the universe in all its parts and is present everywhere at once. The Bible teaches the omnipresence of God (Ps. 139:7–12; Jer. 23:23–24; Acts 17:27–28).

**omniscience.** The attribute of God by virtue of which he perfectly and eternally knows all things that can be known—past, present, and future. God knows how best to attain to his desired ends. God's omniscience is clearly taught in Scripture (Ps. 147:5; Prov. 15:11; Isa. 46:10).

**Omri** (om'rī). The name of several men in the OT, most prominently the sixth king of ISRAEL, founder of an important dynasty c. 885 BC (1 Ki. 16:16–28). Omri was an unscrupulous but able king who made SAMARIA the capital of the northern kingdom. He was succeeded by his son AHAB.

**Onesimus** (oh-nes'uh-muhs). A SLAVE of PHILEMON in the city of COLOSSE. He evidently robbed his master and made his way to ROME, but there he met PAUL and became a Christian. Paul then wrote to Philemon, asking him to receive Onesimus back as a brother (Phlm. 10–19; cf. Col. 4:9).

**Onesiphorus** (on'uh-sif'uh-ruhs). An Ephesian believer whose fearless ministry to PAUL during his second Roman imprisonment was held up as a model of Christian kindness (2 Tim. 1:16–18; 4:19).

**Ophel** (oh'fel). An area in the original SE hill of JERUSALEM (2 Chr. 27:3; 33:14; Neh. 3:26–27; 11:21). The name probably refers to a narrow part of the city's E ridge that expands NE from DAVID's initial town (the original Mt. ZION) toward the TEMPLE.

**Ophir** (oh'fuhr). A region, probably in ARABIA (some say India), known for its export of fine woods, precious stones, and especially gold (1 Ki. 9:28; 10:11; Ps. 45:9; Isa. 13:12). It is possible that the name derives from Ophir, son of JOKTAN (Gen. 10:26–29).

**Ophrah** (of'ruh). **(1)** A grandson of OTHNIEL (1 Chr. 4:14). **(2)** A town within the tribal territory of BENJAMIN (Josh. 18:23; 1 Sam. 13:17); it was probably near BETHEL. **(3)** A town within the tribal territory of MANASSEH that was the home of GIDEON (Jdg. 6:11, 24; 8:37); it was probably near MEGIDDO.

**oracle.** A message or answer given by God or a PROPHET; the word is used often in this sense by such versions as the NIV and the NRSV (e.g., Num. 23:7 [TNIV "message"]; 2 Sam. 23:1 [TNIV "inspired utterance"]; Isa. 13:1 [TNIV "prophecy"]). The KJV uses the word in the sense of "shrine" (e.g., 1 Ki. 6:5).

Looking NW toward the Ophel in Jerusalem. The southern wall of the temple mount is visible to the right. 

**ordain.** In addition to the meanings "appoint, establish, issue an order," this term has the special religious sense "to invest officially with ministerial or priestly authority" (e.g., Exod. 28:41; KJV "consecrate"). Note also the noun *ordination* (e.g., 29:22).

**ordinance.** An authoritative decree (e.g., the Passover feast, Exod. 12:14). In Christian theology, the term *ordinance* also has a specialized meaning referring to BAPTISM and the LORD'S SUPPER.

**Othniel** (oth'nee-uhl). Nephew of CALEB and the first of the JUDGES (leaders) of ISRAEL (Josh. 15:17–18; Jdg. 1:13–14; 3:9–11; 1 Chr. 4:13). Because of the sin of the Israelites, God delivered them into the hand of Cushan-Rishathaim (Jdg. 3:8–11), king of MESOPOTAMIA. In their distress they prayed to the Lord, who raised up Othniel to rescue them. He so restored Israel that a period of forty years of peace set in.

O

# P

**Paddan, Paddan Aram** (pad′uhn, pad′uhn-air′uhm). KJV Padan. The area of Upper MESOPOTAMIA around HARAN, upstream of the junction of the rivers EUPHRATES and Habor (Gen. 25:20; 28:2–7; 31:18).

**Palestine** (pal′uh-st*in*). Another name for CANAAN, that is, the region lying between the E coast of the MEDITERRANEAN Sea and the JORDAN RIVER (but sometimes considered to include the area E of the Jordan); often called "the Holy Land." The name occurs four times in the KJV where the reference is to PHILISTIA (Exod. 15:14; Isa. 14:29, 31; Joel 3:4); it is not found in modern versions of the Bible.

Palestine.

**Pamphylia** (pam-fil′ee-uh). A lowland district situated halfway along the S coast of Asia Minor (modern Turkey). At the time of the NT it was a small Roman PROVINCE, bounded by CILICIA to the E, Lycia to the SW, and PISIDIA to the N. PAUL and his companions visited Pamphylia on the first missionary journey, when he preached at PERGA, the chief center of the territory (Acts 13:13; 14:24).

**Paphos** (pay′fos). The capital city of CYPRUS, located at the extreme western end of this large island. Here PAUL and BARNABAS encountered the wiles of the Jewish sorcerer ELYMAS in the court of Sergius PAULUS, the Roman governor, who was converted to Christianity (Acts 13:6–13).

**papyrus.** A reed or rush that grows in swamps and along rivers or lakes. The term refers also to the writing material made from the stalk of the plant. There is little doubt that the NT books were originally written on papyrus (plural *papyri*).

**parable.** A saying or story that seeks to drive home a point the speaker wishes to emphasize by illustrating it from a familiar situation of common life. The OT contains some parables (e.g., 2 Sam. 12:1–12), but the term is used especially of the frequent stories told by Jesus, many of which had to do with the nature of the KINGDOM OF GOD (e.g., Matt. 13).

**paradise.** This term occurs three times in the NT, always with reference to the ultimate place of spiritual bliss (Lk. 23:43; 2 Cor. 12:4; Rev. 2:7).

**Paran** (pay′ruhn). A broad central area of desert in the SINAI Peninsula. It was the district settled by ISHMAEL (Gen. 21:21) and crossed by the Israelites at the EXODUS (Num. 10:12; 12:16; 13:3–26). DAVID fled into Paran after the death of SAMUEL (1 Sam. 25:1). Mount Paran (Deut. 33:2; Hab. 3:3) could refer to any one of a number of prominent peaks in the mountains in the southern Sinai Peninsula.

**parchment.** The skin of a sheep (or goat) prepared in such a way that makes it suitable for writing. Because parchment was more durable and expensive than PAPYRUS, it was used for important or valuable documents. When PAUL asked TIMOTHY to bring him his SCROLLS, he added the comment "especially the parchments" (2 Tim. 4:13), which may be a reference to the apostle's personal copies of the OT Scriptures.

**pardon.** See FORGIVENESS.

**Parthians** (pahr′thee-uhnz). On the day of PENTECOST, some of the people who heard the apostles speak in foreign languages were from Parthia, a territory in PERSIA (Acts 2:9).

**passion.** This English term—which in modern usage means primarily "emotion, ardent affection," and the like—used to have other senses, including "suffering." It often refers specifically to the last sufferings and death of CHRIST (cf. Acts 1:3 KJV).

**Passover.** See FEASTS.

**pastor.** This English term (from a Latin word meaning "shepherd") occurs once in the NT with reference to spiritual leaders (Eph. 4:11; in the KJV it occurs also several times in Jeremiah). The Greek term behind it is used in a similar sense elsewhere (e.g., Heb. 13:20; 1 Pet. 2:25). See ELDER.

**Pastoral Letters.** A common designation applied to three letters written by the apostle PAUL in the early 60s, probably after he was released from his first imprisonment in ROME (many scholars believe that they were written by a disciple of Paul after his death). Two

P

## OVERVIEW OF 1 TIMOTHY

**AUTHOR:** The apostle PAUL.

**HISTORICAL SETTING:** Probably written after the apostle's first Roman imprisonment (thus c. AD 63, perhaps from MACEDONIA) to his spiritual son TIMOTHY, who was ministering in EPHESUS.

**PURPOSE:** To encourage and instruct Timothy in his pastoral responsibilities, especially with regard to sound teaching and matters of church organization and worship.

**CONTENTS:** Warnings against heresy (1 Tim. 1); the need for prayer and worship (ch. 2); church leadership (ch. 3); further warnings about false teaching (ch. 4); pastoring different groups within the church (ch. 5); final instructions (ch. 6).

## OVERVIEW OF 2 TIMOTHY

**AUTHOR:** The apostle PAUL.

**HISTORICAL SETTING:** Written during the apostle's final imprisonment in ROME (c. AD 66) to timid TIMOTHY, whose spirit may have been waning in the face of difficulties.

**PURPOSE:** To encourage Timothy as he experienced conflict and suffering in EPHESUS; to warn him regarding heresy; to ask him to come quickly to Paul, whose martyrdom is near.

**CONTENTS:** Timothy's faith and responsibilities (2 Tim. 1); the nature of the pastoral ministry (ch. 2); opposing heresy and teaching sound doctrine (3:1–4:5); Paul's approaching death (4:6–22).

## OVERVIEW OF TITUS

**AUTHOR:** The apostle PAUL.

**HISTORICAL SETTING:** Written from NICOPOLIS (a city in W GREECE), probably after the apostle's first Roman imprisonment (thus c. AD 63), to his spiritual son TITUS, who was ministering on the island of CRETE.

**PURPOSE:** To instruct Titus to complete the appointment of ELDERS over the various congregations in Crete; to warn him of false teaching; to give instructions about Christian conduct.

**CONTENTS:** Church organization (Titus 1:1–9); false teaching (1:10–16); pastoring different groups within the church (ch. 2); final instructions (ch. 3).

P

of these epistles were addressed to TIMOTHY and one to TITUS, who were Paul's special envoys sent by him on specific missions and entrusted with concrete assignments. Common to all three letters are instructions to help these pastors fulfill their ministry.

**patience.** God's patience is evident in that he is "slow to anger" (e.g., Ps. 86:15 [KJV "longsuffering"]; cf. Rom. 2:4 [KJV "forbearance"]; 2 Pet. 3:9). Thus believers are exhorted to "be patient, bearing with one another in love" (Eph. 4:2; Col. 1:11; 3:12). This is possible only as a result of the Spirit-filled life (Gal. 5:22), and Christ's own endurance is the Christian's model (Heb. 12:1–2).

**Patmos** (pat′muhs). A small island off the SW coast of Asia Minor (modern Turkey) to which JOHN the apostle was banished; here he received his vision and wrote the APOCALYPSE (Rev. 1:9–11). See REVELATION, BOOK OF.

**patriarch.** The father or head of a family, tribe, or clan. In the NT the term usually refers to ABRAHAM, ISAAC, JACOB, and the twelve sons of Jacob (e.g., Jn. 7:22; Acts

7:8–9; Rom. 9:5; Heb. 7:4), but in one passage it is used of DAVID (Acts 2:29).

**Paul** (pawl). A leading APOSTLE in the early church whose ministry was principally to the GENTILES. Born of Jewish parents in TARSUS, he was given the Hebrew name SAUL; his Latin name Paul reflects the fact that he was also a Roman citizen (Acts 21:39; 22:25–29). He moved to JERUSALEM at an early age, distinguished himself as a leading RABBI, and became a persecutor of Christ's followers (8:1; 9:1–2; 22:3–5; Gal. 1:13–14), but on his way to DAMASCUS he received a REVELATION from Christ himself and accepted the Christian faith (Acts 9:3–20; Gal. 1:15–17). The second part of the book of ACTS (Acts 13–28) is devoted almost exclusively to his missionary labors through much of the Roman empire. Paul also became the most eminent theologian of the early Christian church, and his teaching has been preserved in his letters to various churches (e.g., see ROMANS; CORINTHIANS; GALATIANS).

Paul's second missionary journey.

P

Patmos, the island where John wrote the book of Revelation.

**Paulus, Sergius** (paw′luhs, suhr′jee-uhs). The Roman PROCONSUL of CYPRUS who was converted to Christianity under PAUL and BARNABAS (Acts 13:6–12). See also ELYMAS.

**pe** (pay). Also *peh*. The seventeenth letter of the Hebrew alphabet (פ, transliterated as *p*), used to begin each verse in Ps. 119:129–36.

**peace.** The Hebrew word *shalom* in the OT indicates "completeness" or "soundness" and can refer to well-being and security (Jdg. 3:11; Ps. 122:7) as well as the calmness of a mind stayed on God (Ps. 29:11; Isa. 26:3). The MESSIAH is a bringer of peace (Isa. 9:6). According to the NT, peace results from God's FORGIVENESS (Phil. 4:7), is a fruit of the HOLY SPIRIT (Gal. 5:22), and marks the ideal relation among believers (2 Cor. 13:11).

**Pekah** (pee′kuh). One of the last kings of ISRAEL (2 Ki. 15:25–31). Pekah usurped the throne by murdering his predecessor, PEKAHIAH; his reign of twenty years is described as evil.

**Pekahiah** (pek′uh-hi′uh). Son of King MENAHEM; he succeeded his father on the throne but reigned for a short period, c. 741–740 BC (2 Ki. 15:22–26).

**Pelethite** (pel′uh-th*i*t). The name of a people group that possibly should be identified with the PHILISTINES. See KERETHITE.

**Peniel** (pen′ee-uhl). See PENUEL.

**Peninnah** (pi-nin′uh). Wife of ELKANAH and rival of his other wife, HANNAH (1 Sam. 1:1–7).

**Pentateuch** (pen′tuh-ty*oo*k). A term applied to the first five books of the Bible, traditionally attributed to MOSES (GENESIS, EXODUS, LEVITICUS, NUMBERS, and DEUTERONOMY). See also TORAH.

**Pentecost** (pen′ti-kost). This name (from a Gk. word meaning "fiftieth") refers to the OT Feast of Weeks (Exod. 34:22; Deut. 16:9–11), also called the Feast of Harvest (Exod. 23:16) and the Day of Firstfruits (Num. 28:26), when the initial grain harvest was formally dedicated. It fell on the fiftieth day after the Feast of the Passover (see FEASTS). The events recorded in Acts 2 transformed the Jewish festival into a Christian one, for on that day the HOLY SPIRIT was poured upon the CHURCH in fulfillment of Jesus' promise (Acts 1:8) and of OT prophecy (2:16–21, quoting Joel 2:28–32).

**Penuel** (peh-ny*oo*′uhl). A place on the JABBOK River, 8 mi. (13 km.) E of the JORDAN, where JACOB wrestled with the ANGEL

Remains of the Temple of Trajan in Pergamum.

Jon Arnold Images Ltd/Alamy

(Gen. 32:22–32; cf. also Jdg. 8:8–9, 17; 1 Ki. 12:25). The NIV always uses the spelling "Peniel" ("Penuel" is used as a personal name, 1 Chr. 4:4; 8:25).

**Perez** (pee'riz). KJV Pharez and Phares. Son of JUDAH by his daughter-in-law TAMAR; his twin brother was ZERAH (Gen. 38:28–30). Perez was an ancestor of DAVID (Ruth 4:18–22) and of JESUS (Matt. 1:3; Lk. 3:33).

**perfection, perfect.** God alone is perfect in the full sense of the term, but the Hebrew word behind it can refer to wholeness or completeness, and this quality often is ascribed to a person (e.g., KJV Job 1:1 and Ps. 37:37, where modern versions have "blameless") or to the heart of an individual (e.g., KJV 1 Ki. 8:61; NIV "fully committed"). In the NT the word describes God himself (Matt. 5:48), his will (Rom. 12:2), his gifts (Jas. 1:17), etc. In some passages the idea is clearly that of reaching Christian maturity (e.g., 1 Cor. 14:20; Heb. 5:14).

**Perga** (puhr'guh). The chief city in the district of PAMPHYLIA. PAUL and BARNABAS passed through Perga during the first missionary journey (Acts 13:13–14; 14:24–25).

**Pergamum** (puhr'guh-muhm). KJV Pergamos. An important city in the region of MYSIA (part of the Roman province of ASIA), located 15 mi. (24 km.) from the Aegean Sea. The use of PARCHMENT (a word derived from the name Pergamum) as a writing material originated here. One of the seven letters in the book of Revelation is addressed to the Christian community in this city (Rev. 1:11; 2:12–17).

**Perizzite** (per'uh-zit). A collective term for one of the older population groups of PALESTINE that lived in the hill country of JUDAH (Gen. 13:7; 34:30; Exod. 23:23; Josh. 9:1; 12:8; Jdg. 3:5; 1 Ki. 8:20).

**persecution.** Harassment, oppression, or punishment, especially as a result of religious views. Jesus pronounced a blessing on "those who are persecuted because of righteousness" (Matt. 5:10–12). Before his conversion, SAUL (PAUL) was a persecutor of Christians (Acts 22:4), but as an APOSTLE he himself suffered persecution (2 Cor. 4:9) and warned believers that they would suffer in a similar way (1 Thess. 3:4).

Persepolis served as the capital of the Persian empire.



**perseverance.** Patient endurance (e.g., Rom. 5:3–4; see PATIENCE). In Christian doctrine, the term has a specialized sense, referring to Jesus' promise that "no one can snatch them [my sheep] out of my Father's hand" (Jn. 10:29; cf. Rom. 8:38–39; Phil. 1:6; 2 Tim. 1:12) and that therefore true believers will endure until the end. This doctrine, sometimes referred to as "eternal security," is not accepted by some because certain passages seem to allow for the possibility that believers may fall away (esp. Heb. 6:4–6; 10:26–27). See also APOSTASY.

**Persia** (puhr'zhuh). A country of SW Asia, to the E of Babylonia (modern Iran). The Persians became dominant in the sixth century BC and conquered BABYLON in 538 (cf. Dan. 5:30–31). See CYRUS; DARIUS.

P

**Peter** (pee′tuhr). An APOSTLE who acted generally as the leader of the twelve disciples of Jesus. His name was SIMON, but Jesus gave him the surname Cephas (ARAMAIC) or Peter (GREEK), both of which mean "rock" (Mk. 3:16; Lk. 6:14; Jn. 1:42). Peter was outspoken and had an intense faith (Matt. 16:16–19), but sometimes he had to be rebuked (16:21–23). He vigorously promised total allegiance to Jesus (26:35), yet he denied the Lord three times (26:69–75). After the RESURRECTION he became the most prominent leader of the CHURCH in JERUSALEM (Acts 1–5; 10; 12). See also PETER, LETTERS OF.

**Peter, Letters of.** Two of the CATHOLIC EPISTLES. The first of these is specifically addressed to Christians scattered throughout much of Asia Minor (modern Turkey) and who were undergoing PERSECUTION; it conveys a beautiful message of hope and encouragement. The second letter reads

## OVERVIEW OF 1 PETER

**AUTHOR:** The APOSTLE Simon PETER (though some believe the work is pseudonymous).

**HISTORICAL SETTING:** Probably written from ROME (the "Babylon" of 1 Pet. 5:13) in the late 50s or early 60s, but an earlier date is not impossible. Addressed to Christians in various regions of Asia Minor who were undergoing severe persecution.

**PURPOSE:** To encourage holy conduct in the face of suffering by assuring the readers of their coming reward.

**CONTENTS:** The greatness of our SALVATION (1 Pet. 1:1–12); the call to SANCTIFICATION (1:13–2:12); the need for submission (2:13–3:12); the proper response to suffering (3:13–5:14).

## OVERVIEW OF 2 PETER

**AUTHOR:** The APOSTLE Simon PETER (though many believe the work is pseudonymous).

**HISTORICAL SETTING:** Since the writer views his death as imminent (cf. 2 Pet. 1:13–15), the letter must have been written shortly before Peter's martyrdom (c. AD 65–67), probably from ROME. The letter was addressed to Christian communities that were being threatened by false teaching.

**PURPOSE:** To warn the readers against APOSTASY by stressing true KNOWLEDGE over against the message of the false teachers.

**CONTENTS:** Spiritual growth and true knowledge (2 Pet. 1); denunciation of false teachers (ch. 2); the coming of the DAY OF THE LORD (ch. 3).

## OVERVIEW OF PHILEMON

**AUTHOR:** The apostle PAUL.

**HISTORICAL SETTING:** Probably written from ROME during the apostle's first imprisonment in that city (c. AD 61–63). The letter was motivated by the conversion of ONESIMUS, a runaway slave.

**PURPOSE:** To persuade Philemon to forgive Onesimus and receive him back.

**CONTENTS:** After introductory comments (Phlm. 1–7), Paul makes his case (vv. 8–21) and adds concluding remarks (vv. 22–25).

almost like the last will and testament of the apostle (cf. 2 Pet. 1:13–15), reminding his readers of the truth of the GOSPEL, warning them about false teachers, and reassuring them that the Lord will return as he promised.

**pharaoh** (fair′oh). Title of the kings of ancient EGYPT. Pharaohs are mentioned in various OT contexts (e.g., Gen. 12:10–20; 41:1–45; Exod. 5–11; 1 Ki. 3:1; 14:25–26; 2 Ki. 17:4; 23:29–35; Jer. 44:30).

**Phares, Pharez.** See PEREZ.

**Pharisee** (fair′uh-see). Name of the most influential religious group among the Jews in NT times. The Pharisees probably originated in the second century before Christ. They had intense loyalty to the Mosaic LAW but also gave great importance to "the tradition of the elders," human interpretations that sometimes tended to neutralize God's commands (see Mk. 7:1–13). Their views were usually stricter than those of the SADDUCEES, but the Pharisees were not as rigid as the ESSENES. Pharisees individually mentioned in the NT include NICODEMUS, GAMALIEL, and PAUL (see Phil. 3:5).

**Philadelphia** (fil′uh-del′fee-uh). An important city in the region of LYDIA in NW Asia Minor (modern Turkey). One of the letters of Revelation was addressed to the Christian church in Philadelphia (Rev. 1:11; 3:7–11).

**Philemon, Letter to** (fi-lee′muhn). A brief letter written by the apostle PAUL, asking Philemon to welcome his runaway slave, ONESIMUS, as a brother.

**Philip** (fil′ip). **(1)** Son of HEROD the Great who ruled some areas NE of the Holy Land (Lk. 3:1). **(2)** Another son of Herod (by a different wife) whose full name may have been Herod Philip (Matt. 14:3; Mk. 6:17). **(3)** One of the original twelve APOSTLES (Matt. 10:3, etc.); he is mentioned several times in the Gospel of John (Jn. 1:43–48; 6:5–7; 12:21–22; 14:8–9). **(4)** An EVANGELIST whose name first appears in the list of seven DEACONS chosen by the JERUSALEM church (Acts 6:5). He ministered in SAMARIA (8:5–6), explained the gospel to the Ethiopian EUNUCH (8:26–39), and settled in CAESAREA (8:40). He had four unmarried daughters who had the gift of prophecy (21:8–9).

**Philippi** (fi-lip′*i*, fi′li-p*i*). A city of MACEDONIA visited by the apostle PAUL (Acts 16:1, 12–40; 20:6; Phil. 1:1; 1 Thess. 2:2). Philippi was apparently the first European city to hear a Christian missionary. Here Paul and SILAS established a Christian

P

Archaeological excavations at the site of Philippi. Todd Bolen/www.BiblePlaces.com

church with the help of LYDIA. Because Paul expelled a spirit out of a woman, he and Silas were put in prison, but the jailer was converted after an earthquake. See also PHILIPPIANS, LETTER TO THE.

**Philippians, Letter to the** (fi-lip′ee-unz). A letter written by the apostle PAUL to the church in the city of PHILIPPI. The letter was occasioned by a gift (probably finances and clothing) that EPAPHRODITUS brought from Philippi to Paul in prison. The apostle took the opportunity to thank the Philippians for this gift and other favors, but he also urged harmony and UNITY in aim and work (Phil. 1:27–29), HUMILITY as exemplified by Christ (2:1–11), the cultivation of joy and gladness amid difficulties (3:1; 4:1, 4–7), and the pursuit of noble virtues (4:8–9). Of special theological importance are the so-called Christ hymn (2:6–11) and the discussion of FAITH and RIGHTEOUSNESS (3:1–14).

**Philistia** (fi-lis′tee-uh). Name given to a territory on the coastal plain of CANAAN, extending approximately from GAZA in the S to JOPPA in the N (Exod. 15:14; Ps. 60:8; Joel 3:4). See PHILISTINE.

**Philistine** (fi-lis′teen). The name of a warlike people who probably came from the islands of the Aegean Sea and who occupied a territory in SW PALESTINE known as PHILISTIA. Their period of greatest importance was 1200–1000 BC, when they were the principal enemy of ancient ISRAEL (Jdg. 10:6–7; 13:1; 1 Sam. 4:1–7:14; etc.). The five large cities of the Philistines were ASHDOD, GAZA, ASHKELON, GATH, and EKRON (Josh. 13:3; 1 Sam. 6:17).

**Phinehas** (fin′ee-huhs). **(1)** The son of ELEAZAR and grandson of AARON (Exod. 6:25); he was a PRIEST of obvious integrity and deep moral passion. Phinehas played an important part in several incidents both in the wilderness and after the conquest

## OVERVIEW OF PHILIPPIANS

**AUTHOR:** The apostle PAUL.

**HISTORICAL SETTING:** Probably written from ROME during the apostle's first imprisonment in that city (c. AD 61–63), but some scholars prefer an earlier date and place (EPHESUS or CAESAREA). The letter was occasioned by Paul's receipt of an offering from the church at PHILIPPI and by news of discontent and divisions within that community.

**PURPOSE:** To thank the Philippians for their moral and financial support and to update them concerning his situation; to impress upon them the need for HUMILITY and UNITY within the church; to relieve their anxieties and urge contentment whatever their needs.

**CONTENTS:** After a thanksgiving and prayer (Phil. 1:1–11), the apostle reports on his imprisonment and prospects (1:12–26), issues a call for SANCTIFICATION (1:27–2:30), deals with doctrinal problems (ch. 3), and gives final admonishments (ch. 4).

of CANAAN (Num. 25:1–13; 31:6; Josh. 22:9–34; cf. Ps. 106:30). **(2)** Son of ELI the priest who, along with his brother HOPHNI, engaged in gross immorality and was condemned by a "man of God" (1 Sam. 2:11–36). **(3)** A postexilic priest (Ezra 8:33).

**Phoebe** (fee'bee). KJV Phebe. A woman from the church in the small town of CENCHREA (near CORINTH) whom PAUL commended to the church in ROME (Rom. 16:1–2). She is described as a "servant" (NIV) or "deacon" (TNIV), but there has been much debate on whether or not the Greek term here denotes a church office.

**Phoenicia** (fi-nish'uh). KJV Phenicia and Phenice. An ancient country that occupied a strip of seacoast stretching about 120 mi. (190 km.) N from Mount CARMEL; most of this area is occupied by the modern state of Lebanon. Its two main cities were TYRE and SIDON. The Phoenicians turned their attention to the sea because of the pressure on the agricultural lands in the narrow lowland strip, never more than 20 mi. (32 km.) wide. Thus they became the most notable sailors of the ancient world, spreading their trading posts around the African coast from Carthage westward all the way to Spain. In the OT they are usually referred to as Sidonians (Deut. 3:9; Josh. 13:6; etc.). Likewise, "the gods of Sidon," BAAL and ASHTORETH (Jdg. 10:6), were the gods of the Phoenicians generally.

**Phrygia** (frij'ee-uh). An extensive territory in W Asia Minor (now part of modern Turkey) traveled by PAUL in his missionary journeys (Acts 13:13; 14:24; 16:6; 18:23).

**phylactery** (fi-lak'tuh-ree). A small box containing strips of PARCHMENT on which were written those passages of Scripture that enjoin the Israelites to put God's words on the hand and the forehead (Exod. 13:1–10; 13:11–16; Deut. 6:4–9; 11:13–21). Interpreting this command literally, Jewish men often wore such boxes (also called *tefillin*) on the forehead. Jesus condemned the SCRIBES and PHARISEES who used especially large boxes for outward display (Matt. 23:5).

P

This inscription, which dedicates a temple to Emperor Tiberius, contains a reference to Pontius Pilate (Pilatus, second line). © William D. Mounce

**Pilate, Pontius** (pī′luht, pon′shuhs). Roman GOVERNOR of JUDEA who held office AD 26 to 36 and who sentenced CHRIST to death by crucifixion (Matt. 27:2–65; Lk. 3:1; 13:1; Acts 3:13; 1 Tim. 6:13).

**pillar.** This term is used in various ways. (1) An upright support for a building, such as the TABERNACLE or the TEMPLE (Exod. 27:10–17; 1 Ki. 7:2–42). (2) A column used as a monument or memorial, usually in connection with WORSHIP, either legitimate or idolatrous (Gen. 28:18–22; Exod. 24:4; Lev. 26:1 [NRSV; NIV "sacred stone"]). (3) Figuratively of anything that gives support, such as an influential and important person (e.g., Jer. 1:18; Gal. 2:9; Rev. 3:12), the foundations of WISDOM (Prov. 9:1), the CHURCH (1 Tim. 3:15), etc. (4) The column of cloud and fire that guided ISRAEL out of EGYPT and through the wilderness (Exod. 13:21–22; 14:19–20, 24; 33:7–11; see CLOUD, PILLAR OF).

**Pisgah** (piz′guh). A height in the mountains of ABARIM, NE of the DEAD SEA (Num. 21:20; 23:14; Deut. 3:27; 34:1). Pisgah may be the same as Mount NEBO, or it may refer to a nearby peak.

**Pisidia** (pi-sid′ee-uh). A small and mountainous Roman PROVINCE in S Asia Minor (modern Turkey), just N of PAMPHYLIA. Within its borders was the important city

Many scholars believe that Pisgah should be identified with the N shoulder of Mt. Nebo, shown here (with the N end of the Dead Sea in the distance). © Jon Arnold Images Ltd/Alamy

of ANTIOCH, visited by PAUL and BARNABAS (Acts 13:14; 14:21–24).

**pit.** A hole in the ground, sometimes dug for water but also used for other purposes (e.g., as a trap, Jer. 18:22). The word may be used to describe the place of physical BURIAL, a hole with graves dug into the sides. In a figurative sense it can refer to calamity (e.g., Ps. 40:2), and the expression "go down to the pit" means to die without hope, alluding to the nether world of departed spirits (Ps. 28:1). See also ABYSS.

**pity.** See KINDNESS; MERCY.

**plague.** This term often refers to an epidemic disease, but in the Bible it usually denotes a disastrous affliction sent by God as punishment. Especially significant were the ten plagues against the people of EGYPT (Exod. 7–12; see also Ps. 78:43–51; 105:26–36; Acts 7:36; Heb. 11:28).

**pledge.** This term may refer simply to a promise (1 Tim 5:12) or more specifically to personal property held by a creditor to secure payment of a debt (Gen. 38:17–18, 20). The OT Mosaic LAW protected the poor by stating that if an outer garment was taken as a pledge, it had to be restored at sunset for a bed covering (Deut. 24:12–13; for other similar regulations, see vv. 6, 10–11, 17–18).

**Pollux.** See CASTOR AND POLLUX.

**polygamy.** A MARRIAGE in which a person has more than one spouse. The OT mentions some men (e.g., ABRAHAM, JACOB, DAVID) who had more than one wife, but this practice seems inconsistent with God's purpose at creation (Gen. 2:24; Matt. 19:4–6; Eph. 5:31–33) and is evidently disallowed in the NT (1 Tim. 3:2, though some interpret this verse differently).

**polytheism.** The practice of worshiping more than one god, strongly condemned in the Bible (e.g., Exod. 20:3).

**Pontius Pilate.** See PILATE, PONTIUS.

Modern reproduction of the Tower of Antonia, on the NW corner of the temple mount. This structure may be what the Gospels refer to as the Praetorium.
Berthold Werner/Wikimedia Commons

**Pontus** (pon′tuhs). A large PROVINCE of N Asia Minor (modern Turkey) that lay along the Black Sea just E of BITHYNIA (Acts 2:9; 18:2; 1 Pet. 1:1).

**possession, demoniacal.** See DEMON.

**Potiphar** (pot′uh-fuhr). The Egyptian official who purchased JOSEPH and placed him in charge of his household (Gen. 37:36; 39:1, 4–5). He was probably leader of the bodyguard.

**Potiphera** (puh-ti′fuh-ruh). An Egyptian priest who became the father-in-law of JOSEPH (Gen. 41:45, 50; 46:20).

**potter's field.** See AKELDAMA.

**Praetorium** (pri-tor′ee-uhm). This Latin term denoted initially the tent or headquarters of a military commander and later the residence of a provincial governor. The corresponding Greek term is used in the Gospels with reference to PILATE's headquarters in JERUSALEM (the NIV renders it "Praetorium" in Matt. 27:27 and Mk. 15:16, but "palace [of the Roman governor]" in Jn. 18:28, 33; 19:9). The same Greek word occurs in Phil. 1:13, where it refers either to a palace or to the praetorian guard (an elite group of bodyguards).

**praise.** A general term for expressions that exalt either human beings (Prov. 27:21) or God, especially in song (Exod. 15:2).

**prayer.** A spiritual response to God that involves addressing and petitioning him but also contemplating and waiting for him. In the Gospels there are many references to Jesus' praying (e.g., Lk. 3:21; 6:12–13; 9:18; 22:39–40), and he had much to say about prayer (Matt. 6:5–6; 18:19–20; Lk. 11:2–8; 18:1–8). The apostles too emphasize this theme (Rom. 8:26; 12:12; Eph. 3:13–21; 6:19; Phil. 4:6–7; Jas. 5:13–18; 1 Pet. 3:12).

**preaching.** The proclamation of the word of God as found in the Bible, calling sinners to be reconciled to him (2 Cor. 5:20). Much of Jesus' ministry involved preaching the GOSPEL (good news) of the KINGDOM OF GOD, demanding that the hearers repent and believe (Matt. 9:35; Mk. 1:14, 15; Lk. 4:43). In the preaching of the APOSTLES the focus is Christ himself as divine Lord and Redeemer (Acts 2:22–36; 5:42; 11:20; 17:3; 1 Cor. 1:23–24; 2 Cor. 1:19; 4:5).

**predestine.** To determine or choose beforehand (Rom. 8:29–30; Eph. 1:5, 11). See ELECTION.

**Preparation Day.** This phrase (or "the day of Preparation") is used several times in the account of Jesus' trial and death (Matt. 27:62; Mk. 15:42; Lk. 23:54; Jn. 19:14, 31, 42). It normally refers to the sixth day of the week (Friday), when everything had to be made ready to observe the day on which no work was permitted, the SABBATH.

**Presence, bread of the.** See SHOWBREAD.

**press.** A device used for extracting liquids from certain fruits from which WINE and OIL were made (Isa. 16:10).

**prevent.** This English term, which now means "to hinder, to keep from happening," is used by the KJV in the archaic sense "to come or go before, to anticipate," a rendering that can be confusing in a number of passages (e.g., Ps. 119:147; Matt. 17:25; 1 Thess. 4:15).

**pride.** Although this English term can be used in such positive senses as "self-respect" and "delight" (e.g., "I take great pride in you," 2 Cor 7:4), in the Bible it usually refers to a deep-seated sin associated with vanity, presumption, haughtiness, and arrogance. Pride deceives the heart (Jer. 49:16) and brings destruction (Prov. 16:18). "God opposes the proud but gives grace to the humble" (Jas. 4:6). See also BOAST.

**priest.** A person authorized to perform religious rites and to represent human beings before God (Heb. 5:1). The formal priesthood in ISRAEL began with the time of the EXODUS, when AARON was appointed as HIGH PRIEST and his sons as priests under him (Exod. 28–29). Aaron's descendants formed the priestly line, assisted by the LEVITES. The priests led Israelite WORSHIP, which involved primarily the offering of SACRIFICES, but they had many other responsibilities, including matters of health (e.g., Lev. 13). The Aaronic priesthood was set aside when Christ, through his perfect ATONEMENT, became the only priest that believers need (Heb. 7:11–28).

**principality.** This English term is used a number of times by the KJV to translate a Greek term that means "authority" or "ruler" (e.g., Eph. 3:10; Col. 1:16) and that refers to supernatural and angelic powers. See ANGEL; DEMON.

**Priscilla** (pri-sil′uh). Also Prisca (2 Tim. 4:19 KJV). The wife of AQUILA, with whom she is always mentioned in the NT. PAUL met these Jewish Christians in CORINTH (Acts 18:2); they instructed APOLLOS in EPHESUS (18:24–26; see also Rom. 16:3–4; 1 Cor. 16:19).

**Prison Epistles.** Term used to refer to a group of letters traditionally thought to have been written by the apostle PAUL during his first Roman imprisonment: EPHESIANS, PHILIPPIANS, COLOSSIANS, and PHILEMON.

**proconsul.** The title given to a MAGISTRATE functioning in place of a consul outside ROME; it was applied to the governor of a Roman PROVINCE, such as Sergius PAULUS (Acts 13:7) or GALLIO (18:12).

**profane.** To defile, desecrate. The word occurs especially in LEVITICUS and EZEKIEL, where the issue of ritual purity is prominent (e.g., Lev. 20:3; Ezek. 7:21–22). See PURIFICATION.

**promise.** In the Bible this term is used often in the special sense of God's design to bring SALVATION in the person of his Son. This promise was first given to EVE (Gen. 3:15) and was repeated to ABRAHAM (12:2, 7), DAVID (2 Sam. 7:12–13, 28), and others (e.g., Isa. 2:2–5; 4:2; 55:5). In the NT all these promises are regarded as having their fulfillment in Christ and his people (2 Cor. 1:20; Eph. 3:6). In addition, there are many promises of blessing to believers, among them the KINGDOM (Jas. 2:5), eternal LIFE (1 Tim. 4:8), and Christ's coming (2 Pet. 3:9; see ESCHATOLOGY).

**prophet, prophetess.** In the Bible these words refer primarily to those who were appointed by God to communicate his word with divine authority. Sometimes the prophetic message involved predicting the future, but this aspect was subordinate to the main purpose of revealing God's will: correcting, warning, instructing, and encouraging. God, who could choose a prophet even before birth, put his own words in the prophet's mouth (Jer. 1:2–10). The prophets therefore spoke under divine INSPIRATION, being moved by the HOLY SPIRIT, and Christians are told to pay attention to their message (2 Pet. 1:19–21).

**propitiation and expiation.** The verb *propitiate* means "to (re)gain someone's favor, to appease," and thus the noun *propitiation* refers either to "the act of pacifying a person or deity" or to "something, such as a sacrifice, that brings about conciliation" (this noun is used by the KJV in Rom. 3:25; 1 Jn. 2:2; 4:10; modern versions translate "sacrifice of atonement" or the like). The related term *expiation* refers to the removal of SIN. See ATONEMENT.

**proselyte.** In the KJV NT this term is applied specifically to GENTILES who joined themselves to the religious life of ISRAEL, thus the NIV translates "convert" (Matt. 23:15; Acts 2:10; 6:5; 13:43).

**prostitute.** A person who engages in sexual activity in exchange for money or other personal profit. In ISRAEL, legal measures were in force concerning prostitution (e.g., Lev. 19:29; 21:7, 14; Deut. 23:18), and the Bible elsewhere warns against the practice (Prov. 6:25–26; 1 Cor. 6:15–16).

Depiction of the prophets Zephaniah, Joel, Obadiah, and Hosea by John Singer Sargent (1865-1925).

Courtesy of the Trustees of the Boston Public Library/Rare Books

## OVERVIEW OF PROVERBS

**AUTHOR:** King SOLOMON is represented as the source for most of the book, but some sections are attributed to others, and much of the material has no certain attribution.

**HISTORICAL SETTING:** The earliest sayings go back to the Solomonic period, c. 950 BC, but the book could not have taken final form prior to the reign of HEZEKIAH, c. 700 (Prov. 25:1).

**PURPOSE:** To impart true WISDOM, especially to the young.

**CONTENTS:** After a preamble that identifies the FEAR of the Lord as the beginning of wisdom (Prov. 1:1–7), the first major sections consist of discourses on wisdom from a father to his son(s) (1:8–9:18), followed by sayings specifically attributed to Solomon (10:1–22:16), anonymous sayings (22:17–24:34), sayings of Solomon transcribed by "the men of Hezekiah" (chs. 25–29), and sayings of Agur and Lemuel (chs. 30–31).

## OVERVIEW OF PSALMS

**AUTHOR:** More than half of the psalms, primarily in Books I and II (Ps. 1–72), are attributed to King DAVID; one to MOSES (Ps. 90); two to SOLOMON (Ps. 72; 127); a dozen to ASAPH (Ps. 50; 73–83); one to ETHAN (Ps. 89). Many have no ascription.

**HISTORICAL SETTING:** Aside from Ps. 90 (attributed to Moses), the poems were composed over several centuries, from the Davidic period (c. 1000 BC) to postexilic times (c. 400 BC, though some scholars have argued that various psalms are as late as the 2nd cent. BC).

**PURPOSE:** To provide God's people with a collection of poems appropriate for WORSHIP, expressing praise, thanks, confession, lament, and confidence, as well as encouraging obedience and faith.

**CONTENTS:** The collection consists of five parts (alluding to the PENTATEUCH), each of which concludes with a doxology: Book I (Ps. 1–41), Book II (Ps. 42–72), Book III (Ps. 73–89), Book IV (Ps. 90–106), Book V (Ps. 107–150).



**Proverbs, Book of.** One of the poetic books of the OT, consisting of admonitions and sayings about WISDOM. Its central text is "The fear of the LORD is the beginning of knowledge" (Prov. 1:7). The bulk of the book is said to have come from SOLOMON (1:1; 10:1; 25:1; other authors are mentioned in 30:1 and 31:1). The vehicle of instruction is a favorite Semitic device—teaching by contrast, especially between SIN and HOLINESS. Numerous specific topics are covered.

**providence.** God's support, care, and supervision of all CREATION. This doctrine opposes the view that events take place by chance or because of some impersonal fate. Divine providence encompasses the government of the entire universe but especially of human beings (Deut. 10:14; 32:8; Neh. 9:6; Dan. 4:35). The Son of God is represented as "sustaining all things by his powerful word" (Heb. 1:3; cf. Col. 1:17).

**province.** An administrative district of government. The provinces of ROME, such as ASIA and JUDEA, were acquired over a period of more than three centuries.

**Psalms, Book of.** The longest book in the Bible, quoted by the NT more often than any other OT writing. Both for public WORSHIP and for individual devotional guidance, its 150 poems constitute the height of God-given literature. These were composed by a variety of authors, but especially DAVID. Psalms is organized into five sections or "books": Ps. 1–41; 42–72; 73–89; 90–106; and 107–150. A number of Israel's psalms had specific liturgical usage. For instance, the "songs of ascents" (Ps. 120–134) may have been chanted by pilgrims ascending to Jerusalem; and the "Hallel" ("praise") psalms (Ps. 113–118) accompanied the Passover (cf. Matt. 26:30).

**Ptolemais.** See ACCO.

**publican.** Term used by the KJV meaning "tax collector." In NT times, those who collected taxes and tolls for the Roman empire were regarded by the Jews as traitors, willing tools of the oppressor, and thus among the worst of sinners; yet Jesus was willing to have contact with them and offer them SALVATION (cf. Matt. 9:10–11; 21:31–32; Lk. 18:9–14; 19:1–10).

**Pul** (puhl). See TIGLATH-PILESER.

**purification.** The concept of religious purity was a deeply seated concern for the Israelites. It involved both ceremonial and ethical cleanliness, that is, freedom from any kind of ritual or moral pollution separating a person from God. Special rites of purification were needed for various reasons, such as contact with a corpse (Num. 19:1–10) and certain diseases (Lev. 13:8). The NT emphasizes inner purity (Matt. 5:27–28; 19:3–9; Mk. 10:2–11; 1 Cor. 5:9–13; 6:18–20). See also HOLINESS; UNCLEAN.

**Purim** (poor'im, pyoo'rim). The Jewish festival observed on the 14th and 15th days of the month ADAR (February-March).

King David, author of many psalms, is depicted here with a hand harp. (Detail of a stained glass window from the Victorian period.)

These Jewish men from Morocco, in their traditional costume, are reading the Esther Scroll in celebration of the Feast of Purim.
Z. Radovan/www.BibleLandPictures.com

P

It commemorates the deliverance of the Hebrews from the murderous plans of the wicked HAMAN in the postexilic period (Esth. 9:24–32). This festival is named from the casting of the LOTS to determine the most expeditious time for the mass murder of the Jews (cf. 3:7). See ESTHER, BOOK OF.

**Put** (poot). Son of HAM (Gen. 10:6; KJV "Phut") and ancestor of a country mentioned by the prophets (e.g., Jer. 46:9; Nah. 3:9). Many believe it is the same as LIBYA.

# Q

**qoph** (kohf). The nineteenth letter of the Hebrew alphabet (ק, transliterated as *q*, sometimes *k*), used to begin each verse in Ps. 119:145–52.

**quail.** A small migratory game bird (related to the pheasant), highly valued as food. In response to the complaints of the Israelites in the wilderness, God miraculously provided a great abundance of quail for them but also punished them for their greed (Num. 11:18–34).

**queen.** This term is often applied to the mother or the wife of a king, such as Maacah (1 Ki. 15:13) or ESTHER (Esth. 2:22), but sometimes it refers to a ruling female monarch, such as the queen of SHEBA (1 Ki. 10:1). The only ruling queen the Hebrews had in OT times was ATHALIAH (2 Ki. 11:1–20).

**Queen of Heaven.** A deity worshiped in the time of JEREMIAH (Jer. 7:18; 44:17–19, 25). Some think the reference is to the Canaanite goddess ASHTORETH.

**quick, quicken.** In modern usage the adjective *quick* almost always refers to speed, but the KJV translators used it in its older sense, "alive" (e.g., Num. 16:30; Ps. 124:3; 2 Tim. 4:1; Heb. 4:12). Similarly, the verb *quicken* is used in the KJV with the meaning "revive, make alive" (e.g., Ps. 119:50; Rom. 4:17; Eph. 2:5).

**Quirinius** (kwi-rin'ee-uhs). KJV Cyrenius. Roman governor of SYRIA around the time of Jesus' birth (Lk. 2:2). Historical records suggest that he may not have officially held that title until some years later.

**Qumran.** See DEAD SEA SCROLLS.

# R

**Raamses.** See RAMESES.

**Rabbah** (rab′uh). **(1)** The capital city of AMMON, also known as Rabbath-Ammon (cf. Deut. 3:11 KJV; its modern name is Amman, the capital of the Hashemite Kingdom of Jordan). Rabbah was located about 23 mi. (37 km.) E of the JORDAN RIVER. In the time of DAVID, the king of the Ammonites humiliated a group of Hebrew messengers, an action that led to war (2 Sam. 10:1–13; 12:26–31). Several of the prophets proclaimed judgment against Ammon (Jer. 49:2–3; Ezek. 21:20–21; Amos 1:14). **(2)** A town in the hill country of the tribe of JUDAH (Josh. 15:60).

**rabbi** (rab′*i*). A term that originally meant "my master" and that came to be used as a title by the Jews after the OT period in designation of their religious teachers. Christ was so addressed (e.g., Matt. 26:25, 49; Mk. 9:5), as was JOHN the Baptist (Jn. 3:26). In some of these passages, the use of the term appears to be a form of address corresponding roughly with English *sir.*

Remnants of Roman columns in Rabbah (modern Amman, Jordan).

The title "Rabboni" (Mk. 10:51; Jn. 20:16) is an ARAMAIC form of the same word.

**Rabmag, Rabsaris, Rabshakeh** (rab′mag, rab′suh-ris, rab′shuh-kuh). Babylonian titles held by various officials (see NRSV, 2 Ki. 18:17; Jer. 39:3, 13). The NIV translates these titles with such phrases as "high/chief official" and "field commander."

**Rachel** (ray′chuhl). Wife of JACOB and mother of JOSEPH and BENJAMIN (Gen. 29:6–28; 30:22–25; 35:16–19). Rachel was the younger daughter of LABAN (brother of REBEKAH, Jacob's mother, Gen. 28:2); thus Jacob and Rachel were full cousins. JEREMIAH pictures her as rising from her grave to weep over the children who are being carried to BABYLON, never to return (Jer. 31:15; cf. Matt. 2:18).

**Rahab** (ray′hab). **(1)** A prostitute of JERICHO, at whose house two spies stayed just prior to the conquest of PALESTINE by JOSHUA (Josh. 2:1–21). Because she helped them escape, she and her family were spared (6:25). Rahab became an ancestress of Jesus (Matt. 1:5), and the NT commends her faith (Heb. 11:31; Jas. 2:25). **(2)** Poetic name of a monster (e.g., Job 26:12), used symbolically for EGYPT (Ps. 87:4; Isa. 30:7; 51:9–10).

**rainbow.** In his COVENANT with NOAH, God declared that he would never again send a universal FLOOD to destroy the whole inhabited earth, and that promise was made visible by the rainbow (Gen. 9:8–17).

**Ramah** (ray′muh). The name of several towns, but especially one in the tribal territory of BENJAMIN, not far from the city of BETHEL (Josh. 18:25; Jdg. 4:5). It was probably the same as Ramathaim (1 Sam. 1:1) and therefore the birthplace of SAMUEL the prophet (1:20), who later made it his headquarters (7:15–17).

**Rameses** (ram′uh-seez). Also Raamses. One of the cities in EGYPT that the Hebrews were forced to build (Exod. 1:11); it was from Rameses that they began their journey out of Egypt (12:37; Num. 33:3, 5).

**Ramoth** (ray′moth). The name of several towns, but especially one in GILEAD, and so better known as Ramoth-Gilead. It was one of the CITIES OF REFUGE (Deut. 4:43; Josh. 20:8) and, as a frontier town, a key military outpost in the wars between ARAM and Israel; AHAB was killed in battle there (1 Ki. 22:3–40; see also 2 Ki. 8:28–9:14).

**ransom.** As a verb, this English term means "to free someone by paying a price" (e.g., Lev. 19:20; KJV "redeem"). As a noun, *ransom* refers to "that which is paid for someone's release" (e.g., Exod. 30:12; Matt. 20:2; Mk. 10:4). See ATONEMENT; REDEMPTION.

**rapture.** See TRIBULATION.

**Rebekah** (ri-bek′uh). Sister of LABAN, wife of ISAAC, and mother of ESAU and JACOB. Rebekah's father, Bethuel, was ABRAHAM's nephew (cf. Gen. 22:20–22) and thus Isaac's cousin. Abraham sent his steward to MESOPOTAMIA to find a bride for Isaac from his own family, and the steward's adventure became a classic story of divine PROVIDENCE and guidance (ch. 24). After twenty years of marriage and in answer to prayer, God gave Rebekah twins (25:20–26). She plotted the deception by which Jacob gained his father's formal blessing (ch. 27).

**Recab** (ree′kab). Also Rechab, Rekab. The name of several men in the OT, especially the ancestor of the Recabites, a family that was famous for its rules to abstain from wine, build no houses, sow no seed, and plant no vineyard (Jer. 35).

**recompense.** See RETRIBUTION; REWARD.

**reconciliation.** The act or process of restoring harmony and unity in a broken relationship. The Bible stresses that there is need for reconciliation between God and human beings because of the alienation

The Passage of the Red Sea (lithograph by William Brassey Hole, 1846-1917).


between them, which has its source in SIN. God himself has provided the means of reconciliation through the death of his Son Jesus Christ (Rom. 5:10–11; 2 Cor. 5:17–21; Col. 1:19–22).

**red heifer.** A young cow without defect that was to be sacrificed (see SACRIFICE) and burned outside the camp. Its ashes were used for the removal of certain types of ceremonial UNCLEANNESS, such as that of a leper or that incurred through contact with the dead (Num. 19:2–13). See PURIFICATION.

**Red Sea.** In modern usage, this name refers to the NW arm of the Indian Ocean, separating Africa from the Arabian Peninsula. In the OT, the name is a translation of the Hebrew phrase *yam-sûph*, meaning literally "Sea of Reeds" (the translation "Red Sea" comes originally from the SEPTUAGINT). As used in the Bible, this name appears to refer to several distinct places, including the Gulf of Suez on the W (Num. 33:10–11) and the Gulf of Aqabah on the E (1 Ki. 9:26). The crossing of the waters after the EXODUS (Exod. 14) probably took place among the lakes N of the Gulf of Suez.

**redemption.** A metaphor used in both OT and NT to describe God's merciful and costly action on behalf of his people. The basic concept is that of release or freedom on payment of a price (but that does not mean that God paid a price to someone). In the OT the term is applied primarily to God's deliverance of ISRAEL from EGYPT through the EXODUS (Exod. 6:6; 15:13; Ps. 77:14–15; 106:9–11; Isa. 43:1–4; 51:10–11). But that event was only a shadow of the spiritual deliverance from SIN that would be accomplished through the death of Christ (Mk. 10:45; Rom. 3:24; Eph. 1:7; 1 Pet. 1:18–19). Our final redemption is still in the future (Lk. 21:27–28; Eph. 4:30) and will take place at the RESURRECTION (Rom. 8:23).

**regeneration.** In biblical studies this term refers to the new birth, indicating a radical spiritual renewal brought about by the HOLY SPIRIT (Tit. 3:5). Related expressions are "born again" (Jn. 3:3, 5, 7), "born of God" (Jn. 1:13; 1 Jn. 3:9; 5:1), "gives life" (Jn. 5:21), "made us alive" (Eph. 2:1, 5; Col. 2:13), "new creation" (2 Cor. 5:17), "new life" (Rom. 6:4), and "renewal" (Rom. 12:2; Tit. 3:5).

**Rehoboam** (ree´huh-boh´uhm). Son of SOLOMON and his successor to the throne (1 Ki. 11:43–12:27; 14:21–15:6). Because of the heavy taxes he imposed, the northern tribes revolted and formed what came to be known as the kingdom of ISRAEL. Rehoboam remained king in the southern kingdom of JUDAH, reigning c. 930–913 BC.

**remission (of sins).** Release from guilt. See FORGIVENESS.

**remnant.** Something left over. In the Bible this term is applied to the spiritual kernel of the nation of ISRAEL who would survive God's judgment and become the germ of the new people of God. Thus MICAH saw

General view of the Valley of Rephaim.

Danny Frese/www.BiblePlaces.com

the returning glory of Israel (Isa. 7:3; Mic. 2:12; 5:7–8; Zeph. 2:4–7; Zech. 8:1–8). The apostle PAUL highlighted this concept to explain that the true Israel consists of those who believe (Rom. 9:23–30; 11:5).

**repentance.** The act or process of changing one's mind and turning the course of one's life, especially toward God. As a response to divine GRACE, repentance and FAITH are the two sides of one coin (Mk. 1:15; Acts 20:21). Jesus' disciples are commanded to preach repentance to Jews and Gentiles (Lk. 24:47; Acts 2:38; 17:30).

**Rephaim, Rephaites** (ref′ay-im, ref′ay-*i*ts). **(1)** A strong and numerous race of giants that lived E of the JORDAN RIVER (Deut. 2:10–11, 20; 3:11). The name is also applied to giants among the PHILISTINES who fought against DAVID and his mighty warriors (1 Chr. 20:4). **(2)** The Valley of Rephaim was a basin SW of JERUSALEM whose N end marked the N boundary of the tribe of JUDAH and the S boundary of the tribe of BENJAMIN (Josh. 15:8; 18:16). The PHILISTINES sometimes used it as a camping site in preparation for war (2 Sam. 5:18, 22).

**Rephidim** (ref′i-dim). A stop in the wilderness wanderings of the Israelites near Mount SINAI where God brought water out of a rock; it was here too that AMALEK fought with Israel (Exod. 17).

**reprobate.** This adjective, meaning "corrupt" or "depraved," is used by the KJV in several passages (e.g., Rom. 1:28; 2 Tim. 3:8; Tit. 1:16). The Greek word it translates means "not standing the test, and so rejected."

**resh** (reysh). The twentieth letter of the Hebrew alphabet (ר, transliterated as *r*), used to begin each verse in Ps. 119:153–60.

**rest.** God is said to have "rested from all his work" (Gen. 2:2). He commanded that the seventh day, the SABBATH, was to be one of rest (Exod. 16:23; 31:15) and that the land was to have its rest every seventh year (Lev. 25:4). God promised rest to the Israelites in the land of Canaan (Deut. 12:9). The word is sometimes used in the sense of trust and reliance (2 Chr. 14:11). Christ offers rest of soul to those who come to him (Matt. 11:28). Hebrews 4 says that God offers to his people a rest not enjoyed by those who died in the wilderness.

**restoration.** The act of bringing back to a former state. This term is especially applied to the period of Hebrew history following the EXILE, when the Israelites returned to their land and rebuilt JERUSALEM and the TEMPLE (c. 515–450 BC). The verb *restore* is sometimes used of Jesus' healing (e.g., Matt. 9:30; 12:13), of spiritual renewal (Gal. 6:1), and of God's work in the end time (Acts 1:6; 3:21).

**resurrection.** The divine miracle of restoring a deceased person to life in body and soul, either to temporal LIFE, as was the case with LAZARUS (Jn. 11), or more properly to ETERNAL, glorified life, to which Christ was raised and to which those who are his will be raised at his return (Matt. 22:31; Lk. 20:37; Acts 4:2; 17:32; Rom. 8:11; 1 Cor. 15:1–58). Scripture also teaches a resurrection to eternal PUNISHMENT in body and soul of those who lived and died without Christ (Matt. 10:28; Jn. 5:28–29; Acts 24:15).

**retribution.** The act of paying back to someone according to that person's just deserts. The word is not found in the English Bible, but the idea is expressed in reference to JUDGMENT from God when he "will give to each person according to what he has done" (Rom. 2:6).

**Reuben** (*roo*′bin). Firstborn son of JACOB (born to LEAH, Gen. 29:31–32). As an adult, Reuben committed incest with his father's CONCUBINE (35:22; cf. 49:4). On the positive side, he delivered JOSEPH from death (37:19–22; 42:22) and later offered his sons as surety for BENJAMIN (42:37). The name Reuben is also applied to the Israelite tribe that descended from him. The Reubenites occupied land E of the Jordan (Num. 32).

**revelation.** In Christian theology, this term refers to God's disclosure of himself in nature (general revelation) and in Scripture (special revelation). The former focuses on the fact that God exists and must be honored as sovereign—a truth that is known, and has always been known, by all human beings everywhere, rendering them without excuse when they ignore him and do what is evil (Ps. 19:1–6 [cf. 14:1]; Rom. 1:18–20). Special revelation, on the other hand, focuses on SALVATION—truths about SIN, GRACE, ATONEMENT, FAITH, and so on.

## OVERVIEW OF REVELATION

**AUTHOR:** An early Christian named JOHN, probably to be identified with John the apostle.

**HISTORICAL SETTING:** Written from prison on the island of PATMOS. The earliest Christian traditions date the book to the time of PERSECUTION under Emperor Domitian c. AD 95, but some scholars prefer a date during the reign of NERO c. AD 65.

**PURPOSE:** To encourage Christians in the midst of opposition and suffering by assuring them that CHRIST will be victorious over the forces of evil.

**CONTENTS:** After an introduction that includes a vision of Christ (Rev. 1), the book conveys messages to seven specific churches in Asia Minor (chs. 2–3), followed by a series of visions: the heavenly court, the scroll, and its seven seals of judgment (4:1–8:1); seven angels with seven trumpets (8:2–11:19); a woman and a dragon, two beasts, and other figures (chs. 12–14); seven bowls of wrath (chs. 15–16); the fall of Babylon and the final battle (chs. 17–19); the reign of Christ and the new Jerusalem (chs. 20–22).

Christ is presented as the ultimate revelation (Jn. 1:18).

**Revelation, Book of the.** The last book of the NT, frequently called *The Apocalypse of John* from the use of the Greek word *apokalypsis* ("unveiling, revelation") in Rev. 1:1. The author, named John, described himself as a brother of those who were suffering persecution (1:9), and traditionally he has been identified as JOHN son of Zebedee, one of Jesus' disciples. Revelation was written for the express purpose of declaring "what must soon take place" (1:1), in order that the evils in the churches might be corrected and that they might be prepared for the events that were about to confront them. The book provided a new perspective on history by showing that the KINGDOM of Christ was eternal and that it would ultimately be victorious over the kingdoms of the world. There are four main schools of interpretation. The *preterist* holds that Revelation is simply a picture of the conditions prevalent in the Roman empire in the late first century. According to the *historical* view, the book represents in symbolic form the entire course of church history from the time of its writing to the final consummation. The *futurist* interpretation is that most of what the book describes refers to those events that will attend the return of Christ and the establishment of the city of God. The *idealist* or *symbolic* school treats Revelation as a dramatic picture of the conflict of good and evil, which persists in every age but which cannot be applied exclusively to any particular historical period.

**revenge.** See AVENGER OF BLOOD; VENGEANCE.

**reward.** Something given in return for an action, whether good or evil. The Bible makes clear that OBEDIENCE to God results in both spiritual and physical benefits (Rev. 22:12); moreover, it teaches degrees of rewards dependent upon the individual's faithfulness to God's commands (e.g., Matt. 25:14–30; 1 Cor. 3:12–15). The fundamental principle, however, is made clear by PAUL: "It does not, therefore, depend on human desire or effort, but on God's mercy" (Rom. 9:16 TNIV). Ultimately, God himself is the believer's reward (Gen. 15:1).

**Rezin** (ree′zin). King of ARAM (SYRIA) who supported PEKAH, king of ISRAEL, in his fight against JUDAH (2 Ki. 5:37; 16:5; Isa. 7:1). Rezin is also credited with recovering ELATH (2 Ki. 16:6). He was the last Aramean king to rule DAMASCUS (16:9).

**Rhoda** (roh′duh). The name of a young servant in the house of MARY, the mother of John Mark (see MARK, JOHN), who came to answer the door when PETER arrived there after his miraculous deliverance from prison (Acts 12:13–15).

**Rhodes** (rohdz). A large island c. 12 mi. (19 km.) off the SW coast of Asia Minor (modern Turkey). It is generally thought that the

The Acropolis of the city of Lindos, on the E coast of Rhodes.

inhabitants of Rhodes are meant by the name Rodanim (Gen. 10:4; 1 Chr. 1:7). When PAUL passed that way, traveling from TROAS to CAESAREA (Acts 21:1), Rhodes was little more than a port of call with a degree of prosperity and distinction as a beautiful city.

**righteousness.** Morally right behavior or character. The Lord God always acts in righteousness (Ps. 89:4; Jer. 9:24). His people are placed in right relationship with him through REPENTANCE and FAITH (Gen. 15:6; Hab. 2:4; Lk. 18:14; Rom. 1:16–17). See JUSTIFICATION.

**Rimmon** (rim′uhn). The name of a person (2 Sam. 4:2–9), of a deity in SYRIA (ARAM; 2 Ki. 5:17–19), and of several places (Josh. 15:32; 19:13; Jdg. 20:45, 47).

**Rizpah** (riz′puh). A CONCUBINE of SAUL (2 Sam. 3:7; 21:8–10).

**rock.** Because of their abundance due to soil erosion, the rocks of PALESTINE repeatedly play a part in the Bible story, and even God is frequently referred to as "the Rock" (e.g., Gen. 49:24; Deut. 32:4, 13–18; Ps. 18:31). In the NT Christ is called "the spiritual rock" from which his people drank (1 Cor. 10:4; cf. Exod. 17:6). See also PETER.

**rod, staff.** A piece of tree limb used for support, as a weapon, for measuring, etc. Staffs became symbols of authority (Jer. 48:17). MOSES carried one when he returned to EGYPT (Exod. 4:2); upheld, it brought hail and lightning (9:23) and locusts (10:13), and it caused the sea to divide (14:16). PUNISHMENT is symbolized by the rod (Ps. 89:32; 125:3; Prov. 13:24; 22:15; 29:15). The victorious believer will rule with a scepter or rod (Rev. 2:27).

## OVERVIEW OF ROMANS

**AUTHOR:** The apostle PAUL.

**HISTORICAL SETTING:** Written from CORINTH during the third missionary journey (probably the winter of AD 56–57) to the Christian church in ROME, which was facing challenges related to Jewish-Gentile issues. The apostle was about to travel to JERUSALEM to deliver a contribution from the GENTILES for the poor Jewish churches in JUDEA, after which he planned to visit Rome on his way to Spain (Rom. 15:23–33).

**PURPOSE:** In preparation for his visit, Paul needed to clarify the nature of his message of grace to the GENTILES over against the objections of Jewish opponents; he also wanted to deal with doctrinal and practical problems faced by the Roman church.

**CONTENTS:** After an introduction that summarizes his GOSPEL and ministry (Rom. 1:1–17), the apostle demonstrates the universal need for God's RIGHTEOUSNESS in view of the SIN of both Gentiles and Jews (1:18–3:20), expounds and defends his message of JUSTIFICATION by FAITH (3:21–5:21), develops the doctrine of Christian SANCTIFICATION (chs. 6–8), and deals with the difficult problem of ISRAEL's unbelief (chs. 9–11); he then addresses specific issues involving the Christian life (12:1–15:13) and concludes with a summary of his plans, greetings, and final exhortations (15:14–16:27).

Aerial view of the modern city of Rome, with the Coliseum on the bottom left (the Basilica of St. Peter is in the background).



**roll.** See SCROLL.

**Romans, Letter to the.** The longest of the thirteen NT epistles bearing the name of PAUL. Although Romans is often viewed as a theological treatise, it is a real letter, written in preparation for the apostle's visit to ROME (see Rom. 15:19–32). It is true, however, that this document preserves Paul's most complete and systematic exposition of the GOSPEL, explaining the fundamental doctrines of the Christian faith.

**Rome.** Originally a city-state in the Italian peninsula, eventually becoming the capital of the Roman empire. Founded in the eighth century BC on the banks of the Tiber River, it grew to surround seven hills. In population the city probably passed the million mark even before NT times, and a very important Christian church was founded there (see ROMANS, LETTER TO THE). PAUL was imprisoned in Rome on two separate occasions (Acts 28:16; 2 Tim. 2:9), and from there he wrote several letters (the PRISON EPISTLES and 2 Timothy). Both he and PETER are said to have suffered martyrdom in Rome.

**root.** That part of the plant that penetrates the soil and draws up sap and nourishment for the plant. Roots near water symbolize prosperity (Job 29:19; Ezek. 31:7); the opposite is a "withered" root (Hos. 9:16). A root growing old in the ground (Job 14:8) signifies loss of vitality, while "to take root" or "be rooted" denotes becoming or being firmly established (2 Ki. 19:30; Eph. 3:17). Jesus is described as "the Root and the Offspring of David" (Rev. 22:16; cf. 5:5).

**Rufus** (*roo'*fuhs). **(1)** Son of SIMON of Cyrene (who was forced to carry Jesus' cross) and brother of ALEXANDER (Mk. 15:21). **(2)** A Christian in ROME to whom PAUL sent greetings (Rom. 16:13). Possibly he is the same as #1.

The story of Ruth is depicted in these three panels by Thomas Matthews Rooke (1842-1942). Tate, London/Art Resource, NY

**Ruth, Book of.** A short OT book that records how NAOMI's daughter-in-law, Ruth, who was from MOAB, came to be married to BOAZ, an Israelite. This story demonstrates the PROVIDENCE of God at work in the life of an individual, and it exalts family loyalty. It shows how a GENTILE became part of DAVID's ancestry (Ruth 4:17–21); thus Ruth is cited in Matthew's genealogy of Jesus Christ (Matt. 1:5).

## OVERVIEW OF RUTH

**AUTHOR:** Unknown.

**HISTORICAL SETTING:** The story takes place in the time of the judges (Ruth 1:1; see JUDGES, BOOK OF), probably c. 1100 BC. The book may have been written during the reign of DAVID or shortly after (though some scholars date it centuries later).

**PURPOSE:** To demonstrate God's PROVIDENCE in the lives of ordinary people; to show that the Moabite ancestry of DAVID was divinely overseen and thus does not invalidate his kingship; to inculcate filial devotion.

**CONTENTS:** NAOMI's bitterness and Ruth's devotion (Ruth 1); Ruth gleans grain in BOAZ's fields (ch. 2); Ruth requests kinsman-redemption from Boaz (ch. 3); Boaz becomes Ruth's kinsman-redeemer (ch. 4).

# S

**Sabbath** (sab′uhth). The Hebrew weekly day of REST and WORSHIP, observed on the seventh day of the week, beginning at sundown on Friday and ending at sundown on Saturday. The Sabbath was instituted at CREATION (Gen. 2:2–3) and included among the Ten Commandments (Exod. 20:8–11; Deut. 5:13–15; see COMMANDMENTS, TEN). It was meant to be a day of "joy in the LORD" (Isa. 58:13–14). Because Jesus rose from the dead on the first day of the week, most Christians observe this day of rest by meeting for worship on Sunday (cf. 1 Cor. 16:1–2).

**sackcloth.** Strong, rough cloth woven from the long, dark hair of the oriental goat or the camel. It was used to make bags, articles of clothing, etc. Since it was dark in texture, sackcloth was appropriate for times of grief (Gen. 37:34; 2 Sam. 3:31) and to show REPENTANCE (Neh. 9:1; Matt. 11:21).

**sacrifice.** The killing of an animal, usually on an ALTAR, as an offering to God, for the purpose of dealing with SIN (see ATONEMENT). In the OT, such sacrifices included (1) the burnt offering (Lev. 1); (2) the fellowship offering (ch. 3; KJV "peace offering"); (3) the sin offering (4:1–35; 6:24–30); and (4) the guilt offering (5:14–6:7; KJV "trespass offering"). These rituals were a shadow of Christ's perfect sacrifice (Heb. 9:11–15). In a figurative sense, a humbled heart is the sacrifice God wants (Ps. 51:17); Christians offer their own bodies as "living sacrifices" (Rom. 12:1); and even financial gifts can be "a fragrant offering, an acceptable sacrifice" (Phil. 4:18).

Remnants of an ancient synagogue in Capernaum. Although the structure is later than the NT, this may have been the site where Jesus was criticized for healing on the Sabbath (Mk. 3:1-6).

**Sadducee** (sad′*joo*-see). A member of an important Jewish sect during NT times. More political and aristocratic than religious, the Sadducees were opposed by the popular party of the PHARISEES, with whom they differed on various doctrinal questions. For example, the Sadducees denied the RESURRECTION of the body and the existence of ANGELS (Mk. 12:18; Acts 23:8).

**saint.** This term means literally "a holy person," that is, someone sacred or consecrated to God (e.g., Ps. 16:3; see CONSECRATION; HOLINESS). In the NT it refers to members of the Christian church. *All* believers are called "saints," though the term is applied normally to the group of Christians constituting a CHURCH, rather than to one individual Christian (e.g., Acts 9:13; Rom. 8:27; Rev. 5:8). The reference is to those who belong to God as his own. In some instances, however, their saintly character becomes prominent (e.g., Rom. 16:2; Eph. 5:3).

**Salamis** (sal′uh-mis). A harbor on the W coast of the island of CYPRUS. PAUL and BARNABAS preached in the SYNAGOGUES there on the first missionary journey (Acts 13:5).

**Salem** (say′luhm). An abbreviated form of JERUSALEM (Gen. 14:18; Ps. 76:2; Heb. 7:1–2).

**Salome** (suh-loh′mee). **(1)** One of the women who ministered to Jesus in GALILEE and

An artistic representation of the sacrifice offered by Noah (oil on canvas by Daniel Maclise, 1806–70).

who after the crucifixion went to the tomb to anoint his body (Mk. 15:40–41; 16:1). Apparently she is the same as the wife of ZEBEDEE (Matt. 27:56) and therefore mother of JAMES and JOHN. **(2)** The daughter of HERODIAS and Herod PHILIP (Matt. 14:3–11; Mk. 6:16–28); her name is not mentioned in the Gospels but it is given by Josephus, a first-century Jewish historian.

**salvation.** This word (as well as the verb *save*) can refer to everyday types of deliverance, as from enemies, disease, and danger (e.g., 1 Sam. 10:24 [KJV]; Ps. 72:4). In the Bible, however, it is applied primarily to God's special involvement in human history, as in the EXODUS (Exod. 14:13 KJV) and ultimately in the saving work of Jesus Christ, who saves his people from their sins (Matt. 1:21; Lk. 2:11, 30; Acts 4:12; 1 Thess. 5:9). Sinners receive salvation when they repent and believe (Lk. 19:9; Rom. 10:10), but believers continue to enjoy God's salvation throughout their lives (Phil. 2:12–13; 1 Pet. 2:2), and their final salvation is still in the future (Rom. 13:11; 1 Pet. 1:5).

**Samaria** (suh-mair'ee-uh). The capital city of the northern kingdom of ISRAEL. Built c. 875 BC by King OMRI (1 Ki. 16:24), it was located on a hilltop c. 40 mi. (65 km.) N of JERUSALEM and c. 25 mi. (40 km.) from the MEDITERRANEAN. The city was destroyed by the Assyrians in 721 BC but later rebuilt. The name was applied also to the general region in which the city was located. See also SAMARITAN.

**Samaritan** (suh-mair'uh-tuhn). An inhabitant of the territory of SAMARIA; the term may also signify the religious sect associated with that region. After the fall of the northern kingdom of ISRAEL, most of the inhabitants were deported, while people from other nations were brought in, leading to intermarriage and also a mixed religion (2 Ki. 17). Thus the Samaritans and the Jews felt separated by race and religion, and this situation is reflected in the NT (Matt. 10:5; Lk. 10:30–37; 17:11–19; Jn. 4:4–42).

**samech** (sah'mek). The fifteenth letter of the Hebrew alphabet (ס, transliterated as *s*), used to begin each verse in Ps. 119:113–20.

**Samson** (sam'suhn). A leader and hero of Israel, famous for his prodigious strength displayed against the PHILISTINES (Jdg. 13–16; Heb. 11:32). He may have been the last of the JUDGES of ISRAEL prior to SAMUEL. His birth was announced by the ANGEL of the Lord beforehand to his mother, who was barren. Samson was dedicated as a NAZIRITE (cf. Num. 6:1–21), and the Spirit of the Lord came on him to accomplish great deeds. But he also showed some moral weaknesses, and his relationship with a non-Israelite woman named DELILAH led to his fall and eventual death.

**Samuel** (sam'*yoo*-uhl). The last of the Israelite JUDGES (leaders) prior to the monarchy; Samuel also served as PRIEST and PROPHET (1 Sam. 1:1–16:13). Born in response to the prayers of his mother, HANNAH, who had been barren, Samuel was dedicated to God as a child. He led the Israelites in victory over the PHILISTINES and was commissioned of God to anoint SAUL and DAVID, the first two kings of ISRAEL.

**Samuel, Books of.** Two historical books of the OT that cover a period of more than one hundred years, from the birth of SAMUEL to shortly before the death of DAVID. The authorship and date of the books are unknown. These books describe the establishment of the kingship in Israel, marking the transition from judgeship to monarchy. The primary concern, however, is not to present historical facts but to demonstrate God's care for his people and to summon the people to repentance and faithfulness.

S

Nebi Samwil (5 mi. W of Jerusalem), traditional burial place of the prophet Samuel, marked by a modern-day minaret.

Z. Radovan/www.BibleLandPictures.com

## OVERVIEW OF 1–2 SAMUEL

**AUTHOR:** Unknown.

**HISTORICAL SETTING:** Covers the period from the end of the era of the judges (c. 1050 BC) to the end of the Davidic period (c. 970). The work must have been composed sometime after the division of the kingdom (c. 930) and possibly as late as the period of EXILE (c. 550).

**PURPOSE:** To provide a historical-theological account of the Hebrew nation during the judgeship of SAMUEL and during the reigns of SAUL and DAVID; to give an account of the rise of the Israelite monarchy; to stress the importance of faithfulness to the COVENANT.

**CONTENTS:** Birth and judgeship of Samuel (1 Sam. 1–7); Saul's rise, triumphs, and failures (1 Sam. 8–15); David's rise, his years as fugitive, and the death of Saul (1 Sam. 16–31); the establishment and successes of David's reign (2 Sam. 1–10); David's sin and its consequences (2 Sam. 11–20); other events during David's reign (2 Sam. 21–24).

S

**Sanballat** (san-bal′at). A man in SAMARIA who opposed NEHEMIAH's efforts to rebuild JERUSALEM (Neh. 2:10, 19; 4:1–9; 6:1–14).

**sanctification.** The process or result of being made holy (see HOLINESS). When things or people are sanctified, they are consecrated and set apart for God's use (see CONSECRATION). When applied to people, the word often has a moral and ethical dimension, especially in the NT. Thus believers are described as already sanctified in Christ (1 Cor. 1:2; 6:11), but they are also called to show holiness in their lives (1 Thess. 4:3; 5:23; Heb. 10:14).

**Sanhedrin** (san-hee′druhn). The COUNCIL or governing body that met in JERUSALEM in NT times and that constituted the highest Jewish authority in PALESTINE prior to AD 70 (e.g., NIV at Mk. 14:55; Acts 4:15). It was composed of seventy members plus the president, who was the HIGH PRIEST.

**Sapphira** (suh-fi′ruh). Wife of ANANIAS. The couple sold a piece of property and pretended to bring the money to the APOSTLES. For their hypocrisy in pretending not to have kept any of the money for themselves, they both died suddenly within three hours of each other, much to the fear of the early church and of all who heard about it (Acts 5:1–11).

**Sarah, Sarai** (sair′uh, say′ri). KJV NT Sara. The wife of ABRAHAM (Gen. 11:29–30) and also his half sister on his father's side (20:12). Sarai was her original name. Still childless at the age of seventy-five, she induced Abraham to take her handmaid HAGAR as a CONCUBINE (16:1–3). Years later God affirmed that Sarai would bear a son and changed her name to Sarah as a mark of his promise (17:15–16). In due time she gave birth to ISAAC, the son of the COVENANT (17:21; 21:1–3). Sarah is mentioned several times in the NT (Rom. 4:19; 9:9; Gal. 4:21–5:1; Heb. 11:11; 1 Pet. 3:6).

**Sardis** (sahr′dis). The chief city in the region of LYDIA. A Christian congregation in Sardis was one of the churches to which the book of Revelation was addressed (Rev. 1:11; 3:1–6).

**Sargon** (sahr′gon). A name found only once in the Bible (Isa. 20:1), where it refers to King Sargon II of ASSYRIA, son of TIGLATH-PILESER III and father of SENNACHERIB. Sargon was responsible for the fall of SAMARIA (2 Ki. 17:1–6).

**Satan** (say′tuhn). A Hebrew term meaning "adversary" or "accuser," and used as the name of the DEVIL, "that ancient serpent," the greatest enemy of God and human beings (Rev. 12:9; 20:2). He is described as "the evil one" (Matt. 13:19, 38; 1 Jn. 2:13; 5:19); "the father of lies" (Jn. 8:44); "the god of this age" (2 Cor. 4:4); "the prince of this world" (Jn. 12:31; 14:30);

This relief of Sargon II from the palace of Khorsabad (c. 710 BC) pictures the king wearing the royal tiara and holding a staff as he faces a high official or crowned prince.

Marie-Lan Nguyen/Wikimedia Commons

Relief of Sennacherib on a magnificent throne watching prisoners being brought before him from the capture of the city of Lachish during the time of Hezekiah (from Nineveh, 7th cent. BC).



"the ruler of the kingdom of the air" (Eph. 2:2); "the tempter" (Matt. 4:3; 1 Thess. 3:5). Although Satan was judged at the CROSS (Jn. 13:31–33), he is still permitted to carry on the conflict, often with startling success. But his revealed doom is sure (Matt. 25:41; Rev. 20:1–10).

**Saul** (sawl). **(1)** The first king of ISRAEL (1 Sam. 9–31). Although his rule was initially promising, later events revealed serious flaws in his character, such as a lack of full OBEDIENCE to God (ch. 15) and personal jealousy (18:8–12; see DAVID). Both he and his sons died in battle (ch. 31). **(2)** Saul of Tarsus. See PAUL.

**savior.** One who saves, delivers, or preserves from any evil or danger, whether physical or spiritual, temporal, or eternal. Human beings cannot save themselves, so the Lord alone is the Savior (Ps. 44:3, 7; Isa. 43:11; Hos. 13:4). Savior is preeminently the title of the Son (Matt. 1:21; Lk. 2:11; 2 Tim. 1:10; Tit. 1:4; 2:13; 3:6; 2 Pet. 1:1, 11; 2:20; 3:2, 18; 1 Jn. 4:10). See SALVATION.

**scapegoat.** Traditional rendering of the Hebrew word *azazel*, the meaning of which is uncertain. It is applied to a goat that symbolically bore the sins of the people on the Day of ATONEMENT (Lev. 16:8, 10, 26). The high priest laid his hands on the head of the goat while confessing "all the wickedness and rebellion of the Israelites" (16:21); then the goat was sent into the wilderness to carry the sins away (16:22).

**scribe.** An official secretary (e.g., 2 Sam. 8:17 KJV). The Hebrew term (*sopher*) is applied especially to professional copyists who produced manuscripts of the Hebrew Bible. Scribes were regarded as scholars and were involved in religious instruction. Accordingly, the NIV sometimes uses the rendering "teacher" in the OT (e.g., Ezra 7:6), and in the NT it consistently uses "teacher of the law." In the Gospels, scribes are sometimes found in connection with the priestly party, that is, the SADDUCEES (e.g., Matt. 2:4), but most of them were associated with the PHARISEES (5:20).

**Scripture.** See BIBLE; NEW TESTAMENT; OLD TESTAMENT.

**scroll.** Sheets of PAPYRUS or PARCHMENT joined together in long rolls and used for various kinds of documents in ancient times. The material could be rolled between two wooden rollers. The Bible often makes reference to books or scrolls (e.g., Ps. 40:7 [cited in Heb. 10:7]; Jer. 36:22–23; Ezek. 2:9–3:3; Lk. 4:17, 20; Rev. 10:8–10).

**Scythian** (sith′ee-uhn). A name designating primarily a nomadic people that inhabited the area E and NE of the Black Sea. The term came to be applied more generally to horse riders who raised livestock in that region and farther N and who were viewed as uncivilized (Col. 3:11).

**security of the believer.** See ASSURANCE; PERSEVERANCE.

**Seir** (see′uhr). See EDOM.

**selah** (see′luh). A Hebrew word of uncertain meaning that occurs frequently in the book of PSALMS (e.g., Ps. 3:2, 4, 8; 4:2, 4). Many believe it indicates some kind of pause in the music or recitation.

**Sennacherib** (suh-nak′uh-rib). Son of SARGON II and king of ASSYRIA, 705–681 BC. During the reign of HEZEKIAH, Sennacherib captured many cities in JUDAH and threatened JERUSALEM, but God delivered his people (2 Ki. 18:13–19:17; 2 Chr. 32:1–22; Isa. 36:1–37:38).

**Septuagint** (sep′*too*-uh-jint). Traditional name given to the primary Greek translation of the Hebrew Bible (commonly abbreviated with the Roman numeral LXX). The term means "Seventy," reflecting a tradition that seventy (or seventy-two) translators produced the translation of the Pentateuch c. 250 BC in ALEXANDRIA. The rest of the OT was translated over the next two centuries in various locations. Since the NT authors wrote in Greek, it was natural for them to use the Septuagint in most instances when quoting or alluding to the OT.

**seraph, seraphim** (ser′uf, ser′uh-fim). There are only two references in the Bible to the seraphs (Isa. 6:2, 6; the form *seraphim* is the plural in Hebrew). Each seraph is said to have six wings, a face, hands, and feet. The seraphs are apparently an order of angelic beings (see ANGEL) similar to the CHERUBS, possibly related to the living creatures of Rev. 4:6–8.

**Sergius Paulus.** See PAULUS, SERGIUS.

**Sermon on the Mount.** Traditional title given to Jesus' discourse recorded in Matt. 5–7. It includes the well-known BEATITUDES and many other ethical teachings that are paralleled in various passages elsewhere (e.g., Lk. 6:17–49, sometimes called the Sermon on the Plain).

**servant.** See SLAVE.

**Servant of the Lord.** Although this phrase can refer to various individuals in the OT (e.g., MOSES, Josh. 1:1), scholars apply it primarily to a messianic figure mentioned repeatedly in Isa. 42–53 whom God calls "my servant." In most Christian interpretation, the "Servant Songs" are understood as a prophecy of Jesus Christ (e.g., Isa. 42:1–4 is quoted as fulfilled in Matt. 12:18–21; and parts of Isa. 53 are often quoted or alluded to in the NT).

**Seth** (seth). Third son of ADAM and EVE and ancestor of the godly messianic line that

A view of the Sea of Galilee from the Mt. of Beatitudes, where tradition says that Jesus preached the Sermon on the Mount. Jon Arnold Images Ltd/Alamy

S

Basalt statue of Shalmaneser III (from Ashur, 9th cent. BC).


descends from him (Gen. 4:25–26; 5:3–8; Lk. 3:38).

**sex.** See ADULTERY; FORNICATION; MARRIAGE; PROSTITUTE.

**Shadrach** (shad'rak). The Babylonian name given to HANANIAH, one of DANIEL's companions taken by NEBUCHADNEZZAR to be trained in his palace as counselors to the king (Dan. 1:3–7, etc.).

**Shalmaneser** (shal'muh-nee'zuhr). The name of several Assyrian kings, though the only one mentioned in the OT is Shalmaneser V (reigned 726–722 BC), son of TIGLATH-PILESER III. He attacked the northern kingdom of ISRAEL (2 Ki. 17:3–5; 18:9–11).

**Shamgar** (sham'gahr). One of the Israelite leaders during the period of the JUDGES (Jdg. 3:31; 5:6).

**Sharon** (shair'uhn). The largest of the coastal plains of N PALESTINE, with a length of about 50 mi. (80 km.) and a variable width of 9–10 mi. (14–16 km.). The "splendor" of Sharon (Isa. 35:2) suggests the dense vegetation originally associated with the whole plain. The "rose of Sharon" (Cant. 2:1) may have been a type of tulip. Sharon is also mentioned in the NT (Acts 9:35; KJV "Saron").

**Sheba** (shee'buh). The name of several people and places in the OT, but especially of a mountainous and fertile country in S ARABIA, now Yemen. Sheba gained wealth through control of the trade in perfumes and INCENSE, which were important in the life and religion of the ancient world (Job 6:19; Isa. 60:6; Jer. 6:20; Ezek. 27:22). The queen of Sheba visited SOLOMON, bringing as gifts gold, precious stones, and spices (1 Ki. 10:1–13; 2 Chr. 9:1–12).

**Shebna, Shebnah** (sheb'nuh). A royal secretary under King HEZEKIAH; he was among those who negotiated with the besieging Assyrian army (2 Ki. 18:18–19:7 = Isa. 36:3–37:7). The Lord accused him of pride and predicted his fall (Isa. 22:15–19).

**Shechem** (shek'uhm). An ancient Canaanite town and then one of the Israelite CITIES OF REFUGE in the hill country of EPHRAIM (Josh. 20:7) in the neighborhood of Mount GERIZIM (Jdg. 9:7), being about 30 mi. (50 km.) N of JERUSALEM. It is the first place in CANAAN to be mentioned in connection with the arrival of ABRAHAM (Gen. 12:6–7). Later JACOB settled down at Shechem, where he purchased land from a Canaanite family (33:18–19; Shechem was also the name of a ruler there). The city played a prominent role in Israelite history (cf. Josh. 24:25; Jdg. 9; 1 Ki. 12:1, 25; Hos. 6:9).

**shekel.** The basic unit of weight in OT times, equal to approximately 11.5 grams (0.4 ounces). Because the term *shekel* by itself could mean "shekel of silver," it was also a monetary unit (cf. 1 Ki. 7:1).

**Shekinah** (shuh-k*i*′nuh). A postbiblical Hebrew term meaning "dwelling," applied especially to the divine presence, in particular the manifestation of God's GLORY in the TABERNACLE (Exod. 40:34–35) and the TEMPLE (1 Ki. 8:10–11). The concept is alluded to in other passages (e.g. Isa. 60:2; Matt. 17:5; Jn. 1:14; Acts 1:9; Rom. 9:4).

**Shem** (shem). Son of NOAH, possibly his firstborn (Gen. 5:32; 9:23–27; 11:10–11; Lk. 3:36). The names of his descendants (Gen. 10:21–31) suggest that he may have been the ancestor of Semitic people groups, including the Hebrews (the modern term *Semite* is derived from *Shem*), but historical ethnic distinctions are difficult to determine with precision.

**Shema, the** (shuh-mah′). Name given to the confession found in Deut. 6:4–9 (recited with 11:13–21 and Num. 15:37–41 in SYNAGOGUE services). This designation derives from the first word of the passage, *shema'*, which means, "Hear!" (The word *Shema* is also the name of a place and of several persons.)

**Sheol** (shee′ohl). The Hebrew name of the place where the dead were believed to dwell. The NIV usually renders this word as "the grave" (e.g., Gen. 37:35), but other renderings include "death" (Job 17:16) and "depths" (Ps. 139:8). See also HADES.

**Shiloh** (sh*i*′loh). A city in the territory of EPHRAIM, 20 mi. (32 km.) NNE of JERUSALEM, that served as an important religious center. The TABERNACLE was located there from the time of JOSHUA through that of SAMUEL (Josh. 18:1; 19:51; Jdg. 21:19; 1 Sam. 1:24).

**Shimei** (shim′ee-*i*). The name of many persons in the OT, but especially a relative of SAUL who cursed King DAVID (2 Sam. 16:5–12; 19:16–23; 1 Ki. 2:8–9, 36–46).

**shin** (shin). KJV *schin*. The twenty-first letter of the Hebrew alphabet (שׁ, transliterated as *š* or *sh*), used to begin each verse in Ps. 119:161–68.

**Shinar** (sh*i*′nahr). A designation for the land of BABYLONIA (Gen. 10:10); here was built the city and tower of BABEL (11:2).

**showbread.** The consecrated UNLEAVENED BREAD ritually placed on a table in the TABERNACLE (and TEMPLE) each SABBATH. The NIV and other versions use the more literal rendering, "the bread of the Presence" (e.g., Exod. 35:13). The loaves reminded the people of God's supply of daily need for bread and their continued dependence on God's provision for spiritual as well as physical needs.

**Shunammite** See SHUNEM.

**Shunem** (sh*oo*′nuhm). A town about 3 mi. (5 km.) N of JEZREEL and just S of Mount MOREH (Josh. 19:18; 1 Sam. 28:4). ABISHAG, DAVID's nurse who cared for him shortly before his death, was a Shunammite (1 Ki. 1:3). The prophet ELISHA lodged frequently at Shunem in the home of a well-to-do family (2 Ki. 4:8–37).

**Shushan.** See SUSA.

**Sidon** (s*i*′duhn). KJV usually spells it Zidon in the OT. An important, coastal city-state of PHOENICIA about 25 mi. (40 km.) N of TYRE. Sidon was well known for its craftsmanship (ivory, silver, etc.), com-

The village of Shunem, located on the SW side of Mt. Moreh in the Jezreel Valley. Z. Radovan/www.BibleLandPictures.com

merce, and seafaring (cf. Isa. 23:2), but it came under God's judgment for its IDOLATRY (Jdg. 10:6; Ezek. 28:21–23). It is mentioned a number of times in the NT (e.g., Matt. 11:21–22; 15:21; Acts 27:3).

**sign.** In Scripture this word has several meanings, but it often refers to an event that gives evidence of a divine power, that is, a MIRACLE (e.g., Exod. 4:8); the word is used in this sense especially in the Gospel of John (e.g., Jn. 2:11; 3:2; 20:30; in these cases the NIV, but not the TNIV, uses the phrase "miraculous sign").

**Sihon** (*si'*hon). A king of the AMORITES defeated by the Israelites on their way to CANAAN (Num. 21:21–30). This event became a powerful reminder of God's protection (e.g., Deut. 2:24–37; 31:4; Josh. 13:21; Neh. 9:22; Ps. 135:10–12).

**Silas, Silvanus** (*si'*luhs, sil-vay'nuhs). A prominent member of the JERUSALEM church (Acts 15:22, 27, 32) and companion of the apostle PAUL on most of his second missionary journey (15:40–17:10). In several of his letters, Paul mentions Silas together with TIMOTHY (2 Cor. 1:19; 1 Thess. 1:1; 2 Thess. 1:1). PETER commends Silas for his assistance (1 Pet. 5:12).

**Siloam** (*si*-loh'uhm). A pool and tower in biblical JERUSALEM (Neh. 3:15 NIV [KJV "Siloah"]; Lk. 13:4; Jn. 9:7, 11). Today the term is applied also to the water tunnel constructed under King HEZEKIAH (2 Chr. 32:30).

**Simeon** (sim'ee-uhn). The name of several men in the Bible; the two most prominent are the following: **(1)** Second son of JACOB and LEAH (Gen. 29:33) and ancestor of the Israelite tribe that bears his name. Simeon was the brother whom JOSEPH held hostage until BENJAMIN should be brought to him (42:24). Toward the end of the wilderness wanderings, the tribe of Simeon appears to have been the smallest (22,000 men, Num. 26:14). Possibly for this reason, the Simeonites were not accorded a separate inheritance in the land; their villages were located in the southern area of JUDAH (Josh. 19:1–9). **(2)** A devout man of JERUSALEM who had been promised by God that he would see the MESSIAH before he died (Lk. 2:25–32). See also SIMON.

**Simon** (*si'*muhn). Greek form of the Hebrew name SIMEON. Almost ten men in the NT bear this name, the most prominent of them being the following: **(1)** One of the twelve disciples of Jesus. See PETER. **(2)** Another of the disciples of Jesus, called "the Zealot" (Matt. 10:4; Mk. 3:18; Lk. 6:15; Acts 1:13). See CANANAEAN. **(3)** A PHARISEE in whose house a sinful woman anointed the feet of Jesus with her tears and ointment (Lk. 7:36–50). **(4)** A man who practiced sorcery in SAMARIA and who tried to purchase the power of the HOLY SPIRIT from the APOSTLES (Acts. 8:9–24).

**sin.** The biblical writers portray sin with a great variety of terms because they have a powerful sense of the purity and holiness of the living God. Thus sin may be viewed, for example, as a transgression or violation of the divine law (Matt. 15:3; 1 Jn. 3:4), but also as disobedience (Rom. 5:19; Heb. 2:2), rebellion (Ps. 78:17; Isa. 58:1), wrongdoing (Lev. 5:19; 1 Jn. 5:17), and especially as a personal offense against the Lord himself (Gen. 13:13; Exod. 32:33; Ps. 51:4; Jer. 3:25; Rom. 8:7–8). Sin is both a pervasive condition of the heart (Gen. 6:5; Jer. 17:9) and the practical outworking of that condition in thoughts, words, and deeds that offend God. All human beings are sinners (Rom. 3:10–12, 23) except for Jesus Christ, who made FORGIVENESS and SALVATION possible (2 Cor. 5:21; Heb. 4:15; 7:26–27).

Staircase leading to the depression that once functioned as the Pool of Siloam. www.HolyLandPhotos.org

Pinnacle of Jebel Musa, traditional site of Mt. Sinai.



**Sin, Desert of.** This region—not to be confused with the Desert of ZIN in the northern NEGEV—was on the route followed by the Hebrews when they left EGYPT (Exod. 16:1; 17:1; Num. 33:11–12). The hebrew name *Sin* is not related to the English word *sin*.

**Sinai, Mount** (si'ni). The name of the sacred mountain before which Israel encamped and on which MOSES communed with God and received the COVENANT and the LAW (Exod. 19:1–2, 11, 16–20; 34:1–29; cf. Heb. 12:18–24). This mountain is also known as Horeb (Exod. 3:1; 33:6; Deut. 5:2; 1 Ki. 19:8).

**Sisera** (sis'uh-ruh). Commander of the army under JABIN, the Canaanite king of HAZOR (Jdg. 4:2–22). Sisera oppressed Israel for twenty years, but was then defeated by the Israelites under DEBORAH and BARAK.

**slave, slavery.** Among the Hebrews, slaves could be acquired by capturing prisoners of war (Num. 31:7–9), by purchase (Lev. 25:44), by the voluntary decision of the person wanting to be a slave (Exod. 21:6), and so on. They could gain their freedom in a number of ways (Exod. 21:2–27; Deut. 15:12–23). Slavery continued in NT times, but the love of Christ seemed to argue against its continued existence (Eph. 6:5–9; Gal. 3:28; Phlm. 15–16).

**Smyrna** (smuhr'nuh). A port city on the W coast of Asia Minor (modern Turkey). Smyrna was famous for science, medicine, and the majesty of its buildings. One of the letters in the book of Revelation was addressed to the Christian church in this city (Rev. 2:8–17).

**Sodom** (sod'uhm). One of the cities destroyed by God because of the people's sin (Gen. 18:20; 19:24–25). ABRAHAM's nephew, LOT, had earlier chosen to live in Sodom and suffered for it (19:1–10), but he was delivered from destruction. Throughout the Bible, Sodom and GOMORRAH are mentioned together often as examples of wickedness and of God's judgment (e.g., Isa. 1:9–10; Jer. 50:40; 2 Pet. 2:6).

**Solomon** (sol'uh-muhn). Son of DAVID and third king of ISRAEL (c. 970–930 BC). Solomon received special WISDOM from God (1 Ki. 3:3–14; 4:29–34), built a great TEMPLE for the Lord (chs. 6–8), and enlarged the kingdom of Israel to its greatest geographical extension and material prosperity (4:20–28; 10:14–29). Unfortunately, he also arranged a series of marriage alliances with pagan countries, and these were his eventual undoing (11:1–13).

**Song of Solomon.** Also known as Song of Songs (from the opening verse) and as Canticles, this biblical book centers on the joys and distresses of the love relationship between a man and a woman. The work appears to be attributed directly to King SOLOMON (Cant. 1:1), though the Hebrew can be understood to mean, "The Song of Songs which is for [*or* concerns] Solomon." The book is difficult to analyze, and there is also a great diversity of interpretations.

Many have thought that it is an allegorical description of the LOVE of God and his people ISRAEL (or of the love of CHRIST and the CHURCH). Others think that the book presents actual history and nothing more. It seems better to hold that the book is historical, presenting the purity and wonder of true human love, but that it also directs us to the greater love of Christ.

**Sosthenes** (sos′thuh-neez). Ruler of the SYNAGOGUE at CORINTH during PAUL's first visit there (Acts 18:17). Many believe that he became a Christian and that he is the same person mentioned in 1 Cor. 1:1.

**soul.** This term usually refers to the immaterial essence of human beings, especially their moral and emotional nature (Deut. 6:5; 1 Sam. 1:15; Ps. 23:3; 42:1–6; Matt. 10:28; 26:38; Heb. 6:19). On the basis of several passages (especially 1 Thess. 5:23; Heb. 4:12), some believe that the soul and the SPIRIT are two substantive entities. Others argue that both of these terms (as well as HEART, MIND, etc.) refer to the single immaterial self from different perspectives.

**sovereignty of God.** A phrase that does not appear in the Bible but that summarizes the biblical teaching about God's supreme authority over his creation, in human history, and in the work of salvation (e.g., 1 Ki. 12:15; Isa. 46:20; Rom. 9:20–21; Eph. 1:11).

**spirit.** This English term (from Latin *spiritus*, "breath") is usually the rendering of Hebrew and Greek words that also mean "air, blowing, breath, wind" (e.g., Job 41:16; Ps. 18:15; Jn. 3:8; 2 Thess. 2:8). When used with reference to the human psychology, *spirit* is one of several nouns denoting the nonmaterial self (see SOUL). This word is used especially when the direct relationship of the individual to God is the point of emphasis (e.g., Rom. 8:16). See also HOLY SPIRIT.

**spiritual gifts.** See GIFTS, SPIRITUAL.

**Stephanas** (stef′uh-nuhs). A Corinthian Christian who, with his household, was one of the few persons baptized personally by the apostle PAUL in CORINTH (1 Cor. 1:16; 16:15–18).

**Stephen** (stee′vuhn). The first Christian martyr. Stephen had a Hellenistic (i.e., Greek-speaking) Jewish background and was one of the seven men appointed to look after the

## OVERVIEW OF SONG OF SONGS

**AUTHOR:** The work was probably written by King SOLOMON, but some scholars disagree.

**HISTORICAL SETTING:** The subject matter is the life of Solomon (c. 950 BC). The date of the composition of the book, if not written by Solomon himself, is uncertain.

**PURPOSE:** To celebrate human LOVE, probably as a reflection of the love between God and his people.

**CONTENTS:** The lovers praise each other (Cant. 1:1–2:7); deepening of their affection (2:8–3:5); arrival of Solomon and marriage (3:6–5:1); the wife's longing for the return of her husband (5:2–6:9); the beauty of the bride (6:10–8:4); the wonder and permanence of love (8:5–14).

S

Partial reconstruction of the synagogue at Korazin (2nd or 3rd cent. AD). © Baker Publishing Group

daily distribution to the poor in the early Jerusalem church (Acts 6:1–6; see DEACON). He also gave powerful witness to the GOSPEL, as a result of which he was falsely accused of blasphemy (6:8–15). His speech before the Jewish COUNCIL (7:1–53) provoked his hearers to stone him (7:58–60).

**Stoics** (stoh´iks). In the NT the Stoics are mentioned only once (in Acts 17:18, with the EPICUREANS), but other portions of the NT, especially the epistles of PAUL, use Stoic language or indirectly allude to concepts associated with this school of philosophy. The Stoics sought to live in harmony with nature by accepting without complaint the things that we cannot control (the only thing we have power over is our own soul).

**submission.** See OBEDIENCE.

**Succoth** (suhk´uhth). **(1)** A city within the tribal territory of GAD, just N of the JABBOK River and about 3 mi. (5 km.) E of the JORDAN RIVER (Gen. 33:17; Josh. 13:27; Jdg. 8:5–16). **(2)** A city in EGYPT not far from RAMESES; it was the first stop of the Israelites at the time of the EXODUS (Exod. 12:37; 13:20; Num. 33:5–6).

**suffering.** See PERSECUTION; TRIBULATION.

**supplication.** An earnest request, especially to God. See PRAYER.

**Susa** (*soo*´suh). KJV Shushan. One of the oldest cities of the world; ancient capital of ELAM and later of PERSIA (Ezra 4:9; Neh. 1:1; Esth. 1:2). Enjoying its delightful climate, Persian kings resided in Susa during the winter, and here DANIEL had a vision (Dan. 8:2).

**swaddling clothes.** Strips of cloth (as in NIV) in which a newborn baby was wrapped (Lk. 2:7, 12 KJV).

**swearing.** See OATH.

**sycamore, sycomore.** The sycamore-fig tree, often called the fig-mulberry, is a large spreading tree, producing sweet fruit (1 Ki. 10:27; Amos 7:14; Lk. 19:4). It is not the same as the tree called a "sycamore" today.

**synagogue.** A Jewish institution for the reading and exposition of the Holy Scriptures. It originated perhaps as early as the Babylonian EXILE. Synagogues had at least two officials. The ruler of the synagogue was responsible for the property and for the general oversight of the public worship (cf. Lk. 13:14; Acts 13:15). The minister or attendant (cf. Lk. 4:20) was a paid officer whose special duty was the care of the synagogue building and its furniture, in particular the rolls of Scripture.

**Syntyche** (sin′ti-kee). A woman in the church at PHILIPPI who, with EUODIA, had labored together with PAUL; these women needed to be reconciled with each other (Phil. 4:2–3).

**Syria** (sihr′ee-uh). This name is usually applied to the territory N and NE of PALESTINE, covering roughly the area now occupied by the modern state of Syria (and a small part of SE Turkey). Some Bible versions use this name to translate the Hebrew term for ARAM, which most frequently refers to the city-state of DAMASCUS and the neighboring territory.

**Syrophoenician** (s*i*′roh-fi-nish′uhn). This term is used to describe a woman encountered by CHRIST when he journeyed to the region of TYRE in the territory of PHOENICIA (Mk. 7:24–26 KJV and most versions; the NIV translates, "born in Syrian Phoenicia").

S

# T

**tabernacle.** This term, which means "tent," refers specifically to the portable sanctuary built by the Israelites in the wilderness (Exod. 25–27). It is also referred to as the Tent of Meeting (e.g., 27:21). The tabernacle was made after the pattern shown to Moses on the mount (25:9; 26:30; Heb. 8:5). See also HOLY OF HOLIES; TEMPLE.

**Tabernacles, Feast of.** See FEASTS.

**Tabitha** (tab′i-thuh). See DORCAS.

**table.** This term is often used by the KJV with reference to the tablets of stone on which God himself wrote the law (e.g., Exod. 31:18; 32:19; 34:1; Deut. 4:13; 2 Cor. 3:3; Heb. 9:4).

**Tabor, Mount** (tay′buhr). A hill about 10 mi. (16 km.) SW of the Sea of GALILEE in the Valley of JEZREEL (Josh. 19:22; Jdg. 4:6, 12–14; Ps. 89:12; Jer. 46:18). Some think Jesus' TRANSFIGURATION took place here, but a more likely place is Mount HERMON.

**Tamar** (tay′mahr). **(1)** A town or region of uncertain location (Ezek. 47:19; 48:28). **(2)** The daughter-in-law of JUDAH (Gen. 38:6–30; Matt. 1:3). **(3)** A beautiful daughter of DAVID, sexually assaulted by her half brother AMNON (2 Sam. 13). **(4)** A beautiful daughter of ABSALOM (2 Sam. 14:27).

**Tarshish** (tahr′shish). A region apparently named after a grandson of JAPHETH (Gen.

The reconstruction of the tabernacle shown here was built at the Timna Nature Reserve (on the southern tip of Israel).

Todd Bolen/www.BiblePlaces.com

10:4). In some passages Tarshish is associated with ships and ports (e.g., 1 Ki. 10:22). It was viewed as a very distant place (cf. Jon. 1:3; 4:2) that developed trade in minerals (Jer. 10:9; Ezek. 27:12). Many think it was located in SW Spain.

**Tarsus** (tahr′suhs). A important city of CILICIA in SE Asia Minor (modern Turkey), some 10 mi. (16 km.) inland. Tarsus, an intellectual center in the first century, was the birthplace and early residence of the apostle PAUL (Acts 9:11; 21:39).

**tassel.** The Israelites were instructed to make tassels (KJV "fringes") on the corners of their garments as a reminder of God's commands (Num. 15:38–39); Jesus condemned the misuses of this practice (Matt. 23:5). See also PHYLACTERY.

**tau** (tou). Also *tav, taw.* The last (twenty-second) letter of the Hebrew alphabet (ת, transliterated as *t*), used to begin each verse in Ps. 119:169–76.

**tax collector.** See PUBLICAN.

**teaching.** The importance of teaching is emphasized throughout the Bible. Parents must teach their children what God has said and done (Deut. 4:9–10). The PROPHETS and PRIESTS were expected to instruct the people (1 Sam. 2:23; 2 Chr. 17:7; Ezra 7:20; Ezek. 44:23). The psalmists often asked God to teach them his way and his word (Ps. 25:4–5; 86:11; 119:12, 66, 108). Jesus was viewed preeminently as a teacher (Matt. 4:23; 17:24; 22:16; 26:18; see RABBI). In the Christian church, teaching plays a fundamental role (Acts 4:2; 5:42; 13:1; Rom. 12:7; 1 Cor. 12:28; Eph. 4:11; 2 Tim. 2:2; Jas. 3:1).

**Tekoa** (tuh-koh′uh). A town in JUDAH some 5 mi. (8 km.) S of BETHLEHEM on a prominent elevation c. 2,700 ft. (820 m.) high. It was the hometown of the prophet AMOS (Amos 1:1; see also 2 Sam. 14:2–4; 2 Chr. 11:6; 20:20; Neh. 3:5, 27; Jer. 6:1).

Model of the Jerusalem temple during the NT period. © William D. Mounce

**Tel, Tell.** The Hebrew and Arabic words for "mound." They are frequently found as the first element in the names of archaeological sites, so named because of the accumulated ruins and occupation debris of ancient settlements.

**Tema** (tee′muh). Son of ISHMAEL and grandson of ABRAHAM (Gen. 25:15; 1 Chr. 1:31). Tema is also the name of a place that was apparently founded by him or his descendants (Job 6:19; Isa. 21:14; Jer. 25:23), identified with modern Teima in N ARABIA.

**Teman** (tee′muhn). A city in EDOM possibly founded by a grandson of ESAU (Gen. 36:11). Its inhabitants were noted for their WISDOM (Jer. 49:7; Obad. 8–9; see also Ezek. 25:13; Amos 1:12).

**temperance.** The prime meaning of this word is self-control (Acts 24:25; 1 Cor. 9:25; Gal. 5:23; 2 Pet. 1:6). It is not limited to abstinence from liquor.

**temple.** A building used for religious WORSHIP. For several centuries, the center of Hebrew worship was the TABERNACLE, a portable tent. King DAVID purposed to build a permanent house or temple for God (2 Sam. 7), and his son SOLOMON was

T

Traditional site of the Mount of Temptation.



able to fulfill this desire (1 Ki. 6–8). This building was destroyed in 586 BC but then rebuilt by ZERUBBABEL (Ezra 5:2) and greatly expanded by HEROD the Great (Jn. 2:20). Herod's temple was destroyed by the Romans in AD 70.

**temptation.** This English term today means "enticement to do something wrong," but the KJV uses it (and the verb *tempt*) in the sense of "testing, trial," whether the intention is good or bad. Thus God is said to have tested ABRAHAM to draw out his FAITH (Gen. 22:1); the Israelites tested God's goodness in the wilderness (Exod. 17:7; Num. 14:22); SATAN tested/tempted Jesus by trying to weaken his faith in the Father (Matt. 4:1–11); the testings/temptations that Christians go through are never greater than we can bear (1 Cor. 10:13; see also Jas. 1:1–2, 12–15).

**Ten Commandments.** See COMMANDMENTS, TEN.

**Tent of Meeting.** See TABERNACLE.

**Terah** (ter′uh). Father of ABRAHAM (Gen. 11:24–32; Josh. 24:2; Lk. 3:34).

**teraphim** (ter′uh-fim). A Hebrew word (plural form) used with reference to the images of household gods (KJV Jdg. 17:5; 18:14–20; Hos. 3:4; the same Heb. word occurs also in other passages, e.g., Gen. 31:19, 34–35; 1 Sam. 15:23).

**Tertius** (tuhr′shee-uhs). The SCRIBE to whom PAUL dictated his epistle to the ROMANS (Rom. 16:22).

**Tertullus** (tuhr-tuhl′uhs). A lawyer hired by the Jews to state their case against PAUL before FELIX (Acts 24:1–9).

**test.** See TEMPTATION.

**testament.** See COVENANT.

**testimony.** This English word is sometimes equivalent to "witness" (2 Tim. 1:8 KJV) or to "evidence" (Acts 14:3 KJV). The term is used also with reference to God's REVELATION and COMMANDMENTS (Ps. 78:5 KJV), and the ARK of the covenant is often called "the ark of the Testimony" because it contained the tablets of the Ten Commandments (Exod. 25:22).

**tet** (tet). Also *teth.* The ninth letter of the Hebrew alphabet (ט, transliterated as *ṭ*), used to begin each verse in Ps. 119:65–72.

**tetrarch.** Title given to the ruler of some small provinces in the Roman empire (Matt. 14:1; Lk. 3:1, 19; 9:7; Acts 13:1).

**Thaddaeus** (thad′ee-uhs, tha-dee′uhs). One of the twelve APOSTLES (Mk. 3:18). According to some Greek manuscripts of Matt. 10:3 (cf. KJV), he was also called Lebbaeus. On the basis of Lk. 6:16 and Acts 1:13, many believe that Thaddaeus is the same person as JUDAS #3.

**thankfulness, thanksgiving.** The Bible stresses the importance of having a sense of gratitude and of expressing that gratitude to God for his gifts (1 Chr. 16:4–8; Ps. 30:12; 95:2; 136:1–3; Matt. 14:19; Rom. 1:21; 2 Cor. 9:11–15; Phil. 4:6).

T

**Theophilus** (thee-of′uh-luhs). A man to whom the Gospel of LUKE and the ACTS OF THE APOSTLES were addressed (Lk. 1:3; Acts 1:1). The expression "most excellent" perhaps indicates that Theophilus was a respected Roman official; he may have been a recent Christian convert who needed further instruction.

**Thessalonians, Letters to the.** With the possible exception of GALATIANS, 1 and 2 Thessalonians are the earliest letters surviving from the correspondence of PAUL. They were written to the church in THESSALONICA, which was founded by Paul on his second journey (Acts 17:1–4). Both of the letters were probably written from CORINTH, after SILAS and TIMOTHY rejoined him (18:1–5). In the first letter Paul defends himself from the attacks of his Jewish enemies (1 Thess. 2:1–6, 10, 14–16) and encourages the Thessalonians to grow in the faith. Sometime later, the apostle needed to write to them again because they had been disturbed by the arrival of a letter falsely attributed to him (2 Thess. 2:2). The second letter serves to

## OVERVIEW OF 1 THESSALONIANS

**AUTHOR:** The apostle PAUL.

**HISTORICAL SETTING:** Written from CORINTH during the second missionary journey (c. AD 50) in response to a report from TIMOTHY (1 Thess. 3:6).

**PURPOSE:** To reassure the recently converted Christians in THESSALONICA of Paul's love for them; to exhort them to holy living; to comfort them by providing instruction concerning Christ's return.

**CONTENTS:** After an introduction (1 Thess. 1), the apostle explains the nature of his ministry and his concern for the Thessalonians (chs. 2–3), and then proceeds to deal with problems in the church.

## OVERVIEW OF 2 THESSALONIANS

**AUTHOR:** The apostle PAUL (though some modern scholars dispute this attribution).

**HISTORICAL SETTING:** Written from CORINTH during the second missionary journey (c. AD 51) in response to news of further problems in the church at THESSALONICA.

**PURPOSE:** To provide additional instruction regarding the coming of Christ and appropriate Christian living.

**CONTENTS:** After an introduction (2 Thess. 1), the apostle clarifies that certain events must take place before the coming of the DAY OF THE LORD (ch. 2) and exhorts the Thessalonians to pray, be industrious, and exercise church discipline (ch. 3).

Excavations of the cardo (main street) at Thessalonica. Snowdog/Wikimedia Commons

clarify further the problems of the first one and to confirm the confidence of the readers.

**Thessalonica** (thes′uh-luh-*ni*′kuh). The capital city of the Roman province of MACEDONIA. The population included a large Roman element and a Jewish colony. Paul visited Thessalonica after PHILIPPI (Acts 17:1–9), then returned to Macedonia during his third journey (19:21) and again after he was released from his first Roman imprisonment (1 Tim. 1:3).

**Thomas** (tom′uhs). One of the twelve APOSTLES (Matt. 10:3; Mk. 3:18; Lk. 6:15; Acts 1:13); in the Gospel of John he is also called Didymus, which is the Greek word for "twin" (Jn. 11:16; 20:24; 21:2). Thomas was evidently a questioning, but sincere, disciple (see Jn. 11:16; 14:5; 20:25–28).

**thorn in the flesh.** The apostle PAUL uses this phrase (along with "a messenger of Satan") to describe something (or someone) that afflicted him so that he might not become boastful (2 Cor. 12:7). Some have thought that he was referring to temptations or to persecution, but it seems more likely that he meant some kind of physical malady.

**threshing.** The process of separating seed from the harvested plant, usually on a "threshing floor" (e.g., Ruth 3:3; 2 Sam. 24:18–25). The word also had a figurative use (Isa. 21:10; 41:15; Mic. 4:12–13; 1 Cor. 9:10).

**Thummim.** See URIM AND THUMMIM.

**Thyatira** (thi′uh-*ti*′ruh). A city and major commercial center in NW Asia Minor (modern Turkey), some 20 mi. (32 km.) ESE of PERGAMUM. LYDIA, whom PAUL met in PHILIPPI, was a Thyatiran seller of purple dye (Acts 16:14). The church in that city was one of the congregations to which the book of Revelation was addressed (Rev. 2:2:18–28).

**Tiberias** (ti-bihr′ee-uhs). A city on the western shore of the Sea of Galilee, halfway down the coast of the lake (see GALILEE, SEA OF). Named after Emperor TIBERIUS, the city itself is mentioned only once in the NT (Jn. 6:23), but the name was extended to the lake, and John uses it twice in that sense (6:1; 21:1).

**Tiberius** (ti-bihr′ee-uhs). Second emperor of ROME and ruler at the time of Christ's ministry (Lk. 3:1). He was born in 42 BC, became emperor in AD 14, and died in the year 37. See CAESAR.

**Tiglath-Pileser** (tig′lath-pi-lee′zuhr). Also Tilgath-pilneser. The name of three kings of ASSYRIA. The only one mentioned in the Bible is Tiglath-Pileser III (745–727 BC), also known as Pul, who threatened both ISRAEL and JUDAH and received tribute from them (2 Ki. 15:19–20, 29; 1 Chr. 5:6, 26; 2 Chr. 28:20–21).

**Tigris** (ti′gris). The eastern river of ancient Iraq, which together with the EUPHRATES formed the alluvial plain of MESOPOTAMIA (Gen. 2:14; Dan. 10:4).

**Timnah** (tim′nuh). The name of several towns, especially one located between BETH SHEMESH and EKRON (Josh. 15:10) and allotted to the tribe of DAN (19:43) but controlled by the PHILISTINES in the time of SAMSON (Jdg. 14:1–2).

**Timothy** (tim′oh-thee). Usually spelled Timotheus by the KJV. PAUL's spiritual child (1 Tim. 1:2; 2 Tim. 1:2), travel companion, and official representative. A native of LYSTRA, he was the son of a devout Jewish mother who taught him the Scriptures (Acts 16:1–2; 2 Tim. 1:5; 3:15). He joined Paul during the second missionary journey (Acts 16:4) and continued to serve the apostle in various capacities (e.g., 1 Cor.

Aerial view of Tiberias.

4:17; 1 Thess. 3:2–6). Later he led the Christian community in EPHESUS (1 Tim. 1:2). How highly Paul esteemed Timothy may be gathered from several passages (e.g., Phil. 2:19–22; 2 Tim. 4:9, 21).

**Timothy, Letters to.** See PASTORAL LETTERS.

**Tirzah** (tihr'zuh). A city within the tribal territory of MANASSEH, possibly settled by Tirzah, daughter of Zelophehad (cf. Josh. 17:1–6). JEROBOAM I maintained a residence at Tirzah (1 Ki. 14:17), and it became the capital of the northern kingdom for a period (1 Ki. 15:21, 33; 16:6, 8–9, 15–18). It was evidently a beautiful town (Cant. 6:4).

**Tishbite** (tish'b*i*t). A term used to identify ELIJAH (e.g., 1 Ki. 21:17; 2 Ki. 1:3), probably because he came from an otherwise unknown town in GILEAD named Tishbe (1 Ki. 17:1 NIV).

**tithe.** The tenth part of produce or property for the support of the priesthood or for other religious purposes (Lev. 27:30–33; Num. 18:21–32; Deut. 12:5–18; 14:22–29; 2 Chr. 31:6; Neh. 13:5; Mal. 3:8–10; Heb. 7:4–9). Many Christians believe that some form of tithing is reflected in the NT principle of proportionate giving (1 Cor. 16:2).

**tittle.** A small mark, such as a point or accent, used to distinguish letters of the alphabet; the word is used by the KJV in Matt. 5:18 and Lk. 16:17 (NIV "the least stroke of a pen").

**Titus** (t*i*'tuhs). **(1)** An early GENTILE Christian leader, mentioned only in the letters of PAUL (Gal. 2:1–3; 2 Cor. 2:13; 7:5–16; 8:16, 23; 12:18; 2 Tim. 4:10; Tit. 1:4). He was involved especially in the difficult relationships between Paul and the church in CORINTH. Later the apostle charged him with organizing the churches in the island of CRETE (Tit. 1:4–5). See also PASTORAL

Rolling stone at Herod's family tomb.



T

LETTERS. **(2)** A Roman general who captured and destroyed JERUSALEM in AD 70; he later ruled as emperor of ROME for a short period, 79–81. He is not mentioned in the NT.

**Titus, Letter to.** See PASTORAL LETTERS.

**Tobiah** (toh-b*i*′uh). An AMMONITE who served as a Persian official and who joined with SANBALLAT and others in persistently opposing the work of NEHEMIAH (Neh. 2:10, 19; 4:3, 7; 6:1, 12–19; 7:62; 13:4–8).

**tomb.** This term may refer to a chamber, vault, or crypt, either underground or above. The Hebrews' BURIALS remained simple, most burying sites being unmarked. Apparently the Jews did not use coffins. Tombs of NT times were either caves or they were holes dug into stone cliffs. A general opening gave access to the vaults; ledges provided support for the stone doors, which weighed from one to three tons (cf. Lk. 24:2; Jn. 20:1).

**tongues, confusion of.** See BABEL.

**tongues, gift of.** A spiritual gift mentioned in Mk. 16:17; Acts 2:1–13; 10:44–46; 19:6; 1 Cor. 12–14. See GIFTS, SPIRITUAL. The miraculous ability to speak in other languages served to authenticate the GOSPEL on three occasions recorded in the book of Acts: PENTECOST (Acts 2:1–13), the GENTILES in the house of CORNELIUS (10:44–46; 11:15–17), and the twelve disciples at EPHESUS (19:6). The gift of tongues is mentioned by PAUL in 1 Cor. 12:8–10, 28–30, and discussed more fully in ch. 14. Some believe that the apostle here is not referring to foreign languages but rather to ecstatic outbursts of prayer and praise that were incomprehensible to the speaker as well as to the audience.

**Topheth** (toh′fit). An area in the Valley of HINNOM where idolatrous observances were held, including the sacrifice of children (2 Ki. 23:10; Isa. 30:33; Jer. 7:31–32; 19:6, 11–14; cf. 2 Chr. 28:3; 33:6).

**Torah** (toh′ruh). A Hebrew term meaning "direction, instruction, rule, law." It refers primarily to a way of life derived from the COVENANT relationship between God and Israel. When used as a name, it designates the PENTATEUCH, that is, the five books of MOSES, but sometimes it refers more generally to the whole OT.

**tower.** A lofty structure used for purposes of protection or attack, such as to defend a city wall, particularly at a gate or a corner in the wall (2 Chr. 14:7; 26:9), to protect flocks and herds and to safeguard roads (2 Ki. 17:9; 2 Chr. 26:10; 27:4), to observe and to attack a city (Isa. 23:13), or to protect a vineyard (Matt. 21:33). God is compared to "a strong tower against the foe" (Ps. 61:3; cf. Prov. 18:10).

**tradition.** The behavior or collective wisdom of any given group or culture, handed down from generation to generation. The term does not occur in the OT, but in the NT it usually refers to authoritative Jewish regulations taught by rabbis and elders (Matt. 15:2–3; Mk. 7:3–4; Gal. 1:14). The truths of the GOSPEL can also be referred to as traditions (the same Gk. word is used in 1 Cor. 11:2; 2 Thess. 2:15; 3:6).

**transfiguration.** A change in form or appearance. The term is used specifically with reference to a unique experience of CHRIST recorded in the Synoptic Gospels (Matt. 17:1–8; Mk. 9:2–8; Lk. 9:28–36; alluded to also in Jn. 1:14 and 2 Pet. 1:16–18). He was with his closest disciples on a mountain (probably Mt. HERMON) when MOSES and ELIJAH appeared; at that point Jesus' face shone brightly and his clothes turned brilliant white. The experience gave encouragement to Jesus, who was setting his face to the CROSS (Lk. 9:51), but it also

Artistic representation of Jesus' transfiguration by Sandro Botticelli (1445-1510). Planet Art

confirmed to the disciples that his teaching had divine authority (Matt. 17:5).

**transgression.** The breaking of the LAW. See SIN.

**travail.** This English term, referring to a woman's labor at birth or more generally to any kind of painful or strenuous work, is used frequently by the KJV. Most of the uses are figurative, portraying the agonies of divine judgment on the wicked (e.g., Isa. 13:8; Mic. 4:9–10), the hard work involved in PAUL's ministry (1 Thess. 2:9), the sufferings of the world until Christ returns (Rom. 8:22), etc.

**treasure.** A collection of objects of value. In the Bible the word often has a figurative meaning; for example, it is used to describe WISDOM (Prov. 2:4), the FEAR of the Lord (Isa. 33:6), the things that we value most (Matt. 6:21), God's KINGDOM (13:44), and the Christian's future REWARD (19:21).

**tree of knowledge, tree of life.** According to Gen. 2:9, God put in the middle of the Garden of EDEN "the tree of life and the tree of the knowledge of good and evil." God commanded ADAM not to eat of the tree of knowledge on penalty of death (2:17). The serpent's temptation of EVE (3:1–5) centered on this command. When Adam and Even transgressed it, they were expelled from Eden so that they might not "take also from the tree of life and eat, and live forever" (3:22). In the book of Revelation the tree of life signifies divine blessings (Rev. 2:7; 22:1–2).

**trespass.** An overstepping of the boundaries, used with reference to the violation of God's commands (e.g., Rom. 5:15–20). See SIN.

**tribe.** A large social group composed of families and clans. In the Bible it is applied specifically to the fundamental divisions of the people of ISRAEL, corresponding to JACOB's sons: REUBEN, SIMEON, LEVI, JUDAH, ISSACHAR, DAN, GAD, ASHER, NAPHTALI, JOSEPH, and BENJAMIN. The descendants of Levi were not considered one of the twelve tribes because they served as PRIESTS and ministers throughout all Israel. To preserve the number twelve, the descendants of EPHRAIM and MANASSEH (Joseph's sons) were regarded as separate tribes.

**tribulation.** This English term, referring to severe distress, usually as the result of oppression, is used frequently by the KJV, especially in the NT (e.g., Matt. 13:21 [NIV "trouble"]; Rom. 5:3 [NIV "suffering"]). The NIV uses it only in the expression "the great tribulation" (Rev. 7:15), which refers to a definite period of unparalleled suffering in the future (see also Dan. 12:1; Matt. 24:21–31). On the basis of 1 Thess. 4:16–17 (and other passages), some believe that Christians will be raptured or caught up to be with Christ prior to the great tribulation. Others believe that Christians will be taken to heaven either in the middle or the end of this period.

**Trinity.** This term (from a Latin word meaning "threefold") does not occur in the Bible, but it is used in Christian theology to reflect the biblical truth that there is only one GOD (Deut. 6:4–5; Rom. 3:30) and that he exists in three persons, the Father, the Son, and the Holy Spirit (Matt. 28:19; 2 Cor. 13:14; Gal. 4:6; 1 Pet. 1:2).

**triumphal entry.** This phrase, which does not occur in the Bible, is used to designate the entrance of Jesus into JERUSALEM like a conqueror and king on the first day of the week in which he was to be rejected and crucified (Matt. 21:1–11; Mk. 11:1–11; Lk. 19:29–44; Jn. 12:12–19).

**Troas** (troh'az). A port city on the Aegean coast of W Asia Minor (modern Turkey). This city is mentioned several times in connection with the ministry of PAUL (Acts 16:8–11; 20:5–56; 2 Cor. 2:12; 2 Tim. 4:13).

**Trophimus** (trof'uh-muhs). A Christian from EPHESUS who, with other believers, accompanied PAUL on his way back to JERUSALEM toward the end of the apostle's third missionary journey (Acts 20:4; see also 21:29; 2 Tim. 4:20).

**Trumpets, Feast of.** See FEASTS.

**trust.** See FAITH.

**truth.** This term is usually applied to that which conforms to reality and thus is factual, accurate, historical, reliable. We read, "It is impossible for God to lie" (Heb. 6:18;

Remains of a bathhouse in Troas.

Todd Bolen/www.BiblePlaces.com

T

Roman columns at the site of ancient Tyre.



cf. 2 Tim. 2:13; Tit. 1:2). PETER affirms that the content of the GOSPEL is not based on "cleverly invented stories" (2 Pet. 1:16). PAUL takes pains to demonstrate the historicity of Jesus' RESURRECTION (1 Cor. 15:3–20). But the notion of reliability can also be applied to a person's character, and Jesus himself is the ultimate manifestation of truth (Jn. 1:14, 17; 14:6). Christians are expected to be trustworthy, always speaking the truth (Eph. 4:25). See also LIE.

**tsadhe** (tsahd′ee). Also *ṣade, tzaddi*, etc. The eighteenth letter of the Hebrew alphabet (צ, transliterated as *ṣ*, used to begin each verse in Ps. 119:137–44. Its sound in Modern Hebrew corresponds to that of English *ts*, but in biblical times it was a so-called "emphatic" consonant (its precise pronunciation is uncertain).

**Tubal-Cain** (t*oo*′buhl-kayn′). Son of LAMECH by his second wife Zillah (Gen. 4:22). It is possible that Tubal-Cain was viewed as the ancestor of the KENITES (15:19), often thought to have been metalworkers.

**Tychicus** (tik′uh-kuhs). A close friend and valued helper of the apostle PAUL. Along with TROPHIMUS, Tychicus was evidently a delegate from the province of ASIA (Acts 20:4–6). Later, Tychicus was with Paul during the latter's Roman imprisonment and was entrusted with the important mission of delivering the letters to the EPHESIANS and the COLOSSIANS with instructions to inform them of Paul's welfare and to encourage them (Eph. 6:21; Col. 4:7–9; see also 2 Tim. 4:12; Tit. 3:12).

**Tyre** (t*i*r). A famous port city in PHOENICIA, some 25 mi. (40 km.) S from the sister port of SIDON and 15 mi. (24 km.) N of the modern Lebanese border with Israel. A king of Tyre, HIRAM, was a friend of DAVID (2 Sam. 5:11) and helped SOLOMON build the TEMPLE (1 Ki. 5:1–12). Later, however, Tyre became an enemy of ISRAEL and came under God's judgment (e.g., Isa. 23; Ezek. 26–28). Both Tyre and Sidon are mentioned in the NT (e.g., Matt. 11:21–22; 15:21; Acts 12:20).

# U

**Ucal.** One of two men—perhaps sons, disciples, or contemporaries—to whom AGUR addressed his sayings (Prov. 30:1). The Hebrew text can be interpreted differently (cf. NRSV, TNIV).

**Ugarit.** An ancient and important city on the coast of SYRIA (the modern name of the site is Ras Shamra). Although it is not mentioned in the Bible, its discovery in 1928 yielded numerous texts and artifacts that have shed much light on the biblical world of the fifteenth and fourteenth centuries BC. The Ugaritic language has contributed to our knowledge of ancient HEBREW.

**unbelief.** See FAITH.

**uncircumcised.** This term is sometimes used figuratively to represent unbelief and disobedience to the COVENANT of God (Lev. 26:41; Jer. 9:26; Rom. 2:25–29). See CIRCUMCISION.

**unclean, uncleanness.** In the Bible these terms refer primarily not to physical filth but rather to that which is ceremonially prohibited (e.g., eating certain animals, Lev. 11) or, in an extended sense, to moral impurity (Isa. 64:6). See COMMON; DEFILE; PURIFICATION.

**unction.** This English term, meaning "the act of anointing," is used once by the KJV with reference to the work of the HOLY SPIRIT in believers (1 Jn. 2:20). See ANOINT.

**undefiled.** A person or thing untainted with moral evil (KJV Ps. 119:1; Cant. 5:2; 6:9; Heb. 7:26; 13:4; Jas. 1:27; 1 Pet. 1:4). See DEFILE.

**unity.** Scripture stresses the unity or union of the believers with their Lord (e.g., Jn. 15:1–8) as well as the unity manifested in the BODY OF CHRIST, that is, the CHURCH (1 Cor. 12:12–27; Eph. 4:2–3).

**unleavened bread.** Bread made without yeast (fermented dough; see LEAVEN). Only unleavened bread was to be eaten for the seven days that followed Passover (Exod. 12:15–20; 13:3–7). By doing so, the Hebrews were reminded of their haste in leaving EGYPT during the great EXODUS. See also FEASTS.

**unpardonable sin.** This is not a phrase used in the Bible, but it is the usual way of referring to Jesus' statement that blaspheming or speaking against the HOLY SPIRIT would not be forgiven (Matt. 12:31–32; Mk. 3:29; Lk. 12:10). Other similar parallels (cf. Heb. 6:4–6; 10:26–27; 1 Jn. 5:16) should probably be understood in the light of that statement. In the context it must mean that when people attribute the work of God to SATAN they cannot be reached with the message of salvation and therefore they continue to call God's TRUTH a LIE. It is not that God will not forgive them, but that, by destroying the very offer of the GOSPEL, they place themselves outside the possibility of FORGIVENESS.

**upper room.** Traditional name given to the room where Jesus celebrated the Last Sup-

This small clay tablet from Ur (c. 2050 BC) is a commercial text in cuneiform that records the purchase of oxen from various merchants. 

per (Mk. 14:15; Lk. 22:12); the teaching recorded in Jn. 14–16 is referred to as the Upper Room Discourse. Large upper rooms with outside and inside staircases above the noise and bustle of the city are mentioned in the OT (e.g., 2 Ki. 1:2).

**Ur of the Chaldeans** (oor). A city in MESOPOTAMIA that was the home of ABRAHAM prior to his family's migration to HARAN (Gen. 11:28, 31; 15:7; Neh. 9:7). It was probably located in S BABYLONIA, on the EUPHRATES River. See also CHALDEA.

**Uriah** (yoo-ri′uh). The name of several men in the OT, but especially a HITTITE officer in the Israelite army who was the husband of BATHSHEBA and who was sent to his death by DAVID (2 Sam. 11:3–26; 12:9–10, 15; 1 Ki. 15:5); he was included in the elite corps called "the Thirty" (2 Sam. 23:39; 1 Chr. 11:41; cf. 2 Sam. 23:13, 23, 24; 1 Chr. 11:15, 25).

**Urim and Thummim** (yoor′im, thum′im). Objects, perhaps stones, placed in the BREASTPIECE of the high priest, which he wore when he went into the presence of the Lord and by which he ascertained the will of God in any important matter affecting the nation (Exod. 28:30; Lev. 8:8). It is unknown what they looked like or how they were used.

**usury.** The lending of money at excessive rates of interest. The English term, however, used to mean simply "interest," and it is used in that sense by the KJV (e.g., Exod. 22:25).

**Uzzah** (uhz′uh). Also Uzza. The name of several men in the OT, but especially a son of ABINADAB who was killed while driving the oxcart that carried the ARK of the covenant to JERUSALEM; his death was attributed to the violation of the sacred character of the ark (2 Sam. 6:3–9).

**Uzziah** (uh-zi′uh). The name of several men in the OT, especially a king of JUDAH (2 Chr. 26) who was also known as Azariah (2 Ki. 15:1–7). Uzziah became king at the age of sixteen and ruled fifty-two years (c. 792–740 BC). He won battles against various nations and was a successful ruler, but he strayed far from the Lord at the end of his life and God struck him with leprosy.

# V

**vain.** This English term occurs in the Bible especially as part of the phrase "in vain," indicating that something has no value (e.g., Lev. 26:16; Ps. 127:1; 1 Cor. 15:58). The commandment not to take God's name in vain (Exod. 20:7 KJV) is rendered in the NIV, "You shall not misuse the name of the LORD your God"; some think it means specifically that one is not to use the divine name to swear falsely.

**vanity.** This word today usually means "conceit" (see PRIDE), but the KJV uses it frequently with the meaning "futility" or "worthlessness," especially in the saying, "Vanity of vanities; all is vanity," which the NIV translates, "Utterly meaningless! Everything is meaningless!" (e.g., Eccl. 1:2).

**Vashti** (vash′ti). Queen of PERSIA and wife of Ahasuerus (XERXES I). Vashti refused to exhibit her beauty to Ahasuerus' lords on the seventh day of a feast, so the king banished her (Esth. 1:9–19); her deposition led to the selection of ESTHER as the new queen.

**veil.** This term means primarily "head covering" (e.g., Gen. 24:65; Exod. 34:33–35), but in the KJV it is used also with reference to the curtain of the TEMPLE that separated the HOLY OF HOLIES from the Holy Place (Matt. 27:51; Heb. 9:3).

**vengeance.** Revenge; PUNISHMENT in repayment for an injury or offense. The motivating force is often WRATH (Prov. 6:34; Nah. 1:2), but in human beings it is usually sinful (Lev. 19:18; 1 Sam. 25:26). The justice of God or the faithfulness of his servants is vindicated by the punishment of enemies (Jdg. 11:36; Ps. 94:1–2; 2 Thess. 1:8). See also AVENGER.

**vessel.** This term, referring to various kinds of containers, is sometimes used figuratively, especially of persons as instruments of God's will (KJV Rom. 9:20–24; 2 Cor. 4:7; 2 Tim. 2:20–21).

**victory.** The OT associates victory with the God of power and glory and majesty, who is in full control of his CREATION (1 Chr. 29:11). FAITH is the victory that conquers the world (1 Jn. 5:4–5), and through it Christians continually know the victory because of what God has done in Jesus Christ (1 Cor. 15:7).

**vine, vineyard.** The common grapevine is mentioned throughout Scripture, often in a figurative sense. The mountain regions of JUDEA and SAMARIA, largely unsuited for grain, were well adapted for vine growing. A vineyard was usually surrounded with a protecting wall of stones or thorny hedges to keep out destructive animals (Num. 22:24; Ps. 80:8–13; Prov. 24:30–31; Isa. 5:5). The HARVEST season was always one of special happiness (Jdg. 9:27; Isa. 16:10; Jer. 25:30; 48:33). Grapes were an important part of the diet of the Hebrews. Figuratively, the vine symbolized prosperity and peace among the ancient Hebrews (1 Ki. 4:25; Mic. 4:4; Zech. 3:10). The vine also symbolized the chosen people, who instead of producing outstanding fruit yielded only wild grapes (Isa. 5:1–7; cf. Ps. 80:8–16). Jesus referred to himself as the only true vine, with whom his disciples are in organic union (Jn. 15).

**virgin.** A woman who has not had sexual intercourse (in Rev. 14:4 it is applied to men). Such figurative expressions as "Virgin Israel" (Jer. 31:4) and "Virgin Daughter of Zion" (Isa. 37:22) allude to the purity of God's people.

**Virgin Birth.** The teaching that MARY was a VIRGIN when she conceived and gave birth to Jesus (Matt. 1:18–25; Lk. 1:26–38). This miraculous event points to the unique relation of the Incarnate Son to the human race he came to save: there is a basic continuity with us in that he shares our flesh and was born in the "normal" way, but there is a basic discontinuity in that he was conceived in a unique way and thus born without a sinful nature.

**vision.** Although this English word may refer to physical sight, in the Bible it normally refers to something extraordinary, such as a divine revelation in the form of a DREAM or a visual image without corporeal presence (e.g., Gen. 15:1; Num. 12:6; 1 Sam. 3:1–18; Ezek. 1:1; Zech. 1:8; Acts 9:10; 10:3; 2 Cor. 12:1).

**vow.** A voluntary promise to God to perform some service or do something pleasing to him in return for some hoped-for benefits (Gen. 28:20–22; Lev. 27:2, 8; Num. 30; Jdg. 11:30) or a promise to abstain from certain things (Num. 30:3). In the OT vows were never regarded as a religious duty (Deut. 23:22), but once they were made, they were considered sacred and binding (Deut. 23:21–23; Jdg. 11:35; Ps. 66:13; Eccl. 5:4). Jesus referred to vows only once, and that was to condemn the abuse of them (Matt. 15:4–6; Mk. 7:10–13). PAUL's vow in Acts 18:18 was probably a temporary NAZIRITE VOW.

**Vulgate** (vuhl′gayt). Name applied to the standard Latin translation of the Bible (the Lat. adjective *vulgatus* means "commonly known, in wide circulation").

# W

**wages.** Compensation to a person for performing some work or service (e.g., Gen. 29:15; Deut. 24:15; Matt. 20:8; Lk. 10:7). The Bible sometimes uses the concept in a figurative sense, as when DEATH is described as the wages due for serving SIN (Rom. 6:23).

**walk.** This word is often used in the Bible figuratively to indicate conduct or manner of life (e.g., Gen. 5:22; 1 Ki. 15:3 KJV; Ps. 1:1; Eph. 2:2 KJV). Modern versions frequently avoid a literal translation and instead use "live" or other equivalents.

**wall.** Because walls provide refuge, this term can be used to indicate God's protection (Isa. 26:1; Zech. 2:5). PAUL speaks of "the dividing wall of hostility" that separated Jews and Gentiles but that was broken down by Christ (Eph. 2:14).

**want, wantonness.** These terms, usually referring to LUST or unbridled passion, are used several times in English Bible versions (e.g., Isa. 3:16 KJV; Ezek. 23:44 NRSV; Nah. 3:4 NIV; Rom. 13:13 KJV).

**watch.** A person or group of persons set to guard a city (Neh. 4:9 KJV). The term can be used also to indicate the divisions into which the hours of the night were divided. The Romans, for example, divided the time between sunset and sunrise into four equal watches (Mk. 6:48).

**waw** (wou). Also *vau, vav.* The sixth letter of the Hebrew alphabet (ו, transliterated as *w*, sometimes *v*), used to begin each verse in Ps. 119:41–48.

**way.** In addition to its use in a literal sense, this word occurs frequently in a figurative sense, denoting processes in nature (Job 38:19; Prov. 6:6), moral conduct (1 Sam. 12:23; Matt. 21:32), human experience (Josh. 23:14; Prov. 3:6), and especially God's will and providence (Job 36:23; Isa. 2:3; Mk. 12:14; Heb. 3:10). In addition, the term "the Way" was used specifically of the Christian faith and manner of life followed by the Lord's disciples (e.g., Acts 9:2). Most important, the term is used of CHRIST as the final and perfect revealer (Jn. 14:4–6; cf. Heb. 9:8; 10:19–20).

**wedding.** The ceremony by which a man and a woman are joined together as husband and wife (Matt. 25:1–13; Jn. 2:1–2). The betrothal was a significant and legal commitment for the forthcoming MARRIAGE (Deut. 20:7), a commitment that could be broken only by death or divorce. The blessings of the end times are compared to a wedding banquet (Rev. 19:6–9; cf. Eph. 5:25–27).

**Weeks, Feast of.** See FEASTS.

**weights and measures.** See chart next page.

**well.** Since the rains in PALESTINE are concentrated in the winter months, the availability of water is a problem through much of the year. The ownership of wells was so important that feuds over them were

## Table of Weights and Measures

| | Biblical Unit | Approximate American Equialent | Approximate Metric Equivalent |
|---|---|---|---|
| **Weights** | talent (60 minas) | 75 pounds | 34 kilograms |
| | mina (50 shekels) | $1\frac{1}{4}$ pounds | 0.6 kilograms |
| | shekel (2 bekas) | $\frac{2}{5}$ ounce | 11.5 grams |
| | pim ($\frac{2}{3}$ shekel) | $\frac{1}{3}$ ounce | 7.6 grams |
| | beka (10 gerahs) | $\frac{1}{5}$ ounce | 5.5 grams |
| | gerah | $\frac{1}{50}$ ounce | 0.6 gram |
| **Length** | cubit | 18 inches | 0.5 meter |
| | span | 9 inches | 23 centimeters |
| | handbreadth | 3 inches | 8 centimeters |
| **Capacity** *Dry Measure* | cor [homer] (10 ephahs) | 6 bushels | 220 liters |
| | lethek (5 ephahs) | 3 bushels | 110 liters |
| | ephah (10 omers) | $\frac{3}{5}$ bushel | 22 liters |
| | seah ($\frac{1}{3}$ ephah) | 7 quarts | 7.3 liters |
| | omer ($\frac{1}{10}$ ephah) | 2 quarts | 2 liters |
| | cab ($\frac{1}{18}$ ephah) | 1 quart | 1 liter |
| **Capacity** *Wet Measure* | bath (1 ephah) | 6 gallons | 22 liters |
| | hin ($\frac{1}{6}$ bath) | 4 quarts | 4 liters |
| | log ($\frac{1}{72}$ bath) | $\frac{1}{3}$ quart | 0.3 liter |

The figures of the table are calculated on the basis of a shekel equaling 11.5 grams, a cubit equaling 18 inches and an ephah equaling 22 liters. The quart referred to is either a dry quart (slightly larger than a liter) or a liquid quart (slightly smaller than a liter), whichever is applicable. The ton referred to in the NIV footnotes is the American ton of 2,000 pounds.

This table is based upon the best available information, but it is not intended to be mathematically precise; it merely gives approximate amounts and distances. Weights and measures differed somewhat at various times and places in the ancient world. There is uncertainty particularly about the ephah and the bath; further discoveries may shed more light on these units of capacity.

settled at times only by a unique covenant service (Gen. 21:25–31).

**whirlwind.** A rotating windstorm, usually of limited extent. Although true tornadoes or severe whirlwinds are rare in PALESTINE, several types of violent storms do occur because of the proximity of mountains and lakes to the hot deserts (see 2 Ki. 2:1, 11; Ps. 77:18; Prov. 1:27).

**whore.** See PROSTITUTE.

**wicked, wickedness.** See SIN.

**widow.** In the OT, widows are regarded as being under God's special care (Ps. 68:5; 146:9; Prov. 15:25). The Hebrews were commanded to treat them with special consideration and were punished if they did otherwise (Exod. 22:22; Deut. 14:29; Isa. 1:17; Jer. 7:6). The CHURCH looked after poor widows in apostolic times (Acts 6:1; Jas. 1:27; 1 Tim. 5:3–10).

**wife.** See FAMILY; MARRIAGE; WOMAN.

**wind.** The standard Hebrew and Greek words for "wind" can also be translated "breath," "spirit," and the like, providing the means for interesting wordplays (e.g., Ezek. 37:9–14; Jn. 3:8). See SPIRIT. The Bible has numerous references to physical wind as under God's control (e.g., Gen. 8:1; Exod. 10:13; Ps. 135:7). See also WHIRLWIND.

**wine.** The fermented juice of the grape is mentioned in the Bible as a common drink (Gen. 14:18), an offering (Lev. 23:13), an intoxicant (Gen. 9:21), a disinfectant (Lk. 10:34), and a medicine (1 Tim. 5:23). It is figuratively used of wisdom (Prov. 9:2, 5), of wrath (Jer. 25:15), and of love (Cant. 1:2; 4:10). The abuse of wine is sternly condemned (e.g., Prov. 4:17; 31:6; Isa. 5:11; Eph. 5:18). See DRUNKENNESS.

**winebibber.** This term, referring to someone who drinks wine excessively, is used by the KJV in three passages (Prov. 23:20; Matt. 11:19; Lk. 7:34). See DRUNKENNESS; WINE.

**winnowing fork.** An implement with two or more prongs used to throw grain into the air after it has been threshed so that the chaff might be blown away (KJV "fan," Jer. 15:7; Matt. 3:12; Lk. 3:17).

**wisdom.** God's wisdom involves an infinite, perfect understanding of all that is or might be as well as the infallible judgment to do what is right (Rom. 11:33–36). In a derived sense, wisdom is given to people through the FEAR of the Lord (Job 28:28; Ps. 111:10). The wisdom of SOLOMON was far-ranging in statesmanship (1 Ki. 10:23–24). Wisdom is personified in Prov. 8 in a way that anticipates the coming of Christ (cf. Jn. 1:1–18; 1 Cor. 1:30; Col. 2:3). The term "Wisdom Literature" is used to describe the OT books of JOB, PROVERBS, and ECCLESIASTES, as well as passages in other books that have a similar style and emphasis.

**wise men.** See MAGI.

**wist.** This archaic word is used by the KJV in the sense "knew" (e.g., Exod. 16:15; Mk. 9:6). The present form *wot* occurs also (e.g., Gen. 21:26; Acts 3:17).

**witness.** See TESTIMONY.

**woman.** The general account of CREATION teaches the full humanity of EVE and her intimate relationship to ADAM as a part of his inmost being (Gen. 1:26–27; 2:18–24). Among OT women that played significant roles are the three patriarchal wives (SARAH, REBEKAH, and RACHEL), MOSES' sister MIRIAM (Exod. 2:1–9; 15:21; Num. 12), the judge DEBORAH (Jdg. 4–5), the Moabitess RUTH, SAMUEL's mother HANNAH (1 Sam. 1:1–2:11), and Queen ESTHER. Godly women stand out in Jesus' life and ministry: ELIZABETH, mother of his forerunner (Lk. 1); the Virgin MARY; ANNA (2:36–38); MARY Magdalene; MARTHA and Mary of BETHANY; the women who accompanied the disciples on missionary journeys and who provided for them out of their means (8:3). Women were the first converts in Europe, including the prosperous businesswoman LYDIA at PHILIPPI (16:13–15). Many women are greeted in Rom. 16, including PHOEBE, who may have been a deaconess.

**word.** The Bible contains much that is literally God's message and so it is called "the word of the Lord" (see REVELATION). That expression occurs hundreds of times in the OT and usually denotes the prophetic word, but it also can refer to the LAW of God (Ps. 147:19–20) and to the creative activity of God, who speaks and causes to be (Gen. 1; Ps. 33:6–9). Once uttered, God's word does not return to him empty but accomplishes what he purposes (Isa.

55:11). In the NT the word of the Lord (or of God) refers to the GOSPEL (Acts 4:29; 6:2; 1 Thess. 1:8). The words of Jesus are the words of the heavenly Father (Jn. 5:24; 8:51; 12:48; 14:24). More fundamentally, Jesus himself is the true Word (Gk. *logos*) who has come to earth from heaven (1:1–14) and who reveals the Father (1:18; 14:9).

**work, works.** Human labor was ordained by God at CREATION (Gen. 2:15) as a reflection of the fact that God also works (Jn. 5:17). After the FALL into SIN, human labor became toilsome and frustrating (3:17–19); nevertheless, God commanded that people should work six days each week (Exod. 20:9), and honest work is enjoined in the NT as well (1 Thess. 4:11–12). The plural *works* can refer to the deeds done by God out of holy love (e.g., Ps. 28:5; 92:5; Isa. 5:12) and to those done by human beings as God's creatures, including good works that spring from thankfulness and FAITH (Eph. 2:10; Col. 1:10). However, the Bible warns against doing works in order to earn the favorable judgment of God (Rom. 3:20; Gal. 2:16; 2 Tim. 1:9).

**world.** This term can refer both to the earth in a physical sense (Ps. 24:1) and to its inhabitants (1 Sam. 17:46). Because the world is affected by SIN, the Bible sometimes uses the word in a negative sense. The Greek term for "world," *kosmos*, is used especially in the Gospel of John (e.g., Jn. 1:9–10, 29; 3:16–19; 4:42), and in some passages there is a contrast between Jesus (or his disciples) and the world (8:23; 14:17–22; 15:18–19; 17:9; 18:36). In his first letter, John exhorts Christians not to love the world (1 Jn. 2:15–16).

**worldly.** See CARNAL.

**wormwood.** A perennial plant with silky leaves; it yields a bitter dark oil used for medicinal purposes and to produce absinthe (a liqueur). The wormwood has come to be used symbolically to describe sorrow, calamity, and even cruelty. This word is used a number of times in the OT by the KJV and other versions (e.g., Prov. 5:4; NIV "gall"); it occurs once in the NT as the name of a star that caused water to turn bitter (Rev. 8:11).

**worship.** The honor, reverence, and homage that we should pay to God for his perfection, greatness, and goodness. God redeemed the Israelites from EGYPT so that they might worship him (Exod. 8:1, 20, etc.). The Psalms often exhort us to worship God (e.g., Ps. 29:2; 95:6). We are warned to do so only as God himself has commanded and not on the basis of human ideas (Isa. 29:13; Matt. 15:9). With the coming of Jesus, worship is not restricted to the TEMPLE in JERUSALEM but must be done "in the Spirit and in truth" (Jn. 4:20–24 TNIV); that is, true worship takes place only through Jesus himself, for he is the TRUTH and he gives us the Spirit of truth (Jn. 1:17; 14:6; 15:26).

**wrath.** See ANGER.

# XYZ

**Xerxes** (zuhrk′seez). Greek form of a Persian name; the Hebrew form is Ahasuerus. **(1)** Father of DARIUS the Mede (Dan. 9:1). **(2)** Son of DARIUS I (Hystaspes) the Great and ruler of PERSIA (c. 486–465 BC; Ezra 4:6; Esth. 1:1 and frequently throughout this book). See ESTHER. In secular history Xerxes is best known for his wars against the Greeks.

**Yahweh, YHWH.** See JEHOVAH.

**Year of Jubilee.** See JUBILEE.

**yod, yodh** (yohd). KJV *jod.* The tenth letter of the Hebrew alphabet (י, transliterated as *y*), used to begin each verse in Ps. 119:73–80.

**yoke.** A piece of timber used to hitch together a team of oxen (or other draft animals) so that they could pull heavy loads evenly. In the Bible, the term is most often used metaphorically to designate a burden, obligation, affliction, or SLAVERY (Gen. 27:40; 1 Sam. 11:7; Isa. 58:6, 9; Lam. 3:27; Nah. 1:13; Matt. 11:29; Lk. 14:19). In contrast to the heavy yoke of the LAW (Acts 15:10), Jesus said that if we take his easy yoke, we will find true rest (Matt. 11:29–30).

**Zacchaeus** (za-kee′uhs). A wealthy PUBLICAN of small stature who was the chief tax collector in the important city of JERICHO. When Jesus was passing through the city, Zacchaeus climbed a tree to see him, then received Jesus into his house with joy and repented of his sins (Lk. 19:1–10).

**Zachariah, Zacharias.** See ZECHARIAH.

**Zadok** (zay′dok). The name of several men in the OT but especially a leading priest during the reigns of DAVID and SOLOMON (2 Sam. 8:17; 15:24–29; 1 Ki. 1:7–8, 32–45). Because of Zadok's prominence, subsequent HIGH PRIESTS were chosen only from the Zadokite line (cf. Ezek. 40:46; 43:19).

**Zarephath** (zair′uh-fath). A town in PHOENICIA where ELIJAH went during a time of drought; here he miraculously provided food for himself and for a widow and her son, and later he raised the son from the dead (1 Ki. 17:9–24; cf. Lk. 4:23–26).

**zayin** (zah′yin). The seventh letter of the Hebrew alphabet (ז, transliterated as *z*), used to begin each verse in Ps. 119:49–56.

**zeal.** The Bible speaks of God's zeal or ardent determination, both in accomplishing his gracious purposes (e.g., 2 Ki. 19:31; Isa. 9:6) and as an expression of his wrath (e.g., Ezek. 36:5). The Bible commends godly zeal in following the Lord's will (e.g., Ps. 69:9 [cf. Jn. 2:17]; Rom. 12:11) but also warns against misdirected zeal (Rom. 10:2).

**zealot.** A person characterized by much zeal, enthusiasm, or partisanship. When capitalized, however, the term Zealot refers to a violent Jewish sect that opposed Roman domination (this sect is not mentioned by name in the NT, but cf. Acts 5:37; 21:38). One of Jesus' disciples was called Simon the Zealot (Lk. 6:15; Acts 1:13; KJV

View of Gath Hepher, home of Jonah the prophet, in the tribal territory of Zebulun. Todd Bolen/www.BiblePlaces.com

"Zelotes"), but this nickname probably indicates that he was "zealous" for the LAW and for God. See also CANANAEAN.

**Zebedee** (zeb′uh-dee). A Galilean fisherman, father of the apostles JAMES and JOHN (Matt. 4:21; 10:2; etc.). Since he had hired servants (Mk. 1:20), he was probably a man of means and influence.

**Zebulun** (zeb′yuh-luhn). Tenth son of JACOB and sixth of LEAH (Gen. 30:19–20; 35:23)

## OVERVIEW OF ZECHARIAH

**AUTHOR:** The prophet Zechariah, son of Berekiah.

**HISTORICAL SETTING:** Postexilic JERUSALEM during the reign of the Persian king DARIUS I (c. 520 BC) at a time when the Jewish returnees had ceased to rebuild the TEMPLE. The second part of the book (Zech. 9–14) may derive from a different, later setting in Zechariah's ministry.

**PURPOSE:** To rebuke the Israelites for their sins but also to encourage them in view of the future blessings promised by God.

**CONTENTS:** Initial call to repentance (Zech. 1:1–6); eight visions and a coronation (1:7–6:15); call to repentance and promise of restoration (chs. 7–8); God's victory over the nations and final deliverance of his people (chs. 9–14).

and ancestor of the tribe that bears his name. After the conquest of CANAAN, the tribe of Zebulun received a northern region in GALILEE that was small but fruitful and strategically located.

**Zechariah** (zek′uh-ri′uh). The name of about thirty men in the Bible, but especially the following: **(1)** Son of JEROBOAM II and last king of JEHU's dynasty. After ruling in SAMARIA for only six months, Zechariah was murdered by Shallum (JEHOAHAZ), who succeeded him to the throne (2 Ki. 14:29; 15:8–11). **(2)** Son of JEHOIADA, who was the high priest during the reign of Joash (JEHOASH) of Judah. A godly man, Zechariah denounced the apostasy of the people from the Lord after his father's death, and Joash ordered him stoned to death in the temple court (2 Chr. 24:20–25). **(3)** One of the writing prophets (Zech. 1:1). See ZECHARIAH, BOOK OF. **(4)** A priest who in his old age became the father of JOHN the Baptist (Lk. 1:5–25; 57–80; KJV "Zacharias").

**Zechariah, Book of.** The eleventh book among the Minor Prophets. The author was a priest who returned from the EXILE in BABYLON (Neh. 12:16; see v. 1). He and HAGGAI served as prophets who encouraged the Jews to rebuild the TEMPLE. Around the year 520 BC, Zechariah uttered his first prophecy (Zech. 1:1–6), and the following year he gave a message consisting of eight symbolic visions, with an appendix (1:7–6:15). Two years later he gave a third message in answer to an inquiry (chs. 7–8). The two prophecies found in chs. 9–14 are not dated and were probably given at a much later period.

**Zedekiah** (zed′uh-ki′uh). The name of several men in the OT but especially the following: **(1)** One of four hundred false prophets who, in opposition to MICAIAH, the true prophet, encouraged AHAB, king of JUDAH, and JEHOSHAPHAT, king of ISRAEL, to go to war against the king of ARAM in order to recapture RAMOTH GILEAD (1 Ki. 22:1–38; 2 Chr. 18:1–19:3). **(2)** Third son of JOSIAH (1 Chr. 3:15) and king of Judah from 597 to 586 BC (2 Ki. 24:18–25:8). He was twenty-one when he began to reign, and he reigned until the fall of Jerusalem, eleven years of continual agitation and sedition (2 Ki. 24:18). In the book of JEREMIAH he is portrayed as indecisive and unable to choose the good by faith (Jer. 34–39).

**Zephaniah, Book of.** The ninth book among the twelve Minor Prophets. Dated in the

## OVERVIEW OF ZEPHANIAH

**AUTHOR:** The prophet Zephaniah, son of Cushi.

**HISTORICAL SETTING:** The southern kingdom of JUDAH in the days of King JOSIAH (641–609 BC), possibly during the early part of his reign prior to the religious reforms that began in the year 621.

**PURPOSE:** To rebuke Judah and warn the nation of future destruction; to announce the coming of the DAY OF THE LORD with both judgment and blessing.

**CONTENTS:** Divine judgment and call to repentance (Zeph. 1:1–2:3); oracles against various nations (2:4–3:8); promise of purification and restoration (3:9–20).

Samples of Philistine pottery. Zephaniah speaks about God's judgment upon the Philistines (Zeph. 9:6). Copyright 1995-2011 Phoenix Data Systems

reign of JOSIAH (Zeph. 1:1), this book was probably written sometime between 640 and 622 BC, before Josiah's religious reformation began. The book is concerned throughout with the DAY OF THE LORD. In Zeph. 1:2–6 this event is seen as a punishment for the IDOLATRY of the people (1:4–6). The eschatological or end-time day of the Lord is described in 1:14–18. Then in ch. 2 the prophet appeals to the humble to return to God, for that great day will involve universal destruction. In the third chapter the prophet includes a message of hope that is centered in a REMNANT of God's people, who will be kept secure throughout the turmoil predicted by the prophet (3:12–18).

**Zerah** (zihr'uh). The name of several men in the OT but especially a son of JUDAH by his daughter-in-law TAMAR; his twin brother was PEREZ (Gen. 38:27–30; 46:12; 1 Chr. 2:4; Matt. 1:3).

**Zerubbabel** (zuh-ruhb'uh-buhl). A prominent Israelite who returned to PALESTINE after the EXILE (Ezra 2:2) and functioned

This elevation in SW Jerusalem is commonly referred to as Mt. Zion, but the name was originally applied to the City of David, just S of the temple mount (to the right of this image). Todd Bolen/www.BiblePlaces.com

XYZ

as the governor of JERUSALEM (Hag. 2:2). He was encouraged by HAGGAI to give proper oversight to the work of rebuilding the TEMPLE (Hag. 2:1–9, 20–23; cf. Zech. 4:6–10).

**Zeruiah** (zuh-*roo*′uh). Sister (or stepsister) of DAVID (1 Chr. 2:16); she is known primarily as the mother of ABISHAI, JOAB, and ASAHEL, who were chief officers in David's kingdom (2 Sam. 2:18; 3:39).

**Zeus** (*zoos*). The chief god of the Greeks. The name occurs in only one NT passage (Acts 14:12–13).

**Ziklag** (zik′lag). One of the southernmost towns of the tribe of JUDAH (Josh. 15:31). In SAUL's time it was under the PHILISTINES (1 Sam. 27:6). King ACHISH of GATH gave Ziklag to DAVID when he was pursued by Saul (1 Sam. 27:6), and David used the town as a base for raids against various groups (1 Sam. 27:8–11; 30:1–3; 1 Chr. 12:1–20).

**Zilpah** (zil′puh). A maidservant given by LABAN to LEAH on the occasion of her marriage to JACOB. At the request of Leah, Zilpah became Jacob's CONCUBINE, bearing to him GAD and ASHER (Gen. 29:24; 30:9–13; 35:26; 37:2; 46:18).

**Zion** (*zi*′uhn). The SE hill of JERUSALEM. Zion is first mentioned in the OT as a Jebusite fortress (2 Sam. 5:6–9). DAVID captured it and called it the CITY OF DAVID. When SOLOMON moved the ARK of the covenant to the TEMPLE on nearby Mount MORIAH, the name Zion was evidently extended to take in the temple mount (Isa. 8:18; 18:7; 24:23; Joel 3:17; Mic. 4:7). Zion thus came to stand for the whole of Jerusalem (2 Ki. 19:21; Ps. 48; 69:35; 133:3; Isa. 1:8). (In postbiblical times the name *Zion* became erroneously transferred to the SW hill of Jerusalem, and this practice prevails today.) The name is frequently used figuratively for God's people. In the NT it can represent "the heavenly Jerusalem, the city of the living God" (Heb. 12:22).

**Zipporah** (zi-por′uh). Wife of MOSES and mother of GERSHOM and ELIEZER (Exod. 2:21–22; 18:2–4). After Moses' time in MIDIAN, upon his return to EGYPT, Zipporah averted disaster by circumcising Gershom (2:25–26).

**Zobah** (zoh′buh). An ARAMEAN kingdom that flourished during the early Hebrew monarchy. SAUL fought against Zobah (1 Sam. 14:47); subsequently DAVID, when he sought to establish his northern border, clashed with HADADEZER of Zobah and defeated him (2 Sam. 8:3, 5, 12; see also 10:6–19).

## Share Your Thoughts

**With the Author:** Your comments will be forwarded to the author when you send them to *zauthor@zondervan.com*.

**With Zondervan:** Submit your review of this book by writing to *zreview@zondervan.com*.

## Free Online Resources at

## www.zondervan.com

**Zondervan AuthorTracker:** Be notified whenever your favorite authors publish new books, go on tour, or post an update about what's happening in their lives at www.zondervan.com/authortracker.

**Daily Bible Verses and Devotions:** Enrich your life with daily Bible verses or devotions that help you start every morning focused on God. Visit www.zondervan.com/newsletters.

**Free Email Publications:** Sign up for newsletters on Christian living, academic resources, church ministry, fiction, children's resources, and more. Visit www.zondervan.com/newsletters.

**Zondervan Bible Search:** Find and compare Bible passages in a variety of translations at www.zondervanbiblesearch.com.

**Other Benefits:** Register yourself to receive online benefits like coupons and special offers, or to participate in research.